THE 1542 INVENTORY
OF WHITEHALL

for

Mike

THE 1542 INVENTORY OF WHITEHALL

THE PALACE AND ITS KEEPER

Transcribed and Edited by

Maria Hayward

VOLUME I

Commentary

ILLUMINATA
PUBLISHERS

for
The Society of Antiquaries of London

First published 2004 by
ILLUMINATA PUBLISHERS

for
The Society of Antiquaries of London
Burlington House
Piccadilly, London W1J OBE

ISBN 0-9547916-0-6

British Library Cataloguing in Publication Data
A catalogue record for this book
is available from the British Library

Typeset by James Brown at The West Park Press Ltd
Printed and bound by Grafikon, Belgium

CONTENTS

FIGURES

Illustrations can be found after page 122

A family tree of Sir Anthony Denny's immediate family can be found on page 54.

TABLES

ACKNOWLEDGEMENTS

THIS BOOK HAS BEEN SOME YEARS IN THE MAKING, so there are a number of organizations and people to whom I am indebted. I would like to thank the British Academy for a three-year postgraduate studentship (1993–6), and also the Institute of Historical Research, where I held a one-year Scouloudi Student Research Fellowship (1996–7). The final stages of the project have been carried out since my return to the Textile Conservation Centre, University of Southampton. I would like to thank Nell Hoare, Director of the TCC, for all her help during the completion of this book.

I would like to thank the helpful and knowledgeable staffs of the Public Record Office, the British Library Manuscript Room, London University Senate House Library and all the other archives and libraries that I have visited during the course of my research. In addition, I thank the Master and Fellows of St John's College, Cambridge, for allowing me to consult their archive.

Many individuals have contributed to this project, and my grateful thanks go to Charlotte Barrow, Melanie Blake, Siân Cooksey, Jane Cunningham, Dinah Eastop, John Fisher, Diana Greenway, David Grummitt, Mike Halliwell, Kate Harris, Annie Heron, Maurice Howard, Paul Johnson, Malcolm Mercer, Julia Merritt, Stephen O'Connor, Jenny Stratford, Barbara Thompson, Malcolm Underwood, Philip Ward and Martina Krüger and her parents. The reconstructed first-floor plan of the Palace of Whitehall in 1547 (Figure 1) was reproduced by kind permission of Simon Thurley. In addition, I have benefited from being on the periphery of the Henry VIII Inventory Project and I would particularly like to thank Claude Blair, Tom Campbell, Susan Foister, Philippa Glanville, Alexzandra Hildred, Santina Levey, David Mitchell, Lisa Monnas, Frances Palmer, Elspeth Veale and the late Janet Arnold.

At the Society of Antiquaries I should like to thank Kenneth Painter, Arthur MacGregor, the late Janet Clayton and Kate Owen. I am particularly grateful to Alasdair Hawkyard for his expert editing of the text and for compiling the index to the Commentary. The clear layout of the text and skilled production of the book is a credit to James Brown. A key influence has been that of my former supervisor, David Starkey. His penetrating insights into the political and cultural complexities of this period have proved invaluable and for which I am most thankful. I am also indebted to Ann Saunders and James Carley for reading and commenting on the text. Finally, I would like to express my gratitude to my family for their encouragement and support.

Maria Hayward
February 2004

ABBREVIATIONS

Primary sources and related abbreviations

Full publication details of the works listed below can be found in the Bibliography.

APC : Dasent, J R *et al*, *Acts of the Privy Council of England*

BL : The British Library

BM : The British Museum

Bod Lib : Bodleian Library, Oxford

CPR : *Calendar of Patent Rolls*

CSP : *Calendar of State Papers*

CSPD Edward VI : Knighton, C S, ed, *Calendar of State Papers Domestic Series of the Reign of Edward VI, 1547–1553*

DNB : Stephen, S and Lee, S, eds, *The Dictionary of National Biography*

GMR : Guildford Muniment Room, Surrey

HCRO : Hertfordshire County Record Office

HKW : Colvin, H M *et al*, *The History of the King's Works*

HO : A Collection of Ordinances and Regulations for the Government of the Royal Household (Society of Antiquaries of London) 1790

LP : Brewer, J S, Gairdner, J and Brodie, R H, eds, *Letters and Papers, Foreign and Domestic, of the Reign of Henry VIII, 1509–1547*

NUL : Nottingham University Library

PPC : N H Nicolas, ed, *Proceedings and Ordinances of the Privy Council of England, 1386–1542*

PPE : Nicolas, N H, ed, *The Privy Purse Expenses of Henry VIII*

PRO : Public Record Office, Kew (now incorporated into the National Archives)

SA : Society of Antiquaries, London

SP : State Papers

SR : Luders, A D *et al*, *Statutes of the Realm*

VCH : *The Victoria County Histories of England*

General

b. born
c. circa
d. died
ex. executed
g. unspecified grant
gdgc. grant during good conduct
gdp. grant during pleasure
gl. grant for life
gr. grant in reversion
gs. grant in survivorship
m. married
succ. succeeded
v. vacated

Note: in the text, references to item numbers are given in bold. Unless otherwise stated, those in square brackets refer to the 1542 Inventory. Those in round brackets refer to the 1547 Inventory, following the numbering in Starkey, ed, *Inventory*.

INTRODUCTION

ACCORDING TO THE PREAMBLE of the 1542 Inventory, 'In this booke... Ar particulerly expressid all suche our Money, Juelles, Plate, Vtensiles, Apparell, Guarderobe stuff and other our goodes Catalles and thinges / As Anthony Denny keper of our Palloice at Westminster shall stande chargid with'.[1] This Inventory of the Palace of Whitehall, as it was known by contemporaries, is unique within the group of surviving inventories from Henry VIII's reign for two reasons (see Appendix I). Firstly, it is the only extant inventory of the objects used to furnish the king's apartments at a leading royal residence that was taken during Henry VIII's lifetime. There is nothing comparable for Greenwich or Hampton Court. The closest inventory of this type is that taken of the wardrobe of the beds at Windsor Castle in 1539 and it does not compare in terms of the quality, quantity or variety of objects.[2]

Secondly, there are two small, but highly significant, groups of related records that help place this Inventory into a sequence of documentation so that it does not have to be viewed in isolation. The first of these is found in one of the two bound volumes of the post-mortem 1547 Inventory. This extensive, composite inventory records the goods that passed to Henry VIII's son and heir, Edward VI.[3] It includes the entry for Whitehall Palace compiled in 1547 and two later inventories taken at the palace in 1549 and 1550.[4] The second group consists of smaller but equally valuable documents: Denny's discharge from the office of palace keeper in 1547,[5] a summary of Denny's accounts from 1542 to 1548[6] and the 1551 discharge of Denny's widow and executrix.[7] In addition, it is possible to partially recreate Denny's lost Book of Issue or Discharge (see pp. 141–60) by working with the marginalia recorded on the 1542 Inventory. Denny used this Book of Issue to record all of the items passing out of his hands, because of loss, theft or their transfer into the care of another keeper.

The brief quotation given above sums up the key points that the 1542 Inventory sheds light on as a primary source. These points are as follows: the range of objects, the property where these items were kept and used, the man who had overall responsibility for the pieces, the role of the

---

1   PRO E315/160, f. 1r.
2   BL Add MS 10602, fos 1r–6r.
3   See SA MS 129 and BL Harley MS 1419. Philip Ward transcribed the manuscripts and they were published under the editorship of David Starkey as the first volume of Starkey, ed, *Inventory* (essay volumes forthcoming).
4   BL Harley MS 1419, fos 448r–474v (**15421–16068**) and fos 476r–545r (**16069–17533**).
5   PRO E101/427/2.
6   BL Lansdowne Roll 14.
7   BL Lansdowne Roll 15.

palace keeper and the accumulation and dispersal of the objects within the reigns of Henry VIII and Edward VI. These aspects will be introduced here briefly with the aid of a single object that is recorded within the 1542 Inventory and explored in more depth in the subsequent text.

I. Objects in Denny's Charge

Amongst the 4,156 entries recorded within the 1542 Inventory, there appears a reference to 'oone <great> table with the Picture oof the duches of Mylayne being her whole stature' [675].[8] Although the painter is not identified, it is very likely that this refers to the portrait that Hans Holbein the Younger, the king's painter, painted of the widowed sixteen-year-old Christina, Duchess of Milan, in March 1538.[9] The brevity of the entry can be augmented by an examination of the portrait. This process provides some details relating to the materials, construction and dimensions. Holbein executed this large, framed portrait using an oil medium, on an oak panel that measures 1,790 × 825mm. Further, technical information of this type is not available for many of the other entries recorded in the 1542 Inventory because the objects they describe no longer exist. In most cases, extra details can only be suggested by reference to comparable pieces that do survive.

The 1542 Inventory does not provide any clues as to where Henry displayed the Duchess's picture in his palace or the range of other objects placed in the same room, because the objects are recorded according to type rather than by location. Even so, it is likely that her picture was placed either in a gallery or one of the private rooms within the king's privy lodging. However, there is also the possibility that the picture was not on permanent display and so it may have been periodically in store. While the location is not known, a small insight into how some of the pictures were displayed at the palace is provided. Paned silk curtains were hung before certain pictures but Christina's portrait was not one of these. One reason for the use of these curtains was to create a dramatic effect when the curtain was pulled back as can be seen from the use of curtains before Poussin's *The Seven Sacraments*. Paul Fréart de Chantelou displayed all seven canvases in the same room but only uncovered one picture at a time because the whole set were 'too much for the eye to take in'.[10]

Holbein was resident in England from 1526 to 1528 and 1532–43 and he painted Christina's portrait during the second period. While many of the details of Holbein's career are well known, this book does not seek to provide a detailed chronological and stylistic analysis of the objects found within the 1542 Inventory, many of which also appear in the 1547 Inventory. Such an analysis will appear in the forthcoming essay volumes to the transcript of the 1547 Inventory.[11] The various objects recorded within the 1542 Inventory are discussed here in different terms. They have been examined for what they can reveal about how the contents of the Palace of Whitehall were built up and by whom, how the palace was furnished and used and the range of tasks carried out by the keeper and his staff.

---

8   Henry actually had two portraits of Christina; see also **743**, 'oone table with the Picture of the duches of Mylane'.

9   NG 2475. Christina was the second daughter of Christian II, deposed king of Denmark. At the age of 13 she had married Francesco Maria Sforza, Duke of Milan but he had died within twelve months. She was the niece of Charles V and the great-niece of Henry VIII's first wife, Catherine of Aragon; Scarisbrick, *Henry VIII*, 358–9.

10 Thackray, *Poussin*, 8.

11 An extended bibliography relating to the types of object found in the 1542 Inventory has been included in this volume in order to provide an introduction to the objects, prior to the publication of the forthcoming essay volumes.

II. The Physical Context for the King's Possessions: Whitehall Palace

Henry VIII's new palace of Whitehall was referred to as the Palace of Westminster in most formal documents, such as the 1542 Inventory. This reflects the position outlined in the 1536 Act of Parliament which declared that the sprawling new palace was 'to be taken reputed deemed called and named the king's palace at Westminster'.[12] In keeping with modern research, the palace will be referred to in the introductory text, and in the index to that text, as Whitehall but as Westminster in the index to the manuscript.[13]

Henry VIII had added the various galleries and rooms of the privy lodging onto the core of York Place that he had acquired from Cardinal Wolsey in 1529, during several distinct phases of building. However, very little of the palace remains above ground level because Henry VIII's palace was destroyed by fire at the end of the seventeenth-century. Consequently, an indication of the number, size and organisation of the rooms has been pieced together by archaeologists and historians. The 1542 Inventory provides just a few hints to solve the puzzle. These clues are combined here with an overview of current research on the evolution of the palace to provide a glimpse of the physical structure within which the objects recorded in the Inventory were housed.

III. Sir Anthony Denny: the Man and his Offices

Sir Anthony Denny was appointed as keeper of the Palace of Whitehall in 1536.[14] The portrait of the Duchess of Milan was likely to have entered his hands at sometime in 1538. However, it appears that no documentary record of Denny's charge was compiled until 1542, six years after his appointment. Although he cared for her portrait, Denny never met Christina. But Denny did attend Henry's marriage in January 1540 to Anne of Cleves, the woman eventually selected as the king's fourth bride.[15] Holbein had also painted Anne but this portrait proved to be an unsatisfactory likeness.[16] Denny gave evidence at the hearing that annulled Henry's the marriage of just six months to Anne.[17] Although elements of Denny's career have been studied before – namely his role within Henry VIII's privy chamber and his interest in reformed religious ideas – this partial view does not provide a satisfactory picture of the man.[18] So a fuller study of Denny's life is given here because it demonstrates the qualities he needed to succeed in the post of keeper of the king's leading residence and the rewards he received as a consequence.

Denny's personality is never fully accessible because so little of his private correspondence has survived. Equally, his portrait, painted by a follower of Holbein, hints at his appearance but does not clearly record his features. In contrast Holbein's portrait of Christina conveys an acute sense

---

12   28 Hen VIII, c. 12; also see Starkey, 'Tudor Government', 923–4.

13   This style was used in the index to the 1547 Inventory, see Starkey, ed, *Inventory*, I, 443.

14   *LP* X, 226.34.

15   *LP* XV, 14.

16   This is likely to be the portrait of Anne of Cleves that now belongs to the Louvre, Paris. Holbein painted Anne's portrait, along with an image of her sister Amelia, in 1539 at Düren. It is painted in tempora worked over with oil on parchment that has been laid down on panel. Although Henry did not retain any portraits of Anne, Denny's charge at Westminster did include 'two Lowe Cheirs serving for women of cloth of gold reysid with crymsen vellat … eche of them having the kinges Armes crowned Joyned with the armes of Cleveland and H. & A. enbraudred in the backe' [**251**].

17   *LP* XV, 825, 850 and 860. Christina married her second husband François, duc de Bar, later Duke of Lorraine, in 1541.

18   See p. 56, n. 5.

of her intelligence and wry sense of humour. If Denny's personal papers and portrait provide poor pickings, the body of evidence relating to his office as keeper of the new Palace of Whitehall is much more substantial.

IV. The Role of Palace Keeper

The portrait of Christina, Duchess of Milan, is the only surviving full-length portrait of a single sitter by Holbein. As such, it is unique within the corpus of Holbein's extant work. The significance of the 1542 Inventory has already been highlighted but this document did not appear in isolation. It forms part of a group of seventy-two surviving inventories taken during Henry VIII's lifetime that recorded the king's possessions (see Appendix I). This is a relatively small but significant group of inventories, yet in comparison with the quantity of comparable materials from Henry VII's reign, it is a vast resource. The inventories are in a range of formats, moving from single sheets of paper via rolls to bound volumes. The vast majority record the items placed into the charge of a particular, named individual. There is just one other list of objects passing out of a keeper's care. This is James Worsley's 'boke of delyuerance and discharge'. Worsley was yeoman of the Robes and the book recorded all of the 'kinges Riche Robes' that had been given away at Henry's instigation between 20 December 1516 and 17 January 1521.[19]

Most of the object types found within the 1542 Inventory were represented in this selection of documents. They were usually recorded individually, such as the jewellery in the keeping of Sir William Compton taken in 1519 or more rarely in groups, such as the range of furnishings kept at the king's manor of Beaulieu listed in September 1516.[20] However, paintings were not recorded in any of the documents so the 1542 Inventory provides the first surviving record of paintings owned by an English monarch. Evidence from a number of these inventories has been used to illustrate where the 1542 Inventory differs from other inventories and where there were similarities. This group of inventories also highlights just how special the group of documents relating to Denny's period in office and his surrender of this post are.

In addition, the office of keeper brought Denny a number of responsibilities that centred upon the Palace of Whitehall but also extended beyond there to include a number of Henry VIII's properties and parks. Most of these were in and around the London area but a few were further afield in the Home Counties. The extent of Denny's remit can be garnered from his accounts that are published in this volume.

V. The Development, Maintenance and Dispersal of objects in Denny's Charge

The various methods of acquisition for the objects owned by the king can be guessed at but a series of letters reveal how Christina's portrait came into Henry's possession.[21] The painting was commissioned by the king from his royal painter, Holbein, as part of his quest for a fourth queen consort. Henry sent Holbein with Philip Hoby of the privy chamber to Brussels, where Christina was living with Mary of Hungary, her aunt and Regent of the Netherlands. The king expected Holbein to acquire a good likeness. Holbein did so, even though he was only given one three hour sitting to

---

19 BL Harley MS 2284.

21 *LP* XIII.i, 419, 507, 583.

20 PRO SP1/29, fos 191r–205v and E101/622/31.

draw Christina.[22] Christina ultimately declined Henry's offer of marriage on the grounds that 'her Council suspecteth that her great aunt was poisoned, that the second [wife] was innocently put to death, and the third lost for lack of keeping in her child-bed'.[23] The fact that the king chose to retain the portrait of the elusive Christina is interesting, especially as the 1542 list of portraits reveals that Henry did not keep any images of the woman he married in her place.

It is rare to be able to document with such precision how individual objects entered Henry VIII's hands or those of the keepers ultimately responsible for the king's possessions. Even so, one section of the 1542 Inventory does shed some light on how a number of items came into Denny's hands between 1542 and 1546.[24] The document frequently provides details such as the name of the supplier, the date of acquisition, the quantity and appearance of the items. For example, Anthony Carsidony gave Henry VIII a map or 'the discription of Florence vpon stayned cloth' in June 1543 [**3471**].

The marginalia on the 1542 Inventory reveals the types of damage that some of the pieces suffered while in Denny's hands. There is no notation of this type against Christina's portrait but comments written against other paintings, terracotta panels, stained cloths and embroidered pictures record lost curtains [e.g. **740**], missing frames [e.g. **825**] or the complete disappearance of the item [e.g. **820**]. When pictures were damaged it was not unknown for repairs to be carried out. In 1530 Anthony Toto, the king's serjeant painter, was paid 13*s* 4*d* 'for sundrye colours by hym employed and spent uppon theold payntyd tablis in the kinges prevy closet'.[25] Not all of the damage to the paint layer was necessarily caused by mechanical means. Certain pigments, such as smalt, are sensitive to light and they change colour as the result of prolonged exposure. Holbein used smalt to create the blue background to his portrait of the young prince Edward, aged eighteen months, and with time this has discoloured to grey-brown.[26] In contrast, blue grounds painted with a more light fast blue pigment like azurite, such as that on the portrait of the Lady Mary attributed to Master John, have retained their original colour.[27] The silk curtains placed before some of the pictures may also have had a protective role.

The extensive marginal notation on the 1542 Inventory also records which objects passed out of Denny's hands during the king's lifetime and what happened to the items after Henry's death. The paintings were amongst the group of objects that remained part of Denny's charge when his responsibilities at Whitehall were reduced after the accession of Edward VI.[28] After 1547 the marginalia stops and the next clue as to the whereabouts of the painting appears in the document recording the release of Denny's widow and executrix from responsibility for any missing items in 1551. This indicates that Christina's portrait had passed out of the royal collection by that time because the list of items to be accounted for included

C1 Tables - Furste the picture of thole stature of the Duches of Millane - one.

C1 *RM*: This Table Therle of Arundell hathe of the kinges Majesties gieft as he saithe.

22 *LP* XIII.i, 507. The resulting picture was described as 'very perfect', ibid.
23 *LP* XIV.ii, 400.
24 PRO E315/160, fos 120v–138v.
25 PRO E36/241, p. 106.
26 Hearn, *Dynasties*, pp. 41–2.
27 Ibid, p. 47.
28 Each folio on which the paintings are record is annotated with a variant on 'Ex' to sir Anthony Denny vpon his new chardge'; PRO E315/160, f. 53r.

Although no date is given for the gift, a marginal note written on the 1547 Inventory reveals that Edward VI gave a 'A kniffe the shethe garnished with siluer guilte with A Chayne to the same' (**11191**) to 'therle of Arundell lorde Chamberlayne 12 Novembre 1549'.[29] It is possible that Henry Fitzalan, Earl of Arundel, received the portrait at the same time but if this is the case there is no marginal note against the picture to that effect. On the basis of this evidence, the date of removal can be no more precise than at some point during 1547–51. Some time after the portrait of the Duchess of Milan passed out of royal hands, it descended into the collection of Thomas Howard (1585–1646), Earl of Arundel, who was a passionate collector of Holbein's work.

A number of Henry VIII's possessions had left the Palace of Whitehall during the king's lifetime and at his request. A larger group of items was given to keepers at other royal properties between January and September 1547. This pattern of dispersal and reorganisation reveals some interesting points about how the contents of Henry's leading palace were viewed by the king, who drew them all together, and his successor, who used them to suit his own ends. Evidence of this continuing during Edward's reign is much more limited but, staying with Holbein, one point is pertinent here. It was Edward VI who removed 'A booke of paternes for phiosionamyes' (**11170**) from the study next to the king's old bedchamber at Whitehall.[30] This book has been interpreted as containing the selection of Holbein's drawings that now form the basis of the Royal collection.[31]

Christina's portrait is a physical reminder of a small interlude in the political manoeuvres that took place while Henry sought a new wife after the death of Jane Seymour. Christina was not inclined to consider Henry VIII's suit and is reputed to have said that 'If I had two heads one would be at the disposal of the English majesty'.[32] And a number of Henry's relatives by marriage, court circle and household would have echoed this sentiment. None more so than Catherine Howard, Henry's fifth wife, whose chapel goods were placed in Denny's hands after her execution in 1542 and appear in his inventory.[33] In this way, the objects listed in the 1542 Inventory reveal far more than suggestions about the appearance of a mid-sixteenth-century English royal interior. These objects can provide insights into the pomp associated with royal weddings and the spectacle linked to royal deaths, both natural and unnatural. The objects also highlight some other underlying themes such as Henry VIII's need for and use of magnificence, the role of the Palace of Whitehall and Denny's place in the group of keepers who were responsible for the king's possessions and properties.

29 BL Harley MS 1419, f. 158r.
30 The marginal note records that the book was 'taken by the kinges majestie hym selfe 12 Novembre 1549', BL Harley MS 1419, f. 157r.
31 This is asserted by a number of authors including Roberts, *Holbein and the Court of Henry VIII*, 20.
32 Quoted in Roberts, *Holbein*, 15.
33 PRO E315/160, fos 99v–101r.

I
OBJECTS IN DENNY'S CHARGE

ALTHOUGH THE PHYSICAL STRUCTURE of Henry VIII's Palace of Whitehall no longer exists, the objects used to convert the architectural shell into a royal residence are still accessible via the text of the 1542 Inventory. Indeed, the presence of these objects at the palace is the reason why the document was compiled. Working with the text of the Inventory, supporting documentation and evidence drawn from comparable surviving objects, it is possible to explore various questions relating to what the interior of Henry VIII's palace looked like. For example, the profusion and quality of the items listed in the Inventory vividly suggest the sumptuous appearance of the lost interior, and indicate how many objects were recorded in the Inventory and how many of the rooms within the privy lodging could be furnished with the pieces at Denny's disposal. Moving on from that basis, the objects can also shed light on specific activities that the king and his household undertook at the palace, such as eating, sleeping and religious observance. The Inventory also highlights one of the frequently overlooked aspects of Denny's role as keeper. He was responsible for the purchase and distribution of a substantial yardage of expensive silk cloth that was stored at the palace. In this respect the palace was more than just a repository for objects that were used to promote an image of grandeur and provide sufficient comfort for the king. It was also used as a store for a valuable raw material that was converted at a later date into clothes and furnishings.

The Appearance of the Palace's Interior

The appearance of the interior of Whitehall Palace is highly elusive. This is because the palace no longer exists; there are no definitive visual representations; there are no detailed contemporary descriptions; and the survey of the palace in 1547 recorded the bulk of the objects by type rather than by location.

The validity of this point can be demonstrated by briefly examining the evidence for the king's privy chamber. The first hints can be gleaned by consulting the entries in the 1547 Inventory for the privy chambers at Greenwich and Hampton Court. These reveal that the basic furnishings were wooden tables, forms, stools and cupboards. At Greenwich they were supplemented with a mirror, a pair of regals, a tables board and fire furniture (**9442–9451**) and a similar group of items was present at Hampton Court (**12248–12259, 12387–12391**). In both cases all the textiles were in store.

Moving to Whitehall, it is possible to make some suggestions about the type of furnishing textiles and other decoration that might have been found in the privy chamber. First, sets of tapestries were hung here because the Great Wardrobe accounts refer to the repair of several sets that were used in this room.[1] Secondly, there is one reference in the 1542 Inventory to a hanging made for the privy

---

1 PRO E101/423/10, f. 74r, a reference to 'twelve pieces of good tapestry pro privata camera Regis'.

chamber from the celure of a cloth of estate. The hanging was made from cloth of gold tissue raised with purple velvet and paned with crimson velvet [**237**]. However, it did not appear in the 1547 listing for Whitehall because it was delivered to the Tower Wardrobe on 9 July 1547 (**9218**). Finally, and possibly more spectacularly, from 1537 onwards, the privy chamber contained Holbein's dynastic mural depicting Henry with his third wife, Jane Seymour, and his parents, Henry VII and Elizabeth of York. The figures, which were larger than life size, would have dominated one side of the room.[2]

The most intriguing scrap of information dates from 1550, when James Rufforth died. His charge at Whitehall was surveyed and it included several rooms not covered by the earlier inventories, including the privy chamber. Only one item in the privy chamber was described, and it was set into the wall:

> a thinge artificiallie made like a rocke wherin is many straunge deuises of friers and diuerse other thinges hauing in it a fountayne of allablaster … and vppon the toppe of the fountayne a rounde Balle of christall wherin was three heddes of golde … and xiij stones made like heddes … whiche was supposed to be Camewes being sett abowte in a Border euery one of the compase of a grote all whiche fountayne and rocke is locked vpp with two Leaues like windowes the whiche leaues ar garneshed with peerle and golde threde pirled (**16922**).

The effect this must have created is reminiscent of the Paradise Chamber at Hampton Court.[3] But even with these shreds of information, the appearance of the privy chamber remains elusive, as does the appearance of the whole palace, so some of the elements of Denny's charge will now be considered: carpets, wall hangings, traverses, curtains, fire furniture, candles and other means of lighting and sanitary arrangements. The results shed further light on how the whole of the privy lodging of Whitehall Palace was furnished.

A useful place to start is by looking at data collected during recent archaeological digs on the palace site. The work has provided a footprint for the palace and Simon Thurley has used this, in combination with evidence from the building accounts, to suggest the size and arrangement of the rooms on the ground and first floors (see Figure 1). Working with Thurley's scale drawings it is possible to produce a set of approximate dimensions for the principal first-floor rooms (see Table 1), providing a very rough sense of the space within which Denny and his colleagues worked. The initial impression is that this space was sizeable, both in terms of the number of rooms and the available floor and wall space.

Continuing in this vein, the 1542 Inventory is not particularly helpful. Several rooms are mentioned in the Inventory – the bain or bath house, the bedchamber, the high library, the privy chamber, the secret jewel house, the withdrawing chamber and the queen's bath house.[4] But there is no indication of their specific contents, location or size. It is possible to glean more information

2 The cartoon is dated 1537: *HKW*, IV, 311. The Whitehall mural was destroyed by fire in 1698 but its appearance can be gauged from a section of the cartoon depicting Henry VII and Henry VIII (National Portrait Gallery 4027), and a copy made by Remigius van Leemput in 1667 (The Royal Collection). The surviving section of the Whitehall cartoon measures 2,570 × 1,370mm and it has been estimated that the original dimensions were c. 2,700 × 3,600mm: Thurley, *Royal Palaces*, 211.

3 According to Justus Zinzerling, the Paradise Chamber 'captivates the eyes of all who enter, by the dazzling of pearls of all kinds' and Paul Hentzer added that 'besides that everything glitters so with silver, gold and jewels as to dazzle one's eyes, there is a musical instrument made all of glass, except the strings': Rye, *England as Seen by Foreigners*, 134, 204.

4 'oone Bedstede withowte pillours to close vp in a wall … serving for the Queines Bayne' [**453**].

from the 1547 Inventory, using both direct and indirect evidence, although once again, the inferences that can be drawn from Greenwich and Hampton Court are vital. Thirteen rooms at Greenwich, starting with the privy chamber and progressing via a series of rooms and galleries to the library, were listed as being within the charge of the palace Keeper, Nicholas Dowsing. Four of these rooms – the privy chamber, the withdrawing chamber, the bedchamber and the gallery – were described as being specifically for the king. At Hampton Court the sequence of rooms once again started with the privy chamber. However, the list was more extensive, with twenty-five rooms, and included a number of chambers from the queen's lodging.

The view of Whitehall is much more fragmented as it is spread between the inventories taken in 1547, 1549 and 1550. The first entry for 1547 recorded the secret wardrobe, the secret jewel house, 'the study at the hether ende of the Long Gallorie',[5] 'the kynges secrete studie called the Chaier house',[6] the glass house, the study next to the king's old bedroom and the old jewel house. Although no new rooms were listed in the 1549 palace inventory, there were additional entries in 1550 for a chamber next to the still house, the privy chamber, the privy gallery, the armoury and the 'litle Study called the newe Librarye'.[7] While this rather disjointed list of rooms does not provide a detailed picture of the privy lodging at Whitehall, it does suggest that it was at least as large as that at Hampton Court. It also indicates that there was a similar combination of principal rooms, galleries, studies, closets and connecting chambers.

Another way of seeking an impression of the privy chamber is to start with the various groups of objects and consider where and how they might have been used. Following the theme of the size of the rooms, and extending it to consider how many Denny could have furnished from the items in his charge, the groups of objects listed above will now be examined. This will in turn shed some light on the floors, walls, doors, windows and fireplaces at Whitehall.

CARPETS   The floor coverings used at Whitehall Palace are both accessible and elusive. The building accounts record numerous purchases of rush mats for the rooms at Whitehall, and a fragment of this sixteenth-century matting was recently discovered under the floorboards at Hampton Court.[8] However, on occasion carpets were put down on the floor. Full-length portraits of Henry invariably depict the king standing on a carpet and there were 'ij olde Carpettes vppon the flower' (13843) at the former London house of the Knights of St John at Clerkenwell in 1547.[9] The 1542 Inventory includes seven 'foot carpets', which may have been placed on the floor [434]; their condition, which was described as 'sore woren', certainly suggests regular use.

Not all carpets were intended to be put on the floor, however. In the sixteenth and seventeenth centuries the word 'carpet' referred to a flat textile used as a cover.[10] Examples of this type of carpet also appear in the 1542 Inventory, including the group of fifty-five cupboard carpets [435] and 'oone Carpet of grene Satten enbraudred vpon with sondry of the kinges bestes / Antique heddes grapes and birdes' [422].

5 BL Harley MS 1419, f. 113r.   6 Ibid, f. 115r.   7 Ibid, f. 186r.
8 The matting is illustrated in Thurley, *Royal Palaces*, 320.
9 E.g. the surviving fragment of the Whitehall cartoon; in *The Family of Henry VIII* by an unknown artist, the king's chair of estate stands on a carpet.
10 Thornton, *Interior Decoration*, 109.

TABLE 1

SUMMARY OF THE APPROXIMATE DIMENSIONS FOR THE KEY GROUND- AND FIRST-FLOOR ROOMS AT WHITEHALL, C. 1547

The dimensions given below have been taken from the reconstructed first-floor plan of Whitehall Palace, 1547 (Figure 1) which has been reproduced from Thurley, *Whitehall Palace*, p. 63, fig. 72.

Room	Room dimensions in feet (metres)	Floor space/area in square feet (metres)	Room circumference in feet (metres)
OUTER ROOMS/COMMUNAL SPACE			
Great hall	80 × 40 (24 × 12)	3,200 (288)	240 (72)
Chapel	70 × 30 (21 × 9)	2,100 (189)	200 (60)
Chapel closets	50 × 20 (15 × 6)	1,000 (90)	140 (42)
Gallery to the water gate	110 × 10 (33 × 3)	1,100 (99)	240 (72)
Subtotal	—	7,400 (666)	820 (246)
THE KING'S ROOMS			
Guard chamber	60 × 30 (18 × 9)	1,800 (162)	180 (54)
Presence chamber	60 × 20 (18 × 6)	1,200 (108)	160 (48)
Privy chamber	45 × 20 (13.5 × 6)	900 (81)	39 (130)
Closet	10 × 10 (3 × 3)	100 (9)	40 (12)
Withdrawing chamber	50 × 20 (15 × 6)	1,000 (90)	140 (42)
Privy gallery	200 × 10 (60 × 3)	2,000 (180)	420 (126)
Privy closet	20 × 20 (6 × 6)	400 (36)	80 (24)
Dressing room	30 × 20 (9 × 6)	600 (54)	100 (30)
Dining room	40 × 20 (12 × 6)	800 (72)	120 (36)
Bedchamber	40 × 20 (12 × 6)	800 (72)	120 (36)
Study/library	30 × 20 (9 × 6)	600 (54)	100 (30)
Bedchamber	40 × 20 (12 × 6)	800 (72)	120 (36)
Gallery	130 × 20 (39 × 6)	2,600 (234)	300 (90)
Chair house study	40 × 30 (12 × 9)	1,200 (108)	140 (42)
Upper library	40 × 30 (12 × 9)	1,200 (108)	140 (42)
Subtotal	—	16,000 (1,440)	2,290 (687)

TABLE 1 (CONTINUED)

Room	Room dimensions in feet (metres)	Floor space/area in square feet (metres)	Room circumference in feet (metres)
THE QUEEN'S ROOMS			
Presence chamber	50×20 (15×6)	1,000 (90)	140 (42)
Privy chamber	35×20 (10.5×6)	700 (63)	110 (33)
Bed chamber	30×20 (9×6)	600 (54)	100 (30)
Privy lodging	45×40 (13.5×12)	1,800 (162)	170 (51)
Gallery	170×20 (51×6)	3,400 (306)	380 (114)
Subtotal	—	7,500 (675)	900 (270)
OTHER LODGINGS			
Guest lodgings (?)	100×20 (30×6)	2,000 (180)	240 (72)
Courtier lodgings	195×20 (58.5×6)	3,900 (351)	430 (129)
Subtotal	—	5,900 (531)	670 (201)
TOTALS	—	36,800 (3,312)	4,680 (1,404)

Denny's charge initially consisted of 100 carpets and they varied widely in their means of manufacture, condition and size [221, 420–435]. 'Frameworke' carpets formed the largest group, with sixty-two examples [434–435]. In addition there were twenty-three made from verdure [221], six made from dornix painted to resemble carpets of 'turkey making' [427–431], five of 'turkey making' [424–426, 432–433],[11] two with embroidered designs [422–423] and two executed in needlework [420–421].

While the king owned a few high-quality pieces many (62 per cent) of his carpets were in poor condition, as a consequence of poor storage and heavy use, or they were made using cheap materials such as painted dornix. In addition, most of the carpets were quite small, for example 'one turkey Carpett of silke Rowed / being in length two yerdes / and in bredith iij quarters di of a yerde' [425]. These references provide hints as to the type of textiles that might have been put down on the floor of rooms like the presence chamber, the privy chamber or studies used solely by the king. It certainly seems that carpets were desirable objects, if the king was willing to have painted versions as a substitute for the genuine article and if many of the carpets which he did own were well-used.[12]

---

11 The more common name for English imitations of Turkish carpet or rugs was 'turkey work': ibid, 110.

12 It is noteworthy that these carpets are described as being painted, while the stained cloths kept with the king's pictures were described as stained, rather than painted.

WALL HANGINGS Thomas Campbell has demonstrated that wall hangings were used in a hierarchical manner during the sixteenth century, with the most expensive being set in the most intimate rooms of the privy lodging, except on occasions of state, when the best hangings were displayed throughout the suite of royal apartments.[13] The terminology used to describe the hangings reflected their ranking: 'arras' was used to describe tapestry-woven hangings made with wool, silk and metal thread, 'tapestry' indicated hangings combining wool and silk thread, while 'verdures' were predominantly woven with wool only.[14] In addition, arras and tapestry usually had complex narrative designs, while foliate patterns predominated on verdures.

However, the structure of Henry VIII's inventories reveals that embroidered silk hangings were prized even more highly than arras, as they are listed first. Eight sets of silk hangings with matching window pieces were listed in Denny's charge [171–186], in addition to four sets that were specifically described as tent hangings [187–192]. The combination of expensive velvets, embroidery and fabrics with metal threads like tissue and cloth of gold gave these hangings their high status. They were made of panes of contrasting colours and decorated with the king's letters, devices and badges. The descriptions imply that each set consisted of one large hanging with two to four matching window pieces. The width of the hangings is given in panes rather than yards so it is hard to tell their exact size.[15] However, if each pane was made from a full loom-width of fabric the hangings would have ranged in width from 57ft 6ins (18.89m) to 130ft 4ins (43.37m). Expressed another way, the hangings would have been made up from 30 to 68 widths of fabric [181, 173]. The depths were fairly uniform ranging from 3½yds (3.2m) to 4¾yds (4.34m) and the accompanying window pieces ranged from ⅞yd (0.8m) to 1⅛yds (1.03m). Hangings of this size would have fitted in the larger principal rooms, such as the presence chamber and privy chamber. In order to accommodate the doorways, the panes must have been joined along the top edge of the hanging with some of the vertical seams left open. This construction would also be suited to the tent hangings, where versatility and flexibility were important key features.

However, it is possible that some of the hangings were much smaller, as indicated by the dimensions given for three later entries for silk hangings. The depth and width are given for two (7½yds (8.37m) by 5¼yds (4.8m) and 4½yds (4.11m) by 3¾yds (3.43m)), while the area is given for the third (24¾ square yds (20.58 square m)). Hangings of this size would fit readily on a wall in most of the rooms within the privy lodging. In addition, these hangings were figurative. Two are described as 'serving for a Churche', and while one of them had an image of the Passion [1228], the other was 'wrought with bestes birdes and sondry other Armes of golde Silver & silke' [1227]. The third combined an interesting selection of materials and techniques: 'oone pece of hanging of cloth of Silver stayned with thistory of Joseph borderid rounde aboute with cloth of Golde' [3333].

As with the three figurative silk hangings, the majority of the sets of arras and tapestry had religious subjects, with a predominance of New Testament subjects (see Table 2). After that, classical

---

13 Campbell, 'Cardinal Wolsey's tapestry collection', 114–19.
14 Campbell, 'Tapestry quality'.
15 For the following calculations, a pane has been taken to be a loom-width of cloth; as the width of looms was not standardized at this period, the figure 23ins (584mm) has been chosen, from the fifteenth-century Florentine *braccio*, one of the smallest *braccio* measurements used in Italy: see Monnas, 'Loom widths'.

TABLE 2

THE RELATIONSHIP BETWEEN HANGING TYPE AND SUBJECT

Type	Arras	Tapestry	Verdure	Total
Allegory	—	2	—	2
Classical	1	5	—	6
Genre	1	—	—	1
Hunting	—	1	—	1
Miscellaneous	—	2	—	2
Religious	5	4	—	9
Broad blooms	—	—	9	9
Small flowers	—	—	1	1
'Of the better sort'	—	—	1	1
'Old stuff'	—	—	1	1
'Sundry sorts'	—	—	1	1
TOTAL	7	14	13	34

subjects were most numerous. The sets of verdures were predominantly of the new, fashionable, broad-bloom style and those that were not were described in rather dismissive terms, including 'sundry sorts' and 'old stuff'.

The dimensions given in the inventory for the arras, tapestry, verdure and textile wall hangings are neither standard nor particularly helpful for a building where the room dimensions are uncertain. The arras, tapestry and verdure were recorded in terms of their area in square Flemish ells.[16] While this indicates the quantity of wall space covered, it is not possible to work out the actual dimensions of the hangings. The figures are as follows: 1,415 square Flemish ells 1¾ nails of arras (795⅝ square yds); 2,898¼ square Flemish ells ¾ nail of tapestry (1,630⅛ square yds) and 3,836¼ square Flemish ells 1 nail of verdure (2,157¾ square yds). If the pane width of the silk hangings is taken to be 24ins, then Henry VIII had over 1,670 square yds of this type of hanging.[17] In addition, there were 88 square yds of hangings made of scarlet woollen cloth [223], 16⅞yds of scarlet window pieces [224] and thirteen stained cloths for which no dimensions were given [809–811, 814–823].

If all the hangings were in use simultaneously, they could cover at least 5,638⅝ square yards of wall space. To put this figure in context, it is necessary to estimate the amount of wall space within the principal rooms at Whitehall on the ground and first floors (see figures in the final column, Table 1). Taking an average room height in the mid-sixteenth century of 10ft, there would be approximately 15,600 square yards of wall space, so Denny's hangings could cover a little over

16 A Flemish ell measures 27ins.
17 Based on the calculations of loom widths in n. 15,, the approximate area for entries 171–192 is 1,445 square yds. Dimensions are given for entries 222, 225 and 3333, so their area can be calculated as 225 square yds.

one third of the available space.[18] If Denny was responsible for furnishing just the king's rooms (the second block of rooms on Table 1), which is probably the more likely scenario, the approximate wall area to be covered would be 7,633 square yards. So, with 5,638⅝ square yards of wall hangings at his disposal, Denny had enough to cover almost three quarters of the total space that he might have to furnish. However, once other types of decoration that could be found on the walls of the king's apartments are considered, it is likely that Denny had enough wall hangings to cover all the areas that he was required to. The wall hangings would have been displayed in a context of painted and moulded decoration of the type represented in a drawing by an unknown artist of an interior designed for Henry VIII c. 1545.[19] While this is thought to be a design for a principal chamber, other rooms would have had large scale paintings such as Holbein's mural in the privy chamber, wooden panelling and smaller decorative item such as paintings, maps and mirrors.

These figures indicate that Denny would have been able to select hangings from his own holdings to create a range of decorative schemes that were appropriate for the events taking place in the palace and the status of the rooms that they were deployed in. For added variety, Denny could have drawn on the hangings in Reed's wardrobe, suggesting that high quality wall hangings were used through out the privy lodging on a day to day basis when the king was in residence. For special occasions Denny could have supplemented his resources with items drawn from the removing wardrobe and the Tower wardrobe such as the set of twelve leather hangings 'layde with golde and silver foyle' (**9033**).

It is not possible to link particular sets of hangings with specific locations, except in a few instances. Nine pieces of tapestry 'of the history of Muliager' were described as 'serving for a Lowe gallarye' [**199**]. Several of the pieces with religious subjects were linked with the chapel, as in the case of a piece of arras with the Crucifixion used as an altar frontal [**195**] and two hangings described as 'serving for a Churche' [**1227–1228**]. However, religious subjects were not restricted to rooms with a spiritual function; but while it is not possible to tell where the hangings were deployed, there is evidence for how they were deployed. A special folding ladder was made for the palace in the autumn of 1531 to help the Wardrobe staff furnish the privy lodging.[20]

TRAVERSES   Flexible in terms of construction and the means of deployment, the traverse could be used to cover doorways, to divide rooms or to create a room within a room. Traverses sometimes feature in the background of portraits, suggesting that they were quite a common feature of Tudor decor. They could be hung using rings on a pole, as in the background of Holbein's portrait of Sir Henry Guildford, or from a rope. Richard Gibson's revels accounts for Christmas 1511 include

---

18   This estimage of average room height errs on the conservative side. However, it assumes that the view that the hangings would reach from floor to ceiling, when it is very likely that there would be bare wall above and below them, the equivalent of several feet. Equally, the figures for available wall space do not take doors, windows or fireplaces into account.

19   Cliché des Musées Nationaux, Paris. Simon Thurley believes that this design was produced for Whitehall Palace, see Thurley, *Royal Palaces*, 217. The prominence in the design of the maiden's head badge used by Catherine Parr has been seen as evidence of her interest in architecture and her level of influence; James, *Kateryn Parr*, 162. However, it could just as well indicate Henry's wish to promote his sixth wife. Following on from the point made in the previous footnote, Thurley states that the height of the planned room would have been at least fifteen feet.

20   PRO E36/252, p. 419. The metalwork for the ladder cost 2s. Four other ladders of this type were made for the builders working on the palace.

a payment of 10*d* to replace 'A rope used for the travas in the hall at Greenwich and stolen during the disguising'.[21]

However, there were just six traverses within Denny's initial charge [517–521]. While they were all made from sarsenet, the traverses ranged in width from four to six panes and in depth between 2¾ and 4¼yds (3.88 and 2.51m).[22] As such they are relatively small and it is probable that they were used to cover a door or hang across a corridor. The traverse included with Catherine Howard's chapel stuff contained twelve breadths of sarsenet measuring 7¾yds (7m) which was probably used to form a small closet within in her chapel.

All in all, examining the traverses reveals little about the doors and doorways within the privy lodging at Whitehall. The limited evidence for the locks that would have been fitted to the doors will be discussed below[23] and is equally unrevealing in this context.

CURTAINS   Window curtains have five divergent functions: to provide privacy; to form part of a room's decorative scheme; to exclude daylight; to keep warmth in and to keep out draughts. However, in the sixteenth century window curtains were quite unusual and can be seen as a luxury item. This was true even within royal residences, as the 1547 Inventory indicates – there were five curtains in the Removing Wardrobe, seven at Whitehall in the care of John Reed, twenty-two at Hampton Court and two at The More. There were none in the thirteen other Wardrobes listed in the 1547 Inventory.

The curtains recorded in the 1542 Inventory provide some information about the number and size of the windows in the privy lodging. Denny's initial charge had fourteen sets of curtains, made up of sixty-nine individual items containing a total of 699yds (639m) of 'bridges' satin. By 1547 he had received an additional thirty curtains (a further fourteen sets), comprising a further 366yds (334.5m) in width. If the curtains were gathered, they could have been used for approximately 300yds (274m) of window.

Nineteen of the twenty-eight sets of curtains in Denny's charge were either pairs or single items (68 per cent); seven sets had between three and nine curtains (25 per cent) and there were just two large sets, with twelve and fifteen curtains respectively (7 per cent). The first group could be used in smaller rooms with one or two windows, like studies and closets; the middle group were more suited to medium-sized rooms with several windows; while the last group might have been used in big rooms with many windows, such as the long galleries. The only curtains tentatively associated with a specific room were three curtains of green sarsenet [2351] and one curtain of satin [2352] found amongst 'stuff of sondry natures Aswell founde within the kinges vpper library / as also newly made'.[24]

Curtain lengths were far from standard, suggesting that the heights of windows were equally varied. While the group of curtains in Denny's initial charge [1003–1016] ranged in depth from 3ft 4½ins (1.03m) to 13ft 1½ins (4m), the majority (forty-three curtains, or 62 per cent) were between 6ft (1.83m) and 8ft 3ins (2.51m). There were fifteen shorter curtains (22 per cent) ranging from

---

21 *LP* II.ii, p. 1497.

22 Unlike the chapel traverse mentioned below, there is no real hint as to how wide the panes were; if they were loom widths, they could be between 7ft 10ins (2.37m) and 11ft 6ins (3.51m) wide.

23 See pp. 83–4.

24 PRO E315/160, f. 105v. Only one direct attribution of curtains to a specific room appears in the 1547 Inventory: 'v smalle Courtens of tartaron lyned with buckeram appointed for the kinges pryvey chambre' at Greenwich (**9377**).

3ft 4½ins (1.03m) to 4ft 5ins (1.35m) and eleven longer curtains (16 per cent) measuring between 9ft (2.74m) and 11ft 3ins (3.43m) in length (thirteen curtains of each length). This contrasts with the lengths of the curtains at Hampton Court where, although the overall range was similar (4ft 6ins–13ft 6ins (1.37m)), the vast majority (68 per cent) were between 9ft (2.74m) and 11ft 3ins (3.43m) in length.[25] The range of curtain depths may reflect the fact that there was no attempt to standardize the various phases of building work. It may also be noted that the windows at Whitehall appear to have been slightly smaller than those at Hampton Court. It is likely that the sets of curtains were made for particular windows in a particular royal residence, and were only used in that location.

The width and depth of some of the curtains would have made it difficult to open and close windows. One solution was to use a hooked curtain pole of the type provided for Whitehall in 1532.[26] Denny's own charge included 'thre smale Staves either of them having ij very shorte Graynes of Iron to drawe Curtens with all' [1216].

At Whitehall, with the exception of three green sarsenet curtains, the curtains were made of 'bridges Satten of sondry colours' [1005], suggesting that the colour did not tie in to a specific decorative scheme. This impression is compounded by evidence from the wardrobes at Greenwich, Hampton Court and John Reed's holdings at Whitehall, where the colours were given in the 1547 Inventory. Taking the example geographically closest to Denny, John Reed had two curtains of red and white taffeta, two of purple and white damask, two of red, green, russet and tawny camlet and one of black, yellow and purple 'bridges' satin (9877-9880). Just five lengths of crimson, black, purple and yellow 'bridges' satin [2019-2023] were listed amongst Denny's stocks of fabric. As this cheaper satin was only used to make window curtains at Whitehall, it suggests that the curtains were made from various combinations of these colours.

Almost all the curtains were paned but the width of the panes was rarely recorded. It is possible that loom widths of fabric were seamed together, as in the case of the 'two Courtens of white and redde Tafata paned togethers conteyning vij bredthes of the same Taphata' (9877) in John Reed's Wardrobe. Alternatively, the panes could be much narrower, as in the case of 'Three windowe Curteines of crimesen and yellowe Sarceonett conteyninge xxxv panes di of the same Sarceonet euerie pane beinge one quarter of a yarde brode' at Hampton Court (12183). However, at Whitehall the panes were much larger ranging from 3ft 4½ins (1.03m) to 13ft 1½ins (4m).[27] This use of big blocks of colour would have produced a very striking visual effect.

The curtains certainly appear to have been well used. It is likely that the curtains were newly made for the palace (so making the oldest curtain date from at the earliest 1529), and by 1547 the curtains were described as 'beinge nowe verye olde sore worne and torne' (10567).

As an alternative to, or a substitute for, curtains, cut leafy branches were put over the windows to provide shade in the summer. In August 1547 Nicholas Foscus, groom porter, received 32s for the 'provision of grene bowes for the Kinges majesties pryvie chambre and galleries at Hampton courte' and 46s 8d for the same rooms at St James's.[28]

---

25 There were two curtains 4ft 6ins (1.37m) long, two curtains 7ft 6ins (2.29m) long, fifteen between 9ft (2.74m) and 11ft 3ins (3.43m) long and three between 12ft (3.66m) and 13ft 6ins (4.11m) long (12183-12195).
26 PRO E36/252, p. 631.
27 These figures are the result of dividing the total length of each curtain by the number of panes.
28 Nichols, *Literary Remains*, I, p. xcvi.

FIRE FURNITURE   Warmth was a necessary comfort in the palace, especially as the king became less mobile.[29] Heating was also important in keeping the palace dry when it was empty or during various phases of the building work. John Parker, a tallow chandler, supplied eight earthen pans to Whitehall Palace for burning charcoal 'In the kynges lodgynges the qwhyense and the Gallarysse of the same for the dryng of the moyster of the hangynges there'.[30] While earthern pans of this type did not have a place in Denny's inventory, pieces of ornate, fashionable ironwork did. Surviving examples include a set of firedogs at Knole which were decorated with the badges and initials of Henry and Anne Boleyn, as well as being 'wrought with sondry workes of Antiques' [1129].[31] This fire furniture would have been set into a large fireplace that would have formed an important decorative feature of the rooms. Suggestions of what these fireplaces would have looked like are provided by Holbein's design for a fire surround[32] and the surviving Henrician examples at St James's Palace.[33]

Denny had thirty-six pairs of andirons and thirty-one fire pans of assorted shapes [1126–1141, 3597–3601].[34] The associated tools – seventeen fire forks [1135, 3600], nineteen pairs of tongs [1137, 3601] and fifteen sets of bellows [1138] – were less well represented but these could have been moved fairly easily between rooms. This quantity of fire furniture indicates that Denny was involved in furnishing between thirty and forty rooms, some of which would not have had any heating provision and some of which would have had two fireplaces. Of the twenty-five rooms where an inventory was taken at Hampton Court in the king's and queen's lodgings, only twelve had fire furniture.[35] The areas without heating included the galleries, several small rooms off the galleries and interconnecting rooms.[36] If necessary, temporary heating may have been provided by moving some of the fire pans 'going vpon whelis' into these places [1140]. Beds could be warmed using fire pans, of the type delivered to Henry in December 1543 [159]. The danger of a fire getting out of control was ever present, as indicated by the presence of 'v lardge Squyrtes of copper for water againste fyer' (11689) in the new library at Whitehall.

CANDLES AND OTHER MEANS OF LIGHTING   Daylight was the most important source of light but additional lighting (for the evening, or in winter) could be provided by a variety of means. The most basic was the candle but candles rarely feature in inventories. However, the candlesticks do, and Denny had access to a variety of different types; some were intended for use

29 It was not just the king who felt the cold. In October 1533 the carpenters modifying Anne Boleyn's rooms at Greenwich, prior to Elizabeth's birth, were paid for 'the Stopping of diuerse creves in dores and wyndowes for keping forth the wynd': Bod Lib Rawlinson MS D 776, f. 2r.
30 Bod Lib MS English History b 192/1, unfoliated section between fos 58 and 59.
31 See Blair, 'Royal locks', 494.   32 BM 1854-7-8-1.
33 Several examples are illustrated in Thurley, *Royal Palaces*, 208, 227–9.
34 He also had 'oone Instrument to Raake the fier withall' and a toasting fork [3602–3603].
35 BL Harley MS 1419, fos 244v–253v.
36 The rooms with fire furniture were the privy chamber, the withdrawing chamber, the first bedchamber, the second bedchamber, the bain chamber, the long gallery, the first chamber off the gallery, and the queen's withdrawing chamber, the queen's privy chamber, the king's bedchamber on the queen's side, the privy chamber and the secret jewel house. The rooms not equipped were the library, the little gallery next to the withdrawing chamber, the short gallery, the lobby, the second chamber off the gallery, the little chamber at the end of the gallery, the chamber between the bedchamber and privy chamber, the queen's gallery, the queen's bedchamber, the queen's withdrawing chamber, the privy gallery, the jewel house and the chapel.

at specific times. He had twenty-two silver-gilt chandeliers (a branched support holding a number of candles) [**79–80**] and thirteen candlesticks (three gilt [**103, 113**], six parcel-gilt [**145–146**] and four white [**3749–3750**]) for use when the king was dining and three pairs of gilt altar candlesticks for lighting the king's closet [**131, 139, 3753**]. In addition there were eight glass candlesticks for dining [**1109–1111**] and three for the altar [**1112**]. He also had seventeen gilt metal candlesticks 'to be fastenyd to a wall' [**1147**]. These could be embellished with ropes of Venice gold and silver with decorative tassels 'serving for hanging Candlestickes' [**1224–1225**] and put out with snuffers of iron [**1221**]. More intense lighting could be provided by 'oone braunche of Latten with ix Candlestikes in hit' [**1146**]. The main alternative to candlesticks was the lantern [for example, **1231**].

The candles used in the king's apartments are likely to have been made from beeswax and they could be highly decorated, such as the 'dyuers candelles and peces of candelles of waxe whereof three be painted and gilte' (**9495**). In September 1531, by contrast, 15lbs (6.75kg) of tallow candles were provided for the clerks in the Counting House at Whitehall Palace and for labourers working through the night on the new building work.[37] Tallow was cheaper and burnt with a sootier flame. The diversity of materials for lighting (and heating) is illustrated in the allowances made to the Gentlemen of the Privy Chamber as *bouche* of court:[38] in the winter they received three links, one pricket, one fife, half a pound of white lights, four talfhides and four faggots a week.[39]

While Denny's inventory indicates the possibilities, there do not seem to be enough candlesticks for each room within the privy lodging to have its own lighting. This fits with the pattern at Hampton Court, where there were candlesticks or sconces in only six of the twenty-five rooms; this suggests that certain rooms were provided with permanent lighting, while others relied on lights being brought in as required.[40]

SANITARY ARRANGEMENTS   There are several references to the furnishings provided for the king's bath house or bain, one of the few rooms that recent archaeology has uncovered in detail.[41] Apart from the highly decorative stove that heated the room, the principal feature was the bed. This low bed, without supporting pillars for the celure and tester, had valances of white, tawny and yellow satin embroidered with roses and tawny and white taffeta curtains [**451**].[42] A selection of linen was provided for the king's use while bathing [**570–578**]. There is no evidence of how the bath house was furnished at Whitehall but it is likely that it followed the pattern established at Greenwich. Forty pieces of Henry VIII's glassware were housed in the 'lower study being a bayne' at Greenwich (**9657–9665**), while he kept a painting in the jake's house or privy (**9679**).

37 PRO E36/252, p. 313.

38 *Bouche* of court was the right to eat at the king's expense and to receive fuel and lighting material.

39 *HO*, p. 163. Over the summer they received a reduced allowance. The total value of the wax, white lights, wood and coals per year was £20 13s 0d. The meaning of some of these terms, such as 'fifes' and 'talfhides', is uncertain. 'Links' were torches made of tow and pitch; 'prickets' were candlesticks and so, perhaps, candles by association; 'white lights' were probably more expensive candles, made from beeswax rather than tallow (which is yellow in colour); 'faggots' are bundles of sticks.

40 The candlesticks or sconces were distributed as follows: one candlestick in the privy chamber (**12258**), one candlestick in the short gallery (**12302**), three wall-mounted candlesticks in the long gallery (**12341**), one candlestick in a chamber with the long gallery (**12357**), three candlesticks in the little chamber at the end of the long gallery (**12370**) and two candlesticks in the privy gallery (**12417**).

41 Gaimster *et al*, 'Armorial stove-tiles'.

42 A similar bedstead was listed in the bain at Greenwich in the 1547 Inventory: 'a Trussing bedstedde in the walle for the bayne having Ceeler and tester of blewe and yellowe sarcenet' (**9653**).

OBJECTS IN DENNY'S CHARGE

Denny's charge also included fifteen close stools that were associated with the palace [280–285, 3348]. There were four single items and three sets; the latter consisted of a pair covered with purple velvet, four covered in crimson velvet and five covered in black velvet. A rose embroidered in Venice gold metal thread acts as a unifying theme in their decoration. The close stools listed individually may have been for the king's use. They were well supplied with pewter bowls and cisterns. The sets of close stools suggest that these were orders made in bulk and so possibly were intended for use in the guest chambers.

Furniture: use and deployment

At properties where the 1547 Inventory was taken by room rather than by type of object (for example, at St John's, Clerkenwell, where Denny was Keeper), the impression is that the rooms were not heavily furnished.[43] The hall at St John's, which is likely to have been the largest room at the property, was furnished with

> one Lardge pece of Arras hanginge at thupper ende viij small peces of olde verdoures hanginge vpon bothe sides vj faier Tables vj formes with benches to thesame [,] ... A olde Cubborde with A Carpet [,] ... A beame of woode with latten candelstic- kes ... [and] A litell Bell (13791–13794).

The names of the rooms within Henry's privy lodging at Whitehall indicate that there was an increasing specificity of function. In response to that increased specificity, while some of the furnishings were generic and could be found in all or most of the rooms, others reflected the room's function. Consequently, books were generally placed in the library, the bed in the bedchamber, a cloth of estate in the presence chamber. Some types of object, like paintings, blurred the boundaries and were found both in places to be expected, like long galleries, and unexpected locations, at least for us, like bath houses.

The following paragraphs will examine what types of wooden furniture (such as cupboards, cabinets, seat furniture and suites of furnishings) came within Denny's initial charge, who made it and how it was deployed. It is clear from the outset that if the furnishings in Denny's care at Whitehall were distributed at similar 'density' levels to those found at St John's, they could have been distributed amongst a large number of rooms. The wooden furniture listed as being in Denny's initial charge can be roughly divided into two groups. The first consists of basic furniture made using simple techniques, having little or no decoration and often supplied in bulk. The second covers the more decorative pieces that were often embellished with surface decoration or which had a more complex construction and were purchased individually.

Taking the cupboards as an example, there were 'fourety playne Joyned Cupbourdes olde and newe' [1163] which can be contrasted with twenty-four fancy or more specialized pieces [1149–1150, 1152– 1162]; this leaves one cupboard not accounted for, described as 'playne' [1151]. A particularly fine

43 BL Harley MS 1419, fos 368r–372v. While the former London house of the Knights of St John was not one of Henry VIII's leading properties, the 1547 Inventory gives the impression that the house was furnished at the time the Inventory was taken, or, at any rate, that the listings reflected how the rooms were furnished when in use. Although the quality and age of the pieces reflect the differences between a second-rank property and one like Whitehall, the distribution is likely to have been fairly similar at both categories of residence.

example was made of 'walnuttre myxid with sondry colowrid woddes with this scripture *Humilitatem sequitur gloria* / having in hit thre boxes with covers / for Inke dust and Compters' [1152].[44]

While the purely functional pieces were probably put to use in some of the outer chambers, the more decorative items would have formed part of the display throughout the privy lodging. In April 1532 joiners made a table with a desk and tills, the pillars of which were carved with antiques, for use in the privy gallery.[45] This table seems to have disappeared by 1542, unless it is the 'square table of Waynscott standing vpon an olde fote Antique fashion colourid blewe' [1171]. Tables were often used in conjunction with a desk or standish and the only example of such a combination in Denny's hands was delivered to the king [1164]. A number of standishes were distributed throughout the king's apartments; in 1541 John Avery supplied goose-feather quills for use at Whitehall by the clerks in the Counting House, the clerks of the Works and 'to make pennys for the gallerys for the kynges standishes there'.[46]

CABINETS   Several cabinets were recorded at Whitehall.[47] They could be highly ornate, such as the cabinet with its

> foreparte and sides couered with crymsen vellat garnished in sundrie places with copper gilte with the kinges armes crowned having sondrie tilles of leather within with nyne leaves or dores to the same enameled with pictures of horsemen with iiij leaves to open couered with like crymsen vellat and likewise garnished with copper lyned with grene bridges satten garnished in sundrye places with narrowe passamayne of venyce golde (11574).

The cabinets recorded in the 1542 Inventory were empty, but some of those listed in the 1547 Inventory were in use, albeit mostly for general storage rather than display. The study 'at the hether ende of the Long Gallorie' at Whitehall[48] contained a

> Cabonet conteyning xxiij paier of grete hawkes Bells in one till xxiij tooles of metall of diuerse sortes in another Boxe … being in another tille of the same Cabonet In another tille v bundelles of fine threde and a pece of blacke ribband In another till sundrie tooles the most of them being hafted and stealed withe Brasell In another till iiij Spectacle cases furneshed (10454).

However, a few examples displayed a collection of objects at Whitehall during the king's lifetime, as is revealed by an incomplete document.[49]

Although the preamble is missing, this document almost certainly relates to Whitehall because a marginal note refers to James Rufforth, Denny's assistant. This note indicates that the contents of the two cabinets described were at least partially broken up on the first Sunday in Lent 1544

---

44 The figures break down as follows for the other groups of furniture: eight decorative and forty-nine plain chests, fourteen decorative and forty plain tables, twenty-nine pairs of plain trestles and one single trestle (also plain).
45 PRO E36/251, p. 28.
46 Bod Lib MS English History b 192/1, f. 2v.
47 The following paragraphs draw on Hayward, 'Possessions', 129–30.   48 BL Harley MS 1419, f. 113r.
49 BL Egerton MS 2679, fos 3r–6r.

(2 March). Twenty-six silver and silver-gilt items were removed by the king, 'to what purpose he declared not'.[50] Several of the items listed as being in the cabinets, or pieces that were very similar, appear in the lists of objects removed from the Whitehall secret jewel house on 6 August 1547.[51] These include nine spoons with Cromwell's arms (**1238**), several *pietre dure* cups and jugs, such as 'a Cup of Sarpentyne garnesshid with silver and gilt' (similar to (**729–731**)) and jugs of 'stone' (similar to (**1322**)) and 'iiij peper boxes parcell gilt' (similar to (**442–443**)).[52] Cups of this type had been collected since the late Middle Ages, although they were not an universal taste.[53]

Henry's cabinets also contained more exotic materials, such as a mother-of-pearl shell and 'thre Spones of shelles'.[54] However, the most interesting piece is one of the smallest: 'the picture of prince Edwardes face graven in Agate sett in golde'.[55] Two themes dominated Tudor glyptic art – royal portraits and images of St George – and this entry may refer to a surviving cameo of prince Edward.[56] Classical items, both originals and copies, are notable by their absence from the assortment, as are medals and coins. Although there is no indication as to where these cabinets were kept, they were probably located within one of the galleries or studies. Henry briefly created a cabinet of the type owned by Italian collectors such as Isabella d'Este.[57] The fact that the cabinet was dismantled may reflect that he found this method of display unsatisfactory, preferring to admire his possessions in the context of a room.

The Inventory entries also reveal where cabinets were kept. The example described above was from one of the king's studies. When an inventory was taken of the privy gallery in 1550 only one item remained: 'a Cabonet of crimsen satten allouer laied with siluer and golde passamen withe a [blank] virginall in the bottome' (**16923**). Rooms such as the privy gallery were almost exclusively reserved to the use of the king, so the cabinets were intended for Henry's private interest rather than public display.

SEAT FURNITURE   There is a surprisingly large quantity of seating recorded in the 1542 Inventory. Some of it was strictly functional, such as the forms and wooden stools, while the majority was provided with padding and decorative top covers in a rudimentary form of upholstery.[58] The range of seating included chairs, folding stools, stools, cushions and footstools. Seating was intensely hierarchical, with the low chairs and stools mainly identified as being for women [for example, **251**, **272**] and a single small chair covered with purple velvet for a child [**262**]. As there were few children present at court, it is possible that this was provided for either Prince Edward or the Lady Elizabeth.

---

50 Ibid, f.5v.

51 E.g. SA MS 129, f.17r.

52 BL Egerton MS 2679, f.4r–v.

53 Lightbown, *Secular Goldsmiths*, 59–60.

54 BL Egerton MS 2679, f.4v. Several shells were amongst the plate delivered from Westminster (**408–410**), including 'one Snayle of mother of Perle bourne vp by an Antique man of siluer and guylt the fote of siluer and guilt garnysshed with Rubies Dyamountes and perles the Couer of siluer and guilte with Rubies Dyamountes and perles with a woman holding a Childe sucking at hir brest' (**408**).

55 BL Egerton MS 2679, f.6r.

56 Scarisbrick, *Jewellery in Britain*, 82. There are three surviving early Tudor cameo portraits, of Henry VIII, Henry VIII and Prince Edward, and Prince Edward; they appear to be by the same unidentified artist.

57 Brown and Lorenzoni, '*Grotta* of Isabella d'Este', 161–2; Jardine, *Worldly Goods*, 410–12.

58 The figures break down as follows: sixty-four plain and one decorative forms and seventy-nine plain and thirteen decorative stools. For a fuller discussion of the upholstered seat furniture see Hayward, 'Seat furniture'.

The Inventory includes eighty-four single chairs, cushions, footstools and stools (39 per cent), sixty sets with two-pieces (27.9 per cent) and forty-three sets with three-pieces (20 per cent). These figures (see Table 3) suggest that either seating (whether on chairs, cushions or stools) was only provided for small groups in any one room or, if more people were to be seated, having matching seating was not an important consideration. This point is demonstrated visually in the picture painted to commemorate the Somerset House Conference in 1604, where all the participants were seated on sumptuous chairs, none of which matched.[59] However, the 1542 Inventory also provides an exception to this trend in the form of two sets of sixteen chairs, both of which were covered with cloth of gold raised with crimson velvet [238–239]. It would have required a sizeable room to use either of these sets in its entirety, and the most likely places are the long galleries where the chairs could have been positioned with their backs to one of the long walls.

TABLE 3

BREAKDOWN OF THE SIZES OF SETS OF SEAT FURNITURE, CUSHIONS AND FOOTSTOOLS

Number of items in the set	Chairs	Cushions	Folding stools	Footstools	Stools	Total
1	15	66	—	1	2	84
2	14	29	—	12	5	60
3	4	38	—	1	—	43
4	2	4	—	4	—	10
5	—	4	—	—	1	5
6	—	2	1	1	—	4
7	—	1	2	—	—	3
8	—	—	—	1	—	1
9	—	—	—	1	—	1
10	—	—	1	—	—	1
11	—	—	—	1	—	1
16	2	—	—	—	—	2
TOTAL	37	144	4	22	8	215

SUITES OF FURNISHINGS   One of the problems arising from the objects in the 1542 Inventory being grouped by type is that matching sets of items are split up: a chair is separated from its accompanying footstool and cushion. A number of these sets, however, can be re-established including a

59 NPG 665.

chair covered with cloth of gold 'reysid with Rowes wherin ar flowers of blew vellat' [242], matching cushions [372] and a footstool [277]. Other examples, also with cloth-of-gold covers, include a pair of chairs [246] with two footstools [278]. These sets formed part of Denny's initial charge in 1542 and new similar matching sets were bought some time between February and April 1545 [3702–3710]. This purchase was made up of three matching sets, each consisting of a chair, a cushion and a pair of footstools. These homogeneous groups provide a marked contrast with the more random provision of chairs and cushions and mixtures of colours and fabrics that was apparently the norm in royal wardrobes. However, this shift towards sets of furnishings united by colour and fabric type was short lived. Indeed the majority of the sets had been split up by 1547 (see below).[60]

Objects for Recreation and Intellectual Stimulation

Henry VIII was a highly-educated man with an interest in music, literature and culture generally (see Figure 2). Physically, these interests were manifested in the form of 157 paintings and embroideries [664–808, 812], thirty-one mirrors [861–881, 2240, 2369–2371], twenty-nine maps [837–860, 2358–2359, 3471, 3699–3700], twenty-four pictures made from terracotta, marble or 'blac Towche' [824–836, 2378–2385], ten clocks [1051–1060], 187 musical instruments [888–943, 2353–2355, 3354, 3495, 3701] and 915 books [2398–3305].[61] The best suggestion of how these objects were combined into decorative schemes is provided, once again, by a comparison with the rooms of the privy lodging at Greenwich, the privy lodging at Hampton Court and the studies, library and secret jewel house at Whitehall (see Table 4). This table shows that pictures, maps, musical instruments and clocks were distributed quite freely within the principal rooms of the privy lodging as well as its galleries, studies and closets. There is no reason to think that a similar pattern was not followed at Whitehall. This suggestion will now be explored by looking at several groups of these objects in depth.

'TABLES WITH PICTURES'   The Inventory uses this term to introduce a list of objects – paintings, embroideries and the like – that all include a pictoral image. The clerk used the phrase 'a table with a picture of …' to describe items as diverse as paintings and bas relief sculpture. Stepping away from the presence of an image, this is a very disparate group in terms of the techniques and materials used and includes paintings on panel, embroideries, enamels, low-relief alabaster sculptures and pictures on glass. As Table 5 shows, painting provided the greatest scope in terms of subjects, while religious subjects were executed using the broadest range of materials and techniques. Portraits formed a significant group, with classical subjects and landscapes as small subgroups that added diversity to the collection.

The entries for the paintings provide relatively little detail beyond a brief description of the image and whether a curtain was provided or not. On the whole, information relating to size or construction was omitted, making the few incidental details that do appear all the more interesting. Of the 109 paintings on panel, there were two diptychs [700, 720], nine triptychs (one of which [707] had a lock) [707, 729, 730, 735, 745, 767, 802, 805, 813], two round pieces [717, 740], two square pieces [786, 788], eight little pictures [685, 717, 739, 740, 766, 786, 788, 803], three great pictures [675, 687,

60 See pp. 136–7.
61 For a discussion of the musical instruments, see Blezzard and Palmer, 'Henry VIII'.

TABLE 4

THE DISTRIBUTION OF DECORATIVE ITEMS WITHIN THE PRIVY LODGINGS AT GREENWICH, HAMPTON COURT AND WHITEHALL, WITH REFERENCE TO THE 1547 INVENTORY

Location	Clocks and Dials	Instruments	Maps, Plats and Globes	Mirrors	Pictures
GREENWICH					
Privy chamber	—	—	—	1	—
Closet next to the privy chamber	—	—	—	—	2
Withdrawing chamber	1 clocks	1 regal / virginal	—	—	1, plus 'other pictures'
Closet next to the bed chamber	5 clocks	—	—	—	—
King's gallery	1 clock	1 virginal	—	1	1
A chamber within the gallery	—	—	—	—	1 image cast in metal
Gallery	—	—	1 map	—	—
Closet over the water stair	1 dial	—	1 map, 2 globes, divers plats	1	9
Jakes house (latrine)	—	—	—	—	1
Subtotal	*7 clocks, 1 dial*	*1 regal / virginal 1 virginal*	*2 maps, 2 globes, divers plats*	*3*	*14, plus 'other pictures', 1 image cast in metal*
HAMPTON COURT					
Privy chamber	1 base for a clock	1 pair portatives	—	—	—
Library	—	—	—	—	3
Withdrawing chamber	1 clock	—	—	1	—
Second bedchamber	—	1 virginal	—	—	—
Bath chamber	—	—	—	2	—
Little gallery	1 clock	—	3 plats	—	—
Short gallery	—	—	1 plat	1	'a George in harness'
Lobby between the galleries	1 clock	—	—	—	—
Long gallery	1 clock	1 regal, 8 virginals	1 globe	5	22
First chamber in the gallery	—	—	—	—	1
Second chamber in the gallery	—	1 pair portatives	—	2	1
The little chamber at the end of gallery	—	—	—	1	—
The chamber between the bedchamber and the privy chamber	—	1 instrument	—	1	1
Queen's withdrawing chamber	—	—	—	1	—

TABLE 4 (CONTINUED)

Location	Clocks and Dials	Instruments	Maps, Plats and Globes	Mirrors	Pictures
HAMPTON COURT (CONTINUED)					
King's bedchamber on the queen's side	—	—	—	1	—
Queen's table	—	1 regal	—	2	9
Privy gallery	—	—	—	1	—
Subtotal	*4 clocks, 1 base*	*2 pair portatives, 2 regals, 9 virginals, 1 instrument*	*4 plats, 1 globe*	*18*	*37, plus 'a George in harness'*
WHITEHALL					
The secret jewel house	4 clocks, 1 dial	—	—	6	1
The study at the end of the long gallery	—	—	—	2	—
The chair house study	1 dial	—	—	10	18
The study next to the old bedchamber	—	—	—	13	1
The new library	—	—	1 map, 1 globe	1	1
Subtotal	*4 clocks, 2 dials*	*—*	*1 map, 1 globe*	*32*	*21*
TOTALS	15 clocks, 1 base, 3 dials	1 regal/virginal, 10 virginals, 2 pair portatives, 2 regals, 1 instrument	3 maps, 4 plats, 4 globes and divers plats	53	72, plus 1 image cast in metal, 'other pictures' and 'a George in harness'

750] and one with a cover [688]. More details were given for the embroideries, perhaps reflecting the clerks' familiarity with this medium from their work recording the furnishings. Of the twenty-three embroideries, two had grounds of satin [664, 780], seven had grounds of cloth of gold [716, 728, 752–753, 755], three had grounds of velvet [731, 797, 807], six had borders [752–755], nine were worked with thread of Venice gold and/or silver [676, 683, 701–702, 754, 758, 780, 797, 807], one was worked with flat gold thread [756], three were worked with pearls [716, 731, 757] and two were worked with counterfeit stones [716, 731]. These embroideries may well form part of the English ecclesiastical embroidered tradition that stretched back to the heyday of *opus anglicanum*.

A comparison between the number of pictures and embroideries at Whitehall and those found in the privy lodgings at Greenwich and Hampton Court suggests that Whitehall had far more of these objects. It is possible that some of the pictures and embroideries at Whitehall were not on display, but were kept in a special store. There was a store of this type at Hampton Court, although it was

TABLE 5

THE CORRELATION BETWEEN MATERIALS AND
SUBJECTS FOR 'TABLES WITH PICTURES'

	Allegory	Classical	Landscape	Narrative	Portraiture	Religious	Total
Alabaster	—	1	—	—	—	2	3
Bone	—	—	—	—	—	1	1
Embroidery	—	—	—	—	—	23	23
Enamel	—	—	—	—	—	1	1
Enbossing	—	—	—	—	—	1	1
Glass	—	—	—	—	—	1	1
Marquetry	—	—	—	—	—	1	1
Mother-of-pearl	—	—	—	—	—	2	2
Painting on panel	5	7	—	1	57	38	108
Parchment	—	—	4	—	—	—	4
'Raised with liquid gold and silver'	—	1	—	—	—	2	3
Staining	—	—	—	—	2	2	4
TOTALS	5	9	4	1	59	74	152

not included in the 1547 Inventory entry for that palace.[62] One possible way of distinguishing which paintings and embroideries had been on recent display at Whitehall when the 1542 Inventory was compiled is to examine whether a painting had a curtain.[63] Of the pieces listed in the 1542 Inventory, sixty-one had curtains (see Table 15).[64] If this suggestion is valid, the picture selection had hardly changed between the two inventories. The clerks must have checked whether the curtains were present in 1547 because in four instances they recorded that the curtain had either been removed or lost.[65] It is also possible that, the presence of a curtain may denote those pieces that were hung in the various galleries, while pictures placed in other rooms may not have been covered.

MAPS, STAINED CLOTHS AND TERRACOTTAS   Although the 'tables with pictures' were far from homogeneous as a group, the clerks felt that they were distinct from other types of decorative material, namely maps (including plans and plats), stained cloths and terracottas. One of the paintings came close to crossing the divide with maps, plans and plats. The 'table of the Seege

---

62 The building accounts record a payment for 'a stoke locke sett upon a dour for the sayffe being of the kinges paynted bordes'; PRO E36/239, p. 28
63 I would like to thank Lisa Monnas for discussing this possibility with me.
64 Entries 673–674, 679–681, 689–692, 694, 701, 704–706, 709–713, 715–717, 721, 728, 731–732, 734, 736–738, 740–741, 746–751, 766, 768–772, 774–779, 782, 795–801, 803–804, 806.
65 Entry 736 'deffecit the Curteyne'; and see also entries 740, 800, 806.

TABLE 6

ANALYSIS OF STAINED CLOTHS BY SUBJECT

This table focuses only on the objects described in the Inventory as 'oone cloth stayned' [814]. Staining was also used to create objects that are listed under to other headings: paintings or 'tables' with the design created by staining (710, 786, 809–811) and maps created by staining (834, 841, 843–846, 849–850, 852–853, 3699).

	Allegorical	Classical	Narrative	Portraiture	Religious
Initial list	1	1	1	3	4
Later additions	—	—	—	—	3
TOTALS	1	1	1	3	7

of *Pauy* [804] shared its subject with one of the maps, a 'discription of the Seege of Pavy when the Frenche king was takin' [850]. Yet maps were a distinct group of objects with a strategic and political significance. Their range extended from recording 'dover and Calice' [840], two of the key ports within Henry VIII's territory, to 'the whole worlde' [851].

The maps were also more uniform in terms of the techniques and materials used to produce them. Of the twenty-three maps listed in Denny's initial charge, fourteen were produced on cloth using a staining technique [838, 841, 843-847, 849–850, 852–853, 855–857], six were on parchment [837, 839–840, 842, 848, 854], two were on paper [851, 858] and one was made using a technique that is described in very similar terms to those used for the terracottas: 'the discription of dover made of erth sett in a boxe of wodde' [859]. The single globe listed here was made from metal [860], while the three globes kept in the library were made of wood [2358-2359], one of which was covered with paper [2358].

Stained cloths are sometimes implied to be the poor man's substitute for tapestries. This is not borne out by the 1542 Inventory where those forming part of Denny's initial charge are not listed after the other wall hangings but after the 'tables with pictures' [809–811, 814–823]. Denny received a second group of these hangings 'delyuered owt of the kinges house vnder his privey key' some time between April 1544 and April 1545 [3696–3698].[66] Objects created by staining were also recorded under the two headings 'maps' and 'pictures' (that is, 'tables with pictures'), suggesting that the stained cloths were united by more than just technique: common factors seem to be their larger size, their pictorial rather than topographical subject, and their ephemeral rather than long-lasting nature (see Table 6). Of the initial thirteen stained cloths, three were described as being 'deffecit thole Clothe' [814, 815, 820] by 1547. It is impossible to tell whether this represents pieces that were stolen, pieces that had deteriorated beyond use and/or pieces that had just been misplaced.

The group of terracottas is harder to pin down. Several of the subjects were religious but the majority represented genre studies of women or 'Morian' boys. Between 1542 and 1547 nearly all

66 PRO E315/160, f.135r.

the terracottas in Denny's initial charge had lost their wooden frames. Another group of eleven terracottas was present in the library and added to Denny's charge on 27 May 1542. Perhaps more interesting is the 'square Boxe with thymage of kinge Henrye theight wrought in earth' (**10494**), recorded in the 1547 Inventory as being in 'the kinges secrete studie called the Chaier house'.[67] It has been suggested that this might be the painted terracotta bust of Henry VIII made by the Florentine sculptor Pietro Torrigiano.[68]

BOOKS   Henry had established a library at Whitehall by 1531 at the latest (see Figure 2); in May of that year a new plate-lock was fitted to the door connecting the library with the king's dressing room.[69] The library at Whitehall, like that at Greenwich, was described as being high up, suggesting that a tower location was Henry's preferred site for his libraries.[70] As indicated above,[71] libraries contained more than books, but the books were an increasingly predominant feature. In 1547 the library at Hampton Court was described as having 'a greate nombre of bookes' (**12262**). In addition there were 204 books in the library at Greenwich stored in seven desks (**9668–9681**), with a further 123 books described as being 'vndre the table' (**9675**, **9678**), while two named volumes were in an unspecified location, possibly on the table.[72] In contrast there were 915 books at Whitehall [**2398–3305**] with no real indication of how they were stored. Shelving or desks are possibilities for most of them, while a few could be kept in 'oone Table coverid with grene cloth with sondry Cupbourdes in it to set bookes in with iiij olde Curtens of buckeram frengid with grene silke to hang afore the bookes' [**2365**].

A table would have been a practical addition to any library's furniture, as it provided a place for consulting the books. In the spring of 1531 the joiners at Whitehall made a table with decorative ironwork for the library.[73] It was decorated with nails with rose-shaped heads and eighteen rings embellished with roses. Books were rarely kept in isolation, as the entries for the library at Whitehall in the 1542 and 1547 inventories reveal. In 1542 there were eleven terracottas [**2377–2386**], five mirrors [**2369–2371**] and a globe, but by 1547 only the globe (**11656**)[74] was left in the library. Mirrors, maps and pictures were often found in libraries, studies and long galleries.

67 BL Harley MS 1419, f. 115r.

68 See, for example, Plumb, *Royal Heritage*, 48. The bust in question is in the Metropolitan Museum, New York, but there is another terracotta bust of a boy, *c.* 1500, in the Royal Collection, that has been attributed to Guido Mazzoni and is implausibly considered to be of Henry VIII in his youth.

69 PRO E36/251, p. 106. Similar precautions were taken at Richmond. In the winter of 1535 Henry Romains, the king's locksmith, provided a new plate-lock with two keys and four bolts for the library door: NUL Ne.01, unfoliated, account for Richmond 21 November to 19 December 1535.

70 This was also true of studies and closets. According to Brian Tuke, Henry made use of tower rooms at Hunsdon in the summer of 1528: 'I took [letters from Wolsey] to the king … in the tower, where he sometimes sups apart' (*LP* IV.ii, 4409).

71 See Table 4.

72 They were 'a booke wrytten in parchement of the processe betwene king henry theight and the ladye katheryne dowager' (**9676**) and a copy of the New Testament (**9677**).

73 PRO E36/251, p. 16. The ironwork cost 19*s* 6*d*.

74 Either **2358** or **2359**. The entry in the 1547 Inventory is too vague to distinguish to which of the three 1542 globes it is referring.

The use of furnishings for specific functions

Considering groups of objects in isolation provides only a partial view of how the palace was decorated and functioned. A more complete picture emerges once related groups of objects are examined, in particular those used for significant activities within the king's daily life such as dining, sleeping, and the rituals of the mass and court ceremonial.

DINING   Eating was a central part of court life, for both the king and his household. Henry VIII could eat on a semi-private basis in the privy chamber, or more publicly at larger functions in the privy chamber or the presence chamber, or for events of state in the great hall. *Bouche* of court, which included eating at the king's expense, was granted to about 600 members of the household. The higher household officers, numbering approximately 230, ate outside the hall, with the elite eating in the presence chamber. The large number of tables recorded in the 1542 Inventory indicates that Denny could provide tables and seating for the king and his inner household. He had thirty-eight tables [1177], twenty-five pairs of trestles [1180], sixty-four benches [1182] and seventy-three joined stools [1191]. In addition, Denny had the necessary furniture for large-scale entertaining in the form of 'two Long Tables serving for banket Tables' [1176]. The use of long tables of this type can be seen in the seating plan prepared for the banquet held at Greenwich after a joust in 1517.[75] Twenty-six guests were seated at the long side tables with five on the short top table.

In addition, Denny managed an impressive selection of napery. His basic charge comprised thirty-two tablecloths [579–607], sixty-two napkins [608–610], twenty-nine towels [613–641], three sewer's towels [642–644], fifteen coverpanes [645–656] and four cupboard cloths [611–612]. On 13 May 1542 he received a further eight tablecloths, twenty-three towels, five cupboard cloths, four coverpanes and 245 napkins that had been confiscated from the Lambeth home of the late Duchess of Norfolk [2309–2347]. This quantity of napery corresponds quite well with an order drawn up in January 1542 for Anne Harris, the king's laundress.[76] She was charged with four 'great pieces' (table-cloths?), twenty-eight long and twenty-eight short breakfast cloths, twenty-eight hand towels and twelve dozen napkins.[77] The acquisition of the confiscated material brought Whitehall's stocks of napery up to an acceptable level.

Denny also had lengths of linen cloth that could be made up into new napery: nineteen lengths for tablecloths (totalling 487½ ells (557.21m)), fifteen lengths for napkins (totalling 377¾ ells (431.77m)) and thirteen lengths for towels (totalling 334¾ ells (382.62m)). More interestingly Denny had a large collection of coverpanes [645–656] and, as the 1547 Inventory reveals, with the exception of a single coverpane at Oatlands (12831) they were found only at Whitehall: this suggests that dining habits at Whitehall were particularly sophisticated.[78]

Denny could accommodate at least twenty guests with his resources of silver-gilt plate (see Table 7): it included 'two dossen of plate Trenchers wherof oone dossen hath the kinges Armes / and thother hath thre flowerdeluces' [68], 'Twentie and Six Spones gilt / xxiiij of them with knoppes

---

75   BL Additional MS 21116, f. 44r.

76   *HO*, p. 215.

77   Ibid. Anne Harris was required to wash a quarter of the linen every week and deliver it to the Serjeant or Yeoman of the King's Mouth in the ewery.

78   Mitchell, 'Coverpanes'.

at ther endes' [**64**], thirty-five bowls [**50–58**] and twenty-two cups [**81–94**]. He could also call upon the reserves of banqueting plate in the removing coffers.[79] One notable exception to this wealth of material is the absence of any serious display plate – this could have been borrowed from the Tower jewel house or the Whitehall jewel house as required.[80] Alternatively, the gilt plate could be supplemented with 'divers conceytes for a Bankett made of erthe' [**1125**] and other pieces from Henry's selection of glassware such as 'Twelve Bolles of Glasse with oone cover to them / all wrought with diaper worke white' [**1071**].

In August 1543 Denny received some white (silver) dining plate from the secret jewel house: twenty-seven plates and seventy-five dishes with the king's arms [**3480–3481**] and eighteen saucers with the Duke of Norfolk's arms [**3482**]. For those further down the social spectrum, Denny had forty-eight platters, twenty-four dishes and one charger, all of pewter [**1234–1236**]. After Henry VIII's death this pewter was returned to Richard Frenior by means of a writ of restitution.[81] This group of materials reveals that Denny could cater for a range of individuals both numerically and socially.

Interestingly, Denny also had a small selection of cooking utensils in his care, including 'two Trevettes of Iron' [**1238**] and six wooden bowls [**1239**]. Most likely, these were for use in the privy kitchen, which was situated on the ground floor at Whitehall, close to the chapel. The role of the privy kitchen was to provide meals for the king at times convenient to him. Denny's role was to liaise with the king and his cook.

SLEEPING ARRANGEMENTS   The provision of beds and bedding at Whitehall in 1542 was generous. There were twenty-five bedsteads with apparel and four without, ten trussing bedsteads with hangings, one folding bed, fourteen mattresses, thirty-four counterpoints, nine quilts, seventy-eight pairs of sheets and fifty-seven single sheets, fourteen bolsters, twenty pillows, thirty-five pairs of pillow-beres and thirty-three single. In addition there were also unappointed furnishings for beds in the form of twenty-one celures and testers, and two sparvers. The bedsteads with apparel were listed first and the first few of these were the largest, being 9ft square (2.74m square) or 9ft (2.74m) × 9ft 3ins (2.82m), while the majority were a little smaller, ranging from 6ft (1.83m) to 8ft 3ins (2.51m) in length and 3ft 9ins (1.14m) to 8ft 3ins (2.51m) in breadth. The entries did not record the overall heights of the bedsteads but a rough approximation can be gained from the length of the bed curtains. These ranged from 5ft 3ins (1.6m) to 8ft 3ins (2.51m) in length. In addition, some beds had decorative vanes which would have added more height [**444**], and others had 'Antique Cuppes' [**447–448, 450**].

Often the celure and tester, curtains and counterpoint appointed to some bedsteads were all the same colour. Even so, it was standard practice for the different elements to be in contrasting colours. For example a crimson and purple celure and tester, had yellow, white and purple curtains and a russet and yellow counterpoint [**445**] (see Table 8). This impression of the furnishings often

---

79 Entries **101–103, 129–131, 417, 605–631, 823–825, 993–999, 1070–1077, 1115–1116, 1177–1182, 1227–1228, 1278–1283, 1385–1389, 1525–1530, 1591–1598, 1648–1652, 1670–1671, 1719–1728, 1756–1759, 2001–2002**.

80 For example, 'one Salte of golde the salte being Prasinus greane being thistorie of Adam and Eve dryven owte of paradis by thaungell garnished with rubies Saphires turqueyses and perles standing vppon three balles of Jasper poids xiij oz quarter' (**88**) was delivered to the Tower from the jewel house at Whitehall in 1547.

81 PRO E315/160, f. 76v.

TABLE 7

SUMMARY OF THE PLATE IN DENNY'S CHARGE, 1542–7

Type of plate	Initial charge	Later additions	Total
DOMESTIC PLATE			
Gold			
Casting bottles	2	—	2
Spoons	2	1	3
Gilt			
Basins and ewers	6	1	7
Bowls	35	7	42
Candlesticks	3	—	3
Casting bottles	6	—	6
Chafing dishes	—	1	1
Chandeliers	22	—	22
Clocks	1	—	1
Cruces	2	—	2
Cups	24	3	27
Flagons, pairs	2	2	4
Glasses	2	—	2
Hourglasses	1	—	1
Jugs	3	2	5
Lanterns	2	—	2
Layers	2	2	4
Nuts	2	—	2
Perfume pans	3	—	3
Pots (pairs)	15	2	17
Salts	12	1	13
Snuffers	2	—	2
Spice boxes	1	—	1
Spoons	26	—	26
Strainers	1	—	1
Trenchers	24	—	24
Trenchers, standing	4	—	4
Parcel-gilt			
Barber's basins	1	—	1
Basins and ewers	9	2	11
Bowls	—	5	5
Candlesticks	6	—	6
Chafing dishes	—	2	2
Cruces	—	3	3
Cups	—	1	1
Flagons (pairs)	—	2	2
Goblets	—	6	6
Lavatory basins	2	—	2

Type of plate	Initial charge	Later additions	Total
Perfume pans	2	—	2
Pots (pairs)	—	2	2
Standishes	1	—	1
White			
Barber's basins	3	—	3
Bells	1	—	1
Candlesticks	2	4	6
Cruces	—	1	1
Cups	—	1	1
Kitchen pots	1	—	1
Ladles	1	—	1
Lanterns	—	1	1
Perfume pans	4	—	4
Snuffers	1	—	1
Tastes	1	—	1
Vices	2	—	2
Warming pans	1	—	1
Water pots	3	—	3
Subtotal	*246*	*52*	*298*
CHAPEL PLATE			
Gilt			
Basins	4	2	6
Candlesticks (pairs)	2	1	3
Chalices	2	1	3
Crosses	—	1	1
Cruets	4	2	6
Holy-water pots	1	2	3
Images	14	—	14
Pyxes	3	—	3
Sakering bells	1	1	2
Superaltars	—	1	1
Tablets	1	—	1
Water pots	1	—	1
Parcel-gilt			
Chalices	—	1	1
Holy-water pots	1	—	1
Sakering bells	1	—	1
Subtotal	*35*	*12*	*47*
TOTAL	**281**	**64**	**345**

TABLE 8

THE COLOURS AND COLOUR COMBINATIONS USED FOR BED HANGINGS

Colour	Celures and testers	Curtains	Counterpoints
Black	2	—	—
Blue	3	2	2
Crimson	11	7	7
Green	2	5	2
Purple	8	5	8
Red	1	4	2
Russet	—	—	1
Tawny	2	1	2
Three colours	4	2	1
Two colours	12	14	15
Unspecified	1	—	—
White	5	8	10
Yellow	4	10	7
TOTALS	**55**	**58**	**57**

combining very vibrant colours – first indicated by the colour combinations used for window curtains – is reinforced by much of the evidence relating to bed hangings.

Evidence from the marginalia indicates that the king slept in a bed furnished with crimson satin hangings and curtains that were embroidered with gold thread, pearls and blue stones [**440**]. This bed 'was enlarged mensis Marcii Anno xxxiiij^to ... and thapparell therof made mette to the same bedstede in euery degre / and the thre curtyns ... new euery of them'. While none of the bed linen was identified as being for the king's bed, the most luxurious was probably for his use. This included 'foure Sheetes of lawne ... frengid rounde aboute with a narrowe freng of venice golde / And having iiij smale buttons with Shorte tasselles of like golde' [**557**], 'eight pillowebeeres of holland with brod seames of silke of sondry colours nedleworke' [**565**] and 'oone Pillowe beere of fyne holland wrought with a brode seame of venice golde silver and silke nedleworke' [**566**]. Although the Groom of the Stool was responsible for the king's bed linen, in 1542 Denny had 'two smale Pillowe beeres of holland to cary Lynen for the king his bed in' [**564**].

Further notes suggest that the king's bedchamber was hung with a set of five scarlet wool wall hangings and six window pieces [**223–224**], as these hangings were altered when the bedchamber was enlarged between July and September 1545.[82] Other items that could have been used, if not to match, at any rate to blend with, the hangings include a close stool 'coverid ... with scarlet frengid

---

82 Ibid, f. 9v.

with crymsen silke / and lined with scarlet' [285]. In November 1542 Henry ordered a set of four footstools covered with scarlet [3317] and in September of the following year Denny received 'two lowe Stowles to stande by a bedde', also covered in scarlet [3483]. These stools may have made it easier for the king to get in and out of bed as he became less agile.

It seems likely that Henry used this group of furnishings in his private bedchamber. If this is the case, then it raises several interesting issues. First, the bed – it was sumptuous, but nowhere near as luxurious as the bed taken as a perquisite by the Earl of Warwick, which had hangings of crimson gold tissue [436]. Secondly, the use of wool for the king's furnishings is unique. Even though good quality woollen cloth was expensive and it was dyed scarlet – probably with kermes, the most expensive dyestuff – all of the other comparable furnishings in Denny's charge were made of silk. Thirdly, this use of scarlet woollen cloth would have fitted with contemporary thinking on a healthy lifestyle. Andrew Boorde advised readers in his *First Boke of the Introduction of Knowledge* published in 1547 'Let your nyght cap be of scarlet … and in your beed lye not to hote nor to cold, but in temperence'.[83] Henry owned a scarlet night cap and it looks as though he persued this advice one step further by using scarlet for the furnishings used within his bedchamber. Interestingly, the individual items were not bought or commissioned as a set, but acquired over several years. Lastly, the fact that the king had the bed and the wall hangings altered so that they could expand to fit his changing needs or a new bedchamber, indicates that they reflect his personal choice and one that he wished to retain.

As the quantity of the bedsteads and bedding indicates, there was ample provision for guests and members of the household. The quality of bedstead offered to a guest would reflect the social standing of the individual. Those of the first rank would be treated almost on a par with the king, as is indicated by the bed given as a gift to Lady Margaret Douglas at some time in 1544–5 (36 Henry VIII) [454], presumably on the eve of her marriage to the Earl of Lennox in July 1544. The quality of bedsteads found within the Wardrobes of the social elite can be gauged from those confiscated by the king. George, Lord Rochford, and his wife had a painted and gilt bedstead with hangings of tawny cloth of gold and white satin [2350]. Seven celures and testers were seized from the home of Cromwell at Austin Friars (9171–9177).[84] The first celure had clearly been a royal gift as it was made from purple tinsel, purple taffeta and white satin and it was embroidered with the king's arms (9171).

Two of the furnished trussing bedsteads were given to Anne Bassett [464] and Dorothy Bray [465]. These bedsteads were smaller than those in the first list, measuring approximately 6ft 9ins (2.06m) by 4ft 6ins (1.37m), with hangings of cloth of gold or velvet. These grants indicate that this type and quality of bed was considered suitable for significant members of the queen's household. There were ten such beds, along with seventeen celures and testers of sarsenet, with valances and curtains.

Loans of mattresses from Henry's Wardrobe to leading members of the household or guests were not uncommon. For example, in 1526 the household expenses of Henry, Earl of Devon record a

83 Cunnington and Cunnington, *English Costume*, 47.
84 A sparver (9178) and a canopy (9179), one counterpoint (9180), one bed (9181), five quilts (9182) and three bedsteads (9183) were also seized.

payment to a servant 'to cary ij beddes fro the kynges wardrope to my lordes chamber at Beshoppis Hatfeylde for my yong lord to ly apon, ijd and more for mony leyd aoyt to cary the same beddes a gayn in to the kynges wardrope at the Removyng day ijd'.[85] It seems this practice was established within the Wardrobe of the Beds at Whitehall. The charge of the Keeper, John Reed, included 'xxvj Beddes of Brucell tikes filled withe Fethers and Lined with the Lettres H R' (**9763**).

Denny also had an appropriate quantity of bed linen, including twenty-six single sheets [**547, 549–550, 552, 554–557**] and sixty-six pairs [**543–549, 551–553**] and thirty single pillow-beres [**560, 564–569**] and thirty-five pairs [**559–563**].[86] Some of these were made by individuals involved indirectly with the palace: for example, John Reed's wife was paid for 'making and marking' pairs of sheets for the wardrobe, at a rate of 8d the pair.[87]

Finally, as the privy lodging grew in size, the king was provided with a raying chamber close to his bedchamber. At Whitehall, in January 1532, the garland adorning a bust standing over the chimney of the king's dressing chamber was painted and gilded at a cost of 13s 4d.[88] This architectural development no doubt influenced, and was related to, the shift of control of the Wardrobe of the Robes from the Lord Chamberlain to the officers of the Privy Chamber, between 1536 and 1540.

CEREMONIAL AND RELIGIOUS LIFE   Denny's charge included some unusual items if his remit was confined to the privy or secret lodging and did not extend into some of the more public rooms beyond, in particular the guard chamber and the presence chamber. The Yeomen of the Guard served in the guard or watching chamber, while the Gentlemen Pensioners, founded in 1539, stood in the presence chamber. A number of sets of staff weapons and poleaxes were kept at Whitehall and they would have been used for these duties – 'foure score and eightene pertisaunstes partely gilt garnysshid with crymsen vellat and frengid with red silke' [**957**] and 'twentye and two Pollaxes gilt / the staves coverid with crymsen vellat / frengid with a depe frenge and a narrowe frenge of venice golde and crymsen silke' [**952**]. These weapons would have been offset by the rich livery supplied by the Great Wardrobe to the guards. Denny also had recourse to five banners, all of which were made from quartered crimson and purple silk and were painted with the king's arms [**1142–1144**]. During the course of his time as Keeper, Denny delivered one of the banners to the king.[89]

Cloths of estate were associated with the king's chair in the presence chamber. Denny had eleven clothes of estate at his disposal, including one with 'the Lorde Princes badges' for Edward [**236**]. However, none of the chairs in his charge were identified as chairs of presence or estate, and so it is hard to be certain which chairs were used in the Presence Chamber. An indication of how the Presence Chamber might have been furnished can be gleaned from the list of 'hangynges and chamberynges' that were delivered to William Ruggley, page of the wardrobe of the beds, on 18 December 1519.[90] The set of furnishings consisted of a chair of estate 'for the kinges service', a

85 PRO E36/225, f. 60r. (*LP* IV.i, 1792). The King's Works provided large numbers of tables, forms and stools for members of the household. At Dover Castle the joiners made tables, trestles, stools and cupboards for the king's lodging, for the queen and for every lodging and office in the castle: NUL Ne.01, account 2–30 June anno 28 (1536).

86 These figures do not include the 'Six peir of Sheetes of course holland serving for the king his grace in his Bayne' [**551**].

87 Bod Lib MS English History b 192/1, f. 58v.

88 PRO E36/252, p. 589. At Eltham a door was made leading from the privy chamber into the raying chamber: PRO E101/497/1.

89 PRO E315/160, f. 73r.

90 BL Harley MS 2284, f. 13r.

cloth of estate, eleven tapets and seven cushions, all made of crimson cloth of gold of tissue. In addition there were two cupboard cloths of blue velvet, a tappet of arras and another chair of estate, this time covered in purple velvet and embroidered with roses and portcullises.

The ceremonial weapons could also be used outside, as would two sets of very expensive tent hangings with matching window pieces, one of red and blue cloth of gold and the other of cloth of tissue, cloth of gold, red and white baudekin, red and white gold baudekin and blue cloth of gold [187–192]. When Denny's charge was reviewed in 1547 these hangings, along with cases for cushions [417] and two fire pans [1141], were transferred to the officers of the Tents. Tent hangings of this type were used during summer progresses. The progress of 1541, when Henry went to York with the aim of meeting his nephew James V of Scotland, was probably the most pertinent in the context of the 1542 Inventory. Tents were also used at jousts and tournaments, although these were far less common in the 1540s than they had been in the early years of Henry's reign. While the Guard used many of the weapons kept at Whitehall, others were used by Henry himself. Various items were delivered to the king, including an arming sword [981], a dagger with a crystal haft [994], a battleaxe [966] and a 'Rounde Targatte of Lether coverid with crymsen vellat' [944]. Other pieces were kept within the studies at Whitehall and by the officers of the Wardrobe of the Robes.

Although Henry did not celebrate any of the key festivals (including Christmas and Easter) at Whitehall during the period covered by the 1542 Inventory, he did take part in the ceremonial linked to the two meetings of Parliament held within the larger palace complex. As a consequence Henry's Parliament robes were kept at Whitehall [8–9]. His Garter robes were also kept here [10–11].

The view presented of Henry religious beliefs in the 1542 Inventory is ambiguous. On the one hand, the king owned orthodox religious paintings, tapestries with subjects inspired by the Old and New Testaments and sufficient altar plate to furnish the king's closet, including twelve gilt images [115–119, 126–129, 135–137]. In March 1545 Henry bought from Morgan Wolf (the king's goldsmith) an additional consignment of plate for Whitehall that included further items for the chapel [3752–3760]. The significant purchases, in terms of diversity and their conservative religious nature, were a superaltar [3760] and 'oone Crosse with a great foote to stande vpon an Aulter having the Crucyfixe Mary and John garnesshid in sondry places of the saide Crosse with Agates Camewes Peerles and divers Counterfett stones' [3752]. On the other, there were paintings of an overtly reformist nature including 'oone table of the nakid trueth with the workes of the busshop of Rome setforth in it' [678] and 'oone table with the Picture of the king his highnes standing vpon a Mitre with iij Crownes having a Serpent with vij heddes going owte of it / having a Sworde in his hand wherin is written *Verbum dei*' [726].

The plate was accompanied by a group of luxurious liturgical textiles: thirty-eight vestments in eight colours [1018, 1023, 1025, 1036–1049], twenty-three altar frontals in four colours [1017–1018, 1022, 1024, 1029–1035], two corporal cases [1021, 1027], one sacrament cloth [1019], one silk altar cloth [1028], five linen altar cloths [1051] and two mass books [1020, 1026]. Amongst the list of stools was a 'knelying Stowle of waynscot deske fashion with a standish of Lether partely gilt standing vpon the same' [1189]. Other items brought from elsewhere within Denny's charge would have completed the interior of the king's closet – cushions, hangings, carpets, traverses and pictures. These could be combined to produce an interior of the sort depicted in the miniature of Henry VIII kneeling at prayer within his closet in the Black Book of the Garter (1534–41). This view is reinforced by the list of liturgical textiles delivered to Denny from the former chapel of Catherine Howard and it provides a good insight into the furnishings felt to be necessary for one of Henry's wives.

The development and use of a specific group of objects: the fabric store

The large cache of silk and linen housed at Whitehall Palace is one of the more intriguing features of the 1542 Inventory. During the period covered by the Inventory (that is, 1542–7), Denny had recourse to over 1,100 lengths and remnants of cloth. The vast majority of the fabrics were silk (the chief block is [**1240–2023**]) and they were used for clothing and furnishings. In addition there was a cache of high quality linen containing 1,200 ells 3 nails that was used for tablecloths, towels and napkins [**2038–2084**]. The inclusion of this linen stresses the social and cultural importance of dining within the royal household (see pp. 29–30). There was also a small quantity of fancy trimmings [**2024–2032**] and coarser linen and mixed fibre fabrics (for example [**2085–2094**]). Denny also had a small stock of furs but these were listed with the items of clothing in his hands rather than with the lengths of cloth [**24–28**]. The different fabrics are listed in a strict hierarchy, starting with the highly prized tissues, cloth of gold and cloth of silver.

The concept of having a secondary fabric store in addition to the Great Wardrobe was not new in Henry's reign – indeed there are three other precedents. Firstly, James Worsley's 'boke of delyueraunce and discharge of the kinges standyng Wardrobe of his Robes within the towre of London' recorded items of dress and substantial quantities of cloth distributed by the officers of the wardrobe of the king's robes from the Tower between 8 December 1516 and 25 July 1520.[91] Secondly, this document and an inventory of the king's robes taken in 1520 imply that there was a store of cloth kept at Greenwich.[92] Finally, Thomas Alvard, Denny's predecessor as keeper at Whitehall Palace, appears to have built up and administered a silk store. In addition to buying sizeable quantities of cloth (see p. 113), Alvard also appears to have taken an active part in overseeing its use. A bill dated 1537 refers to a remnant of tawny silk velvet that was part of a piece charged on the late Thomas Alvard.[93] The silk was in the hands of William Green, the king's coffer-maker, and was used to cover a coffer for the Lady Mary. The presence of a silk store at Whitehall prior to the 1542 Inventory is further reinforced by the list of rules relating to the receipt, recording and use of silk kept at the palace by Nicholas Bristow in 1538 (see pp. 95–6).

As indicated above, some of the fabric from the earlier store was used to make new furnishings either for this palace or other royal properties. So it is likely that fabric from this store was issued to the craftsmen who supplied the various new cushions, chairs and other furnishings made for Whitehall between 1542 and 1546 (for example **3352–3352**, **3680**). However, none of the names recorded in the Inventory indicate this. Instead, it is the king and his immediate family that were named as the recipients. So Denny delivered fabric to seven key figures between 1542 and 1547: the king himself, Catherine Parr, Prince Edward, the Lady Mary, the Lady Elizabeth, Henry's niece Lady Margaret and her husband the Earl of Lennox. In addition, two of the queen's women, Dorothy Bray and Anne Bassett, received more modest quantities of cloth.

91 BL Harley MS 2284.
93 Bod Lib MS English History b 192/1, f. 13v.

92 BL Harley MS 4217, f. 1r and BL Harley MS 2284, fos 15r–53r.

The silk store was thus pivotal to many aspects of life at the new palace of Whitehall and beyond. It clothed the leading protagonists and formed an integral part of the décor. Because it was situated within the palace where Henry lived increasingly frequently in the 1540s, the king had much closer control over what was purchased and how it was used. Inevitably, such as store would reduce, if only temporarily, the importance of the Great Wardrobe.

The 1540s: the years of the king's decline

If Greenwich was the site of Henry's youth, then Whitehall witnessed his old age and death. The most tangible evidence of the king's physical decline is provided by the delivery in July 1544 of four purpose-made chairs. Two of the chairs, covered in tawny velvet, were 'for the kinges maiestie to sitt in / to be caried to and fro in his gallaries & Chambers' [**3676**] as was the third, covered with russet velvet [**3677**]. In addition there was a chair of purple velvet 'serving in the kinges howse which goeth vp and downe' [**3680**]. As the king became more sedentary he would have felt the cold more. There were fourteen screens at Whitehall to help keep out draughts, three covered with silk taffeta [**1208–1210**], while the other eleven were made from wicker [**1211**]. Two of the taffeta screens were delivered directly to the king in 1543 (probably in January) and in February 1546 [**1209, 1208**].

Henry also had a group of walking sticks or staves to help him move around, including 'two walking staves <oone of them having a Crosse> vpon thupper end of blac horne with a whistell in either end of the nosse / and thother having a whistill of white bone at thupper end' [**1214**]. The king was painted holding such a staff in his left hand in a portrait dated 1542, by an unknown artist, at Castle Howard. The whistle, a discreet means of calling for help, had its counterparts elsewhere. A pair of curious items was listed with a group of miscellaneous pieces: two trunks 'to showte in', one of which was covered with leather [**1232**] and one of which was 'paintid grene tipped With metall gilt at both thendes' [**1233**]. These trunks 'to showte in' were possibly used as some form of megaphone by the king to summon people when he needed them. However, in the 1547 Inventory the trunks were described as 'one Truncke to shoote in' (**11399**).[94]

Henry's death was, evidently, not a private event. At the time he was sleeping in one of the more ornate and bigger beds at the palace with a celure and tester of purple and crimson velvet embroidered with arabesques in gold thread [**439**]. The bed is identified by a marginal note recording alterations made to two of the pillows 'by the kinges commaundment when his grace lay in his deth bed mensis Januarii'. Afterwards, the bed was moved to Windsor Castle,[95] where Henry had chosen to be buried beside Jane Seymour.

After the king's death, several items from the palace were used during the funeral. One poleaxe from a set of twenty-two, with a gilt blade and a velvet-covered haft, was sent on 13 February 1547 '[t]o be occupied at the kinges herse at wynsor with the kinges hernes' [**952**]. In addition, 'two Vestementes of murrey vellat with Chalices and S. and beames of enbraudry with all thapparell to them' were delivered 'to Wynsor Colledge to be occupied abought therse of king Henrici viij^{ui}' [**1046**].

---

94 In the glossorial index to the 1547 Inventory, the trunks are described as 'cylindrical cases to contain or discharge explosives or combustibles' (p. 472). The location of the entry in each inventory supports either reading, and so is of little help in determining which is the correct definition – trunks for shouting are listed with a group of miscellaneous items in 1542, while trunks for shooting appear with the weapons in 1547.

95 PRO E315/160, f. 29v.

Conclusion

The objects described within the 1542 Inventory were used by Sir Anthony Denny to furnish the principal rooms at the Whitehall Palace and the king's privy lodging. While it is not possible to say for certain where particular objects were used, it is apparent that Denny had enough items at his disposal to furnish the thirty to forty rooms of the privy lodging that have been identified by Simon Thurley (see Figure 1) in an appropriate manner. Many of the elements of the décor could be deployed in a range of ways according to the desired effect. The combinations of objects and the quantity of pieces in particular rooms are hinted at in the entries in the 1547 Inventory relating to the privy lodging at Greenwich and Hampton Court, the king's other leading residences.

The style, colour and use of the furnishings in Denny's charge at Whitehall Palace hint at an interesting development. The abiding sense is of blocks of solid colour and rich fabrics. Items like bed hangings, cushions and window curtains were typified by the juxtaposition of strong colours. Although Henry VIII did not have direct access to the looms that produced the silk fabrics used to create most of the textile furnishings found in his lodgings, it seems that the use of panes of fabric reflects personal preference rather than a necessity forced by limited access to fabric. This is demonstrated by the quantity of fabric listed as part of Denny's initial charge and by some of the king's purchases. In February 1543 Henry bought nineteen lengths of black velvet containing 384⅜ yards from Richard Gresham [**3359–3377**]. In some instances pieces were ordered to form suites of furnishings covered with matching fabric but most of these sets were broken up on Henry VIII's death. Even though they did not have a lasting influence, these sets of matching chairs, cushions and footstools appear to have been a forerunner of the trend that Peter Thornton sees as typical of seventeenth-century interior décor.[96]

---

96 Madame de Rambouillet (1588–1665) has been associated with the promotion of a unified use of colour to furnish rooms. She had a *Chambre Bleue* decorated with blue wall coverings and blue textile furnishings at the Hôtel de Rambouillet during the 1620s and 1630s: see Thornton, *Interior Decoration*, 8. Thornton acknowledges that there were medieval precedents but states that 'it seems to be only from about 1625 onwards that this became a dominant feature of fashionable French interior decoration' (ibid).

II

THE PHYSICAL CONTEXT FOR THE KING'S POSSESSIONS: WHITEHALL PALACE

T HE ORGANIZATION of the objects by type rather than location in the 1542 Inventory means that the Inventory offers very few clues about the names, number or organization of the rooms within the palace where the items were kept and used. Fortunately, there are other sources that do provide evidence for the appearance and layout of the privy lodging on the first floor and the principal rooms on that floor and the ground floor. This section seeks to demonstrate why Whitehall Palace was so important to Henry and why, as a consequence, this building was the repository for the best of the king's possessions. In order to do this, it is necessary to consider the significance of the monarch having a palace in Westminster located close to the royal foundation, Westminster Abbey, and the seat of English government. This will be done by briefly reviewing how the old palace was used and the specialist functions it developed. This will be followed by a review of how Henry VIII temporarily responded to the loss of the residential section of the old palace between 1512–29 and the final solution to the problem that Henry opted for.

The twelfth-century writer William FitzStephen summed up the relationship between the suburb of Westminster and the capital city.

> Among the noble cities of the world that Fame celebrates, the City of London of the Kingdom of the English, is the one seat that pours out its fame more widely, sends to farther lands its wealth and trades, lifts its head higher than the rest … Also upwards to the west the royal palace is conspicuous above the … river, an incomparable building with ramparts and bulwarks, two miles from the city, joined by a populous suburb.[1]

The basic relationship between the City of London and the King's palace in Westminster had remained unchanged for four centuries, with one exception. In 1512 the privy palace housing the royal apartments wasa destroyed by fire. Seventeen years later Henry acquired York Place from the disgraced Cardinal Wolsey. Once in Henry's possession York Place underwent a transformation in name (becoming Whitehall) and in size becoming the king's principal residence.

The old Palace of Westminster

The old Palace of Westminster had been the London residence of English kings from the reign of Edward the Confessor (1042–66) until 1512. Until the transfer Edward had used a house at

---

1   Stow, *Survey*, 22–3.

Aldermanbury in the capital, but on becoming the royal patron of Westminster Abbey, he transferred his main residence to a site adjacent to the church where he would eventually be buried.[2] The primacy of Westminster was indicated by it being the one royal property formally known as a palace before Henry VIII's reign.[3] The palace had a marked impact on the surrounding community. Evidence for the early phases of the development of the palace – whether documentary or archaeological – is relatively limited. The early core of the building consisted of a great hall built by William II between 1095 and 1100, together with a lesser hall and a chamber, which were added in the twelfth century by Henry II.[4] Henry III (1216–72) rebuilt and decorated the king's chamber, which was henceforth known as the painted chamber; he also added new accommodation for the queen.[5] His son, Edward I (1272–1307), began the chapel of St Stephen. This private palace chapel, modelled on the Sainte Chapelle in Paris, was completed and lavishly decorated under Edward III (1327–77). In 1365–6 Edward III also took a plot of abbey land to build for the palace a new jewel tower, which was used to store the monarch's plate and cash reserves. The last major addition was the rebuilding of William II's Norman hall by Richard II (1377–99). It was designed by Henry Yevele, working with Hugh Herland, the master carpenter, who created a hammerbeam roof with a span of 67ft (20.42m).[6]

Just as the history of the City of London was punctuated with fires, so too was the evolution of English royal architecture.[7] According to John Stow,

> a great part of this palace at Westminster was once again burnt in the year 1512…since the which time it hath not been re-edified; only the great hall, with the offices near adjoining, are kept in good reparations, and serveth as afore for feasts at coronations, arraignments of great persons charged with treasons, keeping of the courts of justice etc.[8]

The courts that Stow referred to as being lodged within Westminster Hall were the Courts of Chancery, King's Bench and Common Pleas. Nearby were the Court of Requests held in the White Hall, and the Court of Star Chamber. Between 1536 and 1542 four new courts with financial remits were established: Augmentations (1536), First Fruits and Tenths (1540), Wards and Liveries (1540) and General Surveyors (1542). On 31 January 1537 Denny received £662 from the Treasurer of the Court of Augmentations towards the costs of providing a building at Westminster 'for the officers of our Augmentations'.[9]

As well as its legal function, Westminster Hall also had a place in formal court ceremonial.[10] It was the chosen venue for Anne Boleyn's coronation feast, as well as the feast for the coronation planned for Jane Seymour, but never carried out.

The old palace had a range of other functions, two of which are of relevance here. First, from the fourteenth century, the House of Lords had met in the 'White' or 'Parliament' Chamber in

2   Rosser, *Medieval Westminster*, 14.
3   Thurley, *Royal Palaces*, 1. It is described as 'the old and ancient palace of Westminster' in the 1536 Act (28 Hen VIII, c. 12).
4   Thurley, *Royal Palaces*, 4–5.
5   For developments from the reign of Henry III to that of Edward III, see *HKW*, I, 494–504.
6   Alexander and Binski, *Age of Chivalry*, 506–8.
7   According to FitzStephen 'the only pests of London are the immoderate drinking of the fools and the frequency of fires': Stow, *Survey*, 28.
8   Ibid, 420.   9 *LP* XIII.ii, 457.12.   10 Stow, *Survey*, 420.

the old Palace of Westminster.[11] In contrast, the House of Commons met at Westminster Abbey throughout Henry VIII's reign except during the Parliament of 1523, when it met in the lower frater of the Blackfriars. Until 1544 the Commons used the Abbey refectory but after this date (when the refectory was demolished) it transferred to the dormitory.[12] In 1548, when St Stephen's chapel was dissolved along with the chantries, it was given to the Commons as their regular meeting place.[13] Selected members of the House of Commons attended the opening ceremony for each Parliament, any prorogations and its dissolution, all of which were held in the House of Lords. They were also invited to the presentation of the Speaker in the antechamber next to he House of Lords. On occasion, individual Members of Parliament met the king in the new Whitehall Palace: for example, Sir George Throckmorton was brought before Henry during the Parliament of 1529 to explain his behaviour in the House of Commons.[14]

Secondly, the palace provided office space for various departments of the royal household, including the King's Works. The surveyor and his staff were provided with a new office, for the General Surveyors of Crown Lands, built next to the fish house.[15] To make this a more comfortable working environment William Chapel of London, upholsterer, was paid for leather and feathers, as well as the making of six cushions, faced with arras purchased from John Musteaner, the king's arras maker.[16]

Temporary substitutes for the old palace, 1512–29

After the demise of the old palace, Stow noted that 'princes [were] lodged in other places about the City, as at Baynard's Castle, at Bridewell, at Whitehall, sometimes called York Place, and sometimes at St James's.[17] For, though Henry chose to make Greenwich his principal residence from 1512 to 1529, he could not forgo a London base entirely. Westminster, the western suburb of London, was the home of law and administration and the almost invariable meeting place of Parliament. London itself, with its wealth, was central to royal finance; it was also the focus for royal pageantry including weddings, christenings, state visits (such as that of Charles V in 1522) or celebrations (such as those associated with the peace treaty of 1527; both the last two were shared with Greenwich). All these events required the royal presence. To serve such a purpose, a building had to be large enough to house the king, his guests and his household, and it also had to be grand enough to impress both guests and onlookers.

The first property that Stow mentioned was Baynard's Castle. The castle was located within the City and faced on to the river. It was the traditional London residence of the queen consort and was used as a repository for her wardrobe stuff. The building had ancient origins but it was substantially rebuilt by Henry VII in 1500–1, making it 'far more beautiful and commodius [sic] for the entertainment of any prince of great estate'.[18] In spite of this, neither its size nor its location made it suitable as a permanent substitute for Westminster.

---

11 *HKW* IV, 286.
12 Hawkyard, 'Meeting places', 65, 72, 76–7.   13 *HKW*, IV, 286, 291–2.
14 A Hawkyard (personal communication).   15 *HKW*, IV, 289.
16 BL, Additional MS 10109, f. 47v. Additional purchases included matting for the floor, a green cloth for the table, a pair of bellows, fire shovel, tongs and a pair of creepers.
17 Stow, *Survey*, 420.   18 Ibid, 94.

Bridewell was a more important residence. It lay to the west of the City, in the angle formed by Fleet Street to the north, the Fleet river to the east and the Thames to the south. Most of the site had belonged to the Hospitallers of St John's Clerkenwell, who had leased it to Henry VII's minister, Richard Empson.[19] After Empson's fall, the site was granted to Wolsey,[20] who set about turning it into his main London residence. It became surplus to his requirements in 1515, when his attention shifted to York Place (see below). The half-built house was transferred to Henry VIII, who completed it as a replacement for the residential section of the old Palace of Westminster, lost through fire in 1512. According to Stow, Bridewell was 'a stately and beautiful house' linked to the Blackfriars by a gallery.[21] The building work ran from 1515 to 1523 and cost over £20,000. The design was noteworthy for several reasons: for example, although the building did not have a great hall, there was a processional staircase leading up to the main rooms, and the lodgings were organized vertically. This arrangement of the lodgings was found in a number of properties built between 1500 and 1530, in contrast to the horizontal plan favoured by the king thereafter.[22] The Thames frontage, which supplied the all-important water gate, was elaborately developed on land largely reclaimed from the river, and it was connected to the private apartments in the inner court by a gallery that ran north–south along the garden.

The link with the Blackfriars mimicked the old relationship between Westminster Palace and the adjacent abbey. And it came into its own in the parliamentary sessions of 1523 and 1529: the Lords and Commons met in the monastery while the king resided in Bridewell.[23] However, the house was quite small and its shortcomings were highlighted by comparison with the more spacious homes that Wolsey had at his disposal: York Place and Hampton Court. During the 1520s Bridewell was used to lodge Charles V's courtiers (1522) and for the creation of Henry Fitzroy as Duke of Richmond (June 1525). From the 1530s onwards, the house remained in the king's hands and was often used to accommodate foreign ambassadors. In 1553 its function changed dramatically when Mary I gave Bridewell to the City of London as a workhouse for the poor.[24]

Of the other properties listed by Stow, the new palaces of Whitehall and St James's are discussed below, as they were developed after 1529. However, even though Stow did not mention it, there was one other royal residence available between 1512 and 1529: the Tower, right on the eastern limits of London. Henry stayed there prior to his coronation, as did Anne Boleyn in 1533, but the king did not use the royal apartments at other times. Even so, the 1547 Inventory did list the rooms: the parlour, the king's chamber, the closet, the privy wardrobe, the tower chamber, the hall and the entry.[25] This arrangement did not follow the sequence of rooms generally found in the king's apartments and was not suited to the organization of Henry's household. On a negative note, a royal presence at the Tower was more generally associated with the short and less happy visits of Anne Boleyn in 1536 and Catherine Howard in 1542, as they awaited execution.

---

19 *LP* I.i, 257. 43.   20 Thurley, *Royal Palaces*, 40.   21 Stow, *Survey*, 362.
22 Thurley, *Royal Palaces*, 41.
23 The parliamentary sessions ran from 15 April to 29 July 1523 (including 14 days' break) and from 3 November to 17 December 1529.
24 The process of transfer was initiated by Edward VI but was incomplete at his death.
25 BL Harley MS 1419, fos 417v–418r.

York Place: Wolsey's town house

York Place was the London home of the archbishops of York and it was situated on the Westminster river frontage to the north-east of the abbey. To locate it more precisely, the area of land known as Scotland lay to the north, King Street was to the west and property owned by Westminster Abbey adjoined it to the south. Looking back, our knowledge of York Place is rather obscure but its history began with Walter de Grey, Archbishop of York, who bought a substantial house with a plot of land to the north of Endhithe Lane, in the early 1240s.[26] Simon Thurley has divided the evolution of the site into ten phases, with Phases I–x spanning the period 1240–1698, and the final phase, Phase x, being concerned with a group of 'post-palace' structures such as No. 1 Horse Guards and the Banqueting House staircase.[27] Such an overview is too broad for this study: the focus here is on Phases I–v in general, and Phases IV and V in particular.[28]

In 1520 York Place was one of approximately forty-five aristocratic town houses in the capital that were in ecclesiastical hands.[29] Ecclesiastical town houses, like their secular equivalents, were used as centres of conspicuous consumption and they needed access to the Thames via a water gate, which led to the port and to the markets. All the English and Welsh bishops had a London house except the Bishop of St Asaph. They needed them because of their connections with the court, where many of the bishops held offices, and because of their seats in the House of Lords. These properties were used as an expression of wealth, to manifest their owners' appreciation of fashionable architecture and as evidence of royal service. In terms of size and significance it is appropriate that Lambeth Palace, home of the Archbishop of Canterbury and Primate of all England, outdid York Place. But that was before Wolsey got to work.

The early development of York Place can be summarized as follows. Under Henry III, Matthew Paris recorded that there were domestic buildings, a chapel and a stable on the site.[30] But there is almost no further evidence, written or physical, until the reign of Edward I (1292–1307). Edward I was the first king to take advantage of the proximity of York Place to the Palace of Westminster, and he made use of the archbishop's home during several phases of building at his own palace. Edward modified York Place to suit his needs. During 1295–6 the king was a widower and the rooms provided for the celibate archbishop were sufficient for his requirements. However, the security was inadequate and a new boundary wall was erected, possibly including a water gate.[31] In 1299 Edward married his second wife, the French princess Margaret, but there was no suitable accommodation in London with apartments for the queen, apart from the Tower. Consequently, Edward looked to York Place again and, between 1303 and his death in 1307, a set of lodgings was built for the queen. The new rooms included a hall, a privy chamber and a little chamber, along with space for the queen's maid and her wardrobe.[32] Additional work was carried out on the king's rooms at the same time.

---

26 Thurley, *Whitehall Palace*, 1. What follows is presented in archaeological terms, since much of the current evidence relating to both the property and the royal palace which developed on it is archaeological rather than written: ibid, ix–xv.

27 Ibid, p. xv.

28 Phase I: 1240–1320; Phase II: 1465–76; Phase III: 1480–1500; Phase IVa 1515–16; Phase IVb: 1516–27; Phase IVc: 1528–9; Phase Va: 1530–2; Phase Vb: 1537–58.

29 Barron, 'Centres of conspicuous consumption', 1.

30 Thurley, *Whitehall Palace*, 1.   31 Ibid, 2.   32 Ibid, 3.

The next main period of expansion took place during the tenure of Archbishop George Neville (1465–76), when the size of the house doubled. The building works took place in several areas: a new south range was added in addition to the enlargement and reworking of the great hall and cloister, as well as the chapel. The work was carried out in brick and stone and it is possible that Neville also rebuilt the gatehouse that provided access to King Street. The final pre-Wolsey stage of growth came between 1480 and 1500 when Archbishop Thomas Rotheram was the incumbent. Rotheram's main contribution was the addition of a substantial kitchen, a good indication of the archbishop's sizeable household.

Clearer details survive about the building works carried out by Thomas Wolsey. Not only is the archaeological evidence better but a number of building accounts survive, providing additional detail.[33] These relate to the first flurry of work in 1515–16. Wolsey's development of York Place has itself been subdivided into three sections: 1515–16 (the period of the building accounts), 1516–27 (the major phase of work) and 1528–9 (the final phase, with work on key sections including the great hall and chapel, and also the privy kitchen).

Wolsey, who was created Archbishop of York in 1514 and a cardinal in 1516, used his Westminster house to reflect his status as a royal minister and leading servant of the Church. In this there was the precedent set by three of Wolsey's fifteenth-century episcopal predecessors who also served as Lord Chancellor: John Kempe (1425–52), George Neville (1465–76) and Thomas Rotherham (1480–1500). Wolsey processed from York Place to preside as Lord Chancellor in Star Chamber or Chancery, with all the trappings of his various offices: he wore the red silk of a cardinal, and before him was borne the Great Seal of England and a silver-gilt mace (symbolizing his position as Lord Chancellor), two pillars of silver (symbolizing his position as papal legate) and two crosses of silver (one for his archbishopric and one as legate). Well might John Skelton boldly claim that Wolsey's magnificence outdid the king's. He asked 'Why come ye nat to court?' and replied, 'to the kynges courte? Or Hampton Court?'. He then focused on the role of Wolsey's town house:

> And Yorkes Place,
> With 'My lordes grace',
> To whose magnifycence
> Is all the confluence,
> Sutys, and supplycacyouns,
> Embassades of all nacyons.[34]

All these – the display of magnificence, the confluence (throng) of courtiers, and the reception of suits and embassies – were, it should be said, among the traditional attributes of the king's old Palace of Westminster.

Wolsey's immediate plans for York Place consisted of three specific elements: a new great chamber, a gallery and a processional staircase.[35] These were realized relatively quickly. The great

33 PRO E36/236: they are bound in one volume.
34 Scattergood, *Skelton*, 289.
35 Much of this is based on Thurley, *Whitehall Palace*, 13–36. The different stages of development are best explained by the site plans (see ibid, figs 21, 27, 38, 48): fig. 48 is particularly valuable as it shows the first-floor room arrangement in 1529; Thurley, *Whitehall Palace* supersedes Thurley, 'Domestic building works'.

chamber had a substantial undercroft; it adjoined the cloister and was linked to the great hall by an antechamber. The gallery was placed above the cloister and access from ground level was provided by a new, impressive staircase. These initial additions allowed the house to function in a suitably magnificent manner.

In the eleven years (1516–27) that followed the initial redevelopment Wolsey utterly transformed the fifteenth-century house. In order to realise his aggrandisement Wolsey had to acquire land along the boundaries of his property.[36] One of the first developments was the long gallery that stretched south from the privy chamber towards Endive Lane. Further accommodation for guests was provided in the lodging range. The land around York Place was developed as gardens and orchard, incorporating a number of fashionable features such as a banqueting house. Wolsey then turned to the existing great hall and chapel, which looked increasingly inadequate when compared with the new work. These deficiencies were addressed in 1528–9; the reworked great hall and chapel survived until the palace's demise in 1698. On a more personal level Wolsey added a privy kitchen onto the east end of the house to serve his culinary needs. In order to link the new kitchen with his apartments, a privy stair was built.

The resulting series of apartments for Wolsey's own use consisted of a great chamber, a presence chamber, a privy chamber, a bedchamber and a closet that provided access to the long gallery. The same sequence of rooms was to be found in the king's lodgings in his largest and most up-to-date houses. Wolsey's version of these rooms were designed to impress and had the desired effect on the Venetian ambassador Mario Savorgnano, who recorded that the long gallery had

> windows on each side, looking on gardens and rivers … the ceiling being marvellously wrought in stone with gold and the wainscot of carved wood representing a thousand beautiful figures.[37]

However, there was no equivalent provision for the king, although other guests could be accommodated in the lodging range. Whether Wolsey had plans to address this situation is unknown because on 22 October 1529 he surrendered York Place along with the rest of his property to the king.[38]

York Place transformed into Henry VIII's new Palace of Whitehall

Two days later, on 24 October 1529, the king, Anne Boleyn, her mother and Henry Norris (the Groom of the Stool) visited York Place to inspect the property that Wolsey had vacated.[39] They clearly liked what they saw, for York Place provided Henry with what he had hitherto lacked: the opportunity to create a new royal residence close to London and the remaining administrative sections of the old Palace of Westminster.

Wolsey's existing buildings gave Henry himself accommodation on a fully royal scale – a scale, indeed, that undoubtedly outshone all the king's existing houses. Conspicuously absent, and not surprisingly for an all-male episcopal house, was a queen's side. Accommodation for both

36 Rosser and Thurley, 'Whitehall Palace'. For Henry's building programme at Hampton Court, see Thurley, 'Building of Hampton Court'.
37 *CSP Venetian*, IV, 682.
38 Sylvester, *Life and Death*, 98–9.
39 Thurley, *Whitehall Palace*, 37; *CSP Spanish*, 1529–30, 303–4.

the household and guests was relatively limited. Nor was there a park for hunting, a tilt-yard or the other sporting facilities that Henry wanted.

All this in turn required more space. But space, due to the location of York Place in the heart of Westminster, was at a premium. To the east, the site was bounded by the river, to the west by King Street, and to the north and south by valuable and already densely populated housing. People proved the easiest to move. Continuing a process begun by Wolsey, the boundaries of St Margaret's parish were redrawn and the principal leaseholders of properties on both sides of King Street were bought out by the Crown.[40] Once acquired, the substantial number of private houses on the site were demolished and their tenants evicted.[41] The consequent depopulation was substantial enough to be reflected in the declining membership of the local guild.[42] In contrast, the interest of the principal leaseholders was protected. One such was John Reed, who owned three tenements on the east side of King Street, by Endive Lane. He had acquired the leases from Westminster Abbey in 1516 and in 1532 he received £82 13s 4d in compensation for their loss.[43] Reed, however, was an insider: he had been appointed Keeper of the Wardrobe of the Beds at York Place in 1529.[44]

To the east, in the fullness of time, the river gave way as land was reclaimed from the foreshore and embanked. Only the king's highway to the west proved intractable. King Street remained where King Street had long been and the palace structure was carried over it by two gateways. The northern gatehouse, known as the Holbein Gate, was built in the 1530s and the southern, or King Street Gate, at the end of Henry's reign.[45] This arrangement is clearly illustrated in the mid-sixteenth century woodcut map of London known as the 'Agas' map (Figure 3).[46]

The year 1529 was thus, as Simon Thurley has noted, a turning point in the building history of the reign of Henry VIII.[47] For the Henry did more than seize the site of his fallen minister's palace: he also seized the initiative. Hitherto, Wolsey had been England's principal architectural patron; now Henry himself took this role, developing in so doing a real personal interest in building. Above all, he took over Wolsey's team of experts. Three stand out: James Needham, the master builder, Thomas Alvard, the financial manager and Thomas Cromwell, Wolsey's legal factotum.[48] Cromwell's particular skill, honed in the recent dissolution of monasteries to endow Wolsey's educational foundations, lay in the acquisition of land. Around this core of experts, a larger group of skilled craftsmen was retained in the king's service, including Patrick Kelly, 'plasterer to our works in Westminster', who was granted a livery coat of red broadcloth annually for life.[49]

40 *CSP Venetian*, IV, 665: Rosser and Thurley, 'Whitehall Palace'.
41 Rosser and Thurley, 'Urban cost of princely magnificence', 67–73.
42 The Rounceval Guild, attached to the Rounceval Hospital: ibid, 74.
43 Ibid, 70; PRO E101/420/11, f. 95r.
44 Reed seems to have favoured ecclesiastical landlords because in July 1535 he and his wife Joanna were granted a 50-year lease on the lands of the prebend of St Paul's: *LP* VIII, 1059.
45 The appearance of the King Street Gate was recorded by George Vertue *c.* 1725 for the Society of Antiquaries; the engraving is still in their collection.
46 Three impressions of the 'Agas' map survive: in the Public Record Office, Kew, the Pepysian Library, Magdalene College, Cambridge and the Guildhall Library, London. The eight sheets of the map have been reproduced: see Prockter and Taylor, *A to Z of Elizabethan London*.
47 '1529 was a watershed in the development of the English royal house. It marks an intellectual turning point for Henry who suddenly became more interested in architecture', Thurley, *Royal Palaces*, 49.
48 Thurley, *Whitehall Palace*, 38.
49 PRO LC5/49, f. 12.

Henry's building work on the site falls into two phases: 1530–2 and 1537–47.[50] At first, emphasis was on enlarging, preparing and enclosing the newly acquired site. Walls were built on almost every side: along the river, to the south by Lamb Alley, and along either side of King Street. The need to build in water or waterlogged conditions turned the eastern and southern walls into a major feat of civil engineering. Within the walls, gardens (to the north) and orchards (to the south) were laid out. To the west, on the other side of King Street, the land that the king had bought and turned into a park was also enclosed with walls that Thomas Cromwell, who was not given to hyperbole, called 'sumptuous'.[51] On the King Street side of the park Henry VIII built the largest complex of sporting and leisure facilities in any of his houses. It included a tilt-yard with a viewing gallery, open air and covered tennis courts, a pit for cock fighting and several bowling alleys.[52]

Then to make the whole site usable, the palace and its gardens on the east side of King Street was connected to the park and sporting complex to the west. The gallery from Esher, another of Wolsey's properties, was dismantled, moved to Westminster by water and set up, traversing the site from east to west. Eighty feet of the gallery was erected on the west side of King Street, and the remaining two hundred feet on the east. Where the two parts of the gallery abutted the road, the Holbein Gate was built to join them and carry the structure across the road.

The longer, western end of the gallery, renamed the privy gallery, became the spine of Henry's new palace. Wolsey, as we have seen, had created a private lodging fit for a king. Henry continued to use the two outermost rooms of the sequence, the guard chamber and the presence chamber. Wolsey's third room, the privy chamber, turned to the east, towards the river. Henry, however, wanted his apartments to connect to the new gallery, so a new privy chamber was built to the west. Beyond the privy chamber there were at least four rooms: the king's bedchamber, a dining room, a dressing room and a library. This arrangement did not remain fixed but evolved as the palace developed and these changes were reflected in some of the headings given in the 1547 Inventory, for example 'In the litle Study called the newe Librarye in the chardge of James Rufforthe at Westminster' and the 'Study nexte tholde Bedde chambre'.[53]

This area of the palace, known as the privy lodging, is crucial to the 1542 Inventory as it was here that most of the more or less precious objects in Denny's charge were stored. The privy lodging is also important in the history of palace planning. It was Hugh Murray Ballie who first explicitly linked planning (the architectural arrangement of the rooms) with court etiquette (which assigned a function to rooms).[54] He identified two extreme typologies: the English and the French.

In France, rooms became public or private depending on the time of day, so that the king's bedchamber, for example, was accessible to the public in the day but jealously guarded at night:

---

50 Thurley gives the dates for Phase II as 1537–58 but I have adjusted them to reflect only Henry's contribution. For much of what is contained in the next few paragraphs, see Thurley, *Whitehall Palace*, 37–64. Once again the site plans are of particular interest: see figs 49, 59, 72.

51 *LP* X, 1231.

52 For the archaeological evidence relating to Henry VIII's sporting complex, which was situated on the west side of the palace see Green and Thurley, 'Excavations'. Details are given for the following facilities: the tilt-yard and tilt-yard gallery, the great close tennis play, bowling alleys, the cockpit, the great open tennis play, the small close tennis play, the small open tennis play, a gallery connecting the tennis plays, the pheasant yard, the cony yard and the cock yard.

53 BL Harley MS 1419, fos 186r, 151r.

54 Ballie, 'Ettiquette'. His findings are usefully summarized at 199.

the ceremonies of the *levée* (the royal arising in the morning) and the *couchée* (the king's going to bed) marked the transition between one state and the other. This led Murray Ballie to characterize the French model as being organized on the 'principle of time'.[55]

The English model, on the other hand, was organized on the principle of place. Rooms like the withdrawing chamber and the bedchamber were private at all times, and there was a clear division between the public and private areas of the palace. Early in Henry's reign the divide lay at the outer door of the privy chamber; later the privy chamber acquired some public characteristics and the barrier shifted to its inner door, which led to the privy lodging beyond. The existence of this large private area (whether including or excluding the privy chamber) allowed for the accumulation of the hoard itemized in the 1542 Inventory. The goods were safe because access was limited to only a handful and because even fewer – principally the king and Denny – had keys.

The impetus of the first building programme was maintained by the need to provide accommodation for Anne Boleyn, 'queen in waiting', and to create a suitable backdrop for her coronation in 1533. The queen's lodging was erected in 1533 and it was built at the same height from the ground as the king's. Wolsey's old privy chamber became Anne's presence chamber and beyond that a new sequence of rooms was fitted into what had been Wolsey's long gallery. The low gallery built by Wolsey was extended towards Endive Lane and a new decorative scheme established. It was surrounded by the orchard. At the same time a new privy bridge (that is, a landing stage) was under construction to provide suitable river access to the palace, via the low gallery.[56]

In short, by 1536, when Cromwell drew up his complacent list of 'things done by the king's highness sithens I came into his service', the new 'place' at Westminster, with its park, garden and tilt-yard, was essentially finished. Along with the adjacent St James's on the other side of the park, it was, as he said with justifiable pride 'a magnificent and goodly house'.[57]

Henry's attention now shifted for several years to other building projects, culminating in Nonsuch. These took the newness off the 'new' house at Westminster and left aspects of it looking distinctly old fashioned. In the last five years of his reign Henry turned to Whitehall once more to correct these deficiencies. The works were on the largest scale. The cost was £28,676 3s 4d [**B41**], and Denny was what we would now call the project manager. Most impressive was the development of the waterfront, built with the aim of providing a new river façade (see Figure 4). The process recovered another 4,000 square yards of land from the river frontage to serve as the foundation for the new lodging. In the event, only the southern two bays, out of at least six that were planned, were built. These provided an opulent new lodging for the Lady Mary, Henry's elder daughter.

There were major changes too in the gardens that were such a feature of the palace. The great garden was laid out to the south of the palace and eventually reached down to Lamb Alley. The orchard, which had previously occupied this site, was shifted further south towards Endive Lane. The old low gallery was extended to provide sheltered access into the great garden. In the same way, the privy garden to the north was enclosed with an open cloister.[58] Views of the gardens can be

---

55 'Access to the royal person is measured in temporal, rather than in spatial terms': ibid, 192.

56 For the sequence of the queen's apartments at Hampton Court in 1547 and some of their furnishings see entries **12383–12410**.

57 *LP* X, 1231.

58 For a discussion of the evolution of gardens at this palace in particular and in England in general see Strong, *Renaissance Garden*, 34–9.

seen in the background of the anonymous group portrait of Henry and his family and in Anthonis van den Wyngaerde's sketch of the palace. The sketch reveals that the central feature of the great garden was a large fountain. Wyngaerde's sketch also records the king's new privy water gate in the foreground and diagonally behind it, to the left, the Holbein Gate. Close by were the cockpit, the closed tennis court and the tilt-yard. All these were features of the first building phase.

The most visible feature of the second building phase was the King Street Gate. This was built in a bid to formalize the relationship between the palace and King Street. The effect was to enclose the walled section of King Street between the new gate to the south and the Holbein Gate to the north. The most likely period for the gate's construction is 1542–8 and the design of the domes, windows and pilasters indicates a strong French influence. Finally, there were substantial changes in the layout of the privy lodging. These were designed both to increase the king's privacy and the amount of space available to him. For this second phase, the documents printed below – the 1542 Inventory and Denny's declaration of accounts – form the crucial written evidence.

In a project of this size, building materials were at a premium. The building accounts for the palace indicate that the King's Works drew heavily on local suppliers and labour. Local craftsmen included Ralph Alwood, cooper, Nicholas Starkey, joiner, William Bait, Groom of the Wood Yard and Thomas Swallow, brick maker, all resident in the parish of St Margaret's, Westminster.[59] Others, such as Thomas Tupp, tallow chandler, Ambrose Ford and John Russell, carpenters, and John Tyler, a lime burner, all lived in the neighbouring parish of 'Sente martense Be sydes Charyng Crosse'.[60] Beyond that the craftsmen were drawn from City parishes and from Greenwich, Hampstead, Kingston-upon-Thames and Southwark. Apart from large-scale purchases of new supplies, the King's Works also recycled any available materials. Ralph Williams was employed by Henry 'for the devising and making of engynes for the overthrowing of the walls of the king's old palace of Westminster' and for demolishing 'a Toure of stone and bricke at the king's place within his paleis'.[61] Later in the project, in June 1546 a warrant was issued

> to Mr Canner, surveyor at Westminster and others to deface and take down the church and steeple of St John of Jerusalem beside London and to sell as much therof as he think unmeet for your majesty's buildings at Westminster.[62]

In some royal houses there was a separate lodging for the children. The lodgings provided for the Lady Mary in the final Henrician building phase belonged to that pattern. But the main provision at Whitehall was the nearby St James's, which Henry VIII developed as a home for his heir.[63] Relatively little has been written about St James's Palace because very few of the building accounts have survived.[64] Yet one section of the Tudor palace is still standing, namely the chapel, which retains its original heraldic ceiling celebrating Henry VIII's marriage to Anne of Cleves in 1540.[65]

59 Baker, 'Extracts from royal accounts', 101–4.
60 Ibid, 115, 108, 111.
61 HKW, IV, 287.
62 LP XXI.i, 1165.34.
63 On 9 September 1553 the Spanish ambassador commented in a letter to the Emperor that St James's Palace was 'built by the late king Henry VIII as a residence for the royal children': CSP Spanish, XI, 214. See also Hayward, 'Possessions', 96–7.
64 See HKW, IV, 241–3 and Thurley, Royal Palaces, 81 and other passing references.
65 String, 'A neglected Henrician decorative ceiling'.

TABLE 9

HENRY VIII'S PLACE OF RESIDENCE ON THE GREAT FEAST DAYS
AND OTHER IMPORTANT FESTIVALS, 1542–7

Of the forty-two festivals included here, Henry VIII spent thirteen at Greenwich, twelve at Hampton Court, eleven at Whitehall, three at St James's, two at Windsor and one at Ampthill. At first glance the figure for Whitehall places it a good third: but it is distorted by two factors. First, Henry spent Candlemas in 1542–4 and Easter in 1543 at Whitehall because he was resident at the palace for the parliamentary session. Second, Henry's last illness and death meant that he spent Christmas 1546 and the New Year and Epiphany of 1547 at the palace by default rather than choice.

	1542	1543	1544	1545	1546	1547
New Year's Day (1 January)	Greenwich	Hampton Court	Hampton Court	Greenwich	Hampton Court	Whitehall
Epiphany (6 January)	Greenwich	Hampton Court	Hampton Court	Greenwich	Hampton Court	Whitehall
Candlemas (2 February)	Whitehall	Whitehall	Whitehall	Whitehall	Greenwich	
Easter (variable)*	Greenwich	St James's	Whitehall	Whitehall	Greenwich	
St George's Day (23 April)	Greenwich	Whitehall	Greenwich	St James's	Greenwich	
Whit Sunday (variable)**	Hampton Court	Hampton Court	St James's	Greenwich	Greenwich	
All Saints (1 November)	Hampton Court	Ampthill	Whitehall	Windsor	Windsor	
Christmas (25 December)	Hampton Court	Hampton Court	Greenwich	Hampton Court	Whitehall	

*   Easter: 9 April 1542, 25 March 1543, 13 April 1544, 5 April 1545, 25 April 1546.

** Whit Sunday: 28 May 1542, 13 May 1543, 1 June 1544, 24 May 1545, 13 June 1546.

The shaded areas indicate festivals falling when Parliament was in session.

This table is based on data taken from Henry VIII's itinerary, (PRO OBS 1/1419).

The role of Henry VIII's new palace

The new palace had two roles, which developed sequentially over time. First, it was a working palace, or rather a place where Henry went to attend to the day-to-day tasks associated with governing the country. He set out this view clearly to Ralph Sadler, Cromwell's court agent, in 1536. 'Your lordship', Henry observed to Sadler, 'was in the same case when ye came to the Rolls [Cromwell's London home], as his Grace was when he came to Westminster; for when he is there, he said he had much ado to get thence'.[66] The truth of Henry's remark can be seen from his own itinerary. Even after the first stage of the rebuilding was finished, he chose to spend relatively few of the great holiday feasts (Christmas, Epiphany, Easter, St George's Day and All Saints Day) and other important festivals there (see Table 9) Instead, for those occasions which were celebrated with revels, hunting and other 'pastimes with good company', he preferred other, more congenial palaces, like Greenwich.[67] On the other hand, there is a close correlation between the dates of the parliamentary sessions (now

66 *LP* XI, 1124.

67 Although Henry is no longer thought to have written the piece of music known as 'Pastime with good company', the title reflects Henry's attitude to life: see Blezzard and Palmer, 'King Henry VIII'. Thurley states that Greenwich was the most popular country retreat under the Tudors: 'Greenwich Palace', 20.

TABLE 10

HENRY VIII'S PLACE OF RESIDENCE DURING
THE PARLIAMENTARY SESSIONS, 1542–7

There were two Parliaments during this period. The first sat for three sessions and the second sat for two, before it was terminated by Henry's death.

Session dates	Hackney	Hampton Court	St James's Palace	Waltham	Whitehall
1542: 16 Jan–1 April	2 days	—	—	5 days	75 days
1543: 22 Jan–12 May	—	—	16 days	—	94 days
1544: 14 Jan–29 March	—	—	—	—	75 days
1545: 23 Nov–24 Dec	6 days	1 day	—	—	27 days
1547: 14 Jan–30 Jan	—	—	—	—	17 days
TOTAL	**8 days**	**1 day**	**16 days**	**5 days**	**288 days**

Based on data taken from Henry VIII's itinerary, PRO OBS 1/1419.

invariably held in the old Palace of Westminster and the abbey) and period of the king's residence in the new palace (see Table 10).

Henry's attitude to the business of government, as the thrust of his remark to Sadler indicates, was still pretty ambivalent as late as 1536. But after 1539 his devotion to business became more consistent and his periods of residence at Whitehall correspondingly longer. The palace was now the site of important pieces of political theatre. For instance, shortly before his death, Lord Chancellor Audley sent the Great Seal with Sir Edward North and Sir Thomas Pope 'to the King in his privy chamber at the new palace of Westminster'.[68] Henry received it in the presence of Sir Thomas Heneage and Anthony Denny. The seal was temporarily passed to Sir Thomas Wriothesley until Audley's death on 3 May 1544, when Wriothesley returned the seal to Henry, in his privy chamber:

> Thereupon many gentlemen of the privy chamber and other offices being summonsed,
> the King, sitting on his throne with the bag containing the seal in his hand, redelivered
> the seal to Wriothesley and appointed him Chancellor of England.[69]

At an unofficial level, the balance of power was dominated by the brokering of private arrangements to gain influence and wealth. This process is revealed in a letter from Sir William Paget to Protector Somerset in 1547. Paget wrote 'Remember what youe promysed me in the galerye at Westmynster, before the breathe was out of the body of the king that dead ys'.[70]

Similarly, though the law courts remained in and around the old Palace of Westminster, the new palace assumed a quasi-legal role on occasion. The most famous of these was the trial of John

68 *LP* XIX.i, 459.
69 Ibid.
70 Quoted in Miller, 'Henry VIII's unwritten will', 87.

Lambert, *alias* John Nicholson, on charges of heresy. John Husey, Lord Lisle's court agent, who was present, described the setting:

> In the king's hall of his Grace's manor of York Place, were certain scaffolds, bars and seats made on both sides of the hall, and also a haut place for the king's Majesty, where his Grace sat at the highest end thereof, the said hall being hanged most richly; and about noon, his Grace sitting in his majesty, with the most parts of the doctors divers, with judges, serjeants-at-law, the mayor and aldermen of London, with divers others of worshipful and honest of the Commons, was brought before his Grace one John Nicholson.[71]

It was a cross between the High Court of Parliament and the Court of King's Bench. Henry, clad all in white and speaking from his elevated throne, began the proceedings by interrogating Lambert on his belief in the Real Presence and concluded them, five hours later, by saying that the accused had condemned himself out of his own mouth and ordering Cromwell to read the sentence of death.[72]

But the most important change came eighteen months later, with the condemnation of Cromwell himself on charges which included the same heresy as Lambert's. In the aftermath of the minister's fall, the Privy Council was definitively established as the 'council attendant on the king's person'.[73] It was now a court council: it met at court; its members lodged at court and dined there as a group. And the chief scene of its operations became Whitehall. The exact location of the council chamber under Henry VIII remains unclear. But the council records were stored in the study next to the king's bedchamber;[74] while the secretary, the king's chief assistant in running the council, was lodged near the royal bedchamber too.[75]

This new focus on business was the other side of the coin of the king's physical decline. His health failed rapidly in the period covered by the 1542 Inventory – which failure, as Thurley has shown, had a marked impact on the royal itinerary.[76] Instead of the far-flung progresses of old, the king's movements now concentrated on a handful of houses in and around London. They were equipped with new extended parks, where the game could be brought to the king, rather than him having to ride in pursuit of it. And the most important of these new residences for an increasingly immobile king was Whitehall.

The enhanced residential role of Whitehall led to several changes, both within and without the palace. Denny's position as Keeper gave him responsibility for all the newly acquired parks to the west and north of the new palace. The documents printed here show heavy expenditure on walling, access roads and the maintenance of the king's game. The result was a genuine *rus in urbe*: hunting at Whitehall, despite its urban setting, could not be bettered at any of Henry's more rural houses. Inside the palace, the king gave himself more, and more elaborately organized, private space. Once again, the 1542 Inventory supplies the key evidence. It shows that his bedchamber was extended and his library refurbished to accommodate the books brought in from other, less convenient

71 *Lisle Letters*, V, 1273 (*LP* XIII.ii, 851).
73 *HO*, 159–60.
75 Implied in Starkey, *English Court*, 17–18.

72 Foxe, *Acts and Monuments*, V, 181–250.
74 *APC*, II, 106; *APC*, I, 395, 278.
76 Thurley, *Royal Palaces*, 60.

palaces. It records the equipment installed to cope with his increasing lack of mobility: there were two wheelchairs and a form of lift. A marginal note even establishes in which bed the king died.

The thirteen years following 1529 saw York Place evolve from a substantial, fashionable episcopal property into the leading royal residence in England. This process of extension and embellishment, inside and out, was to continue until Henry's death in 1547. Henry's willingness to spend a lot of money on this new palace reflected the king's need for a house close to the capital and the seat of government. Henry's specific need for this property came from the prolonged sessions of the reformation parliament. As a consequence Henry had plenty of time to build up the library and the other groups of objects that he could use to occupy his time when not involved with events related to the governance of the country (see Chapter V).

THE DENNY FAMILY TREE

This family tree has been compiled from information taken from a variety of sources, including Sir Anthony Denny's will. His children are not listed in chronological order. Denny refers to 'my base son William, in his will and the inference is that William is of age, unlike Denny's other children, as he was left an annuity out of Mettingham, Suffolk.

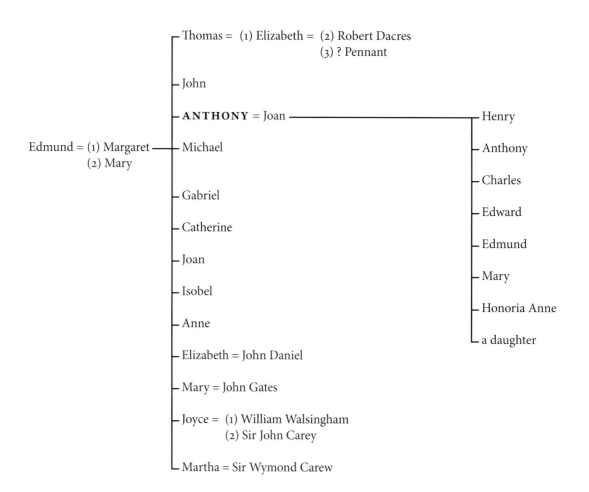

III

SIR ANTHONY DENNY:
THE MAN AND HIS OFFICES

S IR ANTHONY DENNY, as keeper of Whitehall Palace, was one of the two people for whom the 1542 Inventory was principally compiled. The other was the king himself. Denny's relationship with Henry VIII was central to his career during the 1530s and 40s and one that Denny managed with exceptional skill. Although aspects of his personality remain elusive, the aim of this section is to present an overview of his life and to consider some of the reasons for his success at the English royal court. Denny was a consummate administrator and as a consequence he amassed offices. He was the epicentre of a network of friends, associates and connections in the capital and the localities. He acquired sizable estates.

Denny's life

> … if two dewties did not comaund [Denny] to serve, th'one his prince, th'other his
> wiffe, he wold surelie becum a student in S. Johns.[1]

The truth of Roger Ascham's observation is borne out by Sir Anthony Denny's life, a life defined by intellect, duty, industry, family and faith. Yet the finer points of his personality are hard to grasp, as few private letters survive and his home at Cheshunt has been demolished.[2] There is his portrait by a follower of Holbein: it presents a slight, somewhat diffident figure dressed in the black livery of the Privy Chamber (Figures 5–7). However, the picture is dated 1541 and gives Denny's age as 29, but his birth in 1501[3] made him 29 in 1530 and 40 in 1541. If the dating is suspect, how accurately drawn is the image? Perhaps more significant is that, nearly fifty years after his death, the memory of his influence within the royal household was strong enough for Shakespeare to include Denny as a character in his play *Henry VIII*. Shakespeare provides a fleeting verbal image of Denny as an intermediary between Henry and his court.[4] And he roots Denny firmly in London and Westminster. Although his family life was in Hertfordshire and Essex, Denny was strongly bound by a network of clients to his understated, yet integral, role within this court milieu.

1 Ellis, *Original Letters*, 14.
2 The house, possibly built by John Walsh, dated from the mid to the late fifteenth century. It had a hall with a pair of two-storey wings built to the north and south. Beneath the hall was an undercroft, part of which was vaulted. The corbels and capitals of the piers were finished with angels and heads. The house was demolished in 1965: see Smith, *Hertfordshire Houses*, 46–7. For a ground plan of the house see Smith, *English Houses*, fig. 34.
3 *DNB*, V, 823; Denny, 'Biography', 199.
4 *Henry VIII*, V.i. The time-span of the play is of interest as it covers the period from Wolsey's last years in power to the christening of Henry and Anne's daughter Elizabeth. The brief inclusion of Denny fits with his entry into the Privy Chamber.

Anthony Denny was born on 16 January 1501 at Cheshunt in Hertfordshire. He was the second son of Sir Edmund Denny and his second wife Mary Troutbeck, cousin to Anne Boleyn (see family tree, p. 54).[5] Sir Edmund's office as Chief Baron of the Exchequer brought government and City connections, reflected by his decision to educate his son in London at Colet's School of Jesus at St Paul's, where he was taught by William Lily.[6] However, even though tradition asserts that Denny graduated from St John's College, Cambridge, the extent of his further education is uncertain.[7] Although his father left £160 and the income of the family property in Kent 'for his exhibition and finding' it has been proved that Denny was not a Cambridge graduate;[8] nevertheless, he had strong links with Cambridge scholars such as William Butts and Thomas Cranmer throughout his adult life and he sent his son to St John's.[9]

As a young man in his twenties, Denny joined the household of Sir Francis Bryan, a leading member of the king's Privy Chamber.[10] Bryan was another Hertfordshire resident and also a cousin of Anne Boleyn. At this stage Bryan seems to have been an adherent of reformed religious ideas – a view that Denny was to promote throughout his working life, and much more consistently than did Bryan. Finally, Bryan was a confidant of the king, who sent him on various European diplomatic missions. By July 1531 at the latest, Denny's relationship with Bryan had brought him to the king's notice, as Henry referred to letters delivered by him in correspondence with Foxe and Bryan.[11] It is possible that Denny attended Bryan during Henry's visit to France in 1532,[12] when the king preferred Anne Boleyn to Queen Catherine of Aragon as his travelling companion. Shortly afterwards, Denny transferred from Bryan's service to that of the king: on 14 December 1533 livery of a black doublet, jacket and gown was ordered for Denny along with William Brereton, John Carey, John Penne and Nicholas Simpson, his fellow Grooms of the Privy Chamber.[13] Denny also forged direct links with Anne Boleyn, for in August 1535 John Gostwick noted that he had 'delivered the Queen's letter to Mr Denny, although he was in London on the Queen's business.'[14]

In tandem with his court role, Denny probably represented Ipswich in the closing months of the long-running Reformation Parliament (3 November 1529–14 April 1536). An undated letter from the king, attributed to December 1535, promoted Denny's candidature in place of the late Thomas Alvard.[15] Denny was a fitting choice: he was known and trusted by the king, while as an East Anglian landowner he would have had local connections.

5   For simple narrative biographies of Denny see Denny, 'Biography'; *DNB*, V, 823–4; Bindoff, *Commons*, II. 27–9 and Sil, 'Denny'. Some financial aspects of Denny's career were covered by Richardson in his *Tudor Chamber Administration* and *History of the Court of Augmentations*. However, the key analytical work on Denny's career in the royal household was carried out by David Starkey: see 'King's Privy Chamber', 'Representation through intimacy' and 'Intimacy and innovation'. Later contributions include Hoak, 'Secret history'.

6   See Dowling, 'Gospel and the court', 64. John Leland was Denny's contemporary at school and described his (i.e. Denny's) life in his *Encomia*.

7   This traditional view is presented in a number of sources including Denny, 'Biography', 199 and Sil, 'Denny', 191.

8   Bindoff, *Commons*, II, 27; Hudson, *Cambridge Connection*, 40.

9   Hudson, *Cambridge Connection*, 7, 73.

10 The evidence for Denny's early life prior to his entry into the royal household is very limited. Denny is linked with Bryan's household and it is most likely that he joined it during his twenties.

11 *LP* V, 363.

12 Bindoff, *Commons*, II, 27.

13 PRO E101/417/3, no. 18 (102). Each man was granted 14yds of damask for a gown at 9s a yd, a fur of black budge at £6, 8yds of velvet for a jacket and 3yds of velvet for a doublet, both at 16s a yd.

14 *LP* IX, 85.

15 Bindoff, *Commons*, II, 27. Denny was almost certainly Member for Ipswich early in 1536.

In January 1536 Denny obtained the reversion of the keepership of Whitehall with 12*d* a day, a prestigious appointment for a Groom of the Privy Chamber.[16] As Denny followed Alvard in the post of Member of Parliament for Ipswich, so he also succeeded him as Keeper. Indeed, Denny may have been in post on an unofficial footing from Alvard's death: in May 1536, when Anne Boleyn's finances were being resolved after her execution, Denny had the care of some of her possessions at Whitehall, including 'gold and silver plate, a great gold chain [and] many strange pieces of gold'.[17] In the same month Denny's former patron Sir Francis Bryan was made one of the Chief Gentlemen of the Privy Chamber, acting as the junior partner to Sir Thomas Heneage.[18] After Anne's death until 1537 Denny served the new queen, Jane Seymour, who gave him a brooch as indicated by a marginal note in her jewel book.[19]

During this time Denny met and married Joan, the daughter of Sir Philip Champernon.[20] When they met, Joan was a member of Anne Boleyn's household and shared the reformed religious beliefs of her mistress. Later Joan, along with several other ladies at court, was implicated when Anne Askew was tried for heresy.[21] Joan's sister Catherine was governess to the young Lady Elizabeth and became a Woman of the Bedchamber after Elizabeth's accession.[22] Joan probably divided her time between court and family duties after her marriage in 1538. On 13 May 1542 Robert Dacre wrote to Denny from Hertfordshire with the news that 'my sister, your wife, is brought to bed of a fair daughter'.[23] Such letters must have been familiar to Denny: on his death in 1549 he was survived by his wife, five legitimate sons and four daughters.[24]

Denny was well regarded for his learning both within court circles and beyond. He was described as 'a very Maecenas' by Thomas Langley in his *Abridgement of the Notable Works of Polydore Vergil*. In 1538 he worked with the king's librarian William Tildesley and Thomas Cromwell to gain access to Henry's books for Sir Thomas Elyot, to facilitate the preparation of Elyot's dictionary and as a general bid to advance learning.[25] As a consequence of his academic interests a number of books were dedicated to Denny, including Thomas Chaloner's *Homily of Saint John Chrysostom* in 1544.[26] The following year Roger Ascham sent Denny a copy of his *Toxophilus*, while in 1546 Joan was praised in the dedication of William Hugh's *A Sweet Consolation* and the second book of *The Troubled Man's Medicine*.

16 *LP* X, 226.34. He was also granted the post of Keeper of the houses known as Paradise, Hell and Purgatory (ibid, 226.35) and made Keeper of the new park and all the associated sporting facilities with 8*d* a day (ibid, 226.33).

17 Ibid, 912.

18 *LP* IV, 30/5519.

19 BL Royal MS 7C.XVI, f. 27v.

20 Nothing is known of Denny's previous liaisons but there must have been at least one: his will refers to 'my base son William', who was some years older than his other children.

21 The other ladies to be implicated were Catherine Brandon, Duchess of Suffolk; Lady FitzWilliam; Anne Seymour, Countess of Hertford; and Anne Radcliffe, Countess of Sussex. Anne Askew had links with Sir Gawain Carew, Joan's uncle: see Denny, 'Biography', 206–7.

22 Catherine married John Ashley, later to be a Marian exile and then Elizabeth I's Master of the Jewel House.

23 *LP* XVII, 322. Robert Dacre was the second husband of Denny's sister-in-law Elizabeth, whose first husband was Thomas Denny; at this date the term 'brother' and 'sister' could include in-laws, and even close friends, as well as blood relatives.

24 See family tree (above, p. 54).

25 *LP* XXIII.ii, 852.

26 See Dowling, 'Gospel and the court', 65–7. Chaloner was a scholar of St John's.

In September 1537 Denny was granted two additional offices. First, he was appointed Yeoman of the Robes, a post on an equal footing with the Gentlemen of the Privy Chamber.[27] Secondly, he was made Keeper of the Royal Household in the Palace of Whitehall, with *6d* a day.[28] Officially he relinquished the post of Yeoman of the Robes to Richard Cecil early in 1539, but he appears to have stopped carrying out the duties of the post somewhat earlier; Cecil received payment of wages from December 1538.[29] This change surely reflects the situation in the Privy Chamber during the winter of 1538/9. After losing the king's favour Bryan lost the office of Second Chief Gentleman and Denny was named as his successor.[30] This would have left Denny little time for his duties as Yeoman. In his new role, he was present at the reception for Anne of Cleves and some months later he was called as a witness at the annulment of Henry's short-lived fourth marriage.[31]

During this period Denny nurtured his Hertfordshire connections and in December 1540 he was appointed to the Commission of the Sewers with responsibility 'for the coasts of the sea and marsh ground'.[32] As Denny acquired more responsibilities he needed a loyal staff to help him, and in August 1542 he procured a licence to retain in his service twenty gentlemen or yeomen in addition to his household servants, all of whom he provided with food, lodging, livery and wages as long as they were not in receipt of the king's livery or fee.[33]

Denny was equally at the centre of court life. On 12 July 1543 he was present with Heneage, Henry Knevet, the Lady Mary, the Lady Elizabeth and Lady Margaret Douglas for Henry's final marriage to Catherine, Lady Latimer (née Parr), in an upper oratory called 'the Quynes Pryevey closet' at Hampton Court.[34]

Traditionally, Denny has been presented as a key member of the faction promoting reformed religion at court. Such a view can be found in the work of John Foxe:

> So long as Queen Anne, Thomas Cromwell, Archbishop Cranmer, Master Denny,
> Doctor Butts, with such like, were about [Henry VIII], and could prevail with him,
> what organ of Christ's glory did more good in the church than he?[35]

However, this view has been challenged by Jennifer Loach, on the grounds that the beliefs of Denny's wife Joan, which are documented, are often attributed to her husband.[36]

So what evidence is there? From 1536 onwards Denny acquired monastic lands in Hertfordshire and East Anglia. However, this is not necessarily an indication of his feelings about the Dissolution since men of all shades of religious feeling invested in monastic land. Even so, Denny was personally involved in the dissolution of the nunnery at Cheshunt, which he had received before the visit of the Commissioners in March 1537.[37] The indenture for the surrender of the nunnery was signed by Robert Dacre on behalf of Denny, rather than by the prioress.[38]

27 *LP* XII.ii, 796.13.
28 Ibid. This is a different office from those he had been granted previously, at a different rate of pay.
29 *LP* XIV.ii, 781; in March 1539 Richard Cecil received £4 10s 0d to cover his wage from 31 December 1538 to 1 April 1539: BL Arundel MS 97, f. 61v.
30 *LP* XIV.i, 37.144.
31 The documents relating to Denny's involvement in the proceedings include *LP* XV, 825, 850, 860.
32 *LP* XVI, 379.7.
33 *LP* XVII, 714.21.   34 *LP* XVIII.i, 873.   35 Foxe, *Acts and Monuments*, V, 605–6.
36 See Loach, *Edward VI*, 24.   37 *LP* XI, 519.12.
38 *LP* XII.i, 571.5. The indenture is dated 28 May 1536.

There is also evidence by association. Most of his friends and associates, like Dr William Butts, Archbishop Cranmer and Denny's own wife, Joan, were supporters of reformed religious views. In 1543 Denny used his influence within the Privy Chamber to protect Cranmer from the religious conservatives when Gardiner, Bishop of Winchester, initiated the unsuccessful 'Plot of the Prebends'.[39] At a time when religion was so significant, it is very likely that Denny shared the general ideas of the circle he mixed in, even if he was not radical in his approach. Swensen has analysed Denny's use of the dry stamp for evidence of religious patronage but could not find a strong reforming bias.[40] But here, after all, Denny was acting largely as an agent for others, most particularly the king.

However, Denny's will, dated 3 August 1546 (some three years before his death), provides some indication of his personal beliefs.[41] It is highly idiosyncratic, and is suggestive of a commitment to moderate reform. In the phrase that was a touchstone of reformed belief, or rather disbelief in Purgatory, Denny sought to be buried 'without all superfluous funeral charges, or bestowing of black garments'.[42] More revealing still is the evangelical, at times almost Puritan language:

> I cannot but acknowledge my slackness in leaving that undone that I ought still to have done. And my readiness in doing that which I should still have left undone. Lewd fantasy, corrupt flesh, prowess to fall ... have oft wrought their wills in me.[43]

Finally, and crucially, there is his own direct assertion that he had been 'without any mundane respect a more earnest and faithful advancer with all my uttermost force of God's holy and pure Word for my time'.[44]

The striking thing about reformers like Denny is that they combined a fervent faith towards God with an equally passionate patriotism, or as he put it in his will, 'love, fear and true honour to God, and faithful obedience to their sovereign rulers, and love to their native country'.[45] This bellicose, nationalistic religiosity was formed in Henry's wars of the 1540s in which Denny played a considerable role. When Henry led his army to France in 1544 his household formed its core just as it had thirty years previously, in 1514. The involvement of the whole household is indicated by the allocation of tents in July 1544. It included one hall to Denny, another to John Gates for the 'king's majesty's coffers' and a third to Dr Butts 'for hurte and maymed men', while the Wardrobes of the Robes and Beds each received one hall, one round house, one tresance, a passage or corridor, and one hatchment.[46]

---

39   For a summary of the 'Plot of the Prebends' see Guy, *Tudor England*, 194–5.

40   Swensen, 'Patronage', 39. For an explanation of how the dry stamp was used see Starkey, 'Intimacy and innovation', 100.

41   PRO PROB 11/32 (37 Populwell). There is a copy of Denny's will in the British Library, see BL Additional MS 33577.

42   Ibid; such sentiments were not uncommon, as indicated by the wills of Roger Townsend and Henry Brinklow: see Brigden, *London and the Reformation*, 384–5.

43   PRO PROB 11/32 (37 Populwell).

44   Ibid; in addition to the sentiments expressed in his will, he also demonstrated his feelings when he was granted the site and church of the late College of St Mary's, Mettingham in April 1542 (*LP* XVII, 283.43). During 1543–4, very much in the vanguard of ecclesiastical spoliations, the church was stripped of all items associated with unreformed faith, including the high altar and an image of the Virgin with its tabernacle, which were sold to the town of Beccles for 60s, and an image of St John Baptist with its tabernacle was sold to the town of Denton for 3s 4d (BL Additional Roll 63260).

45   PRO PROB 11/32 (37 Populwell).

46   GMR LM 59/101, fos 2r, 1v. The precise definition of these tent terms is uncertain but it is possible that a hall was rectangular or square and a round house was circular (as its name suggests).

Denny was also involved with some of the financial arrangements for Henry's French and Scottish campaigns. In 1544 he delivered three instalments of money to Thomas Cawarden and the other Officers of the Tents, on 12 April (£200), 11 May (£300) and 9 July (£2,000).[47] He put up the whole of the £30,000 that was first assigned to the Scottish expedition and he supplied £8,500 of the £19,500 that was given to Sir John Gresham to purchase arms in the Netherlands.[48]

Denny made a more direct contribution as well. Like his fellow royal servants he drew on his country estates to raise troops, supplying forty-one horsemen, forty archers and 140 billmen for the king's army.[49] This compares favourably with the eighty horsemen, sixty archers and sixty billmen mustered by First Chief Gentleman Heneage.[50] The accounts of Hugh Brown, who administered Denny's Suffolk lands, record additional charges of 60s 8d in the year 1543–4 for the soldiers that Denny provided, besides £4 19s 6d received from the tenth to cover his costs.[51] Presumably he led these men in the field, since he was amongst the select group that Henry knighted at the capture of Boulogne.[52] Two years later, in October 1546, Denny became First Chief Gentleman and Groom of the Stool.[53]

The promotion placed him at the centre of events at the time of Henry's death three months later. Both the nature of what happened and Denny's role in it have been much disputed. One view sees him as a crucial figure in a 'Protestant' coup; the other merely as a reporter of decisions that were genuinely those of Edward. On either view, however, Denny is notable by his prominence. He witnessed Henry's will, being named as one of the key group of fourteen who doubled as executors of the will and as members of Edward's Regency Privy Council, and he was a legatee of the will.[54] It was also Denny who informed the king of his imminent death.[55] He took his seat on the Privy Council on 31 January, the first meeting of the new regime.[56] As befitted his office of First Gentleman of the Privy Chamber Denny was positioned 'At the head of the corpse' in Henry's funeral procession, riding with the coffin in the funeral car.[57] As Groom of the Stool he received a selection of the late king's close stools and associated items [4021–4031] as a perquisite.[58]

47 GMR LM 59/46.

48 Starkey, 'Privy Chamber', 409.

49 LP XIX.i, 275.

50 Ibid.

51 BL Additional Roll 63260.

52 Denny's arms were quarterly one and four, gules a saltire argent between twelve crosses patée or (Denny), two, or, a fess dancette gules in chief three martlets sable and three azure, three trout fretted in a triangle argent, a mullet pierced or for difference. For his crest, he took an arm erect habited azure, charged with a quatrefoil argent, holding in the hand proper a garb (a bunch of wheat) or: Denny, 'Biography', 202. Others so honoured included Thomas Cawarden and Philip Hoby.

53 Starkey, 'Intimacy and innovation', 116. This brought additional responsibilities: for example on 19 January 1547 Denny delivered £100 to Sir Thomas Darcy towards the provision of 'armery against the next jousts and tourney which by the grace of God shall be at the solemn feast of the Prince's creation': LP XXI.ii, 723.

54 Henry VIII's will (LP XXI.ii, 634.1) is a problematic document in terms of its dating and its 'authenticity'; for a discussion of the issues and implications see Ives, 'Henry VIII's will' and Houlbrooke, 'Henry VIII's wills'. For the enrolment of Henry VIII's will and the list of executors see CSPD Edward VI, 11.

55 Foxe, Acts and Monuments, V, 689. 'Master Denny, who was specially attendant upon him boldly, coming to the king, told him what case he was in, to man's judgement not likely to live; and therefore exhorted him to prepare himself to death, calling himself to remembrance of his former life, and to call upon God in Christ betimes for grace and mercy, as becometh every good christian man to do.'

56 Sil, 'Denny', 198–9.

57 Denny shared this place with Sir William Herbert: see CSPD Edward VI, 16 and Strype, Ecclesiastical Memorials, II.ii, 298–9.

58 The selection included 'oone close stowle coverid with tawny vellat pirled frengid with blac silke enbraudred with a Roose of venice gold / and lyned with scarlet' [281].

The claim to the perquisite was presented as a traditional one, but the tradition, like the importance of the office of Groom of the Stool, was probably a recent development. Denny was also instrumental in the organization of Edward's coronation and, along with his colleague as Chief Gentleman, Sir William Herbert, held the pall over Edward's head when Cranmer anointed the boy king.[59] Denny was an active Privy Counsellor in the first few weeks of the reign. But he was not present at the meeting on 13 March 1547 which confirmed the Duke of Somerset's authority as Protector and he was absent from the Council thereafter. In August he lost both the post of Groom of the Stool and that of First Chief Gentleman to Somerset's brother-in-law, Sir Michael Stanhope.[60] Failing health may have been one explanation for this, though he continued to serve as the Member of Parliament for Hertfordshire in the early sessions of Edward's first parliament (4 November 1547– 15 April 1552).[61] But political disfavour was surely another. He only emerged from retirement in early 1549, to play a conspicuous part in the prosecution for treason of Somerset's brother, Thomas, Lord Seymour of Sudeley.[62]

Notoriously, the Lady Elizabeth, Henry VIII's daughter by Anne Boleyn, was heavily implicated in the Seymour affair. The link between Elizabeth and Denny was an old one. In 1539 Lady Lisle had sought to use Denny's wife as an intermediary to place her daughter Anne Bassett in Elizabeth's household.[63] Joan Denny had held out few hopes for the success of the suit on the grounds that the king had already 'said that she had too much youth about her', but she did promise to get Denny to speak to the king directly.[64] Towards the end of Henry's reign Denny himself had better luck, and in 1546 he preferred William Man, 'the eldest groom with my lady Elizabeth to have wages of 4*d* a day which John Belman had'.[65] The link continued after Edward's accession. Elizabeth spent much of the summer of 1548 at Denny's house at Cheshunt. She wrote to Catherine Parr from Cheshunt on 31 July 1548 to wish her well for the birth of her child. She added that 'Master Denny and my lady, with humble thanks, prayeth most entirely for your Grace, praying the Almighty God to send you a most lucky deliverance.'[66]

The following Christmas, Elizabeth, though only fifteen, set up house for herself at Hatfield. But she had scarcely moved outside Denny's sphere of influence: he was Keeper of the house at Hatfield and it lay only four or five miles to the west of Cheshunt, along the ancient road known as the Ridgeway. Early in the 1549, however, Denny arrived at Hatfield to arrest Elizabeth's Cofferer, Thomas Parry, and 'her lady mistress', Catherine Ashley, on charges of complicity in the Seymour affair.[67] But Denny sought to protect Elizabeth's position. This was scarcely surprising, as he was both Elizabeth's protector and Catherine Ashley's brother-in-law. He probably advised Elizabeth on her tactics with the Privy Council; and certainly, according to the evidence of his sister-in-law, she herself had advised Elizabeth to decline Seymour's offer of his London house unless Denny approved.[68] Evidently he did not.[69]

59 See *CSPD Edward VI*, 10 and Loach, *Edward VI*, 36.
60 Murphy, 'Illusion of decline', 124.
62 *PPC*, II, pp. 3–62, 63–4, 236, 258, 262–3.
64 Ibid, 1457a.
65 *LP* XXI.ii, 199.74.
67 *CSPD Edward VI*, 196.
68 Ibid, 195.

61 Bindoff, *The Commons*, II, 28–9.
63 *Lisle Letters*, V, no. 1453.

66 BL Cotton MS Otho C X, f. 236v.

69 Starkey, *Elizabeth*, 79.

In 1547 the Duke of Somerset launched a campaign against Scotland in Edward VI's name. His initial great victory at Pinkie was followed by an increasingly unsuccessful attempt to hold the country down with garrisons. Denny provided six great horse in 1547 and six light horse and six demi-lances in 1548.[70] This was on a par with the contribution of Sir Ralph Sadler, Master of the Great Wardrobe (ten great horses, four light horse and two demi-lances).[71] Although he did not take part personally in the Scottish campaign, Denny joined the force sent by William Parr, Marquess of Northampton to put down the Norfolk rebels in August 1549.[72]

This was his last service for the Crown. On 7 September 1549 Denny added a codicil to his will. Three days later he died and, although the register does not survive to confirm it, he was probably buried in the parish church of St Mary's, Cheshunt.

His offices

The holding of office was integral to success at the Tudor court: it provided an income, a means of access to the social network and the hope of preferment.[73] Preferment could take many forms: grants of land, keeperships of royal parks and properties, annuities and pensions. In addition, most offices within the royal household brought their holder lodgings, along with livery, diets and *bouche* of court. As a member of the Privy Chamber, Denny was eligible for such perquisites and similar provision was made for his wife when, as was customary, she replicated her husband's service to the king in the Privy Chamber of his last wife, Catherine Parr. Denny started as a junior member of the Privy Chamber, before rising to the top. En route, he held a series of posts, often holding two or more offices at a time. The combination of posts was integral to his success at court, providing him with access to the king and the potential to exploit royal patronage for himself and others. To cope successfully with the demands of office, Denny combined personal industry with effective delegation. According to Sir William Paget, Henry recognized the 'painful service Master Denny did take daily with him'.[74] In turn, in his own will Denny acknowledged his debt to his own 'faithful and honest servants that have long and diligently served'.[75]

Lodgings at court were a very important perquisite: space in a palace was at a premium and rents in the adjacent townships like Westminster or Greenwich were high. Once the period of his junior service was over, Denny's rooms were well situated, as befitted his status and office. A list of lodgings for the royal household dated January 1540 recorded double lodgings in the inner, second and outer courts at Hampton Court for the Prince Edward, Heneage, Denny, the Master of the Horse and other leading members of the household.[76] Similarly a record of 'the ordinary to be accustomed to be lodged within the King's majesty's house' from May 1546 included rooms for Denny, and Joan was to lodge with him.[77] His rooms needed to be close to the king so that he could provide regular, prompt attendance.

70 *CSPD Edward VI*, 44, 137.   71 Ibid.

72 Denny, 'Biography', 210.

73 For a summary of the offices, grants and annuities given to Denny see Appendix II below. The desirability of court office, and the livery and regalia associated with it, is demonstrated by the number of individuals who chose to be painted dressed this way: e.g. Thomas Howard, Duke of Norfolk was painted with the white staff and baton that denoted his offices of Lord Treasurer and Earl Marshal (*c.* 1539), and Sir William Palmer in his uniform as a Gentleman Pensioner (*c.* 1546).

74 Quoted in Denny, 'Biography', 209.

75 PRO PROB 11/32 (37 Populwell).

76 *LP* XV, 138.   77 *LP* XXI.i, 969.

Hints of the type of furnishings he had can be gleaned from the inventory of Thomas Culpepper's 'office in the tilt yard' at Greenwich, compiled on 16 October 1541.[78] Culpepper's personal furnishings consisted of a trussing bedstead with a tester, double valances and curtains of tawny velvet and a quilt of tawny taffeta, a round table and a chair.[79] It seems very likely that Denny too would have had a trussing bedstead, for ease of transportation when he removed with the itinerant royal household.[80] Other furnishings would have been limited by what was easy to move and necessary for the effective execution of his office. For Culpepper, the trappings of his office were a harness for the tilt (with its coffer) and two velvet bases. In Denny's case the trappings would have been a desk and writing materials.

The giving of gifts also bound the leading royal officeholders to the king. Members of the royal household, the nobility, the ecclesiastical hierarchy and the leading craftsmen and merchants who traded with him exchanged gifts with the king at the New Year. In 1539 Denny gave his king 'a deske couered with grene veluet enbrawdered with venice golde with diuers necessaries therin', while Joan presented 'a regestre and a shirt with blak worke';[81] although a number of desks covered with green velvet are listed in the 1547 Inventory, it is not possible to identify Denny's gift.[82] In return, Henry gave 'maistres Denny a gilte Jugge with a couer … weing xvj oz quarter di' and 'a gilte Cruse with a couer … And a gilte salte with a couer … Summa xxvij oz di di quarter' to her husband.[83] Five years later, in 1544, Denny chose a more impressive gift: he commissioned an elaborate column timepiece designed by Holbein.[84] Holbein's drawings survive, providing a clear indication of Denny's expendable wealth, his appreciation of the quality of Holbein's work and a good understanding of what the king would enjoy (see Figure 8).[85] The timepiece combined fashionable antique motifs with technical ingenuity, as indicated by the annotations made on the design by Nicholas Kratzer, Henry's astronomer. In his will, Denny displayed a similar understanding of Edward vi, leaving him a gift of 'some such thing apt for a learned King', to be devised by his executors 'or some fine head in invention' chosen by them.[86] The gift was to stand 'in my stead [to] supply the daily service that I have desire to do to his Majesty if life had not left me'.

JUNIOR OFFICES WITHIN THE PRIVY CHAMBER Denny held several posts within the Privy Chamber hierarchy of Groom, Gentleman, Second Chief Gentleman, First Chief Gentleman and Groom of the Stool. His first, and humblest, appointment within the Privy Chamber, that of

78 PRO E314/79, unfoliated.

79 The bedstead also had a mattress, a feather bed, a bolster with one pillow but no pillow-bere, blankets, a pair of sheets and a pair of fustians.

80 In 1541 Denny received some items of clothing from the royal wardrobe that could have been sold or converted into small furnishings such as cushions: *LP* XVI, 402. Edmund Daniel, 'Mr Denys man', collected the items on behalf of his master. In October 1545 Denny preferred Daniel to an office: *LP* XX.ii, 706.51.

81 Folger Shakespeare Library, MS Z. d.11, unfoliated.

82 Likely examples include entries **10435**, **10476**, **10514** and **10540**. All these desks were located within the studies at Whitehall. A desk was clearly considered to be an appropriate gift for a king as Catherine Parr presented her husband with a fine example: 'Item a faire Standisshe with a deske of golde geuen by the Quene at New yeres daie to the kinges maiestie wrought with Astronomie and Geographie with tilles of golde in it put in a case of crymson veluet embrawdred with damaske golde' (**3123**).

83 PRO PROB 11/32 (37 Populwell).

84 BM 1850-7-13-14.   85 Starkey, *Personalities and Politics*, 135.

86 PRO PROB 11/32 (37 Populwell).

Groom, will now be considered; the other, more specialized, offices which he held will be considered below.

According to the Eltham Ordinances of 1526, the Privy Chamber staff comprised six Gentlemen, one of whom was the Groom of the Stool, two Gentlemen Ushers, four Grooms, a barber and a page.[87] When Thomas Cromwell reformed the household structure in the winter of 1539/40 these figures were substantially revised and increased to two Chief Gentlemen, sixteen Gentlemen Ordinary, two Gentleman Ushers, four Grooms and two barbers.[88] So Denny joined the lowest ranks of the Privy Chamber, the Grooms, shortly before a period of revision and change; but while the titles may have changed, the responsibilities of the Privy Chamber staff remained consistent.

The Gentlemen Ordinary, Gentlemen Ushers and Grooms were the king's intimate attendants, helping him to dress and undress, cleaning the Privy Chamber and sleeping at the foot of the king's bed. They provided much of his entertainment, as they were his companions for indoor pastimes and outdoor sports. By their close association with the king, they also came to represent his wishes and authority. As such, they were used as special messengers, diplomats, military commanders and local officials. There is evidence for his fulfilment of all these roles in Denny's subsequent career. But, at least in theory, the Grooms' duties were primarily menial. In the Eltham Ordinances, Wolsey had been at some pains to limit direct physical contact between the Grooms and the king: they were not 'to approach or presume … to lay hands upon his royal person'.[89]

YEOMAN OF THE WARDROBE OF THE ROBES   According to the Black Book of Edward IV the Wardrobe of the Robes, like the Wardrobe of the Beds, came under the auspices of the Lord Chamberlain as part of the Chamber. With the advent of the Privy Chamber during Henry VII's reign, the staff of the Robes brought the king's clothes to the door of the Privy Chamber and then the staff of the new department dressed the monarch. The Eltham Ordinance sought to reinforce the distinction, emphasizing that the servants of the Robes were not to go beyond the threshold of the Privy Chamber.[90] But this distinction too proved impractical and by the 1530s the Wardrobe of the Robes was well on the way to becoming a sub-department of the Privy Chamber.[91] Denny himself played a significant part in the process, for in 1537, while still a Groom of the Privy Chamber, he was appointed Yeoman of the Robes, as successor to John Parker. He received 28s a week, paid on a monthly basis, and was also given a cash reward by the king at the New Year. No inventories survive for Denny's period of office but two draft title pages for an inventory viewed by Sir William Kingston and Sir John Daunce in June 1538 do.[92] Moreover, there is some loosely dated material that does relate to his charge from 1537 to 1538.[93] This includes another, earlier inventory overseen by Kingston and Daunce in May 1537, covering just the accessories and weapons in the care of the Wardrobe.

87   *LP* IV.i, 1939. In 1526 the staff of the Privy Chamber included the Marquess of Exeter, 'which is the King's near kinsman, and hath been brought up of a child with his Grace in his chamber' (ibid), in addition to the fourteen appointed officers.
88   Starkey, 'Privy Chamber', 223–4.
89   *HO*, 156.   90   Ibid.
91   Ibid, 268–72 and Hayward, 'Repositories of splendour', 135.
92   *LP* XIII.i, 1278.
93   *LP* XIII.ii, 1191.

As Yeoman of the Wardrobe of the Robes, Denny had a staff of two: a groom and a page (see Appendix III). In addition he had a part share of a clerk, who also worked for the Wardrobe of the Beds. The split of the clerk's wages indicates the workload, if not the relative importance of the two offices: he received £4 a year for the work of the Robes and £10 for the Beds. The joint responsibilities of the three Robes officers with the occasional assistance of the clerk were to clean and care for the king's clothes, his accessories and some sporting equipment, including a selection of swords and knives.[94] The garments had to be aired prior to being handed over at the door of the Privy Chamber. New orders of clothing were periodically delivered from the Great Wardrobe and other suppliers and craftsmen. As the king removed from one property to the next, the officers of the Robes had to pack and unpack the items in their care.

KEEPER OF WHITEHALL PALACE   Denny obtained the reversion of the keepership of Whitehall Palace in January 1536,[95] and he was only the second incumbent of this post. Thomas Alvard, Denny's predecessor, had been appointed Keeper in February 1530 and died in office five years later, in February 1535. The chief focus of his job had been to oversee the building work at the palace and to furnish it.[96] During Denny's tenure the office expanded considerably. Like all keepers of royal properties, Denny had a number of standard responsibilities but at Whitehall the role exceeded the norm, reflecting the size and importance of the palace. In essence, the role of Keeper at Whitehall was specially enhanced for Denny. The scope and demands of the office during a period when the palace was still under construction required all the skill at Denny's command. On Henry's death, and the consequent reduction in the role of the palace effected by the Duke of Somerset, the need for a Keeper of this type withered and the scope of the office was reduced.

In his, and the palace's, heyday Denny held the keys to the property in the king's absence. In view of the size of the palace by 1547 it is most unlikely that he was the sole key-holder, but he certainly had overall responsibility for the palace and its contents. In addition he negotiated with the King's Works to ensure that the property was well maintained and that any new building work was carried out quickly and economically. In this area, however, Henry's own direct personal interests in the building works meant that Denny played second fiddle until, later, the king's attention shifted to newer projects, like Nonsuch. Denny organized the preparation of the property prior to the king's arrival and its closure after he left. Under him there was also a staff responsible for the Standing Wardrobe, the gardens, orchards and parks (all tasks which the Keeper of a smaller house – like Thomas Carvannel at Beaulieu – had to carry out himself; see Appendix III).[97] In return, Denny received a salary as Keeper, lodgings at the property and a range of other perks such as grazing rights and free warren. Denny's predecessor as Keeper, Thomas Alvard, had a set of rooms off the tilt-yard gallery and lodgings within the new park.[98] Denny perhaps enjoyed a similar allocation, although as he was also a member of the Privy Chamber he was also entitled to accommodation closer to the king.

---

94 For more details see Hayward, 'Repositories of splendour', 140–1, 144–6.
95 For a full discussion of this interesting grant, see pp. 81–2.
96 See below, pp. 113–15.
97 In December 1519 Carvannel received 16d a day as wages and sixty loads of wood a year for the wardrobe: LP III.i, 581.14.
98 Thurley, Royal Palaces, 83.

Finally, it was Denny's duties as Keeper that led to the drawing up of the 1542 Inventory. This aspect of the post of Keeper is discussed separately below.[99]

CHIEF GENTLEMAN OF THE PRIVY CHAMBER   This new post, established in the 1530s, was one of several innovations within the royal household that followed the French model.[100] Initially, there was a single post of Chief Gentleman, which was held concurrently with that of Groom of the Stool. The distinction between the two posts seems to have been between the efficient and the dignified: the Groom of the Stool carried the traditional duties of intimate attendance and running the private administration, while the Chief Gentleman enjoyed the departmental headship of the Privy Chamber. The evidence suggests that Henry Norris, who had succeeded Sir William Compton as Groom of the Stool, was made Chief Gentleman of the Privy Chamber between 1526 and 1532, with first William Carey (d. June 1528) and then Thomas Heneage as his unofficial deputy. His new status was denoted by provision of a new dining table for 'Mr Norris and gentilmen of the kinges Prevy Chamber'.[101] After the fall and execution of Norris in May 1536 the relationship between the Chief Gentleman and his deputy was put on a more official footing: Heneage was appointed Groom of the Stool and First Chief Gentleman, with Sir Francis Bryan as the Second Chief Gentleman. Heneage, as the First Chief Gentleman, held the privy purse and was Groom of the Stool. He was assisted by Bryan, who was the junior partner in this pairing.

When Denny replaced Bryan as Second Chief Gentleman in January 1539 the balance of the relationship between the two offices shifted. Although Heneage was Groom of the Stool, Denny administered the most important part of the king's private finances, known as the privy coffers. The balance shifted back again when Denny was made First Chief Gentleman and Groom of the Stool in 1546. His deputy at this time was Sir William Herbert. The responsibilities of the Chief Gentlemen were extended further by January 1547 when they became ex-officio members of the Privy Council. Stanhope replaced Denny as First, and probably sole, Chief Gentleman in August 1547. After Somerset's fall in October 1549, Stanhope, as his brother-in-law and henchman, was dismissed. There was no single replacement; instead the post of chief gentleman was put into commission between four Principal Gentlemen: Sir Thomas Darcy, Sir Andrew Dudley (soon to be Keeper of Whitehall Palace), Sir Edward Rogers and Sir Thomas Wroth.[102]

GROOM OF THE STOOL   Although there are references to the office of Yeoman of the Stool during Henry VI's reign, the post then lacked much significance within the household structure until 1495 when it was made head of the new Privy Chamber staff in 1495.[103] The Groom of the Stool had responsibility over the Privy Chamber staff of six grooms and a similar number of pages.

99 See pp. 99–105.
100 For a discussion of the English response to the creation of the office of *gentilhomme de la chambre du roi* see Richardson, 'Anglo–French relations'.
101 See Starkey, 'Privy Chamber', 234.
102 Ibid, 239–43.
103 For the period under consideration the holders were Hugh Denys (1495–1509), Sir William Compton (1509–26), Sir Henry Norris (January 1526–May 1536), Sir Thomas Heneage (1536–October 1546), Sir Anthony Denny (October 1546–1547) and Sir Michael Stanhope (August 1547–1549). For changes in the significance of the position see Starkey, 'Privy Chamber', 26–30 and Starkey, 'Intimacy and innovation', 72–6.

By 1526 the Groom of the Stool counted as one of the six Gentlemen of the Privy Chamber in the Eltham Ordinances. With the advent of the offices of the two Chief Gentlemen, the groomship was held in tandem with one of those posts.

Throughout the evolution of this office the Groom of the Stool, at the simplest level, remained the monarch's chief body servant. He personally oversaw the use, maintenance and transportation of the king's close stool.[104] However, from this starting point, the responsibilities grew. He attended the king at all times, acted as his most confidential messenger and controlled access to the king, by holding the keys to the royal apartments. In addition, the Groom of the Stool had a secretarial role: he often procured the king's signature or sign manual, either on his own behalf or acting on instructions from others, he handled much correspondence, particularly relating to the distribution of patronage; and he kept many of the confidential papers, public and private, that were in the king's current use. Finally, he was responsible for the privy purse and cared for the king's personal linen, dining plate and everyday jewels. In fact, if not in name, the Groom of the Stool was the keeper for these items. With the extension of the privy lodging beyond the privy chamber, the Groom of the Stool was the only royal servant allowed into the bedchamber and the rest of the rooms.

The Groom of the Stool was frequently employed as an intermediary, collecting, delivering and transporting messages and items between royal residences. On 21 September 1532 Henry Norris brought seven carcanets, one George and a gold chain from Greenwich to Henry at Hampton Court.[105] Heneage delivered 'clothes of gold clothes of Sylver Tyncelles and other Silkes' to Hampton Court to make 'viij Sparvers and Quisshens' for the French Admiral's visit in 1546.[106]

The keepership of a primary royal residence was often held by the Groom of the Stool: Sir William Compton and Henry Norris were both keepers of Greenwich, the principal palace during their terms of office.[107] But this was not a hard-and-fast rule. William Carey who in 1526 succeeded Compton at Greenwich, although a confidant of the king and husband of Mary Boleyn (an ex-mistress of Henry's), never became Groom. Thomas Heneage, Norris's successor in the office, held the keepership of neither Greenwich or Whitehall. Denny, who had been favoured at Whitehall over Heneage, had held the keepership there for ten years before becoming Groom. He held the two appointments jointly for less than a year.

Denny's appointment as Groom of the Stool and First Chief Gentleman was the apogee of his career. But the fact that Denny only held the former post for the last four months of Henry VIII's reign and the first few months of Edward VI's shows that the office was merely incidental to Denny's position.

---

104 This list of functions is drawn from Starkey, 'Representation through intimacy', 204–7.
105 BL Royal MS 7C.XVI, f. 71r–v (*LP* V, 1335). A carcanet consisted of a series of jewelled or enamelled links, like a collar, but on a smaller scale: see Scarisbrick, *Tudor and Jacobean Jewellery*, 77–8.
106 GMR LM 59/142.
107 Thurley, *Royal Palaces*, 83.

Financial concerns: administration of the king's coffers and the privy purse

Henry VIII's income came from his ordinary revenues such as customs duties and rent from Crown lands, supplemented in times of need by extraordinary taxation of the clergy and the laity.[108] Part of the money went to the Exchequer and other officially established treasuries such as the Chamber, and the Courts of Augmentations and of First Fruits and Tenths. The rest (often including the annual cash-in-hand surpluses of the other treasuries) went directly to the king and it was paid into either his coffers or his own privy purse. During his career Denny controlled both the king's coffers, as a consequence of his being Keeper of Whitehall Palace, and, as Groom of the Stool, the king's privy purse. Denny's notes detailing his administration of the king's coffers between 1542 and 1548 appear in the 1542 Inventory, while the record of his brief administration of the privy purse features in BL Lansdowne Roll 14.

THE KING'S COFFERS   Henry VIII inherited the financial reserve established by his father, which was kept in coffers in treasuries at the Tower, the old Palace of Westminster and in Calais.[109] These coffers played an important role in Henry VIII's finances and he maintained them throughout his reign. But their location changed with the shifts in the king's principal residence from one palace to another. The first change took place in 1512 when, following the fire that destroyed most of the old Palace of Westminster, the treasuries were removed to Greenwich. Greenwich remained both Henry's principal residence and the principal deposit treasury for the first half of his reign. The money was delivered there, usually by boat at 12d a trip.[110] After 1529 Whitehall, or, to give it its formal name, the new Palace of Westminster, in turn displaced Greenwich as the king's principal official or working residence. Denny's role as Keeper of the new palace gave him a central role in the process. Later in Henry's reign, the accounts of the Court of Augmentations record a number of substantial payments made to the king's coffers and delivered by Denny in the period before 1542. To take one example, between 17 May and 19 December 1540 Denny transferred £18,105 7s 8d.[111]

The payments listed in the 1542 Inventory were described as 'Money chargyd by the king his graces commaundement vpon Anthony Denny … whiche shalbe by hym Receauid to his said highnes use'.[112] The king's requirements were many, varied and substantial. During Denny's management of the coffers, a total of £243,423 was received.[113] Denny continued to oversee aspects of Edward's finances until 15 February 1548, although during 1547 the amount of 'Redie money receyved & paid <by the said Sir Anthony>' diminished greatly.[114] This probably reflected the reduction in royal funds and Denny's gradual marginalization within the Privy Chamber.

---

108 For a recent analysis of the sources and extent of Henry's income, see Hoyle, 'War and public finance'. Sybil Jack will be contributing an essay on Henry's finances to one of the forthcoming volumes of the Henry VIII Inventory Project.

109 Grummitt, 'Chamber finance', 239.

110 Coins are heavy and if large quantities were moved it would be easier and safer to transport the money by boat. Between November 1515 and April 1521 the following deliveries were made: two in the last two months of 1515 (PRO E36/215, pp. 410, 415); five in 1516 (ibid, pp. 431, 434, 452, 482, 484); four in 1517 (ibid, pp. 503, 520, 529, 547); seven in 1518 (ibid, pp. 562, 569 and PRO E36/216, pp. 13, 28, 33, 38, 43); nine in 1519 (ibid, pp. 61, 65, 66, 70, 79, 129, 131, 142); two in 1520 (ibid, pp. 223, 227) and five in the first four months of 1521 (ibid, pp. 241, 244, 250, 252, 261).

111 PRO E315/249, fos 46v, 47r, 49r, 50v.

112 PRO E315/160, f. 264r.

113 Ibid, f. 271v.

114 PRO E101/427/2, m. 1.

There was a link between the office of Keeper of the palace and administration of the privy coffers at Whitehall: Denny followed his predecessor, Thomas Alvard, as Keeper of the king's coffers. Hoak has suggested that as Keeper of the palace Denny was responsible for the rooms where Henry kept this financial reserve: the secret jewel house, the withdrawing chamber and the group of studies listed in the 1547 Inventory.[115] However, it seems more likely that these rooms were controlled by the king than by Denny. And their contents were in the king's personal charge as well. Here Denny, for all his overall responsibility for the palace, had no authority. This is shown clearly by the frequent transfers of money and objects from the king's hands to Denny's and vice versa: when Denny delivered goods to the king, he was discharged or exonerated; when he received them, he was charged.[116]

The records in the 1542 Inventory reveal how the money was delivered to the coffers, the various sources the funds came from and the substantial quantities of coinage involved. Similar details appear in BL Lansdowne Roll 14. The deliveries were made by men like Sir Wymond Carew, Treasurer of First Fruits and Tenths, John Gates, who had responsibility for another private treasury known as the removing coffers (see below) and Sir Edmund Peckham, Treasurer of the Mint. In return for the money they received 'a byll subscribed with thand of the said Sir Anthony Denny' [**4129**]. A significant proportion of the money came from other cash reserves held by Henry VIII himself, being either delivered 'owte of his said gracis owne handis' [**4085**], from the removing coffers [**4116**] or from the secret jewel house at Whitehall [**4113**]. Further funds came from government departments like the Court of First Fruits and Tenths [**4143**], from sections of the household like the Chamber [**4090**] or from the Mint [**4110**]. Other sources were linked to individual exercises of the royal perogative, including the fine of £100 imposed on William Roper when he was held in the Tower [**4104**] and the sum of £266 13s 4d paid by William Thorpe for the office of Collector of Customs in the port of Southampton [**4108**]. The king's appropriation of such fruits of 'prerogative' finance is reminiscent of the financial revisions of Cromwell, or, prior to that, of the early days of the privy coffers under Henry VII.[117]

Gates's role as a supplier of money to Denny's account makes another distinction: between the privy coffers (which were largely fixed at Whitehall) and the king's removing coffers, which travelled with him on progress. The removing coffers also contained money. These coffers were managed by John Gates, Denny's colleague, factotum and brother-in-law. When Henry was resident at Whitehall the coffers were housed in the king's withdrawing chamber [for example **4123**]. For ease of use, they were lettered alphabetically and the 1547 Inventory itemizes the monies remaining in coffer L at the time of Henry's death. Subsequent marginal notes to the Inventory record how these funds were later dispersed during Edward VI's reign.[118] Under Henry VIII, money could be transferred from the removing coffers to reserve coffers, either by the king himself or via Gates: on 14 May 1544, Henry delivered £2,000 to Denny [**4106**] and in February 1546 Gates delivered him a further £1,000 [**4129**].

---

115   Hoak, 'Secret history', 211–2.
116   For examples of objects and money being charged to Denny, see the headings on PRO E315/160 fos 135r and 138v; also entry **4119** and the marginal note associated with it.
117   Starkey, 'Privy Chamber', 357–65, 391–3.
118   For example, 'a Silke purse redd and blacke being knitt conteyning Cli. 18 novembre 1549 deliuered to the said sir Edmunde pekham ijCxxxvij angelles at viijs iiijxxxiiijli xvjs Riolles x at xijs vjli In all Cli xvjs' (**2493**).

THE PRIVY PURSE   After the advent of the Privy Chamber, Henry VII's privy purse was administered by Hugh Denys, Groom of the Stool, rather than John Heron, Treasurer of the Chamber. This involved giving Denys responsibility for a range of small intimate purchases which had hitherto been handled by Heron. At first, Denys was reimbursed by Heron item by item, and then by consolidated bills. Only later did he receive lump-sum cash floats. As David Grummitt has demonstrated, there were other such particular treasuries, but the money for the privy purse was the most important of these separate reserves of money.[119] The money from this purse was used to cover a discrete range of expenses: alms, rewards, personal purchases, gambling debts and cash given to other members of the household.[120]

These categories of expenditure remained central to the privy purse for most of its history. But in the surviving accounts of Henry Norris, which run from November 1529 to December 1532, they were dwarfed by other, much larger items: building (£4,931), jewels (£11,268), military and minis-terial expenses (£4,461) and cash transfers to other spending departments (£16,815).[121] Norris's account, therefore, is a hybrid, combining the privy purse as it has been traditionally understood with features more usually associated with the privy coffers.

But the hybrid proved short-lived. The privy coffers were reconstituted, first under Alvard and then under Denny himself as Alvard's successor as Keeper of Whitehall Palace, while under Heneage (who succeeded Norris as Groom of the Stool) the privy purse shrank back to its former size and territory. And it was this limited privy purse that Denny himself administered for the short period in which he held the office of Groom of the Stool.

Heneage resigned, or more probably was dismissed, in October 1546.[122] On 1 October 1546 he handed over £251 7s 2½d to Denny as 'money due vnto his majestie vpon the determynacion of the saied Sir Thomas Henneage Accompte' [B16]. Over the next eleven months, until his own dismissal, Denny paid £1,237 7s 4d for wages and the exhibition of scholars; £166 13s 4d for annuities; £249 16s for rewards and New Year gifts; £83 7s 4d for alms; £175 for debts; £45 for riding and carriage charges; and £665 17s 6d for purchases, giving a total of £2,623 1s 6d.[123] The two aspects of Norris's account were united once more in the same pair of hands. But the developments of the intervening decade and a half had not been in vain. For, despite the fact that their keepers were the same, during Denny's joint tenure the privy purse and privy coffers remained quite distinct institution-ally. Thus his records relating to the king's coffers note that on 30 April 1547 Denny paid 'lxx li. ij^s. vj^d. charged amongst Receiptes of money within hys Offyce of the Gromeshipp of the Stowle' into the coffers, along with money delivered to him by Sir Edmund Peckham [4144].

The accounts of Denny's immediate successor as keeper of the privy purse, Stanhope, conform to the restricted traditional type. This was only to be expected. Edward was a minor with limited needs (at least in the eyes of Stanhope, if not of the king himself). And the Duke of Somerset had shown himself determined to normalize the activities of Henry VIII's private palace administration,

119   Grummitt, 'Chamber finance', 236, n. 32.
120   Starkey, 'Privy Chamber', 360.
121   For Norris's account see *PPE*, a transcription of BL Additional MS 20030. These figures have been recalculated from Starkey, 'Privy Chamber', 384–5.
122   *LP* XX.ii, 331.43, 561.
123   BL Lansdowne Roll 14 [B57–B65]; Denny's total expenditure given in BL Lansdowne Roll 14 (m. 12) is higher, at £3,053 4s.

of which Denny's inflated treasury was the most extreme example. There was an element of 'constitutionalism' in this. But Somerset, as Protector, also took over many of the personal governmental activities which an adult king would have performed. With Peter Osborne, clerk to the four Chief Gentlemen who managed the Privy Chamber under the Duke of Northumberland, the opposite tendency reasserted itself.[124] Faced with royal bankruptcy and political crisis, Northumberland channelled much emergency expenditure through Osborne's hands; but even then the formal distinction between the privy purse and the privy coffers was preserved.[125]

Denny's links with Westminster and London

HIS LINKS WITH WESTMINSTER   The township, later the city, of Westminster was the seat of English government. Denny served as its Member of Parliament twice;[126] as such he was intimately acquainted with the specialized parliamentary, legal and administrative functions that had developed at Westminster during the fourteenth and fifteenth centuries.[127] He himself was a beneficiary of an Act of Parliament[128] whereby the exchange of land between him and the king, which took place in 1546, was ratified. Other aspects of his career made him familiar with the city as a residential and commercial centre.[129] However, Westminster's parliamentary role was the most significant of its three functions, as demonstrated by the intense Reformation Parliaments in the 1530s and 1540s, or those instigated in previous centuries as a result of the financial demands of the Hundred Years War. While Parliament was in session, the king needed to be present in Westminster. It was no accident that Henry's 'Mantill for the Parliament of Crymsen vellat partely furred with powdred Armyns and a Cappe' [8] was kept at Whitehall Palace rather than within the Standing Wardrobe of the Robes at the Tower.

Much of the local government within the manor of Westminster had been the responsibility of the abbey until the Dissolution. After 1540 a secular government gradually developed. The post of High Steward was established in 1545 and the list of office-holders reveals that the appointee was usually a royal favourite, a leading minister or a member of the royal household.[130] Anthony Denny, who was the first holder of the office, qualified admirably on all counts. However, it was not a sinecure and Denny was closely involved in local affairs. He was helped by men like 'henrye Wettaker of Westmynster servante un To maister antonye dennye and renete getherer of the Kynges new Tenementes be Sydes Charyng Crosse'.[131] In 1546 his brother-in-law Sir Wymond Carew was appointed as one of the Commissioners to survey the chantries in Middlesex, London and Westminster.[132]

124   PRO E101/546/19. For a review of Osborne's accounts see Hoak, 'Secret history', 221–3.
125   Murphy, 'Illusion of decline', 124 n. 20, 135–9.
126   See above, pp. 77–9.
127   When Richard II quarrelled with London he removed sections of the legal and financial administration to York, temporarily threatening the development of Westminster as the administrative centre of English government: see Harvey, 'Richard II and York'.
128   HCRO MS 10585.
129   See below, pp. 73–4, 78–9.
130   J Merritt and D R Starkey (personal communications). Also see Knighton, *Acts of the Dean and Chapter*, I, no. 32 and p. 22 n. 69. As Knighton notes, this entry places Denny's appointment as High Steward in January 1545, earlier than given in *History of Parliament*, 1509–58, ii, 27–9.
131   Baker, 'Extracts from royal accounts', 102, 108.
132   Bindoff, *Commons*, I, 581.

Periodically the other local officials challenged Denny's authority, most notably in 1546. While Denny was absent from Westminster, Sir Roger Cholmley, Serjeant at Law and Recorder of London, Serjeant Brown and the Under-Sheriff of Middlesex all ignored Denny's letters concerning the muster within the city and liberties of Westminster.[133] James Rufforth, Denny's deputy as Keeper of the Palace, had to inform his master of their neglect.[134] In spite of difficulties like this Denny retained the stewardship until his death in 1549; the office was then vacant for twelve years until 1561.[135] During Elizabeth's reign the post was secured by Sir William Cecil and then by the Duke of Buckingham under James I. In short, and not surprisingly, the secular administration of Westminster came to be dominated by the leading palace officials, just as the palace physically dominated the city.[136]

HIS LINKS WITH WESTMINSTER ABBEY   Prior to the Dissolution, Denny occasionally worked with William Boston, Abbot of Westminster. In September and October 1537 Denny and Boston investigated rumours that the king had had a liaison with a local woman.[137] However, in 1540 the abbey was converted into a collegiate church and the abbot was replaced by a dean with twelve prebends. The dean and chapter were influential within the life of Westminster, but the dean was usually a royal appointee, further emphasizing the general shift of power from Church to Crown. The 1540s also saw the inception of the short-lived See of Westminster. The sole incumbent was Thomas Thirlby, who was consecrated on 19 December 1540 and resigned on 29 March 1550. The see was then suppressed and became part of the diocese of London, while Thirlby was made Bishop of Norwich.[138]

There were some remaining strands of ecclesiastical government in Westminster, in spite of increasing secularization, and Denny had ties with these. His brother-in-law Sir Wymond Carew presided over the Westminster Leet Court. According to the Chapter Act Book, in May 1547 Carew was allowed to levy fines 'to the use and commodite of the said Dean and chapter', keeping half the money for himself.[139] Carew's duties included the maintenance of the stocks, pillory and ducking stool. In return the dean and chapter paid for the dinners of the steward and other officers of the court when the court was in session.

Sir Anthony also had a number of personal links with the abbey. Most were financial: for example, there was the small annuity (53s 4d) paid to him out of the College of Westminster.[140] There was also the question of the lease of the rectory at Cheshunt, which the abbey had owned and Denny

---

133 *LP* XX.ii, Appendix, 34–5.

134 Ibid.

135 For a general discussion of the office of High Steward of Westminster see Merritt, *Social World*, especially ch. 3.

136 This point was recognized by Grace Fletcher and presented in an unpublished seminar paper: D R Starkey (personal communication).

137 *LP* XII.ii, 764 and Appendix 43. Two years before, in June 1535, Cromwell had noted in his rememberances the end of unspecified discussions between the abbot and Denny: *LP* VIII, 892.

138 Shirley, *Thomas Thirlby*. Thirlby was head of the Chapel Royal and his consecutive appointments at court and at Westminster echo the position of Denny. I would like to thank Alasdair Hawkyard for pointing this similarity out to me.

139 Merritt, 'Early Modern Westminster', 155, n. 9. I am very grateful to Julia Merritt for providing me with this quotation. Also see Knighton, *Acts of the Dean and Chapter*, I, *passim*.

140 Several receipts for this annuity, paid to Denny's servant Roger Leigh, survive as WAM 37118, 37119, 37157 and 37158.

wanted.[141] Between 1544 and 1548 Denny negotiated with the dean and chapter and eventually they agreed an exchange. In return for the rectory Denny provided property of comparable value: Otford chapel and the church of Shoreham in Kent.[142]

Denny also promoted his interest in education and learning within Westminster. In 1546 he supported an application for a royal warrant relating to the abbey. It required the dean and chapter of Westminster to pay an annual stipend of £40 to John Madewe, as Reader of the Divinity Lecture in Cambridge.[143] At a lower level, the king maintained the abbey's school after the Dissolution. In 1546 Denny wrote to the dean asking for a free place for John Dimbleby, kinsman of an officer in the privy kitchen.[144] He assured the dean that his generosity would be rewarded by 'thauthor of all goodness our Lord Ihesus christ, who allways well prosper your vertuous endevors'. Under Elizabeth the school's humanist credentials were strengthened. It was reconstituted as 'a publique school for Grammar Rhetorick Poetrie and for Latin and Greek Languages'. On a charitable note, Denny promoted the application of Thomas Baker for a vacant room within the abbey as an almsman.[145]

HIS LINKS WITH LONDON   Within Westminster, Denny was Keeper of the Palace and the king's appointee in local government. In contrast, his links with the City of London were primarily commercial and personal. His most prestigious post there was a crown appointment, however in March 1541 he was appointed as one of the Customers or Collectors of Tonnage and Poundage in the Port of London, with a licence to act by deputy.[146] As with many of his other offices, the list of previous incumbents included Compton and Heneage. A number of rewards granted to royal servants by the king were payable out of Denny's revenues. In March 1544 he was required to pay an annuity of £20 to John Elder, the king's servant.[147] When the grant was reissued in July of that year, Denny was also described as the collector of a subsidy of 3s a ton and 12d a pound in the Port of London.[148]

After the death of his brother-in-law Robert Dacre in 1544, Denny acquired the freehold of his house with an orchard and garden in the parish of Stepney at Bethnal Green, held from the Bishop of London.[149] Two years later, Denny promoted the suit of John Baker, described as 'Mr Denny's servant', as Surveyor of Customs in London.[150] The same year Denny was granted a lucrative trade concession, to export duty free 2,000 quarters of wheat, 600 tuns of beer, 600 dickers of leather and 600 dickers of calfskin over the next two years.[151] On the borders of the City, Denny was Keeper of St John's, Clerkenwell, the former house of the Knights of St John of Jerusalem.[152] He also had dealings with London merchants and craftsmen on Henry's behalf: according to the account in

141   *LP* XIX.i, 278.25. The late fifteenth-century rectory has a central hall, a parlour in the east wing and a service wing to the west: see Smith, *Hertfordshire Houses*, 46–7 and Smith, *English Houses*, 66.

142   Cheshunt rectory was valued at £40 a year: see *LP* XIX.i, 278.25; WAM 4708, 14298* and 14299. Also see Knighton, *Acts of the Dean and Chapter*, I, no. 82

143   *LP* XXI.i, 963.39.

144   WAM 43046. Denny hoped that by intervening personally he had 'prevented thoccasion of molesting the kinge majestie herin'.

145   *LP* XXI.i, 963.54.

146   *LP* XVI, 678.27 (*LP* I.i, 94.27, *LP* III.i, 405.2); see also *LP* XIX.i, 278.71.

147   *LP* XIX.i, 278.71.   148   *LP* XIX.i, 1035.10.

149   HCRO MS 10585, p. 12.   150   *LP* XXI.i, 1165.49.

151   *LP* XXI.ii, 648.60. A dicker was equivalent to ten dozen (120) items.

152   Denny was named as the Keeper of St John's in the Augmentation accounts, PRO E321/44/45, and in the 1547 Inventory (BL Harley MS 1419, f. 368r).

BL Lansdowne Roll 14 Denny paid £2,356 2s 2½d 'to merchaunttes of London for Silkes' [B53]. Other men with whom he came into close contact included 'William Holte of London marchaunte Taylor', 'Sir Richarde Gresham knight of London mercer' and 'William Lock of London mercer'.[153]

The importance of Denny's servant/client network

Sir John Cheke described Denny as 'able to mould Henry's mind, now mixing the useful with the sweet, now weaving the serious things with the light one, great with small'.[154] Wolsey was also credited with similar skills, but in his case trenchant observers like Polydore Vergil often interpreted their effect as manipulative.[155] With a remarkable capacity for handling those with whom he dealt, Denny developed a network of friends and connections: members of his extended family, fellow officers of the royal household, retainers within the counties where he had a landed interest and the mercantile community. Denny also took on individuals from other men's households: evidence of this can be seen in a letter from the Duke of Norfolk to the Privy Council in December 1546, in which the Duke referred to a letter 'found by a servant of [Bishop Foxe] who is now with … Denny'.[156]

THE FAMILY NETWORK   Denny came from a large family (see family tree, page 54) and as his sisters married he acquired a network of close links with other families of similar rank and similar aspirations: Joyce first married William Walsingham and then Sir John Cary, cousin of Henry VII; Mary married John Gates; and Denny's youngest sister, Martha, married Wymond Carew, Treasurer of the Court of First Fruits and Tenths (1545–9). In addition, Denny's sister-in-law Elizabeth took Robert Dacre as her second husband, after the death of Thomas Denny in 1528. Dacre was Master of the Court of Requests, which brought him into close official contact with members of the Privy Council.

As Denny's star went into the ascendant, these family connections revolved around him, like planets round a sun. And the planets had their satellites too – like Gates's parents-in-law, the Jocelines, who became part of Denny's extended family system. The key manager of the Denny connection, in which ties of family and office were so closely interwoven, was John Gates, who was both Denny's brother-in-law and his acting deputy within the Privy Chamber. Many of Gates's papers have survived, thanks to his conviction for treason under Mary. They document fully the workings of 'the family firm'. On 20 August 1540 Wymond Carew, connected by marriage to both Denny and Gates, wrote to the latter asking for the former's support to gain his release from Anne of Cleves's household.[157] In 1542 Carew wrote to Gates again, this time commenting that 'I moved my brother Denny to get from the king, for my servant William Alexander, the books of Doctor Mallett, who is now in the Tower at the king's pleasure'.[158] Three years later, in

153   PRO E315/160, fos 121r, 124v, 129r.
154   Quoted by Sil, 'Denny', 197.
155   According to Vergil, 'every time he wished to obtain something from Henry, he introduced the matter casually into his conversation; then he brought out some small present or another, a beautifully fashioned dish, for example, or a jewel or ring or gifts of that sort, and while the King was admiring the gift intently, Wolsey would adroitly bring forward the project on which his mind was fixed': quoted in Starkey, *Personalities and Politics*, 60
156   *LP* XXI.ii, 554.   157   *LP* XV, 991.   158   *LP* Add. I.ii, 1571.

1545, Carew was hopeful of the keepership at Havering or the stewardship of the Marquess of Exeter's lands in Devon.[159]

The use of gifts to broker an introduction and foster goodwill was a common part of such negotiations. Some of Denny's more distant relations used small gifts to improve the likelihood of his promoting their suit: in 1543 Dorothy Joceline, who was a famous needlewoman, wrote to her brother John Gates asking him to 'Make my excuse to Mr Denye that I have sent his shirts no sooner, and that he look for none of the other as yet; for the Queen's work troubles me so much and yet I fear I shall scant content her Grace'.[160] Where Denny was given shirts, Gates received smaller tokens: in June 1542 Thomas Joceline wrote to Gates:

> My wife sends you a simple bracelet, being sorry that she cannot send one of gold as easily as one of silk. We trust if the king had taken his progress this way to have had both you and Mr Denny make merry here with us.[161]

This approach was not restricted to family members. Lady Lisle reasoned that she might gain access to Denny via his wife and despatched her agent, John Husey, who met with difficulty: 'I have been twice at Mistress Denny's house to deliver your token, but could not speak with her'.[162]

Other relatives appear to have attracted Denny's interest and patronage more readily. In 1543 Denny periodically received information about the nascent career of his nephew John, who was studying in Venice. According to Edmund Harvel, John 'ceaseth not in diligence to exercise himself daily in luting, vanting and also th'Italian tongue as far as his tender nature can extend'.[163] Although John was described as 'being weak and delicate of nature',[164] in September 1543 he had moved to Cologne and had delivered letters to Bonner for the king.[165] This period of work and travel in Europe was reminiscent of Denny's own youth.

A good marriage was a key step in social advancement and could bring substantial landed and financial interests; like many others, Denny sought to exercise his influence over the marriage market for his own family and others. In May 1544 he received an annuity of £20 out of the Essex lands of his late brother-in-law, Robert Dacre, and the wardship with marriage of Dacre's son and heir George.[166] More significant was the grant to Denny of the wardship of Margaret Audley, daughter and coheiress of Thomas, Lord Audley of Walden.[167] As his will shows, Margaret, one of the greatest heiresses of the day, was intended as bride for his eldest son (see below, p. 80). Lesser figures were not forgotten. In September 1546 he supported a letter to Lady Carew 'in the favour of Mr Champernon for marriage';[168] Denny had ties by marriage to both families and sought to extend them further. However, some individuals did not wish to be linked to the Denny family, as is made evident by the efforts of Sir Thomas Cheyney to break off the proposed marriage between

---

159 Ibid, 1701. 160 Ibid, 1513. 161 Ibid, 1546.

162 *LP* XIV.i, 1120, 1145.

163 *LP* XVIII.i, 725; it is not known whose son John was.

164 Ibid, 576. 165 *LP* XVIII.ii, 126.

166 *LP* XIX.i, 610.5.

167 *LP* XX.i, 465.88. In March 1545 Denny was granted an annuity of £50 a year out of the Hertfordshire manors of Braughing, Corneybury, West Mill and Little Hornmead, which belonged to the Lord Chancellor, Lord Audley.

168 *LP* XXI.ii, 199.28.

his son and a niece of Denny's, which had been brokered by Denny.[169] Cheyney's friends advised caution, stating 'Consider the man to be near about the king and so unmeet to be trifled or mocked with in any cause'.[170]

TIES WITHIN DENNY'S HOUSEHOLD AND THE ROYAL HOUSEHOLD   Livery was a clear indication of a man's membership of a particular household. Denny wore the king's livery and in turn, in 1542, Denny was granted the right to issue livery to members of his own household.[171] In the accounting period 1544–5 a payment of 10s was made 'to Edward Denny bailiff of Howe for the clothe to make hym a cote bicawse he had not his lyuerye sent hym'.[172] While Denny's livery colours are not stated in the accounts, the servant who delivered a gift of money from Joan Denny to Anne Askew was said, at the latter's trial for heresy, to have been dressed in a violet coat.[173] As the man was identified by the colour of his coat, it suggests that this was his livery. If so it was an interesting choice, for violet is close in colour to purple and purple was restricted to the king and his immediate family by sumptuary legislation.[174]

Denny's position within the Privy Chamber and his post as Keeper Whitehall Palace would have brought him into contact with many other people in the king's service. An undated letter to John Gates from Thomas Addington, a Sumpterman with the Privy Kitchen, asked for the support of both Gates and Denny with Sir Anthony Browne, 'for the room of yeoman garneter' with the king's stable.[175] More specifically, many of Denny's links were with the Wardrobe of the Robes. In spite of his relatively short time in office as Yeoman, Denny maintained his links with the officers of the Wardrobe of the Robes after he became a Chief Gentleman of the Privy Chamber. On one level this was because he worked with the current officers on a daily basis within the Privy Chamber; at another it reflects his astute approach to developing networks of clients.

His interaction with these officers and their families took various forms. Denny seems to have secured the appointment of John Parker's wife, Susanna Horenbout, as a chamberer to meet Anne of Cleves.[176] Since Susanna spoke Low German, if not High German, the appointment was a suitable one, but she did not have the necessary financial resources to equip herself properly. Denny therefore wrote to Cromwell, transmitting the king's order 'to set her forth' appropriately.[177] The link continued, and in 1542 Denny acted as overseer of Parker's will along with the executors Ralph Worsley and Richard Turner.[178]

Links could take a simpler form. In March 1540, for example, Richard Browne, a Page of the Chamber, obtained a lease of the manor of Saham Toney and other property in Norfolk, Denny approached the king for remission of the entry fine and William Sherington, a Page of the Robes,

169   LP Add. I.ii, 1794; the letter does not identify Denny's niece by name. The documents relating to the marriage were drawn and engrossed, before Cheyney 'renounced all' (ibid).
170   PRO SP1/245, f.160r (LP Add. I.ii, 1794).
171   LP XVII, 714.21.   172   BL Additional Roll 63264A, unfoliated.
173   LP XXI.i, 1181.
174   For more information on the Henrician sumptuary legislation see Hayward, 'Luxury or magnificence?', 37–46.
175   LP Add.ii, 1799.
176   LP XIV.ii, 297.   177   Ibid.
178   LP XVII.i, 449; also see Foister and Campbell, 'Gerard, Lucas and Susan Horenbout', 725.

conveyed the royal agreement to this to the Exchequer on his instructions.[179] Six years later, in July 1546, Denny, along with Edmund Harman (the king's barber) supported the elevation of David Vincent from the Wardrobe of the Beds to the rank of Groom of the Privy Chamber.[180] The following year the 1547 Inventory records Vincent as Keeper of the Standing Wardrobe of the Beds at Hampton Court.[181]

LOCAL CONNECTIONS IN HERTFORDSHIRE AND EAST ANGLIA While many aspects of Denny's working life were focused around Westminster and London, he also actively acquired lands outside the capital. In 1536 he was granted the site of the nunnery of St Mary's, Cheshunt,[182] which included the rights over the fair held at the chapel of St Giles near Enfield Chase, in Hertfordshire.[183] At the time the 1542 Inventory was compiled, Denny was granted the site of the chantry linked to St Mary's, Mettingham and the group of lands owned by the chantry in East Anglia: Mettingham, Shipmeadow, Ilketshall, Wenhaston and Mellis in Suffolk; and Lyng, Raveningham and Syderstone in Norfolk.[184] These estates were administered for Denny by Hugh Brown, whose accounts reveal a network of lesser stewards and housekeepers.[185] Denny was heavily dependent upon his steward, who in turn consulted 'his masters learned council' in London over a number of legal matters.[186]

The lands had a dual purpose. On a private level they formed part of Denny's network of domestic estates, a resource he could exploit for personal ends. His East Anglian accounts include a number of references to the catching and care of swans, both for his own table and as gifts.[187] This echoes the regular references in the Lisle Letters to the provision of quail for their own enjoyment and for use as gifts.[188] In 1544–5 Denny's steward recorded 'sondry charges concerning the wildfowl sent by John Denny at Mettingham against the marriage of my lord privy seals son' including 'Mr Gawdy his falconers for their pains coming with his hawk to Mettingham to kill pheasants – 20d, for going to Norwich to search for wildfowl – 10d'.[189] Following on these lines the king paid a reward of 2s to 'Mistress Denny's servant for bringing sturgeons'. The maintenance of the fishing and wildfowl was an important consideration and prompted the payment of 20d 'to an otter hunt to serche for the otter in the moted poundes'.[190]

On a public level, as a significant landowner in Hertfordshire and East Anglia, Denny inevitably had an impact on local society and people of all ranks looked to him for patronage. In March 1540

179 *LP* XV, 436.40.   180 *LP* XXI.i, 1382.66.
181 BL Harley MS 1419, f. 206r.
182 *LP* XI, 519.12.
183 Hertfordshire was popular with a number of other royal servants. Cardinal Wolsey owned The More, near Rickmansworth, and Nicholas Bristow also had land in Hertfordshire, as did Sir Ralph Sadler. After the Dissolution a high proportion of Hertfordshire monastic land passed to men with access to royal patronage, including Richard Yngworth, Thomas Birch, John Tregonwell, James Needham, Robert Chester and Humphrey Bourchier: see Doggett, 'Monastic buildings in Hertfordshire'.
184 *LP* XVII, 283.43. The grant indicates that all these lands had been surrendered to the Crown by Thomas Manning, suffragan of Ipswich, previously Master of the Brethren at St Mary's Mettingham. Manning's earlier links with Mettingham explain why Sir Edward North approached Denny to promote him in 1543.
185 BL Additional Roll 63260.   186 Ibid.
187 BL Additional Roll 63260, unfoliated.
188 *Lisle Letters*, II, nos 219, 237, 240a–241.   189 BL Additional Roll 63260.
190 BL Additional Roll 63264A.

the people of the town and parish of Waltham petitioned Denny, asking that the king should grant them the clock and five of the abbey bells for their parish church.[191] Between January and May 1543 Sir Edward North looked to Denny to secure the deanery of Peterborough for Thomas Manning, suffragan of Ipswich, in addition to securing him the grant of Little St Bartholomew's Hospital on the outskirts of London and gaining his release from a debt of £1,000 owed to the king.[192] Denny must have used his influence within Hertfordshire well: on 24 March 1547 John Dudley, Earl of Warwick wrote to Sir William Paget stating that he was

> friendly to Denny, according to his desire for the site and remains of Waltham with certain other farms adjoining Cheshunt. I suppose it will be good for the neighbour-hood to let him have Waltham.[193]

COMMERCIAL CONTACTS   Denny's circle extended far beyond English landed society and indeed beyond England itself. During his Keeping of Whitehall Palace Denny received a number of purchases made by Henry and commissions ordered by him. This would have brought Denny into contact with a broad range of the craftsmen and merchants that supplied the royal house-hold.[194] And most of these, in particular the suppliers of the luxury goods that were Denny's special province, were foreign. Some were linked to Denny on the basis of their commercial transactions, others by a financial retainer. On 29 August 1544 a consignment of hagbuts (hagbushes) intended for Denny was delivered to the English camp by the partner of Dominico Erizo, a Venetian merchant.[195] In September 1545 Erizo was described as Denny's factor when he purchased 2,000 fodders of lead for the king.[196] In November of the same year Denny preferred a duplicate warrant for £1,200 for Erizo and Anthony Carsidony to replace one lost by the negligence of Mr Godsalve's clerk.[197] Erizo, often in partnership with Carsidony, carried out regular business with Denny and his royal master, mainly in silk fabrics. Between 1542 and 1548 they received £16,320 15s 2½d from Denny for 'Jewelles plate Riche clothe of Gold Silver tissue and sondrie sortes of veluettes and silkes' [B53].

A number of the individuals with whom Denny did business were named in BL Lansdowne Roll 14, along with a few of the more significant purchases. Fortunately some of these pieces can be identified within the 1542 and 1547 inventories, which provide more details. In June 1542 Henry paid 'to John Baptiste Galterotte for twoo peces of Riche Arras thone of the Actes of Thappostelles and thother of Antiques M¹ M¹ CCC xxv li xvs vjd ob' [B53]. A marginal note in the 1542 Inventory identifies the following pieces as Henry's purchases: 'Seven peces of hanginges of Arras of thactes

---

191 *LP* XV, 394. The church only had one bell and the parishioners said that they could not afford to buy any more.
192 *LP* XVIII.ii, Appendices 1–3, 10, 11.
193 *CSPD Edward VI*, 28.
194 Indeed, it is interesting that W C Richardson described Denny as a typical example of Henry VIII's financial agents, on a par with John and Richard Gresham, two leading London merchants who often worked for the king: see *Tudor Chamber Administration*, 414 n. 88. In a similar vein John Guy has compared Denny's role with that of Nicholas Bryham, a Teller of the Exchange, who managed the personal finances of Mary Tudor, with £290,000 passing through his hands in 1557–8: see Guy, *Tudor England*, 243.
195 *LP* XIX.ii, 156.
196 *LP* XX.ii, 296.
197 Ibid, 909.20.

of Thappostelles' [**3334**] and 'Fyve peces of Arras wrought with Antiques' [**3335**].[198] Also, at an unspecified date, Denny paid an Englishman – relatively rare in this context – 'Lawrence Warren of London Goldsmythe for a carpett D li' that was transferred to the Tower Wardrobe after Henry's death [**B53**]. Entry **9189** of the 1547 Inventory provides a full description of the carpet:

> a verey fayer Carpett of Crymsen Satten allover enbrawdered with venyce golde garnished with perles in trayles the bordre likewise enbrawdered with venyce golde and perle with six roses and the kinges wordes in the same frengid with venyce golde rounde abowte all thinges being furnished lyned with grene Silke The grounde being white late bought by the kinges Maiesty of Lawrence warren marchaunte.[199]

In all, Denny paid for goods valued at £31,366 5¼*d*. Not surprisingly, the accounting process involved Bristow. The money was recorded 'by seuerall billes … vpon this Accompte examyned & with thesame Nicholas remaynyng' [**B53**].

Denny's links with these men are brought out by a document like the New Year's gift roll for 1539, which treats them as social equals.[200] Denny, along with many other members of the Privy Chamber, was listed in the last category of gentlemen. This category also included many great merchants and craftsmen, so the entries around Denny's gift include the following:

> By Antony Cassidony a broche of golde.
>
> By Cristofer Millyner a russet hatte thromed with silke & gold.
>
> By John Norres gentilman vssher xij fyne handkerchewes.
>
> By Cornelis Heys a paire of gloves garnisshed with golde and twoo small fresshe Sturgions vnsalted.
>
> By Dymocke marchaunt of … white purse of venice making.
>
> By Hanse Holbyne a table of the pictoure of the prince [his] grace.[201]

Unfortunately there are no rolls surviving from after Denny's knighthood that would have recorded his elevation into the category of knights. However, despite his rise in the social order Denny would have retained his close association with the upper echelons of London's commercial community.

Denny's career: a modest success

How do we assess the success of Denny's career? In his biography of Denny's contemporary, Sir Ralph Sadler, A J Slavin offers some useful criteria.[202] Sadler was a royal confidant, rose through the Privy Chamber to the Privy Council and a knighthood.[203] He accumulated a substantial landed estate and acquired a fine country house.[204] He survived the loss of his great patron Cromwell and rode out all political storms to die in his bed. And yet the summits eluded him. He was not ennobled,

---

198 The note reads 'Which xij peces of hanginges of Arras were bought of John Baptist Gaulterote merchaunte of Florence mensis Junii Anno xxxiiijto domini Regis Henrici octaui'. The Acts of the Apostles contained 'CCCClxxix elles iij quarters & iij nailes' and the Antiques 'CCCxxxiiij elles di quarter and quarter of the naile'.

199 The dimensions are given as 'three yardes di and in bredthe twoo yardes quarter and one nayle'.

200 Folger Shakespeare Library MS Z.d.11.

201 Ibid.

202 Slavin, *Politics and Profit*.   203 Ibid, 212.

204 Sadler owned Standon in Hertfordshire.

nor did he become leader of a faction at court. At first sight the parallels with Denny are striking. He too held office in both the Privy Chamber and the Privy Council; he acquired an extensive land-holding; he survived and even thrived on the downfall of his mentors Bryan and Cromwell. But like Sadler, he never quite made it to the top politically or socially as a peer or knight of the Garter.[205]

But in fact it is the differences from Sadler that count. Denny's character made a deep impression on contemporaries. Few other Tudor statesmen, if any, were the subject of so many and apparently so deeply felt encomia while they were alive or so many epitaphs after their death.[206] That of course reflects contemporary judgement, and contemporary judgement can prove fleeting. However, in protecting reform in the last, dangerous years of Henry VIII and, most of all, in the crisis that followed his death, Denny played a historic role of the first rank. Finally, Sadler lived a long life, dying in 1587 at the age of eighty. Denny, in contrast, died at the age of forty-eight. He was cut off in his prime, with his greater and still reasonable ambitions unfulfilled.

To glimpse these ambitions we have to turn, as we have done for most insights into the private man, to his will.[207] His will is focused correctly on providing for his children, both legitimate and illegitimate: their upbringing, education, religion and, above all, with their marriages. For these, with luck, would ensure the family's fortunes. Denny openly admitted that he had acquired his numerous wards, male and female, 'to be coupled in matrimony with mine'.[208] Their status is revealing. Margaret Audley, Lord Audley's eldest daughter and one of the greatest heiresses in the kingdom, he intended for his eldest son. His eldest daughter Anne was to marry the heir of Lord Rich, who lived up to his name; the husband of his second daughter, Mary, was to be young Shelton of Norfolk, and that of his third daughter Douglas, Sir George Somerset's son and heir, 'whom I have certain years nourished with mine in my house for that intent'.[209]

But with his own death these ambitious schemes collapsed and Margaret Audley was instead united with two ducal families: she first married the Duke of Northumberland's son, Lord Henry Dudley, and then, after Dudley's death in 1557, the fourth Duke of Norfolk. On the other hand, Denny's estates in Hertfordshire and Essex, which amounted to 20,000 acres and yielded at least £700 a year, at a very conservative estimate, were sufficient in time to obtain a peerage for his family.[210] His eventual heir, his eldest son Henry, married the daughter of Lord Grey of Wilton and their son in turn was created Earl of Norwich by Charles I. Denny's life, it would seem, had laid the foundation for his family's greatness, which only his premature death had postponed.

205 The English nobility was small and all the Tudor monarchs were quite restrained in the number of new peers they created: there were forty-two in 1509, fifty-one in 1547, fifty-six in 1553, sixty-three in 1559 and fifty-five in 1603: see Guy, *Tudor England*, 46.

206 During Denny's lifetime one Nicholas Wentworth described him as 'a sure friend of truth' (*LP* XIX.i, 19): for other examples see Denny, 'Biography', 199, 211–13.

207 PRO PROB11/32 (37 Populwell).

208 Ibid.

209 Ibid.

210 See Sil, 'Denny', 201 n.71. Denny's annual revenue from his East Anglian lands ranged from £156 to £319. The accounts for these estates survive from 1542 to 1551 and the annual income after deductions was as follows: 1542–3, £319 3s 3½d (BL Additional Rolls 63255, 63256); 1543–4, £202 12s 7¾d (63259, 63260); 1544–5, £189 3s 9¼d (63263, 63264A); 1545–6, £186 13s 11½d (63266, 63267); 1546–7, £156 5s 6¼d (63268); 1547–8, £264 7½s (63271); 1548–9, £269 11s 10½d (63272); 1549–50, £210 7½s (63273); 1550–1, £242 4s 11¼d (63275). In addition, Denny received wages, annuities and fees; his annual income from offices by 1547 was approximately £200: Sil, 'Denny', 194. While the figures for rents and wages are lower than those for Compton and Heneage, they still compare quite well. Compton's gross landed income for 1523–4 was £1,689 3s 3d: see Bernard, 'Sir William Compton', 772. Heneage's landed estate was valued at his death at £1,288: see Sil, 'A forgotten Tudor servant', 172.

IV

THE ROLE OF PALACE KEEPER

S IR ANTHONY DENNY was only the second incumbent in the office of keeper of Henry VIII's Palace of Whitehall. Even so, the office of palace keeper was not a new one and the principal tasks that Denny carried out were well defined. This section will explore the nature of these tasks, the group of people the keeper worked with and the documentation he needed and created while carrying out his duties. While the primary focus of this section is the office, rather than the individual who held it, it is apparent that Henry modified the position to take the most advantage of Denny's talents. It reverted to the more usual format after the accession of Edward VI. In its extended form, the job was far too large for one man and Denny worked with a group of assistants, clerks and accountants.

However, Denny should not be seen in isolation. He was part of a larger group of keepers who cared for the king's possessions and properties (for their scope and number see Appendix III).[1] The keepers were a disparate group with varying degrees of responsibility and lacking a hierarchy as each keeper was ultimately answerable to the king. An appointment as keeper was prestigious. Such offices were usually bestowed as a sign of direct royal approval to men already serving the king within the privy chamber.[2] However, Denny was also far more than just one more member of this rather eclectic group. The range of objects under his care and the kudos associated with Whitehall would have ensured that Denny was at the top of the heap.

The system of Keepers within the old and new palaces at Westminster

As the leading residence of the English monarchy up to 1512, the old Palace of Westminster had a long-established system of multiple Keepers, and at least three separate offices are known. The earliest reference to a Keeper of the 'king's houses at Westminster' dates from 1156, although indirect evidence suggests that the office was operational in 1130.[3] In 1536, according to the 'Act declaring the limits of the King's palace of Westminster' the 'keper of our old Palays of Westmyster' was William Babbington.[4] The Act noted the king's desire not to prejudice Babbington's position by the creation of the new palace and, by implication, the appointment of a new Keeper.[5] The second office was

---

1   This group of keepers was well established by the fifteenth century and fairly stable in terms of areas of responsibility and number, see Hayward, 'Possessions', 132, also appendix 3 'Keepers appointed 1377–1509', 249–61. The one major development was the establishment of the ordnance office, see Gillingham, *The Wars of the Roses*, 26.

2   In contrast the men who received appointments to offices dealing with royal ordnance and ships had relevant experience learned as merchants, ship owners or sailors, see Davies, 'Royal navy', 282–3 and Scammell, 'War at sea', 190–3.

3   Clay, 'Keepership', 1. The Keeper was also responsible for the Fleet prison.

4   SR 28 Hen VIII c.12.

5   Clay, 'Keepership', 17. The office continued until 1884, when the post was taken over by the office of the First Commissioner of the Works.

known as the Keeper of the Privy Palace. As we have seen,[6] most of the privy palace was burned down in 1512 and the surviving rooms, abandoned by the king, were taken over as the (almost invariable) meeting place of Parliament or to house the Court of Requests and the Court of Wards and Liveries. The Keepership of the Privy Palace evolved into the Keepership of the Parliament House. Finally, there was a third office, which appeared towards the end of the fifteenth century; confusingly, this was also known as the Keepership of the Palace.[7] The specific link to the keepership of the houses of Paradise and Hell within Westminster Hall and Purgatory in the immediate vicinity of the hall helped to differentiate it.[8]

Such was the position in about 1530. It was transformed by the king's rebuilding and renaming of York Place. Henry's new buildings required a Keeper. The first, obvious choice for the post was Thomas Alvard. He had run York Place for Wolsey and he supervised its reconstruction for the king.[9] His offices multiplied, piecemeal, like the buildings at Westminster. In February 1530 he was appointed Keeper of York Place; in the following October, Keeper of the King's Garden and Orchard there; and finally, in April 1533, Keeper of the New (that is, St James's) Park, with the custody of the tennis plays and bowling alleys.[10] Alvard had overseen the building of the latter to the west of King Street.[11]

Alvard died in February 1535. No replacement was officially appointed for almost a year. Then on 30 January 1536 three letters patent were issued to Denny. The first gave him the keepership of St James's Park together with the extended sporting facilities,[12] and the second the keepership of both the house of York Place and the gardens and orchards there.[13] Denny now had the entire Alvard succession. But the final letter patent went further and gave him reversion to what has been identified as the third keepership at the old palace, responsible, amongst other things, for the houses of Paradise, Hell and Purgatory.[14]

The purpose of this third grant is made clear by the Act passed in the last session of the Reformation Parliament,[15] which opened on 4 February 1536, a few days after the grant of Denny's patent. Denny himself entered the House of Commons for the first time. His task was presumably to ensure the enactment. The preamble to the Act noted that, because of the 'utter ruin and decay' of Westminster Palace, the king had been moved to acquire the site of York Place and expand and rebuild it into a dwelling befitting 'so noble a prince'. Nevertheless, the old buildings, however ruinous, retained the title of palace, whereas the new, however magnificent, were only a private residence. The body of the Act corrected the anomaly. The name of Westminster Palace was extended to include the whole complex 'for ever'. The boundaries of the palace were similarly

---

6 See above, pp. 40–1.   7 Clay, 'Keepership', 18.

8 Ibid.

9 *HKW*, IV, 306. Alvard was appointed as a Gentleman Usher of the Chamber in November 1529.

10 *LP* VI, 576.25, 24. Caring for household furnishings, if only on a limited scale, was not a new area for Alvard. References in Wolsey's wardrobe book record that he was looking after for some of Wolsey's napery in July 1516, and on 14 April 1529 he took receipt of a table carpet from the gallery at York Place.

11 See above, pp. 46–7.

12 *LP* X, 226.33.

13 Ibid, 226.34.

14 Ibid, 226.35. Later Henry VIII took the houses back, intending them (along with five other properties) to act as a store for exchequer records. As compensation, Denny was granted an annuity of £12 13s 8d on 16 May 1547: *CPR* 1547–8, 248.

15 SR 28 Hen VIII c.12.

extended, from the river to the east to the wall of St James's Park to the west, and from Charing Cross to the north to the limits of the old palace to the south. Finally, the privileges and liberties of the old palace were extended to the whole area. But there was a clear hierarchy: the new palace had priority and the old palace was declared to be 'only … a member and parcel of the said new palace'. Denny's supremacy at Westminster was beyond doubt. He was the only man to hold senior office in both the new and the old palace.[16]

Aspects of the role of Keeper

When Denny was appointed Keeper of Whitehall, he received wages and lodgings in return for carrying out a core group of tasks. These included caring for the fabric of the building (in conjunction with the King's Works), holding the keys, providing a skeleton staff when the house was empty, caring for the contents and managing the gardens, orchards, hunting parks, rabbit warrens, dovecotes and fishponds. Not surprisingly Denny's role went beyond this, reflecting the unusual position of the palace within the network of Henry's properties and of Denny within the royal household. His involvement with the physical structure of the palace is examined above.[17] Other aspects of his role, such as the day-to-day running of the recreational facilities, were delegated to others, as is discussed below.[18] In the following pages several specific elements of Denny's work are explored.

HOLDING THE KEYS   Locks and keys formed a highly significant part of Denny's daily responsibilities. Within the palace, locked doors provided security and privacy.[19] The need for security in some rooms was obvious. In February 1531 a smith from Westminster received 16d for mending locks for the old jewel house at the old Palace of Westminster.[20] At Whitehall, as elsewhere, the king, the Keeper and the Groom of the Stool held master keys, while by-keys, which opened a single lock, were distributed to the relevant household officers. The two references to keys within the 1542 Inventory are both examples of by-keys: one heading refers to the 'Storyes and discription stayned delyuered owt of the kinges house vnder his privey key' and the other reference is to the bath-house key [158].[21]

One reason for only two keys being recorded is that locks could be moved from one property to the next and fitted prior to the king's arrival.[22] In such cases, Henry appears to have retained the keys in his removing coffers. A group of 'xviij keys of the kinges houses' (2384) were kept in coffer F, while in coffer M there was a 'Boxe with tenne small keyes' (2541). Other locks were kept at a particular house, as in the case of 'two Lockes withe two keyes echie locke hauing vppon it three rooses' (16915) that were found by James Rufforth at Whitehall 'in a Chamber next to

16   For an overview of the network of Keepers appointed by Henry VIII to look after his possessions see Appendix III below.

17   See pp. 48–9.

18   See pp. 91–9.

19   Locked doors could also indicate secrecy, as the confession of Margaret Morton to Sir Anthony Browne indicated: in November 1541 she recorded that while the court was at Pomfret [Pontefract] on progress 'Mr Dene [was] sent to the queen [Catherine Howard] from the king one night [and] found it [the door to her chamber] bolted' (*LP* XVI, 1338).

20   PRO E36/216, p. 245.

21   PRO E315/160, f. 135r. The bath-house key is listed with the plate: 'Item two vices with Ringes and a key for the bayne poiz xvij oz'.

22   Thurley, *Royal Palaces*, 83–4.

the Stilhouse'.[23] Decorative locks were not uncommon, as the Beddington lock demonstrates,[24] although door furniture could be purely functional, as in the case of 'a Spring of Iron to dryve to a dore' (**16909**).[25]

CARING FOR THE KING'S POSSESSIONS   Caring for the objects associated with a particular property was a key part of a Keeper's job, either directly or indirectly (for example, through an officer of the Wardrobe of the Beds). Denny's early years in the king's service provided him with a good grounding for his later career. In August 1535 he delivered lengths of cloth of gold and silver, crimson and purple satin and black velvet to the king's sister Margaret, Queen of Scots.[26] Just under a year later Denny took eighteen emeralds and twenty-nine gold letters (*I*s, for Jane), each set with nine pearls, to the king's embroiderer, William Ibgrave, to be stitched on to the sleeves and placard of a doublet.[27]

Denny cared for a vast range of objects, not just wardrobe stuff, a situation that was echoed in the work of the Keepers at Greenwich and Hampton Court in particular and to a lesser extent by the Keepers of other well-visited properties. He was involved with ordering and purchasing a number of new furnishings for the palace. These are listed in the 1542 Inventory. Thirty-four of the deliveries record details about the purchase, the supplier or maker and the date of receipt (for example, folio 121r). A further twelve refer to deliveries of 'stuff new made by the kinges commaundement', but the craftsmen involved are not named (for example, folios 121r–122v). On five occasions objects were transferred from the 'secret jewel house at Westminster' (for example, folio 123r) and on one they came from Hampton Court (folio 120v).

Denny also acquired other types of objects. Between 1542 and 1548 he made many payments, including entry **B53**:

> to Bastya Colcher for one cuppe of cristalle sett in gold Garnysshed with stones CC
> li…Peter Vandellewalle merchaunte of Andawareppe for Jewelles & plate M^l M^l li to
> Fraunces Alberte myllynor for plate dyamoundes and other stuff M^l Dxliiij li viijs vjd qrt.

The reverse side of this process was the maintenance of the items in his care; for example, on 22 October 1547 Denny paid a man for two days' work to repair curtains of bridges satin at 8*d* a day.[28] An account from Sebastian Le Senay, the king's clockmaker, demonstrates how the cycle of repairs within such a large and growing accumulation of possessions was continuous: over a period of months, and on Denny's command, a selection of clocks was delivered to Le Senay for maintenance and repairs.[29]

23   BL Harley MS 1419, f. 516r. According to the 1547 Inventory the locks (and a selection of other items) were 'delyuer[ed] by his executors vpon this Surveye': ibid.

24   This gilt-iron lock is ornamented with bands of geometric cabled designs, with the royal arms supported by a greyhound and a dragon on the keyhole cover. The knob of the catch for the keyhole cover is shaped like a man's face. The lock is so called because it was formerly at Beddington Place, Surrey.

25   Blair, 'Royal locks'. There was 'a locke of golde enameled with a diuise of lettres' (**2871**) in the third of the queen's removing coffers.

26   *LP* IX, 218.

27   *LP* X, 1132.

28   PRO E314/79, Denny no. 21.

29   *LP* Add.I.ii, 1869.

While the furnishings within the Wardrobe of the Beds and those in Denny's care were designated for use at Whitehall, items were loaned out periodically for use elsewhere. In November 1546 Richard Jack, a Yeoman of the Guard, hired a cart in Westminster to take the contents of the king's privy chamber to Oatlands, then back to Westminster, only to return to Oatlands again.[30] This process required careful monitoring to ensure that items did not go astray.

ISSUING PERQUISITES   As Keeper, Denny dispensed the perquisites granted by the king, as the following note from 1542 records: to see 'whether Lames shall buy curtains for the bed that the King gave Mr Heneage for that the old are too short'.[31] Perquisites – that is, items owned by the king which he gave away – were associated with the key stages in a monarch's reign, namely their coronation and funeral. Smaller gifts (new purchases by the king, for the specific purpose of giving them away) would be distributed at the New Year and possibly in association with other significant events, such as a wedding or the birth of a child. Perquisites were expected by two key groups of individuals. First, gifts were given to the monarch's chief body servants, including the Groom of the Stool and the barber, as a reward for loyal service and recompense for the loss of their office on the accession of the new monarch. Secondly, the honorary officers drawn from the nobility, who served at coronations and funerals, claimed rewards in lieu of feudal fees.

Three individuals were listed within the 1542 Inventory as having specifically received perquisites from Denny's charge: Denny himself, as the late king's Groom of the Stool; the Earl of Warwick, for acting as High Chamberlain of the Household at the coronation of Edward VI; and the Earl of Arundel. It is significant that Denny had to account for these three groups of perquisites in his discharge from office.[32] Denny represents the group of recipients receiving a reward or recompense. He received nine close stools, eighteen pewter bowls, ten cisterns and one travelling case [4021–4031]. While symbolic of his office, this gift would only have any financial value to Denny if he sold the items. The Grooms of the Privy Chamber claimed a blue velvet cloth of estate from the Wardrobe at Greenwich (9296); only after selling the cloth of estate could they share the proceeds.

The perquisites were not always furnishings. After Edward VI's death, the officers of the Wardrobe and the royal barber claimed a selection of small jewels as their due. The pieces included

> iiij small rubies set in collettes of golde … vj flowers of golde in euery flower iij perles
> lackinge ij perles garnisshed with small peces of cheynes of golde small beades of
> golde and small seede perles beinge the furniture of a cappe of black velvet.[33]

Such items could be retained as a keepsake or sold for cash.

The rewards given as feudal dues were more substantial and more likely to be kept by the recipient. The nobility would expect to have rich furnishings in their homes and the items would serve

30 Jack was paid 12s for 6 days' expenses plus 7s 6d for cart hire on three occasions: PRO E314/79, Denny no. 4.
31 LP Add.I.ii, 1573.
32 PRO E101/427/2, mm. 5–6 (entries A79–A100). The situation had changed significantly by the reign of Charles I, when the Groom of the Stool claimed the contents of the king's bedchamber on the monarch's death: Sharp, 'Image of virtue', 235. The perquisites claimed by leading members of the household followed a similar pattern; they are best demonstrated by the acquisitions made by Charles, sixth Earl of Dorset, Lord Chamberlain to William III: see Jackson-Stops, 'Purchases and perquisites'.
33 BL Additional MS 46348.i, f. 239r–v. It is unclear whether these items were given as fees by Mary I to her brother's officers or whether she reclaimed them from these men.

as recognition of their loyal service to the Crown. The Earl of Warwick received a bedstead with hangings and a counterpoint, a selection of bed linen, four wall hangings with ten window pieces, three carpets and a chair with matching cushion [**4032–4042**]. In contrast, the Earl of Arundel received only a clock [**4043**].

Formal perquisites of these types account for a tiny fraction of Denny's charge – just twenty-three entries or 0.6 per cent of the total.[34] While the items were significant for the recipients, grants of perquisites did not make large inroads into the holdings at Whitehall and such outgoings were accepted as a traditional aspect of royal service.

DECLARING ITEMS AS REFUSE STUFF   In February 1543 William Tildesley, Keeper of the Wardrobe of the Beds at Windsor, was given a selection of worn bed linen as refuse stuff: it was described as 'olde and broken and unservisable'.[35] Such gifts were part of a long-established practice whereby old or damaged items passed out of royal hands, and the custom was described in Edward IV's household ordinances, known as the Black Book.[36] A Keeper

> shall presume to take nothing by his owne auctoryte tyll the comptrollers haue senne theym so greatly defectyue that they may no longer be amendyd not serue for honeste and suertie of the kynges stuf; and all thinges so delyueryd to be amrkyd in the comptrollers memoranda.

This approach explains why a number of items were recorded as being in poor condition in royal inventories of this period.

The process of declaring items as refuse stuff can be demonstrated from the marginalia of the 1542 Inventory. These show how James Rufforth (Denny's deputy as Keeper) received quite a substantial number of objects described as 'refuse'.[37] The types of items Rufforth received echo those given to Tildesley but they also raise some interesting questions about how and why items were selected for disposal. A number of the pieces were clearly beyond use, including the napery that was collectively described as 'not seruiceable', the footstools 'nowe olde and brokin and vnstuffed' and the carpets 'sore worne and mothe eten'.[38] The four chairs specially made in Henry's later years to help him get around Whitehall Palace were discarded because they were no longer needed. However, other items, including the four trussing beds, the mirrors and counterpoints appear from their descriptions to be in fair condition. Either the descriptions were not updated to reflect the deterioration in their condition or they were disposed of for other reasons. Possibly they were surplus to requirements, and so were granted to Rufforth as an unofficial perquisite. That leads on to the question

---

34   For the sake of this calculation, the total number of entries in the Inventory has been taken as 3,773. This figure excludes all the entries where objects (including the perquisites) are duplicated, the entries summarizing the cloth deliveries made by Denny and the entries recording the money coming into his hands.

35   BL Additional MS 30367, fos 22v, 12v. He also received fifteen pieces of verdure, five celures and testers, four feather beds, four counterpoints and one tapestry tapet: ibid.

36   Myers, *Black Book*, 192–3.

37   Rufforth received seventy-one napkins, twenty-two towels, twenty-two counterpoints, twenty-one assorted sheets, eleven table cloths, four trussing beds with celure, tester, valances and curtains, four chairs, four mirrors, four chests, three wooden bowls, two trivets, two cushions, two remnants of cloth, two carpets, two cupboard cloths, two footstools, one traverse, one coif, one trunk and sundry curtains. His acquitance was listed in the 1547 Inventory (**11796–11871**).

38   BL Harley MS 1419, fos 197v, 195r, 194v.

of why Rufforth was the recipient of these items. The napery was part of his responsibilities and so logically should come to him when it was no longer fit to serve the king. After the revisions to Denny's charge during 1547, Rufforth was at least Denny's equal in terms of caring for the contents of the palace. These objects may have formed a reward for his good service.

PREVENTING PECULATION   Keepers were financially responsible for the goods in their care. When a Keeper, or their heirs and executors, could not provide a satisfactory explanation for an item's absence, they had to replace it. The inventory taken of the Jewel House in 1521 included 'a chalice with a patente gilte … the Cuppe had of Tebbys executours for the Chalis that was loste in Anno primo at the kingis Buriall'.[39] Consequently when items did go missing, the Keepers were quick to apportion the blame, which was duly recorded within the relevant records. Wolsey's Wardrobe inventory had a section headed 'stuff lost and altered', which included 'a large Venetian window carpet and blue velvet window cushion lost by the fault of Mr Wentworth and Ambrose Skelton, gentlemen ushers, during the parliament held at Blackfriars' and 'a black velvet high backed chair burnt in my lordes chamber at Westminster'.[40] Casual theft was also a problem, as the marginal note against a set of 'thre Cusshyons of purple vellat' (**12953**) at Nonsuch indicates. Two of the cushions 'were stolen awaie at the kinges being there … at a standing where the kinge was serued with them'.

Denny faced similar problems, and his discharge from office included a list of items that 'the saide … Accomptaunt dothe Allege to be loste in measure decayed Imbecylede and stollen wherfor he prayeth ~~he~~ to be exonerated and dischardged of ye same'.[41] With the exception of two lengths of kersey that Denny noted had been stolen, it is hard to determine the fate of the missing items. The small, relatively expensive items on the list, such as the gold and silver braid taken from bed hangings and gemstones removed from embroideries and furnishings, seem likely to have been 'Imbecylede and stollen'. Other pieces, including a knife haft, two decorative button tops and an antique head of copper from a mirror, might have been lost accidentally. The glassware may well have been broken, while the disappearance of seventy-seven books may reflect a failure of the recording system for objects rather than theft on a large scale.

MAINTAINING THE SYSTEMS   Within such a busy palace, it was inevitable that a small group of objects would slip through Denny's curatorial net. Indeed, a few pieces were described as being 'in no mans chardge' in the 1547 Inventory (for instance, entries **1117**, **1605**, **2004–2007**). Not surprisingly, the majority of these were at Whitehall. The normal pattern of allocating new acquisitions to a particular Keeper would have been disrupted by Henry VIII dying. The impact of his death would have been most obvious at Whitehall because Denny and many key members of his staff were drawn into the arrangements for Henry VIII's funeral and Edward VI's coronation. Even so, the situation was resolved quite quickly. On 26 July 1547 two unappointed chairs and two carpets found at Whitehall were delivered to Humphrey Orme, for the Wardrobe of the Beds at the Tower, and they appeared amongst his charge in the 1547 Inventory (**9187–9190**).[42]

39   Trollope, 'Henry VIII's jewel book', 182.
41   PRO E101/427/2, m.1.
40   *LP* IV.iii, 6184.
42   BL Additional MS 30367, f.30r.

Other pieces were held by a particular individual without having been formally charged to their care, for example 'a morter of woodde lyned with golde', 'a pestell of woodde thende of golde' and 'six portagues of golde' (**3319–3321**). These items were described as 'Certeyne Parcelles founde at Westminster in the handes of James Rufforth withowte chardge'.[43]

A problem of a different nature was revealed when the silk store at Whitehall was audited in 1547. In spite of Bristow's detailed rules for recording the fabric,[44] the system was flawed. Inaccurate measurement of the fabric lengths occurred throughout the store and this had to be corrected and noted against each colour and type of fabric. The note against entry [**3777**], for purple and blue cloth of gold, reads:

> so remaynyng to be aunsuerid Cxl ^{yerdes} quarter di. To the which is added iij quarters
> di increased in measure & then remaynyng Cxlj yerde quarter.

Similar comments and amendments appeared against every entry [**3774–3862**]. This illustrates that in spite of Bristow's efforts to make the management of the king's goods more efficient, scope for human error remained. Even so, once detected, it seems that problems were resolved fairly quickly.

The system of Keepers at Whitehall Palace

As Keeper, Denny was at the centre of a small group of men who were responsible for Henry VIII's possessions kept within the new palace and this pattern, on a smaller scale, is also found at Greenwich and Hampton Court (see Appendix III). In 1547 Nicholas Dowsing was Keeper of Greenwich and Thomas Maynman, Keeper of the Wardrobe of the Beds, acted as his assistant.[45] It is uncertain whether Dowsing had a deputy as Denny did, but his predecessor had done so. Robert Fowler was paid 15*s* 2*d* for his quarter's wages as Deputy Palace Keeper in March 1538.[46] This basic pattern of a Keeper with a deputy or colleague with whom he worked closely was also echoed at Hampton Court. The Keeper, Sir Thomas Cawarden, worked with David Vincent, Keeper of the Standing Wardrobe and a newly appointed member of the Privy Chamber.

The diversity of objects kept at Whitehall and the size of the palace complex explains why Denny needed help to run the palace and his appointment as Keeper made allowance for the use of deputies.[47] In reality he had just one – James Rufforth. Rufforth acted as Denny's assistant and he was responsible for a large number of goods in his own right. Indeed the letter sent to Rufforth by the Privy Council on 22 July 1545, asking him to send 550 sets of armour to Portsmouth, mistakenly referred to him as Keeper of the Palace.[48] Rufforth clearly had freedom of action, as is borne out by an inventory of jewels dated February 1545 and bearing the comment 'report made hereof to me by James Rufforth'.[49] In 1547 Rufforth took over part of Denny's role, and he gained further

---

43 These pieces were 'in a Coofer of Blacke Fustian of Naples sente to the Towre called the Barbours Coofer', SA MS 129, f. 206r.
44 See below, pp. 95–6.
45 BL Harley MS 1419, fos 54r, 37r.
46 BL Arundel MS 97, f. 10v.
47 PRO C66/666, m. 45 (*LP* X, 226.34). Shaw (*Inventories of Pictures*, 9) was mistaken when he referred to Denny taking office as Keeper in 1542. This error arose because he confused the posts of Keeper of the old palace and Keeper of the new palace.
48 *APC*, I, 214.
49 *LP* XX.i, 247.

responsibility within the palace on the fall of the Duke of Somerset. On Rufforth's own death, the objects in his charge passed to Sir Andrew Dudley, Denny's successor.[50]

From 1529 the Wardrobe of the Beds at York Place (later Whitehall) was managed by John Reed.[51] The holdings were quite substantial and were separate from the furnishings in Denny's charge. On 4 September 1536 Reed was also appointed as Keeper of the Vestry.[52] This appears to have been a specific vestry at Whitehall, separate from the main vestry in the charge of 'Ralph Tapping Serjeant of the Vestry'.[53] Further support was provided by Edmund Pigeon, Clerk of the Wardrobes of Robes and Beds and successor to Nicholas Bristow, who continued to assist and oversee Denny's work in his capacity as King's Clerk. There were also two additional members of the team. Philip van der Wilder, a practising court musician, oversaw the musical instruments, while William Tildesley balanced the role of royal librarian with the post of Keeper of the Wardrobe of the Beds at Windsor.[54] These seven individuals formed the core of the body of men responsible for the care and preservation of the contents of the palace.

The recreational facilities and the armouries also required staff. They were recruited in various ways, which indicates that Denny did not have a monopoly on how people were appointed. He could actively support the petition of an individual, as in the case of John Anthony: in June 1546, Denny supported Anthony's request to be 'keeper of your guns at Westminster' for wages of *6d* a day.[55] However, John Anthony did not remain in office for long. The route taken by his successor reveals that other individuals also saw the palace as a place to secure work for their clients. In December 1545 Alan Bawdeson, a servant of the Earl of Hertford, wrote to Denny about a bow worth *10s* which had been delivered to Henry Parker. By the time the 1547 Inventory was taken, Bawdeson was named as one of the Keepers of the Armouries, having apparently decided that working for the Crown was preferable to supplying the royal household;[56] his position may well reflect the Duke of Somerset's ascendancy at court and his increased access to royal patronage. Sir Thomas Darcy and Hans Hunter, armourer, were also listed in the 1547 Inventory.[57]

Outside the palace were gatekeepers, gardeners and cony-keepers. They too came within Denny's sphere.[58] In 1541 the system of Keepers included: Henry Russell in the privy garden; John Harnes and Philip Welsh in the great garden; William Thomson with the pheasants; John Johnson

50 *CPR Edward VI*, IV, 76. On 24 March 1551 a pardon and release was granted posthumously to Rufforth and to his executors Richard Cook, Edmund Daniel and John Daniel, for any money, plate, jewels, silks utensils, apparel, ornaments and other things in their care.

51 John Reed received the grant as Keeper of the Wardrobe at York Place in February 1529 (PRO E101/420/11, f. 95r). He surrendered this office in September 1533. He was probably then made Keeper of the Wardrobe at Whitehall. On 4 September 1536 he was made joint Keeper of the Wardrobe and the Vestry at Whitehall (*LP* VI, 1195.3) and he was in office as Wardrobe Keeper in 1547 (BL Harley MS 1419, f. 63r). According to the 1541 Subsidy Assessment Reed was living in the half parish of St Matthew in Friday Street, where he was assessed at 100 marks and charged a subsidy of *33s*: Lang, *Two Tudor Subsidy Assessment Rolls*, 65.

52 *LP* VI, 1195.3.

53 SA MS 129, f. 463r. While in no way deserving of the title 'vestry', there was a group of seven vestments in the closet over the water stair at Greenwich that fell outside the charge of the Keeper of the Wardrobe there (**9624**).

54 Philip van der Wilder looked after the musical instruments but the marginal notes in the 1542 Inventory record that on 2 September 1547 he received a small number of furnishings to round out his holdings. These included a mirror [**881**], a table [**1177**], a pair of trestles [**1180**], a chest [**1198**] and two chests for instruments [**1203**].

55 *LP* XXI.i, 1165.78.

56 SA MS 129, f. 431r.   57 SA MS 129, fos 429r, 432r.

58 Bod Lib MS English History b 192/1, f. 3r; also BL Lansdowne Roll 14, m. 8.

at the palace gate; Richard Cathyn overseeing the fish ponds; and Thomas Edgar at the park gate. As a consequence Denny's wage bill was quite substantial. During the accounting period of BL Lansdowne Roll 14 Denny paid wages to porters and keepers at Westminster

> attendinge daylie / Aswell at seuerall Gates within thesaied palace of Westmynster as kepers of the Gardens orchardes phesaunttes and condite hedes … CCCC iiij^{xx} ix^{li} xviij^s viij^d ob. [**B40**]

The nearby royal parks also had staff to care for them and they too came under Denny's remit. In May 1546 he supported the petition of Richard Sawford 'who hath taken vermin in your highness' parks of Marylebone and Hyde these two years' with wages of 4*d* a day during pleasure.[59] However, not all the park keepers were paid out of Denny's budget: between 22 September and 10 October 1540 Thomas Marvyn and Thomas Bridges of Marylebone Park and George Roper and Thomas Free of Hyde Park were paid by the Court of Augmentations.[60]

Keepers sometimes used their personal servants to run errands relating to their office. The servants were paid on a casual basis and the money would have supplemented their ordinary wages. On 22 June 1537 one of Denny's servants hired the king's little boat to transport a bed of arras from Whitehall to Hampton Court for his master.[61] Thomas Condycote, another of Denny's servants, submitted two bills, probably to the Treasurer of the Chamber: one bill was for the sum of 5*s*, for carrying a close stool from Whitehall to Windsor over two days and the other was for the sum of 7*s* 4*d*, for carrying two chests from Whitehall Palace to Windsor.[62] A document relating to the Wardrobe of the Robes in 1540 mentioned a servant of Denny's called Daniel.[63] As these examples make clear, Denny's servants were often used to collect and deliver items, probably because they were reliable and it was quicker to use them than to hire other hauliers. Servants were not restricted to Keepers: Edmund Pigeon was described as Nicholas Bristow's servant in the 1542 Inventory.[64]

One other individual took an unofficial part in the Whitehall system of Keepers: the king. The preamble of the 1547 Inventory stated that a number of the pieces were 'in our saide Fathers owne keaping withowte the chardge of any parson'.[65] While these could have been at any of the king's properties, most of those that can be traced through the 1547 Inventory were at Whitehall. This custom of certain objects being kept directly by the king was not unprecedented: sizeable quantities of jewels and plate had been delivered directly to Richard II within his chamber.[66] In Henry's case, items came into his hands in three main ways: as New Year's gifts, as private purchases or from the charge of one of his Keepers.

The objects in the king's care at Whitehall were most probably located in the rooms of the privy lodging that were Henry's exclusive territory. As there was no concept of formally charging the king with their care, so there was no official record of their location. However, the marginalia of the 1542

59 *LP* XXI.i, 963.93.
60 PRO E315/249, fos 34v–35r. With the exception of George Roper, who received £3, they all were paid £3 10*d* for their half year's wages.
61 Bod Lib MS English History b 192/1, f.14v.
62 *LP* Add.I.ii, 1863.
63 *LP* XVI, 402.
65 SA MS 129, f.1v.
64 PRO E315/160, f. 8v [**212**].
66 PRO E403/478, m. 16.

Inventory reveals that the items listed in sixty-five entries were delivered into the king's hands on 20 separate occasions between 1542 and 1547.[67] It is possible to locate some of them by comparing this group of objects with the items recorded as being in the rooms of the privy lodging in the 1547 Inventory. The carpet, two writing slates, three stools and a silk screen in the study at the 'hether ende of the Longe Gallorie' had all been delivered by Denny to Henry [435, 744, 1188, 1208].[68] A mirror, a screen and a cushion listed as being in the chair house in the 1547 Inventory followed the same path [878, 1209, 392].[69] In addition, a table with a writing desk was delivered to the king during 1542–3 [1164]. It is probably the table in the gallery study, although it also fits the description of the table in the chair house.[70] Henry also received two bells, possibly one for each of the studies [151, 163].[71] One of these [151], a silver-gilt bell with a long copper handle bound with silk, was amongst the pieces delivered by Denny to the Tower on 9 July 1547.[72] By acting as keeper for some or all of the items kept in these studies, Henry created a subset of objects within the palace.

It is equally possible that many of the small, expensive items packed in the removing coffers were 'in the King's charge'. The coffers would have provided a very necessary home for these peripatetic items within a palace structure where rooms and all their contents, however insignificant, were vigorously accounted for. While Henry was responsible for these pieces, it is unlikely that he would have packed the removing coffers himself. John Gates delivered the coffers to the Tower after Henry's death, indicating that he may have had this task during the king's lifetime.[73]

The size of the group Denny was working with meant that effective methods of communication were essential. Conversation would have formed a key part of this – Henry VIII must have discussed his plans for the development, management and furnishing of the palace with Denny on a regular basis. Denny would then have made Henry's wishes known to his own staff. While verbal instructions were probably adequate for much day-to-day business, large projects would have required written instructions and authorization. William Stockley, Clerk of the Crown's Debts received 58s for the parchment and writing and sealing with yellow wax of five principal commissions for Denny, Davy Martin (Comptroller), Thomas Canner (Surveyor of Whitehall), John Molton (mason) and John Russell (master carpenter) together with four small commissions.[74]

The development of a specialized administrative group by Denny

The combination of offices held by Denny was neither accidental nor unique. Indeed, two of Henry VIII's previous Grooms of the Stool, Compton and Norris, had enjoyed similar groupings of offices. Nevertheless Denny's position was peculiar. It was greater in extent than either Compton's

---

67 The deliveries were quite evenly distributed during this period: six in 1542–3, four in 1543–4, three in 1544–5, three in 1545–6 and four in 1546–7.

68 BL Harley MS 1419, f.113r; these equate to entries 10434, 10436–10437 and 10463 in the 1547 Inventory.

69 Entries 10532, 10537 and 10542 in the 1547 Inventory.

70 Entries 10434–10435 and 10540 in the 1547 Inventory.

71 Entry 416 in the 1547 Inventory (entry 163 does not appear in the 1547 Inventory). The bells are evidence of Henry's increased immobility, as are 'Two Chares called Trammes for the kinges maiestie to sitt in / to be caried to and fro in his gallaries & Chambers … and two fote stowles': [3676], (11798).

72 SA MS 129, fos 35r, 52r.

73 Ibid, f.150r. The page is headed 'Money Juelles and other Stuff in the kinges removing coofers late in the Chardge and custodye of sir John Gate knight and by hym deliuered to the lorde greate Master'.

74 Bod Lib MS English History b 192/1, unfoliated section between fos 43r and 53.

or Norris's, since it coincided with Henry's unprecedentedly heavy expenditure on the building and furnishing of Whitehall Palace. And unlike his predecessors, Denny's influence depended primarily on his being Keeper of Whitehall, and not on being Groom of the Stool (a position which he only held latterly and briefly).

The unusual scale of Denny's responsibilities meant that he needed an administrative staff. The main sources of recruitment were his own family and fellow servants of the Wardrobe of the Robes, who acted like another, official family. Denny soon moved on from the Robes, but the connection was maintained. His brother-in-law, John Gates, was appointed Groom of the Wardrobe of the Robes in 1540, a post he held until March 1544.[75] Most important was the professional clerk, Nicholas Bristow, who excelled at secretarial procedures and accounting. Bristow was Clerk of the Wardrobes of the Robes and Beds from 1541 to 1544.

John Gates is better known for the means of his death rather than his actions during his life.[76] Prior to his execution for treason in 1553, he developed his career at court, at first working for his brother-in-law Denny and then in his own right.[77] Gates began his career within the royal household in the Wardrobe of the Robes and then moved into the Privy Chamber, like Denny. In the Wardrobe he appears to have had responsibility for the weapons, girdles and hunting equipment. He also seems to have worked for the Wardrobe of the Beds intermittently. In March 1535 Gates delivered a group of furnishings to John Sandon to equip six rooms in Henry's house at Hackney. They were not of the highest quality because Gates provided 'vj pecys of paynted hangynges' for the little chamber next to the gallery and 'vij pecys of counterfett arras' for the chamber of estate.[78] It is possible that these furnishings came from Whitehall and as such they could reflect the furnishings used there during the early stages of the palace's redevelopment.

Gates acted as an intermediary between Denny and many of the individuals seeking Denny's patronage. He also promoted suits to the king in his own right. In 1542 one of John Gates's lists of 'Things to be remembered' included showing 'the King Nalinghurst's silks'.[79] Relatives were not above exploiting these links. On 9 January 1542 Wymond Carew (who married Martha Denny, Anthony's sister) wrote to Gates stating that his brother Thomas was in Poole with ninety-one fardels of canvas worth over 1,000 marks and he 'will let the king have some if he wishes at a reasonable price, taking a warrant on the receiver of Cornwall for payment'.[80]

---

75 The earliest reference to Gates's holding the office of Groom of the Robes is 27 July 1540: *LP* XV, 917. Thomas Sternold, Gates's successor, was appointed in March 1544: *LP* XIX.i, 275.

76 Sil, 'Sir John Gates'.

77 The level of his success can be gauged from the furnishings at his home Pirgo, in Essex, PRO LR2/119, fos 52r–62v. The hall, dining parlour and gallery were hung with hangings of verdure, say and tapestry but more interesting were the silver bedchamber, the gold bedchamber and the lion chamber, each with their associated inner chambers. Of these the lion chamber was the most luxurious: the Duke of Norfolk claimed the bedstead with its tester of purple velvet paned with purple satin, embroidered with white lions, trimmed with silver spangles and gold and silver lace, along with a chair and two cushions *en suite*. A sense of their worth can be gained from the sale price of the furnished bedstead in the silver bedroom (£33 13s 4d). The five pieces of tapestry, along with two borders, window and chimney pieces, two turkey carpets and a pair of bellows were sold to Sir Robert Rochester for £36 17s 4d: ibid, fos 54v–55r. In addition there was a woman's stool which was stolen before the sale and a court carpet bought by Sir Edward Waldegrave for 2s 8d.

78 PRO E101/421/19. In all Gates provided furnishings for the 'lytell chambre next the galerye', 'the galerye', 'the cheffe bedchambre', the clossett', the 'dynyng chambre' and the 'Chambre of Estate'.

79 *LP* Add. I.ii, 1573.

80 Ibid, 1517.

But despite all this, Gates still carried out the basic tasks of Privy Chamber office himself: 'As Mr Sherington was with you and another of my fellows gone before to Greenwich … I was left alone to truss and to wait upon the king', he wrote to Sir Edward North on 25 December 1546.[81] Gates acquired special responsibility for the king's removing coffers. In 1544 during the French campaign Gates was provided with a hale for the 'king's majesty's coffers'.[82] The 1547 Inventory recorded the receipt of

> Money Juelles and other Stuff in the kinges removing coofers late in the Chardge and custodye of sir John Gate knight and by hym deliuered to the lorde great Master.[83]

Denny's own household servants were used. James Rufforth, who was described as Denny's servant, acted as his deputy at Whitehall Palace. Rufforth served Denny in other areas, public and private. During the accounting period 1542–3 Rufforth collected part of Denny's income from his East Anglian estates.[84] He also helped to protect Denny's interests as Steward of Whitehall. When the sergeant at law challenged Denny's right to call out the muster, Rufforth notified Denny via Gates. On Denny's death in 1549 Rufforth succeeded him as Keeper, a post he held until his own death a year later in 1550. During this period Rufforth continued the administration of the silk house at the palace and he received a substantial delivery of tissue, cloth of gold, cloth of silver, tinsel and velvet from Dominico Erizo in August 1549 (**16143–16159, 16184–16197, 16223–16233, 16258–16261, 16312–16316**).

Finally, as his own career took off and Heneage's declined, Denny was also able to recruit from the affinity of his colleague and precursor. William Clerk began his career as a member of Heneage's household but as early as 1542 Denny created a link with him.[85] On 13 June of that year Denny granted Clerk an annuity of £6 13s 4d from the revenue of his lands in East Anglia.[86] Four years later in 1546 William Clerk, along with Denny and Gates, was appointed to apply the king's signature to some of the more routine paperwork produced by the royal household, using the dry stamp. Clerk actually kept the stamp and used it, while Denny and Gates oversaw how and when he did so.[87]

Clerical support

Some of the most important of Denny's servants, like William Clerk himself, were clerks by training. As the royal household became more bureaucratic, so clerks were increasingly essential to its running. By the mid-sixteenth century, all the clerks serving the king were secular.[88] Long established offices such as the Wardrobes of the Robes and Beds, and the Jewel House had dedicated clerical staff.[89]

81 Ibid, 1784.

82 GMR LM 59/101, fos 2r, 1v.

83 SA MS 129, f. 150r.

84 BL Additional Roll 63255, 'unfoliated'. Some of the money was collected by Edmund Daniel, 'servant of Denny'.

85 For a review of Clerk's career see Sil, 'Sir John Gates', 933 n. 29.

86 BL Additional Roll 63264.

87 *LP* XXI.i, 1536.34.

88 The last celibate clerks, the six clerks of chancery, were removed from office by statute in 1523: see Storey, 'Gentlemen bureaucrats', 108.

89 The clerks of the Wardrobes of the Robes and Beds during Henry VIII's reign were Laurence Gower (27 February 1511: *LP* I.i, 707), John Porth (1 June 1511: ibid, 804.1), John Plofield (April 1529: *LP* V, Treasurer's Accounts of the Chamber), John Briggs (April 1530: ibid, Treasurer's Accounts of the Chamber) (d. July 1537), James Joskyn (g. 5 September 1537: *LP* XII.ii, 796.6), Nicholas Bristow (g. 10 January 1541: *LP* XVI, 503) and Edmund Pigeon (gr. June 1544: *LP* XIX.i, 812.97).

Towards the end of Henry VIII's reign, when several new departments (such as the Navy Board) were established and others (like the Tents and Revels) put on a more permanent footing, the grants of office included the provision of clerical staff. A case in point is the appointment of Sir Thomas Clere as Lieutenant of the Admiralty in April 1546; he received an annuity of £100, expenses of 10s a day when on business, £10 for boat hire and an allowance for two clerks paid at a daily rate of 12d and 8d respectively.[90] Sir Thomas Cawarden, of the Tents, received the services of Thomas Philips.[91] Denny was not to be an exception.

PRECEDENTS: THE WORK OF JOHN PORTH AND JAMES JOSKYN

The other precedent for Denny's clerical staff was the king himself. Henry VIII was well served by a series of clerks, all of whom held office within the Wardrobe of the Robes and Beds for part of their career. One of the most important during the first half of the reign was John Porth or Porte. Porth was listed with the officers of the Jewel House at Henry VII's funeral, while at Henry VIII's coronation he was described as a Squire of the Body, along with Hugh Denys, Groom of the Stool to Henry VII.[92] His career continued during the reign of Henry VIII and he held two clerical offices: Clerk of the Wardrobes of the Robes and Beds (by 1511) and clerk of the Exchange in the Tower (1517).[93] The first real indication of his clerical and administrative skills appears in a grant of February 1508, when Porth was described as 'keeper of certain books of the king' in a grant of the corrody of the free chapel of St Margaret, Conisburgh, Yorkshire.[94] That his role was clerk and accountant, rather than librarian, is made clear when he was described as 'keeper of certain [of] our books of records'.[95]

Porth worked with the Wardrobe staff on a variety of tasks: participating in an inventory of the robes in December 1516 and delivering cloth with Ralph Worsley to Richard Gibson for a revel in February 1520.[96] However, he also carried out other duties for the king. Some were related to his other office within the Tower: in June 1517 Porth and Richard Trees, a servant of John Heron, were paid 8s for receiving the king's money at Westminster.[97] Others were more personal: in November 1516 Porth received 31s 4d for riding on the king's business.[98] Porth was also involved in taking a number of inventories of Henry's possessions, covering a range of the king's goods and including the 1521 inventory of the Jewel House.[99]

During the 1530s and 1540s Henry VIII was served by James Joskyn. Joskyn was the king's servant but he also had other personal ties within the Privy Chamber, especially to its then dominant member, Thomas Heneage. At the Ampthill muster held in October 1536 Joskyn was described as

90 *LP* XXI.i, 718.2.

91 Philips received his grant on 4 May 1546: ibid, 970.15.

92 *LP* I.i, 20, 82.

93 Ibid, 804.1 and *LP* II.ii, 3024.

94 *CPR* 1494–1509, 563. Prior to this Porth had appeared in the patent rolls from 1503, receiving land grants and serving on various commissions, see Ibid, 319, 407, 457, 507, 560 and 635. Porth was appointed to the Commission for the Peace in Derbyshire four times between 1502 and 1504 (nominal fellow commissioners included Arthur, Prince of Wales and Henry, Prince of Wales). He was included on the group enquiring into concealed royal lands in Derbyshire and Nottinghamshire in 1504 and on the Commission to deliver Nottingham gaol in 1506 and 1507.

95 *LP* III.i, 529.24.

96 *LP* II.ii, pp. 1473, 1553.

97 Ibid, pp. 1473, 1474.

98 Ibid, p. 1473.

99 The original manuscript has been lost; it is now known only from a nineteenth-century transcript: see Trollope, 'King Henry VIII's jewel book'.

'servant to Mr Heneage' when he received in prest £9,657 2s 4d.[100] In June of the following year he was appointed as Clerk of the Peace and the Crown in Northamptonshire and Leicestershire and in September as Clerk of the Robes and Beds.[101] During his period in office, Joskyn took an inventory of the Wardrobe of the Beds at Windsor.[102] He also paid money into the king's coffers, including £13,333 6s 8d in April 1540.[103] In July of the same year, Joskyn and his wife Joan were granted the manor of Wiggen Hall in Hertfordshire.[104] In October 1540, Joskyn received on Heneage's behalf annuities and fees owed to him by former monastic houses.[105] The evidence is relatively thin but it does suggest that Joskyn acted as Heneage's financial agent, helping him run both his personal finances and the king's privy purse.

In 1541 Joskyn was made a Teller of the Receipt of the Exchequer.[106] The tellers handled the actual cash in the Exchequer. The experience Joskyn had gained in his work for Heneage qualified him well for the task, and there are signs that he was regarded as the Privy Council's man in what could be a refractory department. During 1545 he was particularly concerned with providing money for victualling at Guisnes, Calais and Boulogne, in September, for instance, carrying over £10,000 in person to Guisnes.[107]

The Denny years: Nicholas Bristow

Joskyn was replaced as Clerk to both the Wardrobes by Nicholas Bristow.[108] Bristow was a professional scrivener. While his entry in the Scriveners' Common Paper is undated, the two entries which precede and follow his suggest that he joined the Scriveners' Company between 13 January and 5 March 1529.[109] The first reference to his presence within the royal household does not appear until 1538, when he drew up twelve guidelines for the management of silk cloth kept at Whitehall Palace; the points are worth recording in full:

1. no silks to be delivered without Bristow's presence;
2. the clerk should note whether silks thus delivered are of the old store or of the new;
3. silks must be marked with the contents and the name of the person from whom they were bought;
4. at the delivery of silks a clerk must write the name of the person to whom they were delivered, to what use, and of what price, upon the bill of contents and book of silks with Denny, and a copy must be given to Bristow;

100 *LP* XI, 937.
101 *LP* XII.ii, 191.48, 796.6.
102 *LP* XIV.i, 607 and 781, f. 61v. Joskyn was paid for 4 days' work in March 1539 when he took the inventory. In March 1540 Joskyn, along with David Vincent and Thomas Maynman, took an inventory of the Wardrobe of the Beds at Greenwich; the job took six days and they were paid at the rate of 2s a day: *LP* XVI, 380, f. 119v.
103 *LP* XVI, 745, f. 46 and *LP* XVIII.i, 436, p. 131.
104 *LP* XV, 942.119. Wiggen Hall, which had estates in Hertfordshire and Middlesex, was part of the property owned by the late monastery of St Albans that was granted to Denny.
105 *LP* XVI, 745, fos 9, 11.
106 Ibid, 503.19.
107 *LP* XX.i, 221 and 259; *LP* XX.ii, 33, 148, 177, 202, 253, 268, 345, 609.
108 *LP* XVI, 503.20.
109 Steer, *Scriveners' Company Common Paper*, 25–6. Although there is no declaration against Bristow's name, there is a marginal note dating from 1563: 'M^d Bristowe abfuit usq' tempus Thome Wytton et tunc Reductus solvens pro omnibus suis arreragiis xls'.

5. the price of silks bought by the king must be put upon the labels;

6. bills for money brought in by any person must be comptrolled by Bristow;

7. such bills must not be paid unless Bristow is present, and he is to enter them in the journal book;

8. all warrants are to be made by Bristow;

9. immediately upon the receipt of a bill, Bristow must make a remembrance of it and in what title he is discharged;

10. no stuff is to be delivered by Hewetson, Mrs Vaughan, Mr Lock or any other which ought to be allowed by Denny, without a bill signed by Denny or his deputy, which the clerk is to enter in his book of remembrance;

11. the clerk is to have a receipt for all money delivered to his master's use;

12. no man shall have a key to the clerk's study except his master or his deputy.[110]

The guidelines suggest that Bristow was systematic to the point of obsession; they also suggest somebody well versed in the problem. Bristow, in other words, had probably been working with Denny for some time as his personal clerk at Whitehall, possibly indeed since Denny's appointment in 1536. In 1541 Bristow's appointment as Clerk of both Wardrobes gave him more of an official footing.[111] A year later, in April 1542, Bristow and Humphrey Orme were granted the keepership of the king's garden, beds and other furniture and little Wardrobe in the Tower of London, with 6d a day as keeper of the garden and 12d a day for the Wardrobe.[112] This grant may have been linked to Bristow's work on the 1542 Whitehall Inventory. In view of his workload, it is likely that Orme carried out the day-to-day duties of this office.

As Clerk of the Wardrobes, Bristow had a core group of duties. He examined objects, compiled inventories and prepared the documentation to discharge Keepers from office. In 1543 Bristow surveyed the Wardrobe stuff at Windsor with William Tildesley, Keeper of the Wardrobe of the Beds at Windsor and the King's Librarian.[113] Bristow also supported the other Wardrobe officers by transferring material between properties and delivering new acquisitions, such as the collection and distribution of furnishings seized from the home of Thomas Cromwell.[114] Apart from the documentation and tracking of goods, Bristow also dealt with the accounts of the Wardrobes of the Robes and the Beds. Sixteen months later, on 29 June 1544, Bristow was granted the reversion of the office of Clerk of the Jewels.[115] His skills were clearly in demand: the records of Sir Thomas Cawarden, Master of the Tents and Revels, indicate that Bristow also worked for him.[116] They had dealings over a selection of confiscated jousting harness, lances and Almain rivets that Cawarden

110   *LP* XIII.ii, 1201.
111   *LP* XVI, 503.
112   *LP* XVII, 283.51. Humphrey Orme was listed as the sole office holder in the 1547 Inventory: BL Harley MS 1419, f. 5r.
113   BL Additional MS 30367, fos 2r–31v (*LP* XVIII.i, 224). Tildesley was a royal servant of long standing. In September 1532 he was granted the messuage known as the henchmen's chamber (above the king's bakehouse) at Whitehall and a cottage at the stair foot adjoining the bakehouse: *LP* V, 1370.21.
114   Edmund Pigeon carried out a similar role in 1547: *LP* XVIII.i, 224. Bristow delivered items received 'from sundry persons attainted' to Windsor Castle on 21 November 1543 and 10 April 1544: ibid.
115   *LP* XVI, 503.20; *LP* XIX.i, 812.103.
116   GMR LM 59/150, f. 4r.

collected from the home of Bristow.[117] These were part of the personal effects of Cromwell, which Bristow had received from the fallen minister.[118]

Bristow's administrative skills also meant that he was drafted onto a number of royal commissions and surveys. His name appears in the accounts of Sir John Williams, Master of the Jewel House. In November 1538 he delivered 3,680½ ounces (114.09kg) of plate and two copies of the Gospels with ornamented bindings from the monasteries of Stratford Langthorn in Essex and St John's, Clerkenwell.[119] In 1546, no doubt valued for his clerical skills and his knowledge of textiles and plate, he was part of the commission appointed to survey the chantries in Essex, Hertfordshire and Colchester;[120] six years later, in 1553, he was part of the team surveying the parish churches of Hertfordshire.[121]

On occasion Bristow's role was more strictly financial. In August 1546 he acted as paymaster for the visit of d'Annebault, the French admiral who came to England to ratify the new Anglo-French peace treaty. The Tents' accounts covering the period of 15 July to 18 October 1546, which he compiled, show him moving the tents from London to Hampton Court and Oatlands and then setting them up.[122] However, a different account reveals that he was involved with the project for a much longer period: he was paid for 188 days' work from February 1546 to February 1547.[123] In addition, Bristow received £2,000 to pay for the materials and workmen's wages required to set up the temporary banqueting house and the tents that were used for the festivities.[124]

In the same year Bristow was given £2,400 for building work at Hampton Court and Nonsuch.[125] The main tent for d'Annebault's visit was erected outside the Palace of Hampton Court, and some of the building work at Hampton Court must relate to this event. The money for Nonsuch was probably linked to the king's visit that year. Henry only visited Nonsuch twice: 5–7 July 1545 and 11–19 December 1546.[126] On the second occasion Odet de Selve, the French ambassador, wrote to Francis I, informing him that Monsieur de la Garde and himself were asked to 'be at Nonsuch on Tuesday night and have audience on Wednesday'.[127] He would have seen the work funded by the money Bristow delivered.

Furthermore, Bristow oversaw the documents relating to the king's private finances and his possessions, dealing in fact with everything apart from the dry stamp (which was administered by William Clerk). He also periodically checked Denny's accounts and warrants. After Sir William Compton had siphoned off Henry's assets while he was Groom of the Stool,[128] his successors

117 Ibid, f. 4r. Interestingly, Edmund Pigeon, Bristow's client, bought one set of Almain rivets, with splints, a gorget and a head piece for 10s: ibid, f. 1r.
118 For the background to Cromwell's fall from power, trial and execution, see Scarisbrick, *Henry VIII*, 375–80.
119 Turnbull, *Monastic Treasures*, 47.
120 *LP* XXI.i, 302.30.   121 *CPR* 1550–3, pp. 393–4.
122 GMR LM 22/1, 22/2.
123 GMR LM 30/3. Bristow was paid at a rate of 3s 4d a day for himself, a clerk and horses. He was working at Hampton Court, Oatlands and Chobham, as well as giving attendance in London.
124 *LP* XXI.ii, 777.   125 *LP* XX.ii, 418.90.
126 PRO OBS 1/1419, fos 73v, 75v (*LP* XX.i, 1117, 1128; *LP* XXI.ii, 532, 768 p. 397).
127 *LP* XXI.ii, 532.
128 William Compton's grant as groom of the stool was dated April 1510 (*LP* I.i, 447.18); his successor, Henry Norris, was in office in 1526: Starkey, 'Intimacy and innovation', 94 and *LP* IV.i, 1906 (18 January 1526 – Compton delivered Henry VIII's New Year's gifts to Henry Norris).

were watched more carefully. This scrutiny extended to Heneage, and Bristow signed Heneage's book detailing all the receipts and payments made 'to or for your Majesty's privy affairs' during 1546–7.[129]

As Denny's clerk, Bristow had an office at Whitehall Palace but he chose to live in the City of London. He received a number of grants from the king, including the house and site of St Mary-without-Bishopsgate for a period of twenty-one years.[130] At the time of the 1541 subsidy Bristow was resident in the parish of St Thomas the Apostle, where his property was valued at £100; as a consequence, he had to pay a subsidy of 50s.[131] He did not regard himself as affluent. When John Gates, his close associate, was selling some land, Bristow hoped to buy some at an advantageous rate. He wrote to Gates stating that 'the price of woods is very sore in London … by reason whereof such poor men as I am are driven to seek ways and means to live'.[132] In addition to his London property he also built up a small land holding in Hertfordshire, the same county as Denny's own home. In 1543 Denny conveyed Little Bibbesworth to Bristow and his wife Lucy.[133] On a separate occasion in the same year Bristow acquired the advowson of the church of St Peter and St Paul, Kimpton, which he kept until his death.[134] On the basis of his landholdings in Hertfordshire, Bristow provided one light horse for the levy of July 1548.[135]

Recognition of Bristow's importance came about in 1540 when he was formally entitled 'king's clerk'.[136] As such he was accountant-in-chief to Denny in his role as head of the private royal financial machine that developed in the last decade of Henry VIII's reign (Figure 9). After Henry's death, Bristow continued to serve each of the late king's children. Bristow's longevity meant that he oversaw the discharge from office of a number of the men named in the 1547 Inventory. In June 1547 he was appointed to 'examine the books of Richard Cecil, yeoman of the wardrobe of the Robes' and discharge him from office.[137] Thirteen years later, in 1560, he was required to review the accounts of David Vincent, Keeper of the Wardrobe at Hampton Court, making allowance for waste stuff and warrants made by Edward VI, Mary and the Privy Council.[138] Finally, in 1565, he considered the accounts of Humphrey Orme, Keeper of the Wardrobe in the Tower.[139] When he died in 1584 Bristow was buried in the church of St Helen's, Wheathampstead, in Hertfordshire.

CONTINUATION: EDMUND PIGEON   In this world, servants also had servants: Bristow assisted Denny and Edmund Pigeon worked for Bristow. A bill for a tent or timber lodging made for the king between July 1543 and March 1544 named Edmund Pigeon as the 'paymaster ys clark'.[140] This work would have brought him to the attention of Bristow, who worked periodically with the

129 *LP* XXI.i, 148.68; 963.116; 1165.65.

130 *LP* XVII, 1154. 50.

131 Lang, *Subsidy Assessment Rolls*, 111.

132 *LP* Add. I.ii, 1797.

133 *VCH Hertfordshire*, III, 31.

134 *LP* XIX.i, 1036.

135 *CPR* 1547–53, 137. In contrast, Sir John Gates provided four light horse and two lances and Sir Thomas Cawarden six light horse and four lances.

136 *LP* XVI, 380, f.132v.

137 *CPR* 1547–8, 261.

138 *CPR* 1560–3, 62. This order was repeated in November 1565 but as David Vincent was dead by then, his son and heir Thomas was held accountable: *CPR* 1563–6, 1084.

139 *CPR* 1563–6, 1238.

140 See GMR LM 11, 59/112.

officers of the Tents. Shortly after the completion of the lodging, in June 1544, Pigeon was named as Bristow's successor as Clerk of the Robes and Beds.[141] The close link between the two men is emphasized further in the 1542 Inventory where Pigeon is described as Bristow's servant.[142]

In September 1546 Pigeon petitioned for the reversion of the office of Groom of the Jewel House, also held by Bristow.[143] The following year Pigeon was involved in the reorganization of the contents of Whitehall Palace (see below, pp. 134–5). Pigeon continued to work with Bristow after Henry VIII's death; in 1560 Bristow, as Clerk of the Jewels, and Pigeon as Clerk of the Wardrobe, looked into David Vincent's affairs.[144]

Documentation associated with Denny's period as Keeper

Denny was granted the Keepership of Whitehall Palace in January 1536.[145] At the appointment of a new keeper, normal practice dictated that an inventory be taken of the goods placed in their charge and this document then acted as the bond between master and servant. A number of inventories have been lost. For example, there are no surviving inventories for the period when Alvard was Keeper of the palace (1530–5). Equally, it is clear that some which we would expect to find for Whitehall were in fact never taken. There is also circumstantial evidence that none was taken on Denny's appointment in 1536. On 21 December 1541 Sir Ralph Sadler wrote that 'As for the money and plate, the King is doubtful whether it is at his palace of Westminster or at Wriothesley's house. It is to be delivered to James, Mr Denny's servant, in bags and chests sealed'.[146] The fact that Henry could not check the whereabouts of the plate and money implies that there was no inventory which he or Denny could consult. Indeed, it seems that Alvard and Denny had to work with just a partial record of the objects in their care. Evidence of this paperwork includes 'a memorial of books in the King's study at York Place' noted by Cromwell in 1533.[147] In addition there is a list of silks and velvets dated 13 April 1537 which may be an example of the 'book of silks with Mr Denny' that was described a year later by Bristow in his memorandum.[148] Denny used this book to manage the silk store at Whitehall.

This situation was not unique. An inventory should have been taken in 1540 when Sir John Williams replaced Cromwell as Master of the Jewel House. However, according to a commission appointed on 12 April 1547, Williams 'hathe not been perfectly charged because there was no survey or charges made or taken of the same sythen the tyme of Sir Thomas Crumwell, late havyng the same office'.[149] This shows that the cycle of inventories was not kept up to date for two key groups of the king's possessions: those kept at Whitehall Palace and those kept at the Tower jewel house.

---

141 *LP* XIX.i, 812.97.
142 For example, PRO E/315/160, f. 9r.
143 *LP* XXI.ii, 199.102.
144 *CPR* 1560–63, 62.
145 *LP* X, 226.34.
146 *LP* XVI, 1466. This letter was sent to the Earl of Southampton and Thomas Wriothesley.
147 *LP* VI, 299 ix.
148 BL Cotton Appendix 89 (formerly 28), fos 54r–66r (*LP* XII.i, 925). For Bristow's memorandum (*LP* XIII.ii, 1201), see above, pp. 95–6.
149 *CPR Edward VI*, I, 138–9.

THE 1542 INVENTORY   The only known inventory documenting Denny's charge at Whitehall was taken over eight years after his initial appointment. The 1542 Inventory was valid from 24 April that year: a new document for a new regnal year. The objects recorded in it were 'deliuerid in charge to the said Anthony Denny in the monethes of Apriell and Maii', possibly indicating that some of the pieces were drawn in from other houses, came from the charges of other Keepers or were new commissions.[150] Four months later Denny was granted a general pardon and discharge for his previous period as Keeper of Whitehall Palace, as Yeoman of the Robes and for the parcels of the king's money, plate, jewels and other stuff which were no longer in his custody on 23 April 1542.[151] Denny's role as Keeper had entered a new phase.

The 1542 Inventory is one of the few inventories taken between 1509 and 1547 to focus extensively on textile furnishings. Earlier surviving inventories are those of Beaulieu (1516), Hackney (1535), Parlands (1536) and Windsor (1539 and 1543).[152] Of these properties, only Windsor was a leading royal residence. However, inventories have been lost: for example, Rowland Riggeley, Thomas Maynman and David Vincent were paid for taking an inventory of the Wardrobe of the Beds at Greenwich in March 1540, but the inventory has not survived.[153] Three months later the Greenwich Wardrobe was supplemented with two cart-loads of furnishings confiscated from Cromwell's house, four miles away.[154] However, the 1542 Inventory also goes way beyond furnishings: it contains the earliest listing of the king's pictures and the first alphabetical list of royal books of any length.

The 1542 Inventory is the largest surviving inventory made during the king's lifetime and it contains just over 4,100 entries (amounting to approximately 8,000 objects). In terms of the number of items recorded and the detail given, it is second only to the 1547 Inventory. The latter has some 17,810 (recto 17,813) entries representing approximately 50,000 objects. The approximate value of the items recorded within the 1542 Inventory is £172,500, in comparison to the estimated worth of around £600,000 of the goods listed in the 1547 Inventory, split equally between the two manuscripts.[155]

The 1542 Inventory is the only inventory taken for one of the three leading royal residences in the course of the reign, and it is set in context by those sections of the 1547 Inventory that deal with Whitehall, Greenwich and Hampton Court. In all three instances the 1547 Inventory records the contents of the Wardrobe of the Beds, followed by the contents of the royal apartments. There

150   PRO E315/160, f. 1r.

151   *LP* XVII, 881.11.

152   Beaulieu, 20 September 1516: PRO E101/622/31 (not calendared in *LP*); Hackney, 5 March 1535: PRO E101/421/19 (not calendared in *LP*); Parlands, June 1536: BL Cotton MS Appendix 89 (formerly 28), fos 54r–66r (*LP* X, 1240: the heading of the document is damaged and the house is not identified in *LP*. Most of the furnishings were later transferred to Oatlands); Windsor, 26 March 1539: BL Additional MS 10602, fos 1r–6r (*LP* XIV.i, 607) and February 1543: BL Additional MS 30367, fos 2r–31v (*LP* XVIII.i, 224).

153   BL Arundel MS 97, f. 119v (*LP* XVI, 380).

154   BL Arundel MS 97, f. 132v (*LP* XVI, 380). The rest of the pieces went to the Wardrobes at the Tower (two carts) and Hampton Court (one cart).

155   The figure for the 1542 Inventory is based on the estimate Sybil Jack made for the 1547 Inventory, see Starkey ed. *Inventory*, I, xi. BL Harley 1419 deals with the wardrobes in general and the palace of Whitehall in particular and represents about £300,000. This manuscript has 6,434 original entries, in comparison to the 3,706 original entries in the 1542 Inventory. (This figure for BL Harley MS 1419 does not include the two sets of duplicate entries for Whitehall and the 1542 figure has had the duplicate entries, textile summary and the figures relating to Denny's management of the king's coffers deducted). So the 1542 Inventory is equivalent to 57.6 per cent of the British Library total, giving an approximate value of £172,500.

is then a section recording the contents of a number of rooms; these contain a mixed selection of objects and there is no attempt to group the objects by type.

The objects recorded in the 1542 Inventory are organized by type and not by the rooms in which they were kept. The majority of the objects at Whitehall were also recorded by type in 1547, but the later document also included items kept in a series of rooms. The most likely reason for the omission of these rooms from the 1542 Inventory is that they fell outside Denny's jurisdiction. Several of these rooms were listed as being in the care of James Rufforth in 1547, including 'The Glasse housse', the old jewel house (where Jane Seymour's clothes were being stored) and the 'litle Study called the newe Librarye'.[156] Rufforth's undated rough book included lists of items kept in a number of the king's studies.[157]

Strictly speaking, inventories are static, backward-looking documents that become outdated as soon as another object is acquired or an old one is disposed of. However, inventories can continue to evolve if they are updated with marginal notes, or if extra sections are added at the end of the main text. Provision for this type of addition would explain why such a large volume (see Volume II, p. 2) was provided for the 1542 Inventory: the initial text of the 1542 Inventory filled approximately half the pages in the volume, leaving plenty of space for fresh acquisitions to be recorded. Both marginalia and additional sections were used to keep the 1542 Inventory current up to 1547.

A number of the items left the palace, but it is significant that the relevant entries were not crossed out. Indeed, it is rare to find items struck out in any good copy of Henry VIII's inventories. There are just two examples of entries being crossed out in the 1542 Inventory [**223, 224**]. Bristow explains that this set of scarlet hangings and the matching window pieces were altered and then 'chargid hereafter in this book in folio 138' [**3763–3764**]. The Inventory therefore preserves the memory of objects that have either passed out of the king's possession or moved from Whitehall to another location. In marked contrast to the lack of deleted entries is the quantity of notation on the 1542 Inventory. It is most unusual compared with most of the rest of Henry VIII's inventories. One notable exception is the section of the British Library copy of the first part of the 1547 Inventory, which records the contents of the king's removing coffers.[158] This is heavily annotated, providing numerous details about when the coffers' contents were dispersed and to whom.

Henry signed the first page of the 1542 Inventory of Whitehall Palace.[159] This use of the king's sign manual or signature on a major royal inventory acted as a symbol of his authority and of the inventory's authenticity; Edward VI signed the documents relating to Denny's discharge as Keeper in the same way and with the same effect.[160] The use of royal signatures on household documents is well documented during the reign of Henry VII, who was well known for his practice of initialling each page of his household accounts.[161] This habit was adopted by his granddaughter Mary I, but generally neglected by his son.[162] The 1516 Inventory of the King's Robes is exceptional: the

156 BL Harley MS 1419, fos 143r, 159r, 186r.
157 PRO E101/419/16.
158 Parallels can be found amongst nobles' inventories, such as the 1561 Inventory produced for William Herbert, 1st Earl of Pembroke. The annotations were chiefly carried out by his secretary, William Jordan: see Turner, 'Lord Pembroke's inventory'.
159 PRO E315/160, f. 1r.
160 BL Lansdowne Roll 14, mm. 1, 12; BL Lansdowne Roll 15, m. 1.
161 See PRO E101/414/6, E101/414/16, E101/415/3 and BL Additional MS 21480; see also Chrimes, *Henry VII*, 332.
162 *PPE Princess Mary* (with a facsimilie of the Lady Mary's signature).

sign manual appears 126 times over the 53 folios;[163] this may mean that the king had a thorough knowledge of his wardrobe, but it was not a practice which Henry VIII chose to pursue diligently with other documents.

The presence of Henry's signatures indicates that the surviving copy of the 1516 Inventory is Denny's own volume, the second 'like booke subscribed with thand of the said Anthony Denny remaynyng with vs'. Counter signatures, inserted by the commissioners or a clerk, could be used as a regulatory measure on inventories: they verified the contents, so giving the document added authority. The system can be seen in operation in the list of Catherine Howard's jewellery and in the 1542 Inventory, both of which were compiled by Nicholas Bristow.[164] Validating signatures were applied to other documents, including the king's last will and testament, which was described as 'bearing date at Westminster the thirty day of December last past, written in a book of paper, signed above in the beginning and beneath in the end, and sealed with the signet'.[165] Henry used his sign manual to authenticate his will and other documents and his signature was accepted at face value. The professional clerks and auditors working for the king often augmented their signature with a 'paraph' or knot device. These marks were developed as a precaution against forgery and they were recorded in registers. Nicholas Bristow's personal paraph was registered in the Scriveners' Company Common Paper.[166] The Scottish notary, Robert Sinclair, authenticated his documents with a knot device very similar in shape to that favoured by Bristow and the sentence 'Ita est Robertus Sinclare Manu Propria'.[167]

THE RELATIONSHIP BETWEEN THE 1542 AND THE 1547 INVENTORIES The 1542 and the 1547 inventories are closely related in terms of the objects covered, the individuals involved and the wording of entries. As demonstrated above, while the 1547 Inventory presents the most uniform overview of Henry VIII's possessions, the organization of a number of the objects reflects the needs of the new king Edward VI and the Protector (the Duke of Somerset) rather than their arrangement during Henry VIII's lifetime. The 1542 and 1547 inventories are most revealing when they are used in combination. While the 1542 Inventory records objects that were almost exclusively for use within the *domus magnificencie* as a whole and the privy apartments in particular, the scope of the 1547 Inventory reflects the broad range of goods owned by a discerning monarch of the day.

While the 1542 Inventory was the work of one clerk, several distinct hands can be identified in the 1547 Inventory. This indicates the scale of the later inventory but it also adds to the sense of it being pieced together. In terms of decoration the 1542 Inventory compares well with the two halves of the 1547 Inventory. The first page of each volume of the letter begins with a large, flourished initial. While these are more impressive than those used in the 1542 Inventory, the other

---

163 These are genuine signatures as opposed to signatures made with the stamp. They vary in length between 580mm and 830mm.

164 BL Stowe MS 559, fos 55r–68r (*LP* XIV, 1389). This process is also described in the accounts of Sir John Williams in relation to the inventory of Sir Anthony Aucher, his predecessor as Master of the Jewel House: see Turnbull, *Monastic Treasures*, 94–5.

165 *LP* XXI.ii, 770.

166 Steer, *Scriveners' Company Common Paper*, 25. Examples of paraphs are illustrated in Jenkinson, *Later Court Hands*, II. I am very grateful to Diana Greenway for these references.

167 Meaning 'This is Robert Sinclair's own hand'. The signature and paraph are illustrated in Barrett and Iredale, *Discovering Old Handwriting*, 85.

folios received little or no embellishment. This contrasts with the 1542 Inventory, where quite a few of the capitals used in the headings were decorated, making the document a fine example of the scrivener's art. Whether the lack of embellishment of the 1547 Inventory reflects a lack of time, a different remit or the indifference of the scribes is impossible to say.

Household inventories were often cumulative and sequential, with one document building on the previous one. The section of the 1547 Inventory that covers Whitehall (**10545–11952**) compares very closely with sections of the earlier 1542 Inventory of the palace. The lists of the musical instruments and of the contents of the glass house are almost identical, thus making the omission of the books from the later inventory particularly odd. Two further inventories relating to Whitehall were written up at the end of the second volume of the 1547 Inventory: a list dated 12 November 1549 (**15421–16068**) and a second dated 31 October 1550 (**16069–17810**).

The 1547 Inventory, unlike that of 1542, contains, embedded in the entries, quite a lot of incidental detail about the suppliers or makers of items. Examples include a 'crucefix nayled with three small dyamountes and in his syde a small rubie gyven by the busshopp of Duresham vppon Newe yeares day anno xxviij^{ui} nuper Henrici octaui' (**190**) and 'twoo small crosses of Siluer having either crosse a small crucefix nayled thereunto thone brokin receaved from the late Monastery of Christchurche' (**191**). This type of detail only occurs in that section of the 1542 Inventory where Denny and Bristow updated the document by recording the merchants and craftsmen supplying goods to the palace and deliveries from other royal properties [**3306–3773**].

OTHER DOCUMENTATION ASSOCIATED WITH DENNY'S OFFICE AS KEEPER OF THE PALACE   The four manuscripts printed below, along with the relevant sections of the 1547 Inventory, provide a unique and detailed insight into how Denny worked as Keeper of the leading Henrician palace in the 1540s. Yet these records represent just a fraction of the paperwork generated by Denny between 1536 and 1549. In part, their survival can be attributed to their being formal records – fair copies of inventories, accounts and the records of his discharge from office. Much of Denny's work required letters, memoranda, warrants and 'diuers perticuler billes and Indentures subscribed with thandes of the perties'.[168] Evidence of the latter is recorded in the 1542 Inventory entries that relate to Denny's management of the king's money: for example, 'a bill subscribed by thande of the said Sir Anthony Denny datid the said daye and yere' [**4132**]. Very few of Denny's working papers have survived, but documents of this type do exist for other offices, such as the bundles of warrants for the Great Wardrobe or the Office of the Tents under Thomas Cawarden: each year, when Sir Andrew Windsor, Master of the Great Wardrobe, presented his accounts he indented with the Auditor of the King's Exchequer for his account book, the warrants and bills he had acted upon and a white leather bag in which they were delivered.[169]

The 1542 Inventory is a substantial document that would probably have been consulted in an office by Denny, Rufforth and other members of the palace staff, rather than being carried around on a daily basis. The good condition of the document supports this proposition. So it is likely that

---

168   PRO E101/427/2, m. 2.
169   A few of these indentures have survived, e.g. for 27 December 1515, 31 December 1522 and 4 January 1536 (PRO E101/417/3, nos 92, 89, 90).

the Keeper of the Palace and, more importantly, his deputy kept rough copies of various sections of the main inventories for everyday use. Rufforth had a small paper booklet into which he had copied details of the cloth stored at Whitehall, as well as the contents of several rooms.[170] In terms of dating, its structure is closer to that of the 1547 Inventory than the 1542 volume but it provides good evidence of this process of making a rough copy.

Denny's book of charge, or 'infra' (the 1542 Inventory) holds the key to a second book that Denny would have needed as Keeper, namely, a book of issue or discharge (also known as a 'book of extra'). This pair of volumes would have been common to all Keepers: a book of infra was used to record a keeper's initial charge and then any additional items that were subsequently delivered into his care, and a book of extra was used to record all items leaving the keeper's charge. A jewel house commission of 1547 referred to plate held by Cromwell at the time of his fall from power as being recorded in his books 'of infra and extra'.[171] Several references to the current jewel house book of extra can be found in the 1547 Inventory. These include 'an Ewer parcell gilte … parcell of John Fremans retorne as apereth in the Bokes of Extra' (**1633**) and 'twelve white Trenchers plaine striken … A parcell of John Fremans retorne as apereth in the Booke of Extra' (**1687**).

Denny would have used his book of issue to record all the items passing out of his hands. The book has not survived but it is possible to partially recreate it, using the marginalia of the 1542 Inventory. Many of the notes record the date when an item passed out of Denny's care, its destination and a folio number. It is likely that this last is the folio in the book of issue on which the entry appeared, so providing a cross reference for Denny and Bristow. When these notes are collated, a series of pages are created, with the entries on a particular folio usually being delivered on the same or similar dates and to one individual or destination. In addition, it is possible to draw up two other lists: one recording objects that left Whitehall after Henry VIII's death, so providing a chronology for the dispersal of many of the palace's furnishings, and one relating to the pieces that remained at the palace, forming Denny's revised charge and Rufforth's new charge.[172]

Other documentation was produced in relation to one particular group of objects – the silk store. Detailed evidence of how the lengths of silk were managed was recorded in 'An order to be taken by Mr Denny touching his business at Whitehall devised by Bristowe'.[173] This list of twelve points, drawn up by Nicholas Bristow in 1538, describes how the store of silks should be administered. It suggests that previously the system had been rather slack. The memorandum mentions several documents including a 'book of silks with Mr Denny', a journal book and a book of remembrance. The summary at the end of the 1542 Inventory, concerning cloth dispersed from the palace between 1542 and 1548,[174] probably drew upon Denny's 'book of silks'. Bristow kept the journal book and book of remembrance along with numerous warrants and receipts. Bristow's journal book may have resembled the daybook kept by Mary Scudamore between 1561 and 1586. This book was used to record items passing out of Elizabeth I's Wardrobe of the Robes, including gifts of clothing

170   PRO E101/419/16.
171   *CPR Edward VI*, I, 138–9.
172   See pp. 158–60, 155–7 below.
173   *LP* XIII.ii, 1201. The points are given in full at pp. 95–6 above.
174   [**3774–3943**].

or jewels, material delivered to the queen's tailor and items 'loste from off the Quenes Majesties backe'.[175] This information could be used in this form or transferred to the main inventory, probably in the form of marginal notes. A few amendments of this type appear in the 1547 Inventory:

> The lardge perle pendaunt pere fasshion was lost frome the flower by the kinges majestie wearing the same in his graces jorney ryding the last sommer frome Tichefeld to Southampton … Whiche perle was afterward founde agayne and rediliuered to thandes of the saide lorde Treasorer (**2209**).

After Henry VIII's death in January 1547, Denny's remit as Keeper changed and he was discharged from his old office[176] and given a new charge, which he held until his death in 1549.[177] Two of the rolls printed below, PRO E101/427/2 and BL Lansdowne Roll 15, list items missing from the 1542 Inventory. These documents relate respectively to Denny's discharge from Henry VIII's service in 1547 and the release of his widow Joan in 1551 from the Edwardian charge. The king's possessions were checked over closely by the commissioners to ensure that Denny did not defraud his master. They were particularly interested in 'percelles … [w]hich be deficient and wantynge … not enploied … to the kynges vse or by his sufficient warrant'.[178]

The roll produced in 1547 has 78 entries (427 items) while the list drawn up in 1551 was much shorter, having just 15 entries (37 items). Most of the items recorded in the 1551 list were of low value, such as 'Anticke Heades of copper and <a> thynne plate of siluer taken of frome a stele glasse – one' [C4] and 'Fete of Tymbre serving for a wicker skryne – j' [C7]. In some instances the commissioners were overzealous. They listed 'the picture of thole stature of the Duches of Millane' as missing but later noted that 'This Table Therle of Arundell hathe of the kinges Majesties gieft as he saithe' [C1]. Ultimately, Denny's widow was granted the following quittance: 'And so thesaied Sir Anthony Denny knight is herof clerely dischardged and Quyett'.[179]

Beyond Whitehall Palace: Denny's broader remit

While Whitehall was his first and most significant charge by 1547, Denny also oversaw a much broader portfolio of royal properties. Within London and its suburbs Denny was financially responsible for St James's Palace, Durham House, Chelsea, The Nete, Stockwell, Highbury and aspects of the Tower of London.[180] He also managed a number of parks, namely Covent Garden, Hyde Park and Marylebone. The latter included a small property and when William, the Keeper at Marylebone Place resigned his post, it created interest: on 13 January 1544 one Jane Wentworth wrote to John Gates expressing her wish to be the 'sole tenant to good Mr Denny' but it is unknown if Denny met her modest requirements of a room and stabling for a horse.[181] Further afield, Denny was responsible for Hatfield in Hertfordshire. In 1542 Gates wrote himself a memorandum 'to know my brother's [Denny's] pleasure whether Hatfield wood shall be palled or hedged'.[182]

175 See Arnold, '*Lost from Her Majesties Back*'; Mary Scudamore was a Gentlewoman of Elizabeth I's Privy Chamber (ibid, 10–12).
176 PRO E101/427/2.
177 PRO E315/160, f. 8v [**211**].   178 PRO E101/427/2, m. 2.
179 BL Lansdowne Roll 14, m. 12.
180 These properties are discussed in greater detail below, p. 107.   181 *LP* XIX.i, 23.
182 *LP* Add. I.ii, 1573.

Linking these properties and the numerous other houses owned by the king was a network of roads and bridges, which Denny oversaw, along with the walls round the properties to keep the king's game in and the general populace out. The scale of the project and the condition of the roads is suggested by Denny's expenditure of £1,683 15s 3¾d in just over six years from 1542 to 1547 [**B41**]. The type of orders Denny issued must have been similar to those given for Henry VIII's last journey. Prior to the departure of the king's funeral cortège, an order was 'taken for the clearing and mending of all the high ways between Westminster and Windsor … and the noisome boughs cut down of every side the way'.[183]

In some instances Denny was formally appointed as Keeper, while in others he was working on a less official footing. Even so, by 1547 this group of houses and parks involved Denny in a large-scale, ongoing scheme of building work and maintenance. Between 11 February and 9 April 1537 he was granted £2,662 1d by the Court of Augmentations for building work and repairs at Whitehall, Chelsea, Hackney and St James's Palace, as well as a contribution towards the cost of the new house for the Court of Augmentations situated within the old Palace of Westminster.[184] The level of expenditure increased dramatically during the period of Denny's accounts (1542–1548), when he spent a total of £32,969 5s 9½d on building materials and wages.[185] The bulk of this sum, namely £28,676 3s 4d, was spent on Whitehall, with £756 6s 5½d being spent on St James's.[186] It was a substantial amount of money and the distribution of the funds reflects the relative importance, size and needs of the two projects. Denny worked closely with Thomas Canner, first Clerk and then Surveyor of Works, and Denny periodically checked Canner's accounts [**B23, 26**]. Denny's involvement ranged from large-scale financial planning to the acquisition of building materials and the implementation of projects in hand. As an example of the latter, Denny preferred a warrant in May 1546 for six score oaks from Endfield Close for the building work at Whitehall.[187]

Not surprisingly, a number of Denny's additional charges were directly related to the palace at Westminster. St James's Palace was developed between 1531 and 1536 and as it formed part of the Westminster complex it readily came under the auspices of the main palace Keeper. This was to change after Henry's death. Richard Coke was named as Keeper of St James's Palace in the 1547 Inventory.[188] The accounts of Thomas Cromwell indicate that The Nete manor was linked with Whitehall and St James's Palace.[189] In 1537–8 Cromwell and several others were lodged at The Nete, which resulted in additional payments for horse fodder and bread for his spaniels.[190] More

---

183 Strype, *Ecclesiastical Memorials*, II.ii, 296.

184 *LP* XIII.ii, 457. The involvement of the Court of Augmentations was not new. On 19 March 1541 Robert Aragon was paid £4 for cages 'to put fowles in at the kinges house in Southwarke' and on the following day Robert Dytling received 17s 4d for making a seat for the privy garden at the same property: PRO E315/249, f. 41v.

185 This figure was broken down as follows: £28,676 3s 4d on Whitehall, £756 6s 5½d on St James's, £46 4s 5¾d on Durham Place, £118 14s 4¼d on Chelsea, £48 14s 5¼d on The Nete, £170 9s 8d on the Tower, £36 4¾d on Stockwell, £170 19s 8d on Hatfield, 42s 8d on Highbury, £24 15s 8½d on Covent Garden, £238 10¾d on Marylebone Park, £996 18s 3¾d on Hyde Park and £1,683 15s 3¾d on roads, gates and bridges [**B41**].

186 This sum is quite small when put in the context of the £376,500 that Henry spent from 1538 to 1539 on fortifications for the south coast, the northern border and Calais: see Starkey, 'Legacy of Henry VIII', 8.

187 *LP* XXI.i, 963.83.

188 BL Harley MS 1419, f. 444r. This section of the inventory is slightly unusual in that it dates from the second year of Edward VI's reign.

189 *LP* XIV.ii, 782 p. 333.   190 Ibid.

illuminating is a letter by John Husey to Lord Lisle dated 8 May 1539, about the city muster.[191] The muster processed from London to Westminster where they were seen by the king, and

> thence about the park where stood my lord Privy Seal and my lord of Oxford, at the back gate of the park which opens towards the Nete and so returned by St James and back again by Holborn and in by New Gate.

Other properties came to the king and then passed to Denny in his capacity as the newly appointed Keeper. In 1536 Henry gained Durham House by exchange with Bishop Tunstal.[192] Like The Nete, Hyde Park came from the Abbot of Westminster in 1538 and it formed part of the block of parkland running from the Whitehall Palace to Hampstead Heath.[193] Denny spent £996 18s 3¾d on Hyde Park [**B41**], which suggests that extensive work was required to make the park suitable for the king's hunting needs. He also created a new road from Charing Cross to Hyde Park, to provide access to St James's Palace.[194] In 1538 Henry acquired Hatfield from the Bishop of Ely, although according to the Augmentation accounts Denny was not appointed as Keeper until 1542.[195] Denny was also made Keeper of Waltham, of Covent Garden in the parish of St Margaret's Westminster and of the house and park at Marylebone.[196] In spite of Denny's work at Durham Place, the 1547 Inventory did not acknowledge his keepership although it did record his responsibility for the dissolved house of the Knights of St John at Clerkenwell.[197]

The Tower and Chelsea, in Middlesex, were also maintained, at least partially, by Denny. The Tower was the oldest royal residence in London and a number of men shared the responsibility for its care and maintenance. Denny's involvement was only on a fairly small scale and possibly confined to the royal apartments. In contrast, Chelsea was acquired from Lord Sandys by exchange in 1536 and was granted to Catherine Parr in 1544.[198] The accounts suggest that Denny maintained the house on her behalf.

While this list is extensive, Denny's remit extended even further. He also funded small projects at other properties where he had no official responsibility. In May 1542 Denny was given £100 as partial reimbursement of the money he had spent enclosing and paling a new park for the king's manor of Waltham.[199] A selection of bills and receipts from 1546 highlight this further. On 5 December Denny delivered £60 to Nicholas Dowsing for the king's gardens and orchards at the Palace of Greenwich.[200] Three days later he gave £40 to Sir Anthony Browne towards palings at Guildford.[201]

191 LP XIV.i, 941. Colvin does not make any reference to The Nete in HKW, IV.
192 HKW, IV, 76.
193 Marylebone manor house was rebuilt by Thomas Hobson c. 1500. In 1538 another Thomas Hobson surrendered the property to Henry VIII, who in turn passed it to Denny. Hobson received land on the Isle of Wight and around Southampton in return: see Saunders, Regent's Park, 150.
194 HKW, IV, 157.   195 LP XVII, app. 17.
196 Ibid.
197 The heading to the entry for Durham Place only refers to 'The Guarderobe stuff beyng the Kinges Majesties when he was Prince remaynyng at Duresham place in the Suburbes of London in the charge of [blank]': BL Harley MS 1419, f. 383r. For St John's, see PRO E321/44/45; also 'The Guarderobe at the house of Sayncte Johns nighe London in the charge of Sir Anthonye Denny knight keper of the house ther': BL Harley MS 1419, f. 368r.
198 HKW, IV, 64.
199 LP XVII, 354.   200 LP XXI.ii, 499
201 Ibid, 512.

TABLE 11

CLOTH ISSUED BY DENNY FROM WHITEHALL, 1542–7

This table is taken from Hayward, 'Possessions', 307, which is based on the summary of the dispersed cloth in the 1542 Inventory (E315/160, fos 139r–147r [**3774–3862**]).

Recipient	Cloth in yards (metres)	Cloth in English ells*	*Passementerie* in pounds and ounces (kilograms)
Henry VIII	7,114½, ½ nail (6,503)	2,607⅞	16lb 11oz (8.27)
Catherine Parr	1,101⅞ (1,001)	12	5lb 7oz (2.69)
Edward: as prince	58 (53)	408	—
Edward: as king	267½ (245)	—	—
The Lady Mary	1,505½ (1,376)	357⅝	3lb ½oz (1.5)
The Lady Elizabeth	1,004½, 1½ nail (918)	538⅝	8lb 5⅝oz and 4 parts of an ounce (4.12)
Lady Margaret Douglas	1,024¼ (937)	25	—
Earl of Lennox	86 (79)	—	—
Dorothy Bray	691¾ (632)	135⅛	—
Anne Basset	433⅛ (396)	159	—
TOTAL	13,287⅛yds (12,146m)	4,243¼ ells	33lb 8⅛oz and 4 parts of an ounce (16.58kg)

*   An English ell measured 45ins in length.
Measures in brackets are approximate metric equivalents

Although Denny was not made Groom of the Stool until 1546, the level of service he provided went beyond that associated with the office of a Keeper. His duties extended to the partial maintenance of Henry's daughters and more limited provision for the king's niece, Lady Margaret Douglas. Denny provided the Lady Mary with an annuity of £166 13s 4d [**B58**] delivered at Christmas and the feast of the Assumption. He also made provision for Anne Bassett and Dorothy Bray, two of the queen's attendants. Both women were given a bedstead and bedding as well as reasonable quantities of cloth (see Table 11).[202] On 26 January 1547 Hugh Aglionby, Collector of the Contribution for the Queen's Household, received £5 paid on behalf of Mistress Bassett by Denny's servant Cokrell.[203] This type of provision for close royal servants was not uncommon. A good example is provided by Will Somer, who served Henry VIII and Edward VI as the king's Fool. Edward VI spent £39 16s 10d on stuff for Will between 1550 and 1552.[204]

202 On 16 June 1542 Dorothy Bray was given a trussing bedstead [**465**], a counterpoint [**497**], a bed [**2360**], a bolster [**2361**], two pillows [**2362**], three quilts [**2364**], one pair of fustians [**2395**], two pairs of sheets [**2396**] and four pillow-beres [**2397**]. On an unspecified date in 1544–5 Anne Bassett received a trussing bedstead with apparel [**464**] and a counterpoint [**495**].

203 *LP* XXI.ii, 750.

204 PRO E101/426/8, m. 2r. This was far from unique. On 9 August 1567 Catherine, Duchess of Suffolk wrote to Sir William Cecil about Lady Mary Keys, a cousin of Elizabeth I, who had been placed in her care. The Duchess was particularly concerned by Mary's lack of possessions appropriate to her status, stating that 'she hath nothing but an old livery feather bed, all to-torn and full of patches, without either bolster or counterpane but two old pillows, the one longer than the other, an old quilt of silk, so torn as the cotton comes out of it': see Gunn, 'Running into the sand', 181.

Henry also paid for items for these five women (the queen, Lady Mary, Lady Elizabeth, Dorothy and Anne) [B52] and some of the goods within the 1542 Inventory were deployed to their benefit. Along with the queen and Prince Edward, they all received silks and linen from Whitehall. After Henry VIII's death, the Lady Elizabeth was provided with her own Wardrobe of the Beds, drawn from the palace's resources.[205]

On one level Denny was just part of the network of Keepers that cared for Henry VIII's property and possessions between 1509 and 1547 (Appendix III) Denny's organization and diligence suited him for this office but these qualities were not unique to him. Indeed, he actually shared these qualities with other equally valued royal officials such as William Gonson, keeper of the naval stores at Deptford and Erith.[206] His organization and diligence were not unique; rather, they were qualities he shared with other key royal servants. Sadly, his ability to cope with the pressures of office was not universal either – in 1544 William Gonson, acting Treasurer of the Navy, committed suicide when the strain of his job became too great.[207]

Denny combined the Keepership of the leading royal residence with his duties within the Privy Chamber, just as Sir William Compton and Henry Norris had. However, the scope of his responsibilities in relation to the king's possessions was unusually broad. Denny was Keeper of Whitehall during its subsequent royal development and he oversaw building work at a number of other properties. A special remit focusing around the Keepership was developed for him between 1542 and 1547. This remit was personal to him. It reflected Henry VIII's style of personal monarchy (Figure 10). After Henry's death in January 1547, the role of Keeper and the organization of the palace changed to meet the needs of the new king and his Privy Council.

Evidence for Denny's Keepership is rich in comparison with that for posts held by others in Henry's reign. The 1542 and 1547 inventories combine to present a highly detailed, indeed unique, view of the evolving charge of one office holder during the 1540s. The marginal notes of the 1542 Inventory allow Denny's lost book of extra to be recreated and in them this reveals how Denny's charge was broken up on Henry VIII's death. These inventories are supported by the presence of three documents that record Denny's discharge from office. The continuity of Denny's employment as Keeper at Whitehall into the reign of Edward VI, albeit in a revised and reduced format, mirrors the links between the 1542 and 1547 inventories. The distinct differences between Denny's charge in 1542 and his charge in the autumn of 1547 reflect the underlying qualities that he brought to the two successive regimes: he was understated but essential for Henry VIII, efficient yet expendable for Edward VI and the Duke of Somerset.

205 PRO E315/160, fos 151v–153v and entries **15259–15299** in the 1547 Inventory.
206 Gonson was both a skilled sailor and an administrator. In October 1536 he was put in charge of the ordnance issued to Charles Brandon, Duke of Suffolk, when the latter was sent to stop the Pilgrimage of Grace. When Gonson returned to the king's service, Suffolk commented that 'we lack him for both putting things in order and for council': *LP* XI.i, 1239.
207 Davies, 'Administration of the royal navy', 271. Almost a century later, in the summer of 1640 Abraham van der Doort took his own life, fearing that he had lost some of Charles I's miniatures and coins: see Millar, *Abraham van der Doort's Catalogue*, xvi.

V

THE DEVELOPMENT, MAINTENANCE AND DISPERSAL OF OBJECTS IN DENNY'S CHARGE

T HE WORKING LIFE of the 1542 Inventory and the processes whereby Henry VIII acquired and disposed of this group of his possessions are revealed by the marginalia written against most of the entries and the section of the Inventory that records new acquisitions. This insight into how the king used and disposed of his possessions raises the question of how Henry VIII had built up the substantial body of furnishings inventoried at his new palace in the thirteen and a half years between October 1529 and April 1542. This section seeks to provide an answer. Once the objects came into the king's possession and the hands of his keepers, they were subject to a range of processes. These included documentation, cleaning, repairs, general maintenance and packing prior to being placed in storage or in carts for transportation as the king removed from one property to the next. The marginalia indicates that a number of items were removed from Whitehall between 1542–6 and this must have been at the king's instigation. A further spate of items left the palace after Henry VIII's death and this had a marked effect on the charge held by the palace keeper.

The development of the palace's contents

THE EARLY PHASE   The earliest record of the furnishings at York Place is Wolsey's wardrobe book, which dates from December 1517 and includes items for both York Place and Hampton Court.[1] Items are recorded under thematic headings rather than in relation to a specific property, which suggests that most pieces were held in common rather than belonging to a dedicated Wardrobe. Exceptions include a set of 21 hangings and 14 window pieces depicting the story of Jacob and Joseph that were 'provided for the Galary in Yorkes places at Westminster', and a short list of items specifically described as being for York Place.[2] In addition, a number of items were 'not charged in any office' before 31 January 1523: twelve tables, forty-nine forms, twenty-four stools, thirty cupboards, nineteen pairs of trestles, forty-two standing beds, one fire screen, one pair of bellows and three paintings and one embroidery for the closet.[3] Possibly there were plans in 1523 to split the pieces between the Cardinal's two main houses. Less exciting, but equally likely, is the possibility that the office of Yeoman of the Wardrobe in Wolsey's household had been vacant for a while.

---

1   BL Harley MS 599. This section draws on Hayward, 'Possessions', 86–9.
2   BL Harley MS 599, f. 11v. This is entry **9719** in the 1547 Inventory.
3   BL Harley MS 599, fos 113r–114r.

While marginalia and additions indicate that the wardrobe book was in use until May 1529, the main sections all predate that time. This may partially explain the high number of hangings made from say[4] and similar, cheaper materials. This group included six pieces of 'beyond see say paned violette and yalow', hangings of buckram and a piece of dornix, a perquisite from the Privy Wardrobe.[5] It is possible that these say hangings were used to furnish the outermost rooms of Wolsey's York Place during the early part of his career and were replaced later with tapestry. No hangings made of say, dornick or buckram featured in the Inventories of 1542 or 1547 for this palace.

When Wolsey surrendered York Place, Hampton Court and The More, he also gave up his possessions to the king. However, Henry VIII took pity on Wolsey and sent him several cartloads of furnishings to decorate Cawood.[6] These were probably drawn from pieces used at York Place and Hampton Court, but after Wolsey's arrest and death in 1530, the pieces at Cawood would have reverted to the Crown. Some may have gone full circle and returned to serve at York Place.[7] It is difficult to make more than tentative links between tapestries listed in Wolsey's wardrobe book and those in the later inventories for Whitehall because the measurements are recorded differently: in Wolsey's wardrobe book the width and depth of each piece is recorded, mostly in yards but with a few instances in Flemish ells, while in the 1542 Inventory the area of each piece is given in square Flemish ells or yards. More certain are items bearing Wolsey's coat of arms or his cardinal's hat. The percentage of such items in the section of the Whitehall Wardrobe held by John Reed in 1547 was quite small, especially when compared to numbers at Hampton Court and The More.[8]

In 1529 Henry VIII acquired York Place and he may have augmented the furnishings that he acquired from Wolsey with holdings from the old Palace of Westminster. Although the privy palace had been destroyed, some of its furnishings had survived the fire of 1512. In 1515 John Pate was appointed as 'keeper of the wardrobe removed from Westminster to Richmond'.[9] However, it is not possible to tell if this Wardrobe survived for long. Items were also brought from other properties to enhance the new palace. In December 1529 the Clerk of the Closet spent 2s on boat hire to transfer goods from Greenwich to York Place.[10] In the following year Thomas Heneage was paid 11s 4d 'for sending twice to Greenwich for York place with a gret boat and 4 oars for divers pictures and the board that stood in the chamber over the library'.[11] Henry VIII also reserved a substantial quantity of Wolsey's confiscated domestic and chapel plate for use at York Place in 1530.[12]

4   Say was a fine cloth. It could be made entirely of silk, entirely of wool or from a combination of the two.
5   BL Harley MS 599, fos 23r–25r.
6   See Sylvester, ed., *Life of Wolsey*, 112, 236.
7   PRO E36/171 and Campbell, 'Cardinal Wolsey's tapestry collection', 131–4.
8   The deployment of sets or single tapestries with the cardinal's arms, as recorded in the 1547 Inventory, is as follows: two out of fifty-eight entries for tapestries (3.4 per cent) and one out of four entries for window pieces at Whitehall (25 per cent); fourteen out of eighty-two entries for tapestries (17 per cent) and one out of fourteen entries for window pieces at Hampton Court (7 per cent); and eleven out of twenty-eight entries for tapestries (39 per cent) and one out of three entries for window pieces at The More (33 per cent).
9   *LP* II.ii, 1002.
10 *PPE*, 14.
11 Ibid, 87.
12 *LP* IV.iii, 6184, p. 2769. It was predominantly gold and silver gilt. The rest was distributed between Hampton Court, Greenwich, The More and Windsor.

THOMAS ALVARD, 1530–5   When Henry VIII appointed Thomas Alvard as Keeper of York Place in 1530, the remit included augmenting the wardrobe holdings.[13] Alvard's accounts for the period 7 May 1531–21 April 1532 mentioned five warrants authorizing the purchase of:

> Riche Apparelles for bedsteedes beddes of downe with their boulsters / fyne mattresses / Pillowes / Fustyans / Sheetes / Pillowberis / Chayers / Cusshyns / Close Stoles / And bedsteedes / As also clothe of golde / clothe of Siluer / Veluet / Satten / Damaske / Taffeta Sarcenette and other.[14]

In all Alvard spent £2,759 13s 9d in ten months on building up the Wardrobe of the Beds and holdings of Italian silks.[15] He also received items from other Keepers including one gown, four doublets and four bonnets, delivered on 16 November 1534.[16] Although the memorandum does not state that these were for Whitehall, five of the items were very similar to objects listed in the 1542 Inventory.[17]

Alvard could look to the staff of the King's Works, as well as independent craftsmen, to make furniture for the new palace. An undated set of building accounts includes a payment of 20d to Nicholas Starkey, joiner, for 'wone pese of Sesoned Crabtre … spente as in making of Cogges and pynnes For … Chayres'.[18] These chairs were partially made by Robert Wilkins, turner, who was paid for the 'wode and Tornyng of viij pyllorse For ij Tornyng Chayres now In makyng To be sett upp In the low gallary'.[19] Other projects were much grander in scale, including 'the kinges grace bedde of Walnuttre', made by William Kendall.[20] It was an expensive project, with the decorative sections taking six carvers ten months to complete at a cost of £60, and a further £16 being spent on gilding. In January 1532 three further beds were painted and gilded at a total cost of 10s and eight decorative vanes were provided for the posts of two of these beds for 29s 4d. Eighteen rods for bed curtains were also supplied measuring 124ft and costing 32s 7d.[21]

The privy purse accounts for 1529–32 reveal what the king was buying, but not for which residence they were intended for. However, as the purchases coincide with Henry's acquisition of York Place and the years immediately following, it is likely that this new property was the focus of his attention. Many of the items bought with money from the privy purse were physically small and were of a type that had not been readily available in the previous century: such objects might have included maps, clocks, scientific instruments, musical instruments, glassware and ceramics. From this list, maps, clocks and musical instruments all appear in the privy purse accounts. The number of items which Henry acquired and the amount he spent may reflect what was offered to him for sale as much as what he wanted to have. He bought only one map or plat, of Rye and Hastings from Vincent Volpe for £3 10s.[22] In contrast he purchased at least twenty-three clocks and four dials from

13   LP IV.iii, 6301.20.
14   PRO E351/3322, p. 3. The first warrant was dated 2 July, the second, third and fourth 24 March and the fifth 5 August.
15   Ibid.
16   BL Royal MS 7 F.XIV, f. 124r (LP VII, 1432).   17   Entries 16–20.
18   Baker, 'Extracts from royal accounts', 102.
19   Ibid, 108.   20   PRO E101/425/14.
21   PRO E36/252, pp. 581, 606; see also p. 607.
22   PPE, 91. See also Auerbach, 'Vincent Volpe', 222–7. Auerbach suggests that 'A Platt for the making the Hauen of Dover' was the work of Volpe: ibid, 225.

TABLE 12

THE ORGANIZATION OF TEXTILE FURNISHINGS AT
THE PALACE OF WHITEHALL, 1542–7

This table is taken from Hayward, 'Possessions', 267, 274–5; some of the original figures have been corrected.

Object	Denny: 1542 Whitehall (PRO E315/160)*	Denny: 1547 Whitehall (PRO E315/160)**	Denny: 1547 Whitehall (BL Harley MS 1419)	Reed: 1547 Whitehall (BL Harley MS 1419)	Rufforth: 1547 Whitehall (BL Harley MS 1419)
Altar cloths and frontals	24	24	—	8	—
Arras	21 pieces	33 pieces	—	39 pieces	—
Beds and bolsters	—	14 beds 13 bolsters	4 beds 4 bolsters	26 beds 26 bolsters	—
Bedsteads with apparel	37	38	—	6	—
Bedsteads without apparel	2	2	—	4	2
Carpets	101	101	—	71	1
Celures and testers	19	21	—	6	19, plus 1 tester and 5 apparels
Chairs	87	95	—	21	—
Close stools	14	15	—	1	—
Cloths of estate	11	12	—	3	—
Corporal cases	2	8	—	2	—
Counterpoints	24	34	4	30	4
Coverpanes	15	21	—	—	24
Cupboard cloths	4	9	—	3	4
Curtains	8 bed 69 window	8 bed 101 window	— sundry window	— 7 window	—
Cushions	248	286	—	53	3
Dorses and redorses	—	5 pairs	—	—	—
Foot stools	24	82	8	8	—
Fustians	1 single —	1 single 1 pair	—	— 14 pairs	—
Hangings, including window pieces	54	55	—	—	—
Napkins	62	307	—	—	228
Pillows	10	20	5	6	8
Pillow-beres	29 single 35 pairs	33 single 35 pairs	— —	19 single 30 pairs	9 single —

TABLE 12 (continued)

Object	Denny: 1542 Whitehall (PRO E315/160)*	Denny: 1547 Whitehall (PRO E315/160)**	Denny: 1547 Whitehall (BL Harley MS 1419)	Reed: 1547 Whitehall (BL Harley MS 1419)	Rufforth: 1547 Whitehall (BL Harley MS 1419)
Quilts	3	10	—	4	—
Scarlets	2	2	—	—	—
Sheets	23 single 66 pairs	23 single 78 pairs	5 single 5 pairs	16 single 48 pairs	16 single 34 pairs
Sparvers	1	1	—	8	—
Stained cloths	10	13	11	—	—
Stools	46	56	4	10	—
Tablecloths	32	40	—	—	50
Tapestries, including window pieces	100 pieces	114 pieces	—	234 pieces	—
Towels	32	55	—	—	55
Traverses	6	7	—	2	—
Verdures	191	213	17 pieces	3	—
Vestments	36	44	—	7	—

*   Items recorded in 1542 when the Inventory was compiled.

**   Includes items acquired between 1542–6 and recorded at the back of the 1542 Inventory, and also the possessions of Jane Seymour, Catherine Howard, Lady Rochford and the dowager Duchess of Norfolk, but excludes the items in Elizabeth's Wardrobe of the Beds.

a number of individuals.[23] Vincent Keney presented a bill of £19 16s 8d for eleven clocks and three dials, whilst Anthony Anthony received £10 10s for a clock in a gold case. In all the king spent £119 9s on clocks.[24] Henry also acquired musical instruments including, shawms, virginals, sackbuts and rebecs, at a cost of £44.[25]

This phase of the palace's development also coincided with the later stages of Henry VIII's quest for the annulment of his marriage to Catherine of Aragon. As a consequence of this, Henry started to acquire theological texts. Most were former monastic books – from Romsey, Sempringham and Evesham – and they were delivered directly to the king. It seems likely that they were collected at York Place.[26] Others were new volumes, including the consignments of books delivered by the king's printer to York Place and Hampton Court in December 1530 and in January 1532 respectively.[27]

23   *PPE*, 91, 161.
24   Ibid, 91, 161. Henry VIII actually spent more than this, but as the prices for individual items were not given on the bill for £50 7s 4d which John Lengar submitted in 1530, it is not possible to include the two clocks he supplied: ibid, 51.
25   Ibid, 25, 26, 37, 110, 114, 131, 169, 187, 201, 210.
26   Ibid, 106, 109, 116, 190; Carley, 'John Leland and English pre-Dissolution libraries: Lincolnshire', 335, 341.
27   Ibid, 101, 189.

ANTHONY DENNY, 1536–47   A list of unappointed furnishings made in May 1540 provides a hint of the quality of the palace Wardrobe before 1542.[28] Arras, tapestry, verdure and bed hangings predominated. Of these, some were new and some had been acquired by confiscation from the Marquess of Exeter, Sir Nicholas Carew and Lord Montague. Other pieces had been brought to the palace from elsewhere, such as the 'perle bed whiche of late cam from Grenewiche and bought of Pierre Conyn'.[29] A few entries were described as 'ollde stuf' and this group included 'a bed called the kinges bed'.[30] Additional beds included one for the queen and 'a Newe bed of riche arras called my lord princes his bed whiche was bought of Petar van de Wall'.[31]

The relative dearth of documentation earlier than 1542 leaves one unprepared for the wealth of the palace's Wardrobe holdings charged to Denny. They included 248 cushions, eighty-seven chairs, eleven cloths of estate, thirty-seven bedsteads with apparel and 366 hangings of tapestry, arras, verdure and silk (see Table 12). Prior to the dispersals in 1547 these figures had increased slightly: a further thirty-eight cushions, twenty-eight window curtains, fifty-eight footstools and 245 napkins were listed. The palace also received the goods of two of Henry's wives. Ralph Worsley delivered 'Certeigne apparell and other Stuff of sondry kindes some tyme apperteignyng to Quene Jane' [2095–2259]. Later the closet stuff of Catherine Howard arrived, in addition to goods owned by the Duchess of Norfolk and 'the Late Lady Rocheford' [2260–2287, 2288–2347, 2348–2350], who were both implicated in her downfall. By 1547 Jane Seymour's clothes and those few items of Henry's attire kept at Whitehall were described as 'Stuff in Tholde Juelhous at Westminster in the Chardge of James Rufforth'.[32]

It is possible to examine the rate of the growth in the palace's contents by comparing the quantity of objects in 1542 and 1547 (see Table 13). Although the two Inventories did not have the same remit, many sections of the 1547 Inventory so clearly build on the 1542 document that comparisons can be made. After just twelve years,[33] the holdings of paintings, embroideries, glass and musical instruments were well developed. Within the next five years, the selection of glass and ceramics had nearly doubled and the holding of clocks increased by well over 300 per cent. The numbers of maps and mirrors also demonstrated a healthy increase (54 per cent and 120 per cent respectively). Other groups, such as paintings and embroideries, stained cloths and terracottas, saw smaller increases of 10–15 per cent. These figures suggest that the main impetus for developing the palace came during the 1530s and early 1540s, when it was Henry's main building project.

Unfortunately, the 1542 Inventory does not include the studies and closets of the privy lodging and so it is not possible to assess how well equipped they were at that time. Evidence from another source indicates how these rooms gradually filled up: in 1535 Henry VIII celebrated Christmas and the New Year at Greenwich and remained there for the whole of January.[34] On 13 January 1536 a list was prepared of 'parcels delivered by the King's commandment by Mr Norris at Westminster'.[35] The

28 BL Royal MS 7C.XVI, fos 60r–64r (*LP* XV, 686).
29 BL Royal MS 7C.XVI, f. 61v.   30 Ibid.
31 Ibid, fos 61v, 61r.
32 BL Harley MS 1419, f. 159r. The attribution of the clothes to Jane Seymour and the late king was not made in the 1547 Inventory but it is possible to identify them by comparing the text of the two inventories.
33 October 1529–April 1542.
34 PRO OBS 1/1419, f. 55v.   35 *LP* VIII, 44.

TABLE 13

THE DEVELOPMENT OF DISCRETE GROUPS OF
OBJECTS AT WHITEHALL, 1542–7

This table is taken from Hayward, 'Possessions', 279.

Object	Number in 1542 Inventory*	Number in 1547 Inventory**
Clocks	10	47 (370% increase)
Glass and ceramics	404	797 (97% increase)
Maps	24	37 (54% increase)
Mirrors	25	55 (120% increase)
Musical instruments	173	378 (118% increase)
Paintings and embroideries	157	182 (15% increase)
Stained cloths	10	11 (10% increase)
Terracottas	13	15 (15% increase)

* These figures reflect Denny's initial charge and do not include items acquired between 1542 and 1546.

** These figures do not include the objects re-recorded a second time in 1549 and 1550, nor items added since 1547.

items included plate, books, carpets and recorders. This particular assortment of objects, together with the date, suggests that these are New Year's gifts being integrated with the king's possessions. The well-stocked studies and closets at the palace suggest that this was a regular practice throughout the reign, regardless of where Henry had actually received his gifts.

An important part of Denny's office was to receive and record new items coming into the palace. The record of the library in 1542 presents the accumulation of books up to that point, but the process of accumulation did not cease at that date. Although no new titles were recorded in the back of the Inventory, other documents reveal the type of acquisitions that were being made. The king's printer delivered a number of books to the palace during 1543.[36] On 11 May Mr James received a great book of paper, 'imperial bound after the fashion of Venice' and another bound 'after the Italian fashion', while on 30 December five board-bound copies of Cicero's *Officiis* and 'one gorgeously gilded for the king' were handed to Mr Jones.[37] These records are interesting for two reasons: they provide details of the type of paper and binding used for the king's books, which were rarely recorded in the 1542 Inventory; and, as mentioned above,[38] they show that Denny used his own servants to collect these items. By 1542 the library at Westminster held over 900 volumes;[39] but while it was the largest royal library, it should not be seen in isolation. At Hampton Court there were 'a greate nombre of bookes' (**12262**), in addition to those at Greenwich (**9668–9678**), Windsor (**13224**) and Beddington (**14026**).

36 *LP* XVIII.ii, 211.
37 See Carley, 'Greenwich and Henry VIII's royal library', 158–9.
38 *LP* XVIII.ii, 211.

39 Entries **2398–3305**.

TABLE 14

ADDITIONS TO DENNY'S CHARGE, 1542–6

Item	Quantity
Andirons	1 pair
Arras	12 pieces
Barehides	2
Beds	2
Bolsters	1
Bowls: pewter	2
Bowls: wood	3
Boxes for the Host	1
Cases	1
Chairs	8
Cisterns for close stools	1
Close stools	1
Cloths of estate	1
Corporal cases	1
Counterpoints	2
Curtains	28
Cushions	38
Damasks	2
Fire forks	1
Fire pans	3
Footstools	58
Forms	1
Halberds	10
Hangings	1

Item	Quantity
Hearths	1
Lutes	3
Maps	3
Passementerie	5lb 2oz
Pillows	6
Plate: gold	3oz
Plate: gilt	1,493⅝oz
Plate: parcel gilt	1,014¼oz
Plate: white	3,359oz
Quilts	4
Rakes	1
Regals	1
Ropes for candlesticks	3
Sables	3 timbers
Stained cloths	3
Stools	10
Tables	3
Tapestry	14 pieces
Textiles: linen	1,501⅛ ells
Textiles: silk	8,131yds
Toasting forks	1
Tongs	1 pair
Verdure	22 pieces
Viols	7

The development process was continuous. Between 13 June 1542 and 13 October 1546 Denny paid for and received a wide variety of new furnishings along with 8,131yds (8,393m) of silk cloth (see Table 14). Impressive as this list is, the details recorded in the 1542 Inventory were not comprehensive. A number of purchases made by Denny for Whitehall and other properties were not given in the Inventory but can be traced via other sources. In 1545 he was involved in the purchase of holland cloth at 12*d* the ell for two quilts 'for the knyghtes beddes' and carded wool to stuff them, along with making and carriage to Windsor, as well as two Spanish blankets at 12s each.[40] He also ordered twenty-six fine ticks for pallets, twelve counterpoints and fifty pairs of sheets for the Wardrobe in June 1546.[41]

Quite a substantial group of items entered Denny's charge between 1542 and 1547. The purchases were recorded in forty-six entries detailing the objects, the supplier or maker and the delivery date (but not the price).[42] The entries indicate that Henry took a keen personal interest in the purchasing, as a number of entries are described as 'Stuff bought by the kinges Majestie … And the same delyverid in charge vnto the said Anthony Denny'.[43] Suppliers included Philip van der Wilder, Keeper of the King's Instruments, and the Florentine, Anthony Carsidony. Twelve of the deliveries were of 'stuff new made by the kyng his highnes commaundement'[44] but unfortunately the makers were not named. It is likely that they were drawn from the group of craftsmen retained by the Crown within the Great Wardrobe and the King's Works. Initially, at least, these pieces were intended for Whitehall and they included substantial quantities of silk and some linen cloth.[45] The textile purchases can be grouped by regnal years as follows: 1542–3 (anno 34) over 625 ells (714.38m) of linen and 1,487yds (1,359.71m) of silk; 1543–4 (anno 35) over 808 ells (923.54m) and 4,913yds (4,490.43m); 1543–5 (anno 35–6) 1,957yds (1,788.7m); and 1544–5 (anno 36) over 849yds (775.99m). This included a little over 12 ells (13.72m) of cambric delivered by Heneage in June 1543, which may have been bought for shirts [3475].

In contrast to this substantial group of purchases, only one gift is identified – a map or 'discription of Florence vpon stayned cloth' [3471] which was '[g]euon to the king his highnes by Anthony Carsidony'.[46] Equally, just one of the entries relates to a confiscation: a table from Thomas Cromwell's house at the Austin Friars.[47] It was 'a Table of Sypers with a border rounde a boute of beyonde See Elme colorid blac with a playne frame of Oke' [3472]. This is the table that Stephen Vaughan encouraged Cromwell to buy in 1529 by describing it as 'the netest pece of worke that I haue seyn'.[48] Not surprisingly, it also appealed to Henry and in 1547 the table still formed part of Denny's charge (10821). Denny also received a few good-quality ex-monastic pieces from the Court of Augmentations: a suit of cloth of gold vestments from Rewley and six yards of cloth of gold from Abingdon valued at £20 and further pieces valued at £26 13s 4d.[49]

A rather odd selection of items came from Hampton Court: two fire pans, three wooden bowls and ten halberds. More significant were the deliveries that came from other sections of Whitehall, including the secret jewel house: the items included plate, sables, stained cloths and linen. Bristow was named once as the intermediary who delivered the items to Denny and this may have been the norm.

---

40 *LP* Add. I.ii, 1724.
41 *LP* XXI.i, 1165.74.
42 Five of the deliveries came from the secret jewel house at Whitehall, and so represent a movement of materials within the palace rather than new purchases.
43 PRO E315/160, f.121r.   44 Ibid.
45 PRO E315/160, fos 120v–134v.
46 Ibid, f.127r.
47 Ibid, 'recyvid from the late Erle of Essex house in London'. Within the main text of the Inventory there were the lists of items confiscated from Lady Rochford and the Duchess of Norfolk.
48 PRO SP1/55, f.68r (*LP* IV.iii, 5860).   49 *LP* XIII.ii, 457.

Housekeeping practices – from an itinerant household to standing houses

In August 1525 Sir Henry Guildford wrote to Wolsey explaining that the Cofferer had left a book of household statutes signed by the king in London on his departure for Sussex.[50] He added that 'Until the king comes to his standing house none can get at them but himself [the Cofferer]'. According to the king's itinerary, which is patchy for this period, Henry was at Windsor on 31 July and Hunsdon on 20 August.[51] The standing house referred to was surely Greenwich. The king had spent a lot of time there between November 1524 and April 1525 and it was his leading residence. Guildford's letter illustrates that the term 'standing house' was in use during the first half of Henry's reign, but the definition is less clear.

By 1603 the situation had developed significantly. In that year Giovanni Carlo Scaramelli, the Venetian ambassador, wrote to the Doge and Senate. He referred to eight English royal properties as standing houses: Greenwich, Hampton Court, Oatlands, Richmond, St James's, Eltham, Somerset House and Whitehall.[52] What identified these properties as standing houses for Scaramelli was that each had its own complete Wardrobe and that the furnishings were not lent out. This is slightly different to the earlier idea of a house being left partially or fully furnished during the owner's absence. Both definitions will now be considered in the face of the available evidence.

Not surprisingly, the evidence from Denny's inventory is contradictory. On the one hand, he had far too much stuff in his charge to even consider moving it all on a regular basis. On the other hand, he had 423 ells (483.49m) of linen canvas to cover the bedsteads while standing [526], which strongly suggests that the main beds were not dismantled. This forms a marked contrast with the entries for Greenwich and Hampton Court in the 1547 Inventory, where there were no standing bedsteads in the bedchambers of either palace. More ambiguously, Denny had a generous supply of packing materials, including 192 cases for cushions [416–418] and sixty-nine cases for chairs [419], that could have been used to protect items either while in storage or while being transported. The most likely reason for these contradictions is that Henry VIII's reign represents the start of the transition from an itinerant royal household, carrying most of its wealth with it, to a monarchy that predominantly travelled between a group of permanently furnished properties located in the valley of the River Thames.

Before considering the change to housekeeping practices that this transition brought about, it is worth establishing the wider context for the situation at Whitehall. Henry VIII was assisted in the development of a group of standing houses with dedicated Wardrobes by the vast influx of furnishings which came into his possession during the 1530s and 1540s.[53] By 1547, the king's Wardrobes had impressive holdings: ninety-seven decorative bedsteads with apparel, 638 carpets, 239 chairs, 687 cushions, 311 counterpoints and 1,264 pieces of tapestry.[54] This greatly reduced the need to pack everything each time the king removed and large bedsteads, which often required a blacksmith to assemble them, could be left *in situ*. In tandem with this increase in holdings, the development of specialist rooms with particular contents made it increasingly impractical to transport even a

---

50 *LP* IV.i, 1572. The following paragraphs draw on Hayward, 'Possessions', 98–101.
51 PRO OBS 1/1419, f. 35v.
52 *CSP Venetian*, X, 102.
53 Henry acquired the furnishings mainly by confiscation and purchase: see Hayward, 'Possessions', 62–7, 73–9.
54 These figures do not include items in the Wardrobes of the king's children: see Table 18 (below, p. 138).

fraction of the king's goods when he removed. It was far simpler to create another group of these specialist rooms at each of his greater houses: prior to the late fifteenth and early sixteenth centuries the number and range of available luxury goods was quite small, but improved trade routes and the influence of ideas associated with the Renaissance resulted in a much greater diversity of objects, including maps, scientific instruments, musical instruments, glassware, printed books, ceramics and medals.[55] Thus at the time of Henry VIII's death there were armouries, libraries, long galleries and a selection of studies and closets at Whitehall, Greenwich and Hampton Court, all specialist rooms unknown in the time of Henry's father. Henry VIII also established four local jewel houses, in addition to that at the Tower, necessitated and facilitated by his growing holdings of plate.

To return to Whitehall: shortly after Edward VI's accession, a payment of 49s was made to Philip Manwaring, Gentleman Usher of the Chamber, and eight others,

> for hanging the Kinges majesties halle at his palais of Westminster, with my lorde
> Protector's lodginges, and diverse other lodginges for the counsaille, for the space of
> three dayes, against the Kinges highnes repairing thither from Hampton courte.[56]

As the king's apartments were not included in the list of rooms to be prepared, it suggests that they have been partially furnished and that Whitehall was gradually developing as a standing house. If this suggestion is correct, there should be evidence of subtle changes in how the household staff cared for the objects in their charge. Such changes in household practices were linked in part to the gradual decline, during the course of the sixteenth century, of the pre-eminence of textile furnishings, which were easy to pack and transport by a peripatetic household. These textiles were replaced by large, ornate pieces of furniture.[57] Medieval inventories list simple seat furniture, such as forms and stools, but by the seventeenth century a wide variety of seating was available. Bedsteads also became increasingly large and complex, such as a bed made for James II in 1688 and now at Knole and William III's bed of 1701 at Hampton Court.[58] As furniture developed in these ways, pieces were left 'standing' rather than being dismantled for storage or packed and moved to the next property with the household.

CANVAS TO COVER BEDSTEADS   In 1542 the Wardrobe at Whitehall contained 'sondrie peces of olde Canvas being cutt and sowed togethers to cover bedstedes <standing> and beddes of downe' containing 423 ells of fabric (483.49m) [526]. Five years later this was split between Whitehall (142½ ells) (162.88m), Windsor (190½ ells) (217.74m), the Tower (27½ ells) (31.43m), The More (24½ ells) (28m) and Edmund Pigeon, clerk of the wardrobes (38 ells) (43.43m). In addition, Nonsuch had six pieces of Normandy canvas for covering beds (12994), there were two covers at Woodstock (13331) and one at Greenwich (9376).[59] This indicates that by the last decade of the

---

55 See Jardine, *Worldly Goods*.
56 Nichols, *Literary Remains*, I, p. xcvi.
57 Thornton, *Interior Decoration*, esp. ch. 7.
58 A sense of scale is provided by two of the bedsteads at Holyrood Palace. The red damask bedstead, *c.* 1680, is 3.35m high, 2.28m wide and 1.98m long. The overall mattress size is 1.93m long by 1.52m wide. The red and yellow velvet bed 1682 is 4.07m high including plumes, 1.78m wide and 2.78m long. For further details see Swain, *Tapestries and Textiles*, 66–7.
59 See also (12995–12996) and (13329–13330).

reign, the king's bedsteads were being left standing at Whitehall when the palace was empty, while other, smaller, items were packed away.

After Henry's death the practice of leaving some bedsteads standing in the king's absence was extended. A substantial quantity of canvas was sent to Windsor in September 1547, and this was probably enough to cover the five sumptuous beds sent at the same time. The Wardrobes at the Tower and The More also received enough canvas to cover one large bedstead or several mattresses, as did Edmund Pigeon, Clerk of the Wardrobes [**526**].[60] While the supplies at Whitehall were limited, the basis on which the decision as to which property should receive fabric from the Great Wardrobe – with Hampton Court, Oatlands and Richmond all excluded – is not clear. Lengths of canvas for the specific purpose of covering bedsteads or mattresses do not appear in the other Wardrobes, apart from those mentioned initially, but this may just be a feature of the records, which seem to omit packing materials.[61] In addition, the Removing Wardrobe contained 'foure paier and one Sheete to hange aboute the kinges highnes bedde' (**14169**), which could have acted as sun curtains.

Unfortunately, the 1547 Inventory does not confirm the use of the canvas bed-covers. Several bedrooms were described – the king's bedchamber at Greenwich and the first bedchamber, the next bedchamber (both in the king's apartments), the queen's bedchamber and the king's bedchamber on the queen's side at Hampton Court – but none of them was furnished with a bedstead.[62] Indeed the only room to contain a bed was the bathroom at Greenwich, which had 'a Trussing bedstedde in the walle … having Ceeler and tester of blewe and yellowe sarcenet' (**9653**). This suggests that during the early months of Edward's minority beds were not kept fully assembled in the king's absence, even at these leading palaces. Or possibly there were standing beds, which were uncovered (accounting for the canvas still being in the Wardrobe), in rooms excluded from the remit of the 1547 Inventory.

Bedsteads were certainly moved on occasion, such as for Henry's trip to France in 1532 and the reception of Anne of Cleves in 1540. By 1547 several of the Wardrobes had special leather cases in which to pack the various components of a bedstead. Of these, the Tower had received one from Whitehall (**9259**), while Woodstock had been given eighteen (**13320–13327**); none was left at Whitehall. The evidence suggests that the king's houses were in a state of transition in 1547.

THE USE OF PROTECTIVE GREEN CLOTHS   Wooden furniture, panelling and decorative carving gradually change colour when exposed to direct sunlight for prolonged periods: dark woods such as ebony fade, while pale woods such as lime darken. Equally, polished surfaces dull with use and can become scratched. The 1547 Inventory indicates that tables, stools, benches and cupboards were left out in a number of the rooms at Whitehall, Hampton Court and Greenwich, even though the decorative textiles had been removed. However, they were generally kept covered with green cloth, an idea borrowed from the *domus providencie*.

60 This assessment of the coverage is based on the entry in the Woodstock Wardrobe for 'twoe canvasses of Soultewiche to couer bedstedes either of them beinge of iij bredthes of soultewiche and in length xij yardes the pece' (**13331**). Each cover contained 36yds (32.9m).

61 Some of the Wardrobes, including that at Richmond, did have large quantities of saltwich, a type of canvas, which may have been used in this way (for instance, **13663**).

62 In contrast, at Leeds Castle in May 1532 celures and testers appeared in twelve, and featherbeds and bolsters in sixteen, of the rooms mentioned: see PRO SP1/70, fos 90r–94r (*LP* V, 1064).

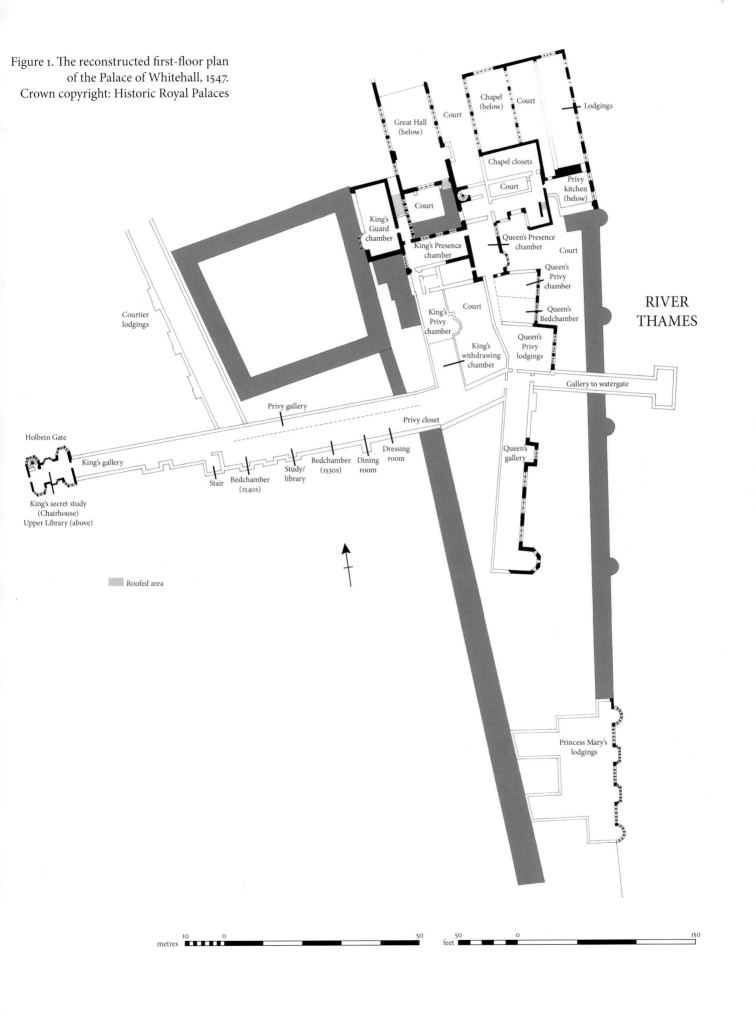

Figure 1. The reconstructed first-floor plan
of the Palace of Whitehall, 1547.
Crown copyright: Historic Royal Palaces

Great Hall
(below)

Court

Chapel
(below)

Court

Lodgings

Chapel closets

Court

King's
Guard
chamber

Court

Privy
kitchen
(below)

King's Presence
chamber

Queen's Presence
chamber

Court

Queen's
Privy
chamber

King's
Privy
chamber

Court

Queen's
Bedchamber

RIVER
THAMES

King's
withdrawing
chamber

Queen's
Privy
lodgings

Courtier
lodgings

Gallery to watergate

Privy gallery

Privy closet

Queen's
gallery

Holbein Gate

King's gallery

Dressing
room

Stair

Bedchamber
(1540s)

Study/
library

Bedchamber
(1530s)

Dining
room

King's secret study
(Chairhouse)
Upper Library (above)

Roofed area

Princess Mary's
lodgings

metres 10 0   50   feet 50   0   150

Figure 2. Henry VIII reading. From Henry VIII's Psalter,
MS Royal A.XVI.f3. By permission of The British Library

Figure 3 (opposite). Section of the copperplate map attributed to
Ralph Agas showing the suburb of Westminster, 1560–70.
Corporation of London, Guildhall Library, Aldermanbury, London

S. Iemes Parke

Charingcrosse

The Courte gate

The Courte

Preuy bridge

Chanon row

Westmynster hall

Starre Chamber

Westmynster

The Quee nts bridge

The olde Palace

Kinges Streate

The Lambeht

Figure 4. View of the Palace of Whitehall from the River
Thames by Anthonis van den Wyngaerde, 1558–62.
By permission of the Ashmolean Museum, Oxford

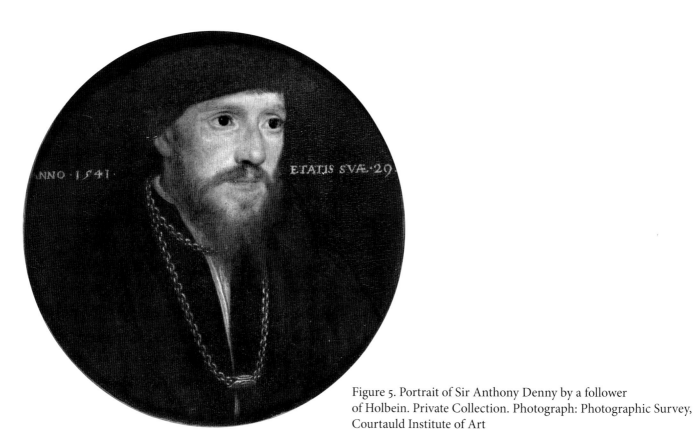

Figure 5. Portrait of Sir Anthony Denny by a follower
of Holbein. Private Collection. Photograph: Photographic Survey,
Courtauld Institute of Art

Figure 6. Engraving of the portrait of Sir Anthony Denny after a follower of Holbein. Private Collection.
Photograph: Photographic Survey, Courtauld Institute of Art

Figure 7. Engraving by Wenceslaus Hollar of the portrait of
Sir Anthony Denny after a follower of Holbein. Private Collection

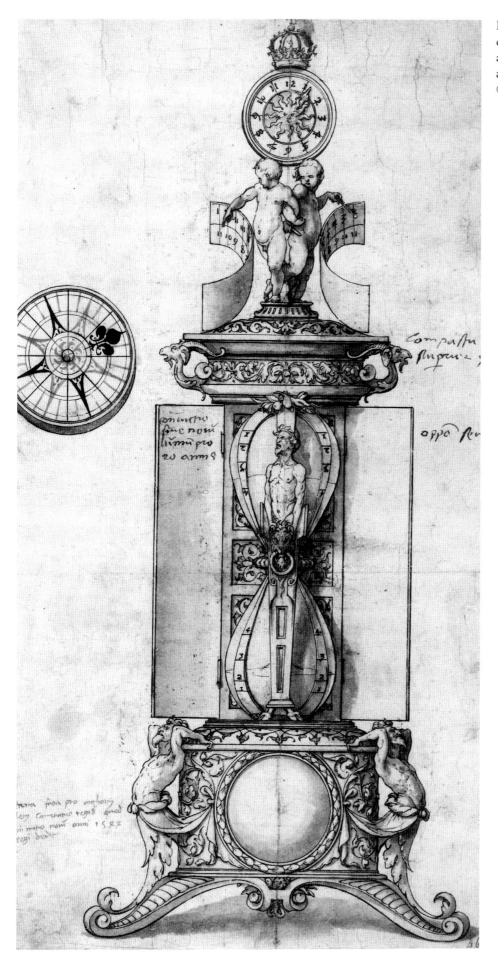

Figure 8. Design by Holbein for a clock salt given by Denny to Henry VIII as a New Year's gift. Department of Prints and Drawings, British Museum © Copyright The British Museum

Figure 9. Miniature of Jacob Fugger 'the Rich', the Emperor's banker, with Matthäus Schwarz, his chief accountant, 1519 Their close working relationship appears to have resembled that of Denny and Bristow. Reproduced by permission of the Herzog Anton Ulrich-Museum, Brunswick, Germany

Figure 10. The family of Henry VIII by an unknown artist, *c.* 1545.
The Royal Collection © 2001, Her Majesty Queen Elizabeth II

Figure 11. Edward VI, attributed to Guilliam Stretes. The Royal Collection © 2001, Her Majesty Queen Elizabeth II

Figure 12. Edward Seymour, Duke of Somerset, Lord Protector,
by an unknown artist, 1547–9. Reproduced by permission from
the collection of the Marquess of Bath, Longleat House.
Photograph: Photographic Survey, Courtauld Institute of Art

Figure 13 (opposite). The first folio of the 1542
Inventory of the Palace of Whitehall, E315/160.
By permission of the Public Record Office, Kew

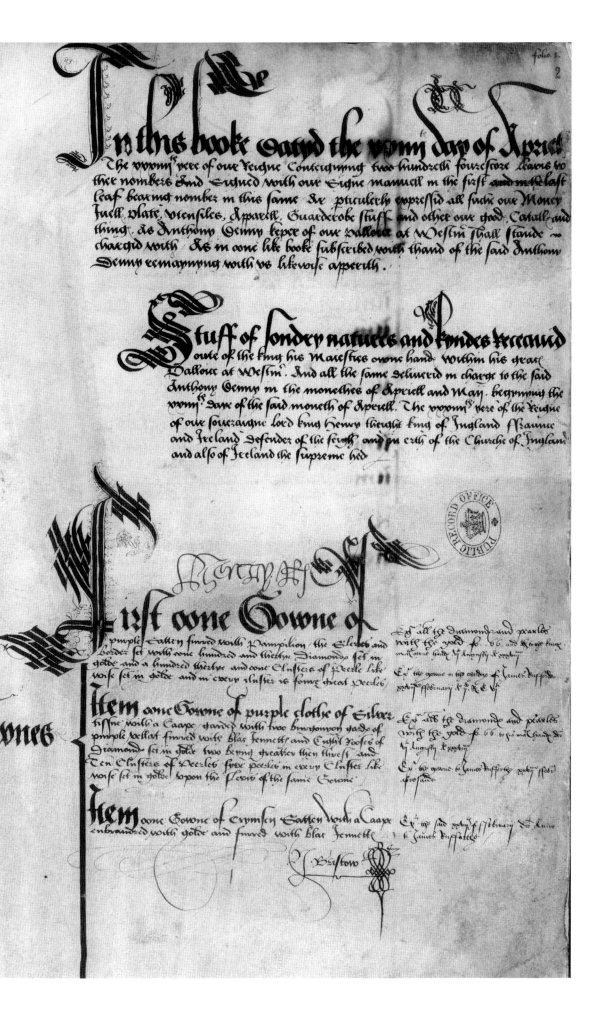

The

In this booke dated the xxviijth day of Aprill
The xxxviijth yere of oure Reigne Conteigninge two hundreth fourescore leaves by
thre nombers And Sealed with oure Signe manuell in the first and in the last
leaf bearing nomber in this same Be particulerly expressid all suche oure Money
Juell, plate, vtensiles, Apparell, Guarderobe stuff and other oure good Catall and
thing. As Anthony Denny keper of oure Pallaice at Westm shall stande
chaegid with As in oone like booke subscribed with thand of the said Anthony
Denny remayning with vs likewise appeereth.

Stuff of sondry natures and kyndes receaued
oute of the king his Maiesties owne hand within his great
Pallaice at Westm. And all the same deliuered in charge to the said
Anthony Denny in the monethes of Aprill and May. begynning the
xxviijth daye of the said moneth of Aprill. The xxxviijth yere of the Reigne
of oure soueraigne lord king Henry theight king of Jngland Fraunce
and Ireland Defender of the feyth, and in erth of the Churche of Jngland
and also of Ireland the supreme hed

Gownes

First oone Gowne of
purple Satten furred with Tampilion the Sleves and
border set with oone hundred and thirtye Diamondes set in
golde and a hundred thirtye and oone Clusters of Peerle like
wise set in golde and in every cluster is fower great peerles

Item oone Gowne of purple clothe of Siluer
tissue with a Caape garded with two burdeures gards of
purple velvet furred with blac Jennetts and Eight Roses of
Diamondes set in golde two beyng greatter then threst and
Ten Clusters of Peerles fyve peerles in every Cluster like
wise set in golde vpon the Pleits of the same Gowne

Item oone Gowne of Crymsey Satten with a Caape
embraudered with golde and furred with blac Jennette

Ex all the diamonds and pearles
with the golde so 66 and by two knyt
my Lorde Gard by Legenty & xxviij

Ex the gowne in ty chardge of James Rufford
whij February Ao 5 E £ vj

Ex all the diamonds and pearles
with the golde so 66 to his wch chardge by
by Legenty & xxviij

Ex tw gowne by James Rufforde whij February
Ao saide

Ex ij the said pohy of February Ao kuin
by James Rufforde

Berstow

Figure 14. Detail from the 1542 Inventory, the watermark, E315/160.
By permission of the Public Record Office, Kew

Figure 15. Detail from the 1542 Inventory showing
Nicholas Bristow's signature, E315/160.
By permission of the Public Record Office, Kew

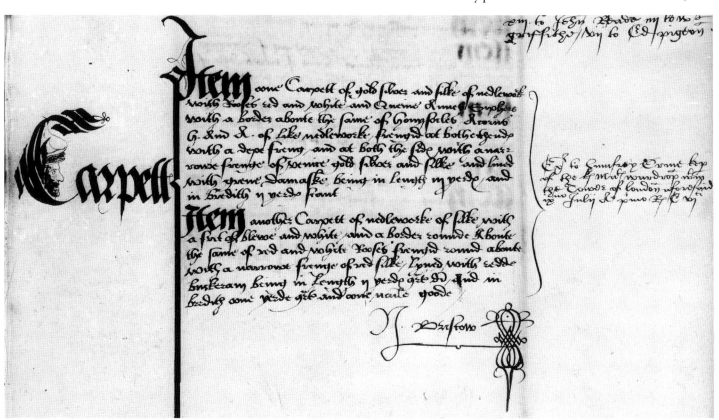

TABLE 15

THE CORRELATION BETWEEN MATERIALS, SUBJECT
AND THE PROVISION OF CURTAINS FOR 'TABLES WITH PICTURES'

	Classical	Narrative	Portraiture	Religious	Total
Alabaster	—	—	—	1	1
Embroidery	—	—	—	4	4
Mother-of-pearl	—	—	—	1	1
Painting on panel	2	1	42	10	55
TOTALS	2	1	42	16	61

The Board of the Greencloth, so named because the table round which they met was covered with a green wool cloth, ran the royal kitchens. Similar cloths were provided, seemingly as a symbol of authority, for clerks and accountants. Denny provided green sarsenet worth £79 8s 1½d for the assayers who worked for him at Whitehall.[63] Within the royal apartments at Hampton Court, four of the thirty-two cupboards and fifteen of the seventeen tables were covered with lengths of green cloth, many trimmed with silk fringe.[64] A few of the stools were also covered in green (**12256**), as was a pedestal for a clock (**12255**). These cloths acted as a protective covering and lent the decor a unifying theme. According to the 1542 Inventory, one of the decorative cupboards [**1149**] and six of the decorative tables [**1164, 1166–1170**] had protective green cloths.

CURTAINS   A selection of the king's pictures and embroideries at Whitehall, Greenwich and Hampton Court were provided with paned silk curtains to protect them from sunlight.[65] In 1542 there were 152 'tables with pictures' listed at Whitehall. Of these, sixty-one had curtains.[66] Because of the meagre nature of the entries for the pictures in both inventories, it is not possible to tell if the use of curtains was associated with particularly fine or prized paintings. However, more panel paintings were treated in this way than any other type of pictures, and more portraits than any other group (Table 15).

The curtains had a dual function: protection and display. They were predominantly made of 'white and yellowe sarcenette' at Whitehall, while at Hampton Court they were green and yellow.[67] The choice of silk for the curtains is significant yet curious: it was relatively expensive, while its

---

63 BL Lansdowne Roll 14, m. 9.
64 The furnished rooms at Hampton Court are covered in the 1547 Inventory by entries **12248–12475**.
65 Paintings kept elsewhere did not have curtains. This is not surprising in most cases, as there are only a few pictures in each location, but their absence at St James's Palace, where there were fifty-six pictures in all (**15364–15419**), is more curious.
66 By 1547 these numbers were 153 and 58 respectively.
67 For Whitehall see entries **10569–10721**; for Hampton Court see entries **12306, 12308–12315, 12318, 12321–12323, 12326–12329, 12335–12337**. Twelve of the paintings at Hampton Court had curtains: eleven were green and yellow and the colour of the twelfth is not given.

susceptibility to sunlight does not actually recommend it as a sun screen. At least some of the curtains were on separate rods, rather than being attached to the frame. In 1531, three curtain rods costing 2s were installed at Whitehall 'to hang curtains before pictures of imagery'.[68]

Protective curtains were also provided for other objects such a 'fyer great Loking steele glasse sett in crymsen vellat richely enbraudred with damaske pirles' at Whitehall, which had 'oone Curtene to the same of blewe taphata enbraudred with venice golde' [862]. In 1542 the highe library at Whitehall included 'oone Table coverid with grene cloth with sondry Cupbourdes in it to set bookes in with iiij olde Curtens of buckeram frengid with grene silke to hang afore the bookes' [2365].[69] Even so, the use of case-covers for furniture was still undeveloped.[70]

STORAGE SPACE   In order to provide sufficient storage space for the objects in his charge, Denny would have needed access to rooms on the ground floor or elsewhere on the first floor. The objects recorded in the 1542 Inventory are organized by type and not by the rooms where they were used or stored. However, when not in use, it is likely that the furnishings were returned to the Wardrobe of the Beds. These rooms would have been on the periphery of the main residential area. While the location of the Wardrobe space in the Tudor period is uncertain, by 1670 the rooms used by the Wardrobe were on the ground floor of the river frontage, close to the privy stairs.[71] It is unlikely that Denny and Reed shared the same Wardrobe space for the objects in their care, or the items could easily have got mixed up.

Several specialist stores were present within Denny's sphere of influence by 1547. For example, the 1547 Inventory refers to 'The Glasse Housse';[72] and the group of musical instruments appear to have been kept together (11872–11952). Other rooms within the privy lodging were demoted to act as storage space, such as the study next to the king's old bedroom.[73] Evidence suggests that this study was used to store some of the papers belonging to the king's Privy Council.[74] From 1547 onwards, the old jewel house was used to store the clothes of Jane Seymour, who had died ten years earlier.[75]

The emphasis so far has been upon the development of Whitehall as the king's leading residence and the use of his possessions there, but the situation was more complex than that. While a steady

---

68 PRO E36/252, p. 631. This use of curtains was not limited to paintings in royal ownership. In 1552 the parish church of Standish, Lancashire has 'one grene say that hangs before a pycture of saynct Wylfryde': Bailey and Fishwick, 'Inventories', 128. The practice continued into the seventeenth century. The portrait of Alice, Lady Le Strange, painted by John Hoskins in 1617 and its pendant of her husband, Sir Hamon Le Strange, are still in their original frames; the frames retain the small hooks used for the curtains: see Hearn, *Dynasties*, 215, no. 144.

69 Green was a very common colour for painting the walls in both public and private libraries and studies in Renaissance Italy, and green cloths were placed under books while they were being read.

70 By the eighteenth century case-covers were in regular use; see, for example, *A Conversation Group* by J H Mortimer (1714–79) in the Yale Center for British Art (Paul Mellon Collection), which shows three men, two sitting on chairs and the other standing in front of a settee, all of which are covered with checked covers.

71 See Thurley, *Whitehall Palace Plan*, 55: four rooms of varying size are marked X to indicate the Wardrobe; they lie to the southeast of the great hall, the chapel and the vestry.

72 BL Harley MS 1419, f. 143r.

73 Ibid, f. 151r.

74 *APC*, I, 278, 395, *APC*, II, 106.

75 Items could also revert to the royal main store on the death of a recipient, as in the case of the clothes of Jane Seymour [2095–2259].

flow of items entered the palace during his lifetime, others equally were leaving on a regular basis. Denny's role as Keeper continually evolved in response to this movement of goods. Using the marginalia of the 1542 Inventory, it is possible to recreate, in part, Denny's book of issue and so to establish a pattern of when objects left his charge and where they went. There are inevitably a large number of small deliveries – a few items going to individuals on isolated occasions. More interesting are the larger groups of objects leaving Whitehall for a particular location or for a specific purpose. Two such groups of objects were considered above – the items going to the king and the lengths of silk and linen distributed to the royal family.[76] A further three will be dealt with here: the first group demonstrates how deliveries of furnishings from Whitehall boosted the Wardrobe holdings at two of Henry VIII's developing properties (Oatlands and Nonsuch: see Appendix IV). The second group consists of objects given to an individual, and the third group contains objects which were being recycled.

Items leaving the palace during Henry VIII's lifetime

TO THE WARDROBES OF THE BEDS AT OATLANDS AND NONSUCH   When William Reed died in 1534 his young son became Thomas Cromwell's ward. This facilitated Henry VIII's acquisition of Oatlands, the Reed family home, which occurred by exchange in December 1537.[77] Henry remodelled the house extensively and he selected the initial furnishings from Parlands, the former home of Sir Henry Norris.[78] Two inventories survive for Parlands.[79] These reveal that some perquisites, including five feather beds and a tapestry carpet 'wrought with the kinges armes' that Norris must have acquired either as Keeper of Greenwich or Groom of the Stool, returned to the king's possession.[80] In the same way, three close stools were a legacy of his time as Groom of the Stool.[81] Only a handful of items were not transferred, including five sets of say hangings and those marked with Norris's initials.[82]

The items from Parlands accounted for 30 per cent of the total furnishings listed at Oatlands in the 1547 Inventory, and as such they were the core of the Wardrobe. On 29 May and 12 July 1543 a number of pieces were sent from Denny's charge at Whitehall (12.7 per cent of the 1547 total). Nicholas Bristow (at that time Clerk of the Wardrobes) delivered the first batch of items, while Edmund Pigeon took the second, much smaller group. The Wardrobe continued to grow and by 1547 the holdings at Oatlands were substantial. They included ten bedsteads with apparel, fifteen chairs, thirty feather-beds, forty carpets, eighty-six cushions, sixty-five pairs of sheets, 199 pieces of tapestry and 252 pieces of verdure. In this instance the contribution from Whitehall did not amount to much but it was significant, and came just over a year after the 1542 Inventory was taken.

---

76 See pp. 90–1 and 108–9.
77 *LP* XII.ii, 1209; *HKW*, IV, 205–6.
78 This is evident from a comparison of the objects at Parlands in 1536 with those at Oatlands in 1547. Sir Henry Norris, Groom of the Stool, was executed in 1536 with Anne Boleyn.
79 BL Royal MS 14B.XLVII (taken in 1533, updated in 1536) and BL Cotton MS Appendix 89 (formerly 28), fos 55r–66r (undated, but post-dating BL Royal MS 14B.XLVII).
80 Ibid.
81 Ibid.
82 Say hangings were quite common in the late fifteenth and early sixteenth centuries. In March 1509 Lady Margaret Beaufort's Wardrobe of the Beds contained seven sets of say hangings: St John's College, Cambridge MS D.91.12, pp. 28–9.

Oatlands did not receive any further pieces from Whitehall after Henry's death, indicating that the size and composition of the Wardrobe was by then felt to be appropriate to the property.

After the modest transfer of items, the process was repeated later at Nonsuch on a larger scale. Nonsuch was a fantastical hunting lodge situated close to Oatlands. It was Henry's last great building project, and followed a new floor plan. Doing away with a great hall, the royal apartments were arranged around a square courtyard. While Nonsuch was Henry's most innovatory palace in terms of decoration and layout, it was a modest, private house, never intended to act as a showcase for the king's possessions. In 1547 there were just two chess sets, a tables board ('a paire of plaieng tables'), a mirror, three paintings ('tables with pictures') and an alabaster sculpture of the Three Magi (**12999–13006**). Henry only visited Nonsuch twice (on 5–7 July 1545 and 11–19 December 1546) and the house was left unfinished at his death.[83] The Wardrobe entry for Nonsuch in the 1547 Inventory reflects its incomplete state – it would doubtless have been larger and more sophisticated had Henry lived longer.

The entry is divided into two sections. Sixty-one out of 145 items on the first list (42 per cent) were among Denny's charge on 9 January 1545, while twenty-two of the twenty-five items on the second list of items (88 per cent), came from Whitehall on 29 September 1547.[84] Edmund Pigeon distributed a third, smaller group of eighteen items taken from Whitehall, at some point after 29 September and before the compilation of the Nonsuch entry in the 1547 Inventory (probably late 1547). Interestingly, the additional eighteen entries appear in both lists. In all, 101 out of the 170 items in the Wardrobe (59.4 per cent) were supplied directly from Denny's charge at Whitehall.[85] The transfer is even more significant if the twenty-two non-textile entries are ignored. In essence, Nonsuch was largely stocked with items apparently surplus to Whitehall, with 68.2 per cent of the textiles present in the 1547 Inventory coming from Whitehall.[86]

The composition of the Nonsuch Wardrobe is interesting. The new additions covered a broad range of furnishing textiles and included fifty-seven cushions, forty verdures, thirty carpets, twenty-nine stools and nineteen chairs. The large number of verdures may partially reflect the highly figurative decorative scheme in the house.[87] Equally, the age and condition of some of the hangings may reflect the on-going building work at the house. Thirteen pieces of highly fashionable broad-bloom verdures were countered by twenty pieces of tapestry and arras that were described as old and worn. Building dust may have been a consideration in the Wardrobe because fifty-seven new buckram cases were provided for sixty-five cushions (**12957**, **12959**) and 18 new cases were provided for chairs (**12969**).[88]

83   PRO OBS 1/1419, fos 73v, 75v (*LP* XX.i, 1117, 1128; *LP* XXI.ii, 532, 768, p. 397).
84   The origins of a few other pieces is revealed in the text, e.g. 'Six peces of verdoures chequered with red and tawny and with the late duke of Norffolk his Armes in the myddes of euerye of them' (**12880**).
85   In Hayward, 'Possessions', 94 the figure given is lower (48.8 per cent) because it does not include the items delivered by Pigeon.
86   The carpenters and joiners employed by the King's Works probably made the wooden furniture for Nonsuch (**13008–13018**).
87   The decorative scheme devised for Nonsuch has been the subject of much speculation and it is of interest because of the move away from a reliance on badges, mottoes and heraldic devices: see *HKW*, IV, 200. There was a figure of Scipio by the entrance to the king's lodging, one of Penthesilea, Queen of the Amazons, on the queen's side, and in the middle of the south side was Henry VIII with his son Edward. Linking these two decorative scenes on the king's side were sixteen scenes from the life of Hercules, while opposite there were the seven liberal arts, the four cardinal virtues, the three theological virtues and *Patientia* and *Humilitas*.
88   A nineteenth chair was added in the second list (**13039**).

The second list in the 1547 Inventory included seven fashionable satin hangings decorated with antiques and the Seven Works of Mercy (**13020**), seven verdures (**13021, 13023–13025**) and thirteen carpets of verdures 'of broad bloom' (**13027**). These high-quality hangings contrast well with the selection of carpets, which included pieces made using a wide range of techniques, such as tapestry weaving (**12883**), embroidery (**13034**) and turkey making (**13035**). In addition there were six carpets made using painted techniques, for example 'two carpettes turquey making of dornix painted chequered with diuerse colours' (**13033**). Painting and staining were used to create a range of furnishings for the cheaper end of the market. Dornix too was a low-quality fabric.[89] The Wardrobe at Nonsuch casually combined the luxurious with the relatively mundane. On a purely practical level taking pieces from Whitehall meant that good-quality furnishings could be transferred at short notice and at no immediate cost to the royal household.

FURNISHING THE QUEEN'S CHAPEL   Following their marriage in July 1543 Henry presented Queen Catherine Parr with liturgical textiles, vestments, plate and service books appropriate for the celebration of mass in her chapel as well as suitable containers for their storage. The grant was substantial: two albs [**2270**], eight altar cloths [**2271**], six altar towels [**2272**], one book [**2284**], three chests [**1198, 2286**], five corporal cases [**2273–2275**], two cruets [**2279**], five dorses, five redorses [**2260, 2262, 2264, 2266, 2269**], two mass books [**2281–2282**], one New Testament [**2283**], one sakering bell [**2280**], one sacrament cloth [**2276**], one low stool [**2285**], two superaltars [**2278**], one traverse [**2277**], one trunk [**2287**] and eight vestments [**2261, 2263, 2265, 2267–2268**]. The pieces were delivered to William Harper, a members of the queen's household.[90]

Most of the items had previously been held by Catherine Howard [**2260–22687**], although two of the chests [**1198**] were drawn from the general list of chapel textiles in Denny's care. From the clues within the list it is evident that some of the objects had been handed from queen to queen. Among these were a dorse and redorse 'garnysshid with sondry of the kinges Badges / and Quene Janes Cognizaunces' [**2260**] and a corporal case 'enbraudred with H. and A.' [**2273**]. These pieces indicate the quantity and quality of textiles that Henry considered suitable for his wives' devotions.[91]

REDISTRIBUTION, REUSE AND RECYCLING OF MATERIALS   So far, we have looked at objects released by Denny to be taken from one property to another, or from one individual to another, but the function of which did not change. However, some of the items leaving his charge did change their character either being transformed into a new object or being reduced to raw components. An example of each type of transformation can be seen within the entries for two significant groups of objects.

First, there is the substantial store of silk cloth held at Whitehall. Many of the lengths of cloth were cut and converted into items of dress or furnishings. This process formed a very positive element of Denny's role as keeper, allowing for the creation of new objects in response to demands

89   There is just one entry for dornix cloth in the lists for the Great Wardrobe: 'Dornixe ij yerdes quarter di' (**15000**).
90   PRO E315/160, f. 99v.
91   Further evidence of Catherine of Aragon's chapel stuff and general Wardrobe stuff can be gleaned from Nichols, 'View of the Wardrobe'.

made by the king, his household or the palace itself. The recycling of textiles is also recorded within the 1542 Inventory. The marginal note after an entry for 'thre kirtilles and thre hoodes of Crymsen vellat lyned with white sarceonet' [11] recorded that 'one kyrtell [was given] to Philippe Lentall being Crimson with the lynyng to couer halbertes'.

Secondly, there are Denny's holdings of plate. The fate of these pieces is revealed by the marginalia of the 1542 Inventory. Plate was transferred from Denny's charge to three individuals between 1542–7: to Sir Edmund Peckham, Treasurer of the mint at the Tower, where it was probably recycled into coinage, on 26 April 1545,[92] to the king on 6 May 1545, 18 February 1546 and various unspecified dates between April 1546 and January 1547[93] and to Sir Anthony Aucher, Master of the Jewel House, on 6 July 1547.[94] The consignment dated 26 April 1545 was by far the most significant and on this occasion Sir Edmund Peckham received 3,800½ ounces (117.81kg) of gilt plate, 852¼ ounces (26.41kg) of parcel gilt plate and 281 ounces (8.71kg) of white plate.[95] Denny was left with 18 ounces (0.551kg) and 2s 6d weight of gold plate, 4,454½ ounces (138.08kg) of gilt plate, 2,195½ ounces (68.06kg) of parcel gilt plate and 508½ ounces (15.76kg) of white plate. This depletion of Denny's plate may partially explain the new delivery of plate that Denny received from the king's secret jewel house in 1546 [3711–60].

The number of items given to the king was much smaller. Henry received 106½ ounces (3.30kg) of gilt plate, 427¾ ounces (13.26kg) of parcel gilt plate and 147 ounces (4.55kg) of white plate. The composition of the group is rather eclectic and probably reflect a particular interest, such as the mazer of serpentine [59] or the fashionable basin and ewer 'wrought with a traile of Antiques with leavis in the bottome of the bason and the lydde of the Ewer' [3730] or need, as in the case of the silver warming pan, presumably for his bed [159].

After Henry VIII's death, the plate remaining in Denny's charge was tranferred from Whitehall on 9 July 1547 to the Tower jewel house.[96] Aucher received a selection of items from Denny's initial charge of plate and almost all of the consignment he received in 1546. In addition there existed a jewel house at Whitehall that was outside Denny's charge, as recorded in the 1542 Inventory, and the plate was collected from there on 10 February 1547 in the presence of Sir Richard Southwell and Sir Thomas Pope.[97] Finally, plate was also collected 'owte of the kinges secrete Juelhous in the olde gallorie next the pryvey garden at Westmynster' on 6 August 1547.[98]

Changes to Denny's role: the consolidation of Edward VI's possessions

Denny's charge changed far more dramatically after Henry's death, when many of the goods in his care were either allocated to others at Whitehall or redistributed among other royal properties.

---

92 The first entry where the date is given in the marginalia is **33**, PRO E315/160 f. 2v. The marginalia also refers to these pieces being recorded on fos 60–61 in the *Book of Issue*.

93 Examples of entries where these dates are given are **59**, **151**, **110**, **3726–3727**, PRO E315/160, fos 3r, 4v, 5v, 136v. These pieces are recorded on folios 18, 61, 64, 67 and 68 in the *Book of Issue*.

94 The first entry where the date is given in the marginalia is **31**, PRO E315/160, f. 2v. In the *Book of Issue* these items appear in the second section, under Aucher's name.

95 These figures compare well with a number of the deliveries made to the Mint by the king's commissioners during the dissolution of the monasteries in the winter of 1538/9. John Freman delivered 5,715oz (177.16kg) of plate, Dr Richard Layton a further 3,538½oz (109.69kg) and Dr Richard Loudon another 4,237oz (131.34kg), see Turnbull, *Monastic*, 9–15.

96 SA MS 129, f. 35r.

97 SA MS 129, f. 8v.

98 SA MS 129, f. 10v.

A comparison of the 1542 and 1547 inventories reveals how the contents of Whitehall Palace under-went marked reduction between the king's death on 28 January 1547 and the start of the work compiling the 1547 Inventory. The 1542 Inventory meticulously records where the items went, and this information shows that a number of Wardrobe holdings were enlarged after Henry's death. So, while the 1547 Inventory recorded the the late king's goods, the deployment of a small but significant percentage of items had changed to suit the needs of the new king and his household.[99]

Henry VIII died on 28 January 1547, but the inventory of his goods was not commissioned until the September of that year.[100] The demotion of Sir Anthony Denny was one factor in this delay. By September of that year Somerset's brother-in-law, Sir Michael Stanhope, had replaced Denny as First Gentleman of the Privy Chamber and as Groom of the Stool, even though Denny had helped the Protector Somerset to secure Henry's cash reserves.[101] Another factor was the war with Scotland: once Edward's property was in safe and reliable hands, this was a primary concern for Somerset and the Privy Council (on which Denny retained his place, although he did not attend regularly).

The new regime was clearly anxious to secure Henry VIII's assets. Plate was gathered in from the jewel houses at Whitehall, Hampton Court, Greenwich, Windsor and Oatlands, and placed in the Tower.[102] While the majority of the gold plate had been kept at the Tower during Henry VIII's life-time, the other jewel houses had only contained a little gold and a selection of pieces from most of the categories of silver-gilt vessels. Plate held by members of the household, such as the Serjeant of the Cellar, the king's barber and the king's apothecary, was recalled.[103] Taking one example, the 1547 Inventory reveals that 471⅛ ounces (14.60kg) of night plate was 'founde in a square house in the long gallorie at Westmnster [sic]' and 387 ounces (11.99kg) 'parcell of the Pothicarie and surgerie plate' was in the hands of Henry VIII's medical team.[104] Both groups of plate were collected up on 11 July 1547. This plate reflects Henry's ill health and it is echoed by the apothecary's accounts from 1546 to 1547.[105]

The Tower jewel house also received 3,404⅞ ounces (105.55kg) of plate that had been in use within Prince Edward's household. This plate was delivered to the jewel house very promptly on 10 and 12 February 1547, shortly before the new king's coronation.[106] In contrast, Edward's Wardrobe stuff was still at Durham House when the 1547 Inventory was taken, although the Keepership there was vacant.[107] Edward's former household was dissolved on his accession and several of his officers were incorporated into the household of the new king, which was organized by his uncle the Earl of Hereford, later Duke of Somerset.[108]

There were several reasons why Somerset and the council opted to empty the five local jewel houses on Henry's death. First, by drawing most of the royal plate into the Tower it was much easier

99 The 1547 Inventory includes a small group of items acquired for Edward VI or remade for him using materials belonging to his father (e.g. **3670–3687**).
100 This and subsequent paragraphs draw on Hayward, 'Possessions', 101–5.
101 Murphy, 'Illusion of decline', 122.　　　　　　102 SA MS 129, f. 5r–v.
103 A list from 1520 indicates this: PRO SP1/232, fos 237r–238v (*LP* Add. I.i, 300).
104 SA MS 129, fos. 24r, 53r.　　　　　　105 PRO SP1/228, fos 146r–162v (*LP* XXI.ii, 768).
106 SA MS 129, f. 32r.
107 See p. 107 n. 197 above.
108 Murphy, 'Illusion of decline', 121. John Ryther became Cofferer, Robert Beverley entered the king's kitchen and Edward Rogers was made a Groom of the Privy Chamber. In contrast, Edward's Wardrobe was still intact at the time the 1547 Inventory was taken: **14027–14128**.

for the king's guardians to control access to, and use of, this cache of bullion, which represented a major cash reserve. This was an important consideration because in the early years of Edward VI's reign the Crown faced a serious financial crisis, generated by Henry's personal extravagance, costly foreign policies and aggravated by his debasement of the coinage.[109]

Secondly, by gathering all the plate into a central depot it was possible to remove 'superstitious' liturgical plate and religious images out from the royal chapels. Interestingly, the group of images kept at Whitehall [**115–119, 126–129, 135–137**] were delivered to Sir Anthony Aucher at the Jewel House rather than Sir Edmund Peckham at the Mint: purging the royal chapels was not a priority in 1547. Once it did become significant, the plate was simply transferred from the Jewel House to the Mint.

Thirdly, Edward VI was a minor and his coronation was described as having 'no very memorable show of triumph or magnificence'.[110] This contrasted with the display and magnificence that his father had maintained. This suggests that Edward's guardians felt that a boy required less display than an adult monarch at his coronation and in his daily routine. The emptying of the local jewel houses forced Edward to rely on the contents of his removing coffers far more. On 9 August 1547 John Gates delivered 6,321⅞ ounces (179.23kg) of gold and silver-gilt plate 'caried in the removing cefers for bankettes' to Sir Anthony Aucher at the Jewel House.[111] Somerset took this policy too far when he kept the king short of funds. His own brother, Admiral Seymour, sought to influence the king by sending him gifts of money.[112]

The armouries were also overhauled. Once again, the changes reflected two factors. The first was Edward's youth. As a boy of nine he had no need for his father's armour and the considerable quantities of hunting equipment accumulated at Greenwich, Hampton Court and Whitehall. The Protector and the Privy Council guarded Edward as anxiously as, two generations before, Henry VII had watched his second son. The rationalization of the armouries was also instigated by the preparations for the war with Scotland.[113] Between 28 May and 16 July 1547, Robert Hemmings received 11s 8d for two days' work with twenty carts for carrying 'handguns, boar spears etc. from the palace of Whitehall to the Tower'.[114] These must be the items recorded at the Tower as 'received out of the chardge of Sir Anthony Denny' (**3854–3870**).[115] Annotations on the 1542 Inventory reveal that other groups of objects were delivered to Sir Philip Hoby, Master of the Ordnance, and Hans Hunter, Keeper of the Armoury at Whitehall.[116] A heading in the 1547 Inventory identifies another group of 'dyuers and sondry kyndes of Munycions and habillementes of warre from the kinges Majesties Palace at westminster the vij[th] of July Anno primo Regis Edwardi Sexti' that had not formed part of Denny's charge (**3800–3885**).[117] At the same time items were being moved from the armouries

---

109 The debasement of the coinage that began in Henry VIII's reign continued under his son. The gold coinage was debased in 1544, 1545, 1546 and 1549, while the silver coinage was debased in 1544, 1545, 1546 and 1551: see Challis, 'Lord Hastings', 232–4.

110 *CSP Spanish*, IX, 47.

111 SA MS 129, f. 20v. There were also four cases of knives with silver-gilt handles of unspecified weight. This set of plate included 124 trenchers, eight layers, seventeen candlesticks and seven pairs of gilt pots.

112 Murphy, 'Illusion of decline', 125–6.

113 These preparations can also been seen in the loans of tentage (**8828–8839**).

114 PRO E101/60/23, unfoliated.   115 SA MS 129, f. 256r.

116 PRO E315/160, fos 64r–66r.   117 SA MS 129, f. 253r.

elsewhere, as is indicated by the 'Harnesse deliuered since the death of the kinge from Hamptoncourte by the said Wolner Armoror at the commaundement of the Counsaill'.[118]

This process of reorganization and retrenchment continued after 1547. The royal fleet was rationalized during 1548 and 1549 when the Privy Council sold ten of Henry VIII's thirteen rowbarges for £165 4s.[119] In 1549 the libraries at Greenwich and Hampton Court were consolidated at Whitehall under the direction of the Librarian, Bartholomew Traheron.[120] A number of duplicate volumes were weeded out, some of these being acquired by Sir Thomas Pope.[121] These extensive cut-backs to the royal holdings of plate, weapons (including some hunting equipment) and armour, ships and books were matched by changes within Whitehall Palace. The revisions and reductions made to the goods of the late king of the type described above reflected in part the limited needs of a boy king, a country at war and a regime that was short of cash. Whitehall underwent a change and declined in importance as a consequence of that change.

The redistribution of the objects in Denny's charge

WHO AUTHORIZED THE CHANGES AND WHY?   The role of Whitehall changed on the accession of Edward VI (Figure 11). For Henry VIII, the palace had been, in part, an expression of his intense, personal rivalry with King Francis I of France and the Emperor Charles V. No one would expect such a stance by a boy king whose religion isolated him from much of Europe, and whose finances were perilous. There is no direct evidence of who authorized the review of Denny's charge, but there are only two real candidates. The first was the new king and the second was the Duke of Somerset (Figure 12) – and the latter, with the backing of the Privy Council, is more likely. Denny's discharge as Keeper noted that after the establishment of his new charge,

> the rest of the saide plate Juelles apparrell Stuff and other gooddes aforesaide so
> remainynge the same commissioners … haue caused him to delyver at sowndrie tymes
> within the tyme of this Accompte to thandes, chardge and custodie of ye master of
> ye kinges Jeuell house, the master of the great Wardrope ye master of Thordinaunce
> & diuers kepers of Guardropes and stufe at sundrie The kynges howsses to be sauely
> keapte to his Majesties vse.[122]

The timing of the process is established by some of the marginalia of the 1542 Inventory. Between 9 July and 29 September 1547 a large number of furnishings were taken from Whitehall Palace to be sent to Greenwich, Richmond, Oatlands, Nonsuch, Windsor and the Tower. A summary of the resulting distribution of key furnishings at Henry's three leading properties – Greenwich, Hampton Court and Whitehall – and the Wardrobe of the Beds at the Tower is given in Table 16.

---

118   Ibid, f. 442v.
119   This particular trend echoed events during the minorities of both Richard II and Henry VI. On 6 September 1380 John de Hermesthope and Robert de Crull were appointed to sell four of Edward III's ships, *La Gracedieu*, *La Mighel*, *La nave Seinte Marie* and an unnamed galley moored at Redcliff, along with their contents and the naval stores kept at the Tower and Redcliff: *CPR 1377–81*, 513–14. In March 1423 William Soper, Clerk of the King's Ships to Henry VI, John Foxholes and Nicholas Banister were required by the Privy Council 'to sell certain of the king's great ships and vessels, as they think most profitable': *CPR 1422–9*, 75. The Council received 1,000 marks as a result of the sale in 1430: Oppenheim, *History of Administration*, 17, 101.
120   Carley, 'John Leland and the royal library', 15.
121   Carley, 'Greenwich and Henry VIII's royal library', 156. Sir Thomas Pope gave a number of books to his foundation Trinity College, Oxford, including twenty-seven books with 'ex Greenwich' and fifteen with 'ex Hampton Court' crossed out.
122   PRO E101/427/2, mm. 1–2.

TABLE 16

THE DISTRIBUTION OF KEY FURNISHINGS BETWEEN GREENWICH, HAMPTON COURT, THE WARDROBE OF THE BEDS AT THE TOWER AND WHITEHALL IN 1547, AFTER THE REORGANIZATION OF DENNY'S CHARGE

This table is taken from Hayward, 'Possessions', 279.

Object	Greenwich	Hampton Court	The Tower	Whitehall
Arras	28	106	103	39
Bedsteads with apparel	8	9	3	8
Cloths of estate	3	2	6	3
Cushions	58	95	59	56
Hangings	—	63	12	—
Tapestry	157	227	40	234
Verdure	16	58	3	—

These figures are based only on items stored in the Wardrobes of the Beds at these properties.

There are two ways of viewing the reorganization at Whitehall. First, it can be seen as an attempt on the part of the Protector to reduce the importance of the palace. John Murphy has demonstrated that by the end of 1547 Somerset had transferred political power from the Privy Council to himself and from Whitehall Palace to Somerset House.[123] Consequently the Privy Chamber declined and the Groom of the Stool was less influential. The new political situation was reinforced at ground level. Somerset requisitioned some of the late king's most private rooms at Whitehall for his own use: the study at the end of the long gallery, the chair house and the secret jewel house.[124] If he did not actually use the rooms in his capacity as Protector, he held the keys, effectively excluding Edward.[125]

In addition, Somerset probably assumed responsibility for the contents, which had previously been overseen by Henry VIII himself. This provided Somerset, his wife and her brother Stanhope with the opportunity to acquire items from the secret jewel house and elsewhere at Whitehall. Such items included a desk of walnut (**10428**), a mirror (**10432**), a copper clock, an ebony box and an hourglass (**10433**).[126] Further to reducing the visual magnificence at Whitehall, Somerset also diverted

---

123 Murphy, 'Illusion of decline', 121–32.
124 BL Harley MS 1419, f. 448r.
125 Even if Edward did have a key to these rooms he had to share them with Somerset.
126 PRO SP10/6, no. 28, PRO SP10/9, no. 53 (*CSPD Edward VI*, 204, 424); Pocock, *Troubles*, 123–4. It is possible to identify some of the missing pieces from the secret jewel house even though the entries refer to groups of objects rather than individual items. However, the object descriptions given for the study are more problematic because of their brevity. Somerset and his wife were accused of stealing a round box (possibly one of the missing compasses (**10449–10450**)), a box containing silver instruments (possibly **10446**) and a comb case.

the most splendid of the chapel goods and furnishings confiscated from Thomas Howard, Duke of Norfolk: these pieces were used to enhance Somerset House rather than put to the service of the king.[127] On Somerset's fall most of the goods that he had acquired from the Duke of Norfolk passed to the Duke of Northumberland rather than to the Crown: like Somerset before him, Northumberland had to be seen in suitable grandeur befitting his status as head of government.

The alternative view of the reorganization is more prosaic. By 1547 Whitehall was undeniably cluttered. Any redistribution of items held there would have made it less overcrowded and less dependent upon a man of Denny's skill to administer. The valuable furnishings that had been amassed there were then available for redistribution amongst Henry's most frequently visited houses. This development of the local Standing Wardrobes of the Beds would also have reduced the demands placed on the Removing Wardrobe of the Beds.

Whatever the reasons behind it, the pre-eminence of Whitehall was undermined by the dispersal of its best furnishings and the reduction in status of its Keeper. This situation was partially reversed on Somerset's fall. The rooms which he had requisitioned returned to the control of the new Keeper, Sir Andrew Dudley, and ultimately the king. After Rufforth's death in 1550, Dudley also took responsibility for the items which had been in Rufforth's care.

THE SHIFT IN THE BALANCE OF POWER   Denny's mandate underwent a drastic reduction during 1547 and as a consequence he shared with Rufforth and Reed responsibility for the goods at Whitehall. Under the new arrangement he was responsible for a few furnishings, the paintings, embroideries and mirrors, some of the clocks and most of the wooden furniture including tables, stools and cupboards.[128] Rufforth oversaw the domestic linen used for dining, washing, sleeping and celebrating mass. He was also charged with the clothing of the late king and Jane Seymour, the glass house, a selection of feathers, the clocks, the library and some wooden furniture (mainly chests).[129] Of these, the feathers had not featured in the 1542 Inventory (**11700–11756**).[130] Rufforth's salary was increased to 2*s* a day from 28 January 1547, in recognition of his greater responsibility.[131] Some of the cloth in the silk store was transferred to the Great Wardrobe but as the 1550 Westminster Inventory reveals, new purchases were also made and delivered to Rufforth.[132] Other pieces, all furnishings, went to Reed.[133] Reed had held the post of Keeper of the Standing Wardrobe of the Beds since 1529, so he was another experienced member of the curatorial team at Whitehall. As Henry VIII spent increasing amounts of time at Whitehall during the 1540s, Reed's responsibilities had grown.

---

127   This transfer is made very clear by the marginalia of the Duke of Norfolk's Inventory, PRO LR2/115.

128   1547 Inventory, entries **10545–10893**.

129   Ibid, **10894–11034**, **11211–11871** (this includes the list of refuse stuff given to him).

130   The list includes New Year's gifts from January 1545 and purchases from Peter van der Wall in May 1546, as well as feathers bought for Edward's coronation. This group of objects reflects a small increase in the Whitehall remit.

131   *APC*, II, 201. On 28 May 1548 the Privy Council authorized payment to Rufforth of £36 10*s* 0*d*, for a year's wages from 28 January 1547 to 28 January 1548.

132   Dominico Erizo delivered large quantities of tissue, cloth of gold and cloth of silver and velvet in August 1549 (**16143–16316**).

133   1547 Inventory, entries **9682–9914**.

In part this three-way split between Denny, Rufforth and Reed was little more than a formal recognition of the way the palace had been managed prior to 1547. It acknowledged the responsibilities of all three men. Denny was frequently absent from the palace, when he tended the king in his capacity as a member of the Privy Chamber, and from 1546 as Groom of the Stool. Reed and Rufforth remained there on a much more permanent basis, attending to much of the everyday management and maintenance.

The working relationship between Denny and Reed is worth exploring (see Appendix V). Between 1536 and 1547 Denny managed the equivalent of a second Standing Wardrobe of the Beds at Whitehall. It is possible that, in the years up to 1547, Denny employed the furnishings in his care within the privy lodging, while Reed tended to the outer chambers of the king's apartments. Alternatively, Denny and Reed could have combined the two sets of furnishings to provide more variety and choice, deploying them throughout the royal apartments. After Henry VIII's death Denny's share of the furnishing textiles was greatly reduced, giving Reed greater responsibility for furnishing the entire palace.

The tapestries held by Reed were of a high quality and pictorial, so the subject matter could be chosen to reflect or set the tone of a particular event. This would have been particularly pertinent if the pieces were displayed in the outer rooms of the palace, such as the guard chamber and presence chamber, to which many members of the court and royal household would have had access. Tapestries hung in the privy chamber and the rooms of the privy lodging beyond, would have been seen by the king, the Groom of the Stool and the officers of the Privy Chamber; here, there would have been an element of preaching to the converted. If their resources were combined, it required Denny and Reed to liaise very closely and regularly maintained paperwork was of the essence. Wall hangings were the most important decorative element within the Wardrobes of the Beds that were held by Denny and Reed at Whitehall. After the changes in Denny's charge in 1547, tapestries with pictorial subjects were transferred from Denny to Reed and formed the predominant type of hanging in the Wardrobe. This shift suggests that responsibility for how and where these pictorial hangings and where they were hung within the palace passed in 1547 from the Keeper of the Palace to the Keeper of the Wardrobe.

In 1547 the items in Reed's custody included most of the usual contents of a standing wardrobe such as hangings, bedsteads, bedding, chairs, curtains and cushions. Reed's charge was liberally supplemented with items from Denny's prior to the list being prepared: 109 of the 233 entries (47 per cent) ascribed to Reed came from Denny. Reed's major holdings were of wall hangings, with 193 pieces of tapestry and arras. Interestingly, there were no pieces of verdure, in contrast to the 213 pieces in Denny's hands prior to the redistribution.

THE REORGANIZATION AT GROUND LEVEL: THE ROLE OF EDMUND PIGEON All the Wardrobe staff, including the Keepers of the Standing Wardrobes at the houses that received pieces from Whitehall, must have been involved in the redistribution of the furnishings. At the very least the Wardrobe Keepers would have checked the delivery, updated their inventories and put the pieces away. It is most likely that Denny, Rufforth and Bristow were involved both in the administrative process of recording where pieces went and in the logistics of getting them from

Whitehall to their new destination. In addition, these three men were party to any discussions as to where pieces went; they certainly had the best knowledge of the objects kept at Whitehall and the strengths and weaknesses of the other Standing Wardrobes. Edmund Pigeon, Clerk of the Wardrobes of the Robes and Beds, periodically acted as their assistant.

The marginalia of the 1542 Inventory reveals that most of the objects left the palace between July and September 1547. For example, Pigeon and Gates delivered four books with fabric bindings (**25**) and a glass of birral (**178**) to the Jewel House Commissioners at Windsor Castle on 25 and 26 July 1547.[134] On 25 August 1547 a substantial group of furnishings was entrusted to Pigeon, who is described in the Inventory as the servant of Nicholas Bristow. This may reflect the fact that Bristow paid Pigeon a financial retainer but it is more likely to indicate that Bristow, as the King's Clerk, was superior to Pigeon, as Clerk of the Wardrobes of the Robes and Beds, and accordingly oversaw his work. In the following month, on 16 September Pigeon returned stuff to Rufforth for Whitehall (**17534–17541**). Later he made two more deliveries of furnishings to Rufforth: on 8 March 1548 (**17542–17560**) and an undated delivery of pieces from the attainted Duke of Norfolk (**17624–17636**).

It is possible to trace the majority of the 144 entries marked as taken by Pigeon and see where they were delivered. Woodstock was the main beneficiary with 22.9 per cent of the entries. As the Wardrobe at Woodstock was without a Keeper in 1547, it is not surprising that Pigeon was responsible for the property.[135] Almost a quarter (24.3 per cent) went to Greenwich, which until then had received very little from Denny's charge: just eight pieces of tapestry and one fire pan on 21 July 1547 [**203, 3307**]. A similar quantity of entries (25.7 per cent) remained at Whitehall and they were essentially split between the charges of Rufforth and Reed. Rufforth received nineteen celures and testers, as well as a selection of cabinets and other furniture.[136] Reed was given additional chapel stuff and further pieces went to Ralph Tapping, Serjeant of the Vestry (5.5 per cent).[137] The return within a short time to Whitehall of about a quarter of those pieces sent away suggests that the initial purging of furnishings had been too drastic. The remaining items (21.6 per cent) were shared between Nonsuch, Windsor, Richmond and The More.[138]

This series of deliveries made by Pigeon suggests that the reorganization of the furnishings at Whitehall was carried out in two distinct, if not chronologically sequential, phases. The first phase saw groups of items sent to specific locations on fixed dates. The second phase may have been to fill in any obvious gaps in individual wardrobe inventories, after the first distribution. Although the pieces involved in the second phase were given to Pigeon part-way through the first, he did not evidently deliver them promptly.

134 The pieces are of interest as they both had links with Anne Boleyn: 'foure bookes whereof three are covered with vellat and one with tynsell one of theym is garnished with A Crowned and one other of gold H and A The thirde of Siluer and gilte and H and A and the fourthe with white Siluer' (**25**) and 'one glasse of birrall garnished with gold with the late Queene Annes armes vppon the cover poids glasse and all viij oz iij quarters' (**178**).

135 BL Harley MS 1419, f. 318r.

136 Celures and testers [**475–492, 2348**]; two bedsteads [**522–523**]; eight bed pillars [**524–525**]; two tables with pictures [**812**]; four tables [**1177**]; three pairs of trestles [**1180**]; two chests [**1198**]; five cabinets [**1204–1207, 2388**]; one sheet [**2307**].

137 Using Concordance II, it is possible to trace a small group of liturgical pieces to the vestry under Reed's charge (two chairs [**267**]; five stools [**273, 275, 291**]; thirty-one cases for cushions [**417–418**]; thirteen cases for chairs [**419**]; lengths of canvas [**526**]; six altar frontals [**1017–1018, 1033**]; five vestments [**1036, 1038**]; one table and three trestles [**1180**]; four chests [**1198**]; one cushion [**3325**]), and to trace a group of Denny's pieces to the vestry under Tapping's charge (one altar cloth [**1028**]; five vestments [**1038, 1040, 1048**]; one folding lectern [**1218**]; two cloths/hangings for a church [**1227–1228**]; one altar frontal [**1229**]).

138 It was not possible to trace five of the entries (3.5 per cent). These pieces may have been granted to Pigeon as a perquisite.

TABLE 17

THE BREAK-UP OF SETS OF SEAT FURNITURE, CUSHIONS AND HANGINGS/ WINDOW PIECES FROM THE 1542 INVENTORY

This table is an extended version of one included in Hayward, 'Seat furniture', 23.

Type of hanging	No. of entries	No. of single items	No. of sets	No. (percentage) of sets left intact	No. (percentage) of sets split up
Arras	9	3	6	6 (100%)	0 (0%)
Chairs	30	9	21	5 (23.8%)	16 (76.2%)
Cushions	123	59	64	42 (65.6%)	22 (34.4%)
Embroidered/appliquéd	25	14	11	11 (100%)	0 (0%)
Footstools	4	1	3	2 (66.7%)	1 (33.3%)
Scarlet cloth	2	0	2	2 (100%)	0 (0%)
Stained cloths	16	16	0	—	—
Stools	18	6	12	6 (50%)	6 (50%)
Tapestry*	14	0	14	12 (85.7%)	2 (14.3%)
Verdure	13	0	13	5 (38.5%)	8 (61.5%)

* These figures do not include the items described as 'a Carpet of fyne tapstry' [210]. These figures do not include the items described as the 'Carpetes of Verdours' [221].

THE BREAK-UP OF SETS OF FURNISHINGS   Some types of furnishing, such as hangings, chairs and cushions, can be made in sets as well as individually. Equally, chairs, footstools and cushions could be covered in the same top fabric to produce a matching suite of pieces. Pieces with the same coverings were intended to be used as an ensemble, so making a more dramatic impact than if they were used individually. Even so, the marginalia of the 1542 Inventory reveal that a number of sets were split up in 1547 when the palace contents were reorganized.

If the different types of wall hangings are considered first (see Table 17) the general trend was for the sets to be kept intact. This reflects the high cost of these hangings and the fact that many of them were figurative in design. While a single piece from a set like the Acts of the Apostles is striking, the narrative force of a set of tapestries is lost if only part of it is displayed. It is significant that the two sets of tapestries which were divided were not strongly narrative in nature: one depicted scenes of hunting and hawking and the other was simply described as 'fyne tapstry Imagrye' [208–209]. The same is true of the verdures, where the individual pieces stood alone and many of the sets were very large, with twenty-four or forty-four pieces.

In contrast, sets of seat furniture like chairs, stools and cushions were split almost routinely.[139] There were twenty-six sets of chairs recorded at Whitehall and 76 per cent of these were divided between two or more Wardrobes, for example:

239   Item Sixtene Chiers of like cloth of golde reyside with crymsen vellat frengid with a freng of red silke / wherof Thertene eche of them having two pomelles of Copper and gilt and thother thre having ther pomelles coveryd with like cloth of gold / And every of the said xvj havinge two Roundelles of wodd with the kinges Armes or Lettres in them payntid and gilte.

239   *LM*: deffeciunt ij Rundelles onelie.

239   *RM*: Ex' vij videlicet vj with pomelles of copper and one with pomelles couered with cloth of gold folio 57.

239   *RM*: Ex' oone with pomelles of copper & gilt folio 72.

239   *RM*: Ex' the vij to Sir Thomas Carden predicto & thone to therle of warwike Lorde Chamberleyn / twoe to the Lady Elizabeth predicto / iij to John Rede predicto / & iij to william griffith predicto.

While the breaking up of such large sets can be justified, sets of two or three chairs were also frequently split and this is less easy to understand. Was the dispersal of these sets a random process, or was it a conscious decision? As the maintenance of the palace had been so efficient under Denny and Bristow, it was out of character for them to take a random approach to redistributing its furnishings had they been left to their own devices. This suggests that the dispersal was intentional and imposed by another party – Somerset perhaps?

The random approach provided the receiving royal Wardrobes with a variety of chairs or cushions rather than one or two suites. This was not consistent with the trend adopted by Henry VIII towards the end of his reign, when he had preferred to buy matching chairs, stools, footstools and cushions. From a positive point of view, this policy ensured the distribution of some new, good-quality pieces, in a range of colours and fabrics, amongst the leading standing Wardrobes. From a negative point of view, however, dividing up many of the sets of cushions and chairs made the dispersal of Whitehall's contents much more final. It also ensured that many of the fine furnishings from Whitehall were dispersed amongst a number of properties. This would fit with Murphy's theory that Somerset deliberately reduced the profile of Whitehall in order to enhance that of Somerset House.[140]

PROVISION FOR THE LADIES MARY AND ELIZABETH   Henry VIII provided Edward with an independent household and his own Wardrobe of the Beds from a very early age.[141] While the contents of his Standing Wardrobe were not as sumptuous as the furnishings at Whitehall, it did have a larger and more varied selection of furnishing textiles than the wardrobes given to his sisters, the Lady Mary and the Lady Elizabeth (see Table 18).[142] Once Edward was head of the family,

---

139   For a discussion of this point see Hayward, 'Seat furniture', 123.

140   Murphy, 'Illusion of decline', 124.

141   Nichols, *Literary Remains* I, xxvii–xxx; Hayward, 'Repositories of splendour', 137.

142   According to the 1547 Inventory, as Prince of Wales, Edward had three pieces of arras, forty-six carpets, one celure and tester, eight chairs, three cloths of estate, ten counterpoints, fifteen cushions, eight single fustians, four pillows, thirteen single pillow-beres, seven quilts, twenty-seven pairs of sheets, one sparver, seventy-nine pieces of tapestry, three traverses, fifteen pieces of verdure and six window pieces: BL Harley MS 1419, fos 383r–393r.

TABLE 18

A COMPARISON OF THE CONTENTS OF THE WARDROBES OF THE BEDS PROVIDED FOR EDWARD, PRINCE OF WALES, THE LADY MARY AND THE LADY ELIZABETH

This table is taken from Hayward, 'Possessions', 276, which is based on BL Harley MS 1419, fos 383r–393r; 433r–438v; 439r–443v.

Object	Edward	Elizabeth	Mary	Totals
Altar frontals / cloths	—	6	1	7
Arras	3	—	—	3
Carpets	46	24	26	96
Celures and testers	1	—	—	1
Chairs	8	2	2	12
Cloths of estate	3	—	2	5
Counterpoints	10	—	22	32
Cushions	15	16	8	39
Fustians	8 single	—	—	8 single
Pillows	4	—	8	12
Pillow-beres	13 single	—	7?	?20 single
Quilts	7	—	—	7
Sheets	29 pairs	—	6 pairs	35 pairs
Sparvers	1	1	2	4
Tapestries	79	26	47	152
Traverses	3	2	2	7
Verdures	15	65	15	95
Vestments	—	6	—	6
Window pieces	6	12	16	34

he too had to provide suitable Wardrobe stuff for his sisters. In particular, the reorganization of the furnishings at Whitehall allowed for the creation of a Wardrobe of the Beds for Elizabeth. Her Wardrobe was described in the 1547 Inventory:

> Stuff deliuered to the Lady Elizabeth ... towardes the furniture of her house after the decease of her said father whiche dothe remayne in the charge of her graces officers at the kinges Majesties plesure.[143]

143 Ibid, f. 439r.

This new Wardrobe drew heavily on Denny's charge, just as the provision of chapel furnishings for Catherine Parr had about three years earlier (although in that case, Denny really only had temporary charge of the items). Elizabeth's Wardrobe either represented a new development or a replacement of any Wardrobe stuff that she might have had.

Its composition, as given in the 1542 Inventory, was very close to its composition listed in the 1547 Inventory (see Concordances I and II). Robert Beverley, Cofferer of the King's Household, received the following items on behalf of the Lady Elizabeth: two chairs [239], two traverses [517, 520], six vestments [1036–1038, 1047–1048], six altar frontals [1018, 1030, 1032], six pieces of tapestry [208–209], eleven carpets [434–435], fourteen cushions [349, 351, 354, 371, 400, 402, 409, 3327, 3330] and seventy-one pieces of verdure [212–213, 216–218, 220]. There are two significant omissions from Elizabeth's Wardrobe. First, she had no cloth of estate, a comment on her relative lack of status in comparison to her brother and sister. Indeed Denny's charge at Whitehall included a cloth of estate for the young prince, who would have been four and a half when the Inventory was compiled: 'The said Ceeler and Tester having the Lorde Princes badges / Images / Antique heddes and Parkeworke enbraudred vpon them' [236]

Secondly, there is a lack of bedding: this probably indicates that she already had bed linen and so did not require a grant from Edward VI.

Mary's Wardrobe was described in similar language to Elizabeth's in the 1547 Inventory,[144] but this presumably reflects the renewal of an existing grant rather than the formation of a new Wardrobe. As an adult Mary would have needed a Removing Wardrobe of the Beds well before 1547. Her relationship with her father was erratic and Mary only received a few pieces from Whitehall during Henry's lifetime: pampilion skins [28], sables [25], one chair [257] and the fabric from a square bed with celure and tester [474] was re-worked and made into two sets of bed hangings, which Mary shared with her sister Elizabeth. She received nothing immediately after Henry's death. Whether the latter was a reflection of a lack of favour or an indication that her Wardrobe was felt to be adequate is uncertain. However, in September 1547 Edward VI gave her a set of five tapestries (13772), two beds of down with bolsters (13776) and two counterpoints (13784–13785) from Nottingham.[145] Mary also received a number of items confiscated from Kenninghall, home of the Duke of Norfolk.[146]

According to Alberti 'There are two principal things that men do in this life, the first is to procreate, the second is to build'.[147] Henry VIII's sixty domestic properties attest to his success with bricks and mortar; the Reformation Parliament reflect his difficulties in providing for the succession. However, it is the evolution of one particular property and its contents that are of interest here. The 1530s saw the rapid development of Henry's Palace of Whitehall as the central focus of his material wealth, as well as his political power and religious supremacy. By 1547 it had became the chief repository for his wealth and possessions, and their management saw the beginning of a gradual shift towards the

---

144 Ibid, f. 433r.
145 Mary received twenty-six tapets from Nottingham in September 1546 (13749).
146 See PRO LR2/115.
147 Quoted in Goldthwaite, *Wealth and the Demand for Art in Italy*, 249. Leon Battista Alberti (1404–72) was author of *De re aedificatoria* [On matters concerning architecture].

development of standing houses in England. The role of the palace was to change in 1547 under the different agenda of Protector Somerset, and Whitehall lost its position as the king's leading palace when many of its contents were re-deployed.

The volume of objects held at Whitehall Palace and the number of properties owned by Henry VIII enabled the English monarchy to begin its transition from an itinerant monarchy with portable possessions to more static royalty, making relatively short distance removals and traveling between furnished properties. Indeed the objects acquired by Henry VIII were to play an influential role in royal life up until the Commonwealth Sale of 1649.

Denny was given an extra-ordinary remit as Keeper of Whitehall by Henry VIII. He continued Thomas Alvard's work in developing the building and its contents. In addition, he had a broader range of responsibilities, managing a group of linked properties. He was also central amongst the officers of Henry VIII's Privy Chamber. Of all the posts Denny held, the office of Keeper of Whitehall Palace was the least dependent on the vagaries of Henry VIII's nature and the most reliant on his own administrative skill. He was well supported by James Rufforth and Nicholas Bristow. Denny's aptitude for the political world is evident in the fact that he continued as Keeper under Edward VI, even if his area of responsibility was reduced and he was no longer Groom of the Stool. Unlike many other men who served Henry VIII, Denny died of natural causes in his bed and his wealth passed to his family.

DENNY'S BOOK OF ISSUE FOR THE PALACE OF WHITEHALL: A PARTIAL RECONSTRUCTION

A CCORDING TO THE PREAMBLES of BL Lansdowne Roll 14 and PRO E101/427/2, Denny had a Book of Issue or Discharge in which he recorded any item that passed out of his charge at Whitehall Palace. This book has been lost, but its format and purpose were described as follows:

> the book of Issues or dischardge hathe in nombre lxviij leves written <ye> first pagine wherof ys signed with thand of the said late kynge and euery pagine of the same Booke <is subscribed> wythe the hande of the said Nicholas Bristowe. And doethe conteine particlerly all and singuler suche of the said plate Juelles <howshold Stuffe> apparrell and other goodes as the said sir Antony Denny hathe delyvered or issued either to his Majesties owne handes or the handes of eny other person or persons.[1]

One of the more remarkable features of the 1542 Inventory is its extensive marginalia. Many of the notes dating from 1542 to 1546 include a folio reference elsewhere. It is a reasonable surmise that this notation refered to Denny's Book of Issue. The inference receives indirect support from the fact that most of the entries relating to items removed after Henry VIII's lack references. After January 1547 the Book of Issue ceased to be kept.

By using the information recorded in the marginalia, it is possible to create a list of the objects delivered to other properties or other individuals by Denny between 1542 and 1547. If we do this, it becomes apparent that the book was started in 1542 and that entries were recorded in order of date. Each new date was given a fresh folio. The dates refer to regnal years rather than calendar years (just as the additions to the 1542 Inventory were recorded by regnal years).[2] This pattern has been followed below. Further information given in the marginalia, such as the number and type of object, the recipient and/or the destination, was also given and is included here; additional information (such as the exact date, or who transported the items) is also sometimes given and is placed here with the general information after the folio number, since it is presumed that it is applicable to all entries on the same folio. It is likely that the original inventory entry was copied out in full in the Book of Issue.

While this may well reflect the construction of Denny's Book of Issue, there is one slight difficulty. Document PRO E101/427/2 mentions that the Book of Issue had sixty-eight pages, while the

---

1   PRO E101/427/2, m.1.
2   For regnal years of Henry VIII and Edward VI, see Volume II, p.11.

marginalia lists entries appearing on folio 2 to folio 138.[3] Even if the clerks were lax in their use of the terms page and folio, the consecutive numbering of the pages would only produce 134 sides. In spite of this, it is worth listing the marginal notes because they give the clearest indication of how objects were dispersed by Denny, when and to whom. It is possible that additional folios were added to the book or that a larger book than originally stipulated was used, and that the change was not recorded in the preamble to PRO E101/427/2.

The second batch of marginalia refers to items removed from Whitehall Palace, presumably under Denny's jurisdiction, between July and September 1547.[4] Again, the notes give the date, the recipient and the destination but no folio number. The lack of a folio number suggests that cross-referencing was considered to be less important in this instance because a new inventory was about to be taken of all the king's goods (the 1547 Inventory). The material is shown in the second list here (pages 148–60), in the same format as the first.

It seems unlikely that the marginalia were only record of the dispersed objects but no other list has survived. The relatively short length of Denny's Book of Issue suggests that this must have been a separate document. The interim list has been recreated here and as no folio numbers were mentioned in the marginal notes, the entries have been listed chronologically. When the 1547 Inventory was compiled, the dispersed objects were listed in their new locations.

---

3 Unfortunately, BL Lansdowne Roll 14 does not indicate how many folios the Book of Issue had.
4 There is a third group of marginal notes which relate to items marked as missing (*defficit*/*defficiunt*) when Denny's discharge was drawn up on Henry VIII's death in 1547.

Items issued by Denny between 1542 and 1547

f. 2   *To the King, 34 Hen VIII*
    288   2 footstools
    291   2 footstools
    895   1 pair of single regals
    To Sir Anthony Browne, 34 Hen VIII
    960   1 pike
    To Sir Anthony Browne and the Lord Privy Seal,
      34 Hen VIII
    968   2 hammers for horsemen
    981   2 arming swords

f. 4   *To Thomas Paston, 18 May 34 Hen VIII*
    975   2 long bows
    976   2 quivers

f. 5   *To the King, 24 May 34 Hen VIII*
    1004   2 curtains
    1012   4 curtains

f. 6   *To the King, 29 May 34 Hen VIII*
    1140   1 fire pan
    1141   3 fire pans
    1239   6 wooden bowls

f. 7   *To Mistress Bray, 16 June 34 Hen VIII*
    465   1 trussing bedstead
    497   1 counterpoint
    2360   1 bed
    2361   1 bolster
    2362   2 pillows
    2364   3 quilts

fos 7, 8   *To Mistress Bray, 16 June 34 Hen VIII*
    2395   1 pair of fustians
    2396   2 pairs of sheets
    2397   4 pillow-beres

f. 9   *To Sir Anthony Browne, 11 July 34 Hen VIII*
    972   1 crossbow

f. 10   *To Prince Edward, 24 July 34 Hen VIII*
    235   1 cloth of estate

f. 11   *No name given 34 Hen VIII*
    919   1 lute with case[5]
    To the Lord Privy Seal, 34 Hen VIII
    947   1 target

f. 12   *To the King, 34 Hen VIII*
    970   3 handguns, 3 cases, 1 horn and 1 purse
    1056   1 clock

f. 15   *To the Lady Elizabeth, 34 Hen VIII*
    2394   1 gilt lye pot

f. 17   *To the King's use, 34 Hen VIII*
    933   1 case with 7 recorders
    (No name given)
    919   1 lute with case
    To Mistress Bray, 25 December 37 Hen VIII
    28   11 dozen and 10 pampilion skins

f. 18   *To the Lady Mary, 25 January 34 Hen VIII*
    28   14 dozen and 2 pampilion skins
    To the King, 34 Hen VIII
    110   1 glass
    163   1 bell
    243   1 chair
    292   2 footstools
    392   1 cushion
    878   1 mirror
    1060   1 clock
    1139   1 fire pan
    1164   1 table
    1209   1 screen
    1222   1 case with instruments
    1223   1 case

f. 20   *To the Lady Mary*
    25   4 sable skins

f. 25   *To Oatlands, 'by the hands of' Nicholas Bristow,*
      23 May 35 Hen VIII
    232   1 cloth of estate
    233   1 cloth of estate
    238   2 chairs
    241   1 chair
    243   1 chair
    245   1 chair
    246   1 chair
    272   1 stool
    419   6 cases for chairs
    3344   1 cloth of estate

---

5   There is a discrepancy in the marginalia for entry **919** — the number of items recorded as being given to new recipients exceeds the number of items in the original entry. In this instance Henry VIII is recorded as having received either 1 lute with case or 2 lutes with 3 cases.

f. 26   *To Oatlands, 'by the hands of' Nicholas Bristow,*
      23 May 35 Hen VIII

280   1 close stool
282   1 close stool
342   3 cushions
351   2 cushions
352   1 cushion
355   1 cushion
356   1 cushion
357   3 cushions
358   2 cushions
362   1 cushion
380   2 cushions
390   1 cushion
657   4 bowls for close stools
660   2 cisterns for close stools
3312   2 footstools

f. 27   *To Oatlands, 'by the hands of' Nicholas Bristow,*
      35 Hen VIII

393   2 cushions
410   1 cushion
417   18 cases for cushions
919   1 lute with case
3322   1 cushion

f. 28   *To Oatlands, 'by the hands of' Nicholas Bristow*
205   6 pieces of tapestry
    To Oatlands
208   7 pieces of tapestry
211   14 pieces of verdure
    To Oatlands 'by the hands of' Edmund Pigeon,
      servant of Nicholas Bristow, 12 July 35 Hen VIII
212   14 pieces of verdure
213   14 pieces of verdure
215   5 pieces of verdure

f. 29   *To Oatlands, 35 Hen VIII*
218   21 pieces of verdure
274   1 stool
283   1 close stool
657   2 bowls for close stools
660   1 cistern for close stools
1198   1 chest
    To Oatlands, 12 July 37 Hen VIII
221   10 carpets

f. 30   *To William Harper, for the use of the Queen,*
      35 Hen VIII
2260   1 dorse, 1 redorse
2261   2 vestments
2262   1 dorse, 1 redorse
2263   2 vestments

2264   1 dorse, 1 redorse
2265   2 vestments
2266   1 dorse, 1 redorse
2267   1 vestment
2268   1 vestment
2269   1 dorse, 1 redorse
2270   2 albs
2271   8 altar cloths
2272   6 altar towels
2273   1 corporal case, 1 corporal cloth
2275   2 corporal cases, 2 corporal cloths
2276   1 sacrament cloth
2277   1 traverse

f. 31   *To William Harper, for the use of the Queen,*
      35 Hen VIII
1198   2 chests[6]
2274   2 corporal cases, 2 corporal cloths
2278   2 superaltars
2279   2 cruets
2280   1 sakering bell
2281   1 mass book
2282   1 mass book
2283   1 New Testament
2284   1 book
2285   1 stool
2286   1 chest
2287   1 trunk

f. 32   *To make beds for the Lady Mary and the Lady*
      Elizabeth, 35 Hen VIII
474   1 square bed/celure and tester

f. 33   *To Richard Cecil, Yeoman of the Robes,*
      35 Hen VIII
991   1 short hanger
993   1 wood knife
    To the King, 35 Hen VIII
994   1 dagger

f. 36   *To Oatlands, 'by the hands of' Nicholas Bristow*
3315   2 footstools

f. 37   *To the Lady Elizabeth, 21 December 35 Hen VIII*
25   1 timber and 3 skins of sable
28   3 dozen pampilion skins
    To the King, at Hampton Court
159   1 warming pan

f. 38   *To Sir Edmund Peckham*
99   1 gilt lantern
100   1 gilt perfume pan
101   1 gilt perfume pan

6   This entry is only noted as going to the queen, with no date or folio. However, fos 30–31 seem the most likely location.

102	2 gilt cruses
105	2 gilt cups
106	1 jug
107	1 jug

To the King, 35 Hen VIII

946	13 targets
947	13 targets
948	1 target
981	4 arming swords
995	2 daggers
996	1 dagger
997	3 daggers
998	4 daggers
999	4 daggers
1000	2 daggers
1001	1 knife
1002	2 knives

f. 39 *To the King, 35 Hen VIII*

861	1 mirror
961	1 morris-pike

f. 40 *To John Reed*

1141	2 fire pans

f. 48 *To Thomas Maynman, Keeper of the Wardrobe of the Beds, Greenwich, 35 Hen VIII*

3547	8 pieces of tapestry
3548	7 pieces of verdure

f. 49 *To Lady Margaret Douglas, 36 Hen VIII*

454	1 bedstead with apparel

To the King's use, 36 Hen VIII

1142	2 banners

f. 50 *To the King, 36 Hen VIII*

944	1 target
966	2 battle axes[7]

To Sir Thomas Darcy, 36 Hen VIII

946	10 targets

To John Rogers, Clerk of the Ordnance, 6 July 36 Hen VIII (to be shipped to Calais)

957	60 partisans
958	18 forest bills
960	32 pikes
962	3 staves
963	4 staves
964	19 halberds
965	2 halberds
966	1 battleaxe
967	6 horse hammers
968	6 horse hammers
978	2 holiness hafts
981	8 arming swords

2387	1 javelin
3487	10 halberds

f. 51 *To Philip Lentall*

11	1 kirtle

To Catherine Addington, 9 July 36 Hen VIII

25	6 timbers and 12 sable skins
26	1 mantle of sable backs and 4 sable skins
27	4 pieces of old sable
28	64 dozen and 2 pampilion skins

To Mistress Anne Bassett, 36 Hen VIII

464	1 trussing bedstead with apparel
495	1 counterpoint

To the King, 36 Hen VIII

950	11 targets

f. 53 *To Sir Thomas Cawarden, 36 Hen VIII*

445	1 bedstead with apparel

To the Queen, 36 Hen VIII

3681	3 sable skins

f. 54 *To Sir Thomas Cawarden, Nonsuch, 9 January 36 Hen VIII*

310	1 cushion
314	2 cushions
320	6 cushions
346	3 cushions
441	1 bedstead with apparel
448	1 bedstead with apparel

f. 55 *To Sir Thomas Cawarden, Nonsuch*

348	3 cushions
353	2 cushions
361	1 cushion
366	1 cushion
368	3 cushions
369	1 cushion
372	3 cushions
378	3 cushions
384	1 cushion
385	1 cushion
387	2 cushions

f. 56 *To Sir Thomas Cawarden, Nonsuch*

241	1 chair
352	1 cushion
364	3 cushions
373	2 cushions
374	2 cushions
380	1 cushion
381	2 cushions
386	2 cushions
389	1 cushion
390	2 cushions

7   The note gives the date 36 Hen VIII but no folio number entry: this location is therefore only a suggestion.

391	1 cushion
396	3 cushions
417	54 cases for cushions
3324	1 cushion

f. 57   *To Nonsuch, 35 Hen VIII*

280	2 close stools

To Sir Thomas Cawarden, 36 Hen VIII

238	3 chairs
239	7 chairs
242	1 chair
244	2 chairs
245	1 chair
246	1 chair
250	1 chair
257	1 chair
272	1 stool
280	2 close stools
282	1 close stool
419	18 cases for chairs
657	6 bowls for close stools
658	3 cisterns for close stools
660	3 cisterns
3311	2 footstools
3314	2 footstools
3549	10 pieces of tapestry
3550	3 pieces of tapestry

f. 58   *To Sir Thomas Cawarden, Nonsuch,*
        36 Hen VIII

275	1 stool
439	1 damask (for a bedstead)
453	1 damask (for a bedstead)
515	1 scarlet
516	1 scarlet
544	3 pairs of sheets
545	1 pair of sheets
554	2 pairs of sheets
561	3 pairs of pillow-beres
562	1 pair of pillow-beres
568	1 pillow-bere
569	1 pillow-bere

f. 60   *To Sir Edmund Peckham, 26 April 37 Hen VIII*

33	1 pair of gilt flagons
35	1 pair of gilt pots
36	1 pair of gilt pots
38	1 pair of gilt pots
39	1 of a pair of gilt pots
40	1 pair of gilt pots
42	1 pair of gilt pots
43	1 pair of gilt pots
44	1 pair of gilt pots
45	1 pair of gilt pots
47	1 of a pair of gilt pots

51	3 gilt bowls
53	3 gilt bowls
54	6 gilt bowls
55	6 gilt bowls
56	6 gilt bowls
57	3 gilt bowls
62	3 gilt basins and ewers
63	1 gilt basin and ewer
64	14 gilt spoons
67	1 gilt snuffer
71	3 gilt salts
72	1 gilt salt

f. 61   *To the King, 6 May 37 Hen VIII*

59	1 mazer

To Sir Edmund Peckham

73	1 gilt salt
74	2 gilt salts
77	1 gilt layer
80	11 gilt chandeliers
82	1 gilt cup
84	1 gilt cup
89	1 gilt cup
91	1 gilt cup
92	1 gilt cup
93	1 gilt cup
94	1 gilt cup
95	1 nut
96	1 nut
97	1 jug
144	9 parcel-gilt basins and ewers
145	2 parcel-gilt candlesticks
146	4 parcel-gilt candlesticks
153	1 white kitchen pot
154	1 white barber's basin
157	2 white candlesticks
158	2 vices

f. 62   *To Sir Edmund Peckham*

98	1 glass

No name given

229	1 cloth of estate

To Sir Thomas Cawarden, 22 June 37 Hen VIII

231	1 cloth of estate
312	3 cushions

To the King, 37 Hen VIII

3480	27 white plates
3481	75 white dishes
3482	18 white saucers

f. 63   *No name given*

187	1 tent hanging
188	1 tent hanging
189	2 window pieces
190	1 tent hanging

191 1 tent hanging
192 2 window pieces
To Sir Thomas Cawarden
417 3 cases for cushions
To the officers of the Tents
1141 2 fire pans

fos 63, *To the Queen*
64 **3681** 15 sable skins
To the Lady Elizabeth
3681 15 sable skins

f. 64 *To the King in his study, 18 February 37 Hen VIII*
151 1 parcel-gilt bell
435 1 carpet
744 1 slate
1188 3 stools
1197 4 chests
1208 1 screen

f. 65 *To the Lady Elizabeth*
882 1 standish
To the King, 38 Hen VIII
3313 2 footstools

f. 66 *To the King, 6 August 38 Hen VIII*
1   the diamond buttons from a gown
2   the diamond buttons from a gown
12   the pearl clusters from a coat
To Alan Bandeson, 22 September 38 Hen VIII
970 1 handgun
971 3 handguns
To Sir Anthony Aucher, 37 Hen VIII
1224 4 ropes for candles
1225 10 ropes for candles
To Sir Anthony Aucher, 38 Hen VIII
3355 6 ropes for candles

f. 67 *To the King, 38 Hen VIII*
3730 1 parcel-gilt basin and ewer
3732 1 pair of parcel-gilt flagons
3733 1 pair of parcel-gilt pots
3735 2 parcel-gilt bowls
3737 1 parcel-gilt goblet
3738 2 parcel-gilt goblets
3742 1 parcel-gilt cruse
3749 2 parcel-gilt candlesticks

f. 68 *To the King, 38 Hen VIII*
3726 1 jug
3727 1 jug

f. 69 *To Sir Anthony Denny as Groom of the Stool, 1 Ed VI*
280 2 close stools
281 1 close stool
282 2 close stools
284 2 close stools
285 1 close stool
657 10 bowls for close stools
658 5 bowls for close stools
659 1 bowl for a close stool
660 5 cisterns for close stools
661 4 cisterns for close stools
919 1 lute with case
3348 1 close stool
3350 1 case for a close stool
3484 2 bowls for close stools
3485 1 cistern for a close stool
Used at the late king's funeral at Windsor,
13 February, 1 Ed VI
952 1 poleaxe
To the Lord Protector
3681 8 sable skins
To James Rufforth
3681 32 sable skins

f. 70 *To the Earl of Warwick, by virtue of his office as*
Lord Chamberlain, by the commandment of the
Lord Protector
434 1 carpet
435 2 carpets
436 1 bedstead
447 1 counterpoint
3763 4 hangings of scarlet
3764 10 hangings of scarlet
To the Lady Elizabeth, 1 Ed VI
910 1 pair of virginals
To Windsor College to be used for the
late king
1046 2 vestments

f. 71 *To the Lady Mary*
257 1 chair
To the Earl of Warwick, Lord Chamberlain, 3 May
1 Ed VI
345 1 cushion
543 1 pair of sheets
550 1 pair of sheets
559 1 pair of pillow-beres
568 1 pillow-bere
To the Lord Protector, 1 Ed VI
921 1 case with 4 flutes and 1 flute
927 1 case with 7 crumhorns
934 1 case with 8 recorders

938	1 sagbut	f. 72	*To the Earl of Warwick, Lord Chamberlain*
3306	1 fire pan	**239**	1 chair
To the King, 1 Ed VI		*To the King, 2 Ed VI*	
972	2 crossbows with case and quiver	**1233**	1 trunk 'to shoot in'
3681	4 sable skins		
3681	43 sable skins[8]	f. 73	*To Sir Thomas Cawarden*
To the Earl of Arundel by commandment of the		**446**	1 bedstead with apparel
Lord Protector, 1 Ed VI			
1053	1 clock	f. 108	*To the King*
To Richard Frenior, by virtue of a writ of restitution		**744**	5 slates
by commandment of the Lord Protector, 1 Ed VI			
1234	1 pewter charger	f. 138	*To the King, 35 Hen VIII*
1235	48 pewter dishes	**960**	27 pikes
1236	24 pewter saucers	*No name given, Sept 37 Hen VIII*	
1237	23 pewter saucers	**233**	5 hangings
		224	6 window pieces

Items removed from Whitehall between July and September 1547 (including items delivered to Sir Anthony Denny, Keeper of the Palace of Whitehall, 'on his new charge')

To Sir Anthony Aucher, Master of the Jewel House, 9 July 1 Ed VI

31	2 gold casting bottles	**83**	1 gilt cup	**128**	1 image
32	2 gold spoons	**85**	1 gilt cup	**129**	1 image
34	1 pair of gilt flagons	**86**	1 gilt cup	**130**	2 gilt altar basins
37	1 pair of gilt pots	**87**	1 gilt cup	**131**	1 pair of gilt altar candlesticks
39	1 of a pair of gilt pots	**88**	2 gilt cups	**132**	1 pair of gilt cruets
41	1 pair of gilt pots	**90**	1 gilt cup	**133**	1 gilt holy-water stock
46	1 pair of gilt pots	**103**	2 gilt candlesticks	**134**	1 gilt chalice
47	1 of a pair of gilt pots	**104**	1 lantern	**135**	1 image
48	1 pair of gilt pots	**108**	1 hour glass	**136**	2 images
49	1 pair of gilt pots	**109**	1 clock	**137**	2 images
50	3 gilt bowls	**111**	1 gilt perfume	**138**	2 gilt altar basins
51	1 gilt bowl	**112**	1 gilt casting bottle	**139**	1 pair of gilt candlesticks
52	3 gilt bowls	**113**	1 gilt candlestick	**140**	1 gilt pyx
58	1 gilt bowl	**114**	1 gilt snuffer	**141**	1 pair of gilt cruets
60	1 gilt basin and ewer	**115**	1 image	**142**	1 gilt chalice
61	1 gilt basin and ewer	**116**	1 image	**143**	1 sakering bell
64	12 gilt spoons	**117**	1 image	**147**	1 parcel-gilt barber's basin
65	1 gilt strainer	**118**	1 image	**148**	1 parcel-gilt standish
66	1 gilt spice box	**119**	1 image	**149**	2 parcel-gilt perfumes
68	24 gilt trenchers	**120**	1 gilt pyx	**150**	2 parcel-gilt lavatory basins
69	4 gilt trenchers	**121**	1 gilt water pot	**151**	2 parcel-gilt bells
70	2 gilt salts	**122**	1 gilt table	**152**	1 parcel-gilt holy-water pot
75	3 gilt salts	**123**	3 gilt casting bottles	**154**	2 white barber's basins
76	1 gilt layer	**124**	2 gilt casting bottles	**155**	3 white water pots
78	6 gilt chandeliers	**125**	1 gilt pyx	**156**	1 white ladle
79	5 gilt chandeliers	**126**	1 image	**160**	1 white taste
81	8 gilt cups of assay	**127**	1 image	**161**	2 white perfumes

8   No folio is given for this entry: this location is therefore only a suggestion.

162	1 white snuffer	3718	3 gilt bowls	3743	1 parcel-gilt cruse
164	2 white perfumes	3719	1 gilt cup	3744	1 parcel-gilt cruse
165	1 superaltar	3720	1 gilt cup	3745	1 parcel-gilt chafing dish
166	1 case of knives	3721	1 gilt cup	3746	1 parcel-gilt chafing dish
167	1 case of knives	3722	1 gilt basin and ewer	3747	1 white cup
168	1 case of knives	3723	1 gilt layer	3748	1 white cruse
169	1 case of knives	3724	1 gilt layer	3750	2 white candlesticks
170	1 mazer	3725	1 gilt salt	3751	1 lantern
1217	2 copper and gilt perfume pans	3728	1 gilt chafing dish	3752	1 gilt cross
2295	2 broad knives and 2 meat knives	3729	1 parcel-gilt basin and ewer	3753	1 pair of gilt altar candlesticks
3711	1 gold spoon	3731	1 parcel-gilt pair of flagons	3754	2 gilt altar basins
3712	1 pair of gilt flagons	3734	1 parcel-gilt pair of pots	3755	1 gilt chalice
3713	1 pair of gilt flagons	3736	3 parcel-gilt bowls	3756	2 gilt cruets
3714	1 pair of gilt pots	3738	1 parcel-gilt goblet	3757	1 sakering bell
3715	1 pair of gilt pots	3739	2 parcel-gilt goblets	3758	1 gilt holy-water pot
3716	1 gilt bowl	3740	1 parcel-gilt cup	3759	1 gilt holy-water sprinkle
3717	3 gilt bowls	3741	1 parcel-gilt cup	3760	1 superaltar

To John Hales, deputy to Ralph Sadler, keeper of the Great Wardrobe, 9 July 1 Ed VI

1143	1 banner
1144	2 banners

To Humphrey Orme, Keeper of the Standing Wardrobe of the Beds at the Tower, 9 July 1 Ed VI

171	1 hanging	230	1 cloth of estate	424	1 carpet
172	2 window pieces	237	1 celure from a cloth of estate	426	1 carpet
173	1 hanging	238	1 chair	438	1 bedstead with apparel
174	3 window pieces	293	2 cushions	440	1 bedstead with apparel
175	1 hanging	294	1 cushion	450	1 bedstead with apparel
176	2 window pieces	295	1 cushion	459	1 bedstead with apparel
177	1 hanging	296	1 cushion	460	1 bedstead with apparel, except the scarlet
178	2 window pieces	297	1 cushion		
179	1 hanging	298	1 cushion	461	1 bedstead with apparel
180	4 window pieces	299	1 cushion	526	canvas to cover bedsteads
181	1 hanging	301	1 cushion	541	1 case for a bedstead
182	2 window pieces	303	1 cushion	1140	2 fire pans
183	1 hanging	304	1 cushion	1198	2 chests
184	2 window pieces	306	1 cushion	3319	1 cushion
185	1 hanging	307	1 cushion	3333	1 hanging
186	2 window pieces	315	1 cushion	3334	7 pieces of arras
193	12 pieces of arras	316	2 cushions	3335	5 pieces of arras
194	2 pieces of arras	318	2 cushions	3345	1 chair
195	1 piece of arras	319	2 cushions	3470	3 quilts
196	2 pieces of arras	321	2 cushions	3496	1 bed and 2 pillows
197	2 pieces of arras	416	1 case for a cushion	3497	1 bed, 1 bolster and 2 pillows
222	1 hanging	417	24 cases for cushions	3702	1 chair
226	1 piece of arras	419	4 cases for chairs	3703	1 chair
227	1 piece of arras	420	1 carpet	3706	1 cushion
228	1 cloth of estate	421	1 carpet		

To Sir Ralph Sadler, Master of the Great Wardrobe, 9 July 1 Ed VI

3863	tissue of gold, silver and silk, all colours	3893	satin, black	3924	sarsenet, double and single, black
3864	cloth of gold, crimson	3894	satin, russet	3925	sarsenet, double and single, russet
3865	cloth of gold, incarnate	3895	satin, tawny		
3866	cloth of gold, purple and blue	3896	satin, yellow	3926	sarsenet, double and single, tawny
3867	cloth of gold, yellow	3897	satin, changeable		
3868	cloth of gold, black	3898	satin, green	3927	sarsenet, double and single, white
3869	cloth of gold, russet	3899	satin, white		
3870	cloth of gold, green	3900	damask, crimson	3928	sarsenet, double and single, green
3871	cloth of gold, tawny	3901	damask, purple		
3872	cloth of silver, all colours	3902	damask, blue	3929	sarsenet, double and single, yellow
3873	baudekin, of gold	3903	damask, murrey		
3874	tinsel, of all colours	3904	damask, black	3930	silk of newmaking, of diverse colours
3875	velvet, crimson	3905	damask, russet		
3876	velvet, red	3906	damask, white	3931	bridges satin, of diverse colours
3877	velvet, murrey	3907	damask, green		
3878	velvet, black	3908	damask, tawny	3932	Milan fustian
3879	velvet, russet	3909	damask, orange	3933	baudekin, of silk
3880	velvet, tawny	3910	damask, yellow	3934	camlet, of silk
3881	velvet, white	3911	damask, ash	3935	Brussels ticks
3882	velvet, green	3912	damask, incarnate	3936	holland
3883	velvet, yellow	3913	taffeta, crimson	3937	Normandy cloth
3884	velvet, incarnate	3914	taffeta, incarnate	3938	nettle-cloth
3885	velvet, purple	3915	taffeta, purple	3939	cambric
3886	velvet, blue	3916	taffeta, black	3940	passementerie, gold, silver and silk, mixed with gold and silver
3887	velvet, newmaking, of diverse colours	3917	taffeta, tawny		
		3918	taffeta, white		
3888	satin, crimson	3919	taffeta, yellow	3941	passementerie, black
3889	satin, incarnate	3920	taffeta, changeable	3942	fringe, of silk
3890	satin, purple	3921	taffeta, orange	3943	Brussels cloth
3891	satin, blue	3922	taffeta, russet		
3892	satin, murrey	3923	sarsenet, double and single, purple, blue and violet		

To William Tildesley, Keeper of the Wardrobe of the Beds at Windsor, 20 July 1 Ed VI

234	1 cloth of estate	330	1 cushion	437	1 bedstead with apparel
238	7 chairs	331	1 cushion	439	1 bedstead with apparel
240	1 chair	332	1 cushion	444	1 bedstead with apparel
241	1 chair	333	1 cushion	452	1 bedstead with apparel
244	1 chair	334	1 cushion	455	1 bedstead with apparel
264	1 chair	335	1 cushion	456	1 bedstead with apparel
267	1 chair	336	1 cushion	518	1 traverse
286	2 footstools	337	1 cushion	526	canvas to cover bedsteads
287	2 footstools	338	1 cushion	527	1 clothsack
288	2 footstools	339	1 cushion	528	1 clothsack
316	1 cushion	340	1 cushion	529	1 clothsack
318	1 cushion	344	1 cushion	530	1 clothsack
319	1 cushion	349	1 cushion	531	1 clothsack
322	2 cushions	358	1 cushion	532	1 clothsack
325	1 cushion	363	1 cushion	866	1 mirror
326	1 cushion	417	24 cases for cushions	867	1 mirror
327	1 cushion	419	12 cases for chairs	870	1 mirror
328	1 cushion	435	16 carpets	871	1 mirror

874	1 mirror	1057	1 clock	3686	1 damask
875	1 mirror	1059	1 clock	3701	1 pair of double regals
1054	1 clock and 1 larum	2350	1 bedstead		
1055	1 clock	3479	2 barehides		

To Thomas Maynman, Keeper of the Wardrobe of the Beds at Greenwich, 21 July 1 Ed VI

| 203 | 8 pieces of tapestry |
| 3307 | 1 fire pan |

To Robert Hobbs, Keeper of the Wardrobe of the Beds at The More, 6 August 1 Ed VI

219	10 pieces of verdure	263	1 chair	526	canvas to cover bedsteads
251	1 chair	265	1 chair	3328	2 cushions
253	3 chairs	363	1 cushion	3329	2 cushions
255	1 chair	379	2 cushions	3330	2 cushions
256	2 chairs	393	3 cushions	3707	1 cushion
258	1 chair	394	3 cushions		
259	2 chairs	419	5 cases for chairs		

To Robert Beverley, Cofferer of the King's household, for the Lady Elizabeth, 6 August 1 Ed VI

209	1 window piece of tapestry
212	9 pieces of verdure
213	2 pieces of verdure

To The Lady Elizabeth, 6 August 1 Ed VI

208	5 pieces of tapestry	400	1 cushion	1036	1 vestment
216	21 pieces of verdure	402	1 cushion	1037	2 vestments
217	24 pieces of verdure	409	1 cushion	1038	1 vestment
218	3 pieces of verdure	434	2 carpets	1047	1 vestment
220	12 window pieces of verdure	435	9 carpets	1048	1 vestment
239	2 chairs	517	1 traverse	3326	1 cushion
349	3 cushions	520	1 traverse	3327	1 cushion
351	1 cushion	1018	2 altar frontals	3330	1 cushion
354	2 cushions	1030	2 altar frontals		
371	3 cushions	1032	2 altar frontals		

To John Reed, Keeper of the Wardrobe of the Beds at Whitehall, 17 August 1 Ed VI

198	6 pieces of tapestry	238	1 chair	274	1 stool
199	9 pieces of tapestry	239	3 chairs	275	2 stools
200	5 pieces of tapestry	245	1 chair	276	1 stool
201	7 pieces of tapestry	247	1 chair	278	1 stool
202	7 pieces of tapestry	248	1 chair	289	2 stools
204	8 pieces of tapestry	250	1 chair	290	2 footstools
206	6 pieces of tapestry	260	2 chairs	291	2 footstools
207	6 pieces of tapestry	264	1 chair	302	2 cushions
209	19 window pieces of tapestry	267	2 chairs	305	3 cushions
233	1 cloth of estate	273	1 stool	308	1 cushion

309	1 cushion	512	2 quilts	1022	2 altar fronts
311	1 cushion	513	2 pillows	1023	2 vestments
317	3 cushions	517	1 traverse	1026	1 mass book
323	3 cushions	521	1 traverse	1032	2 altar fronts
343	3 cushions	526	canvas to cover bedsteads	1038	2 vestments
344	2 cushions	543	7 pairs of sheets	1050	2 altar cloths
345	2 cushions	544	5 pairs of sheets	1140	1 fire pan
347	1 cushion	546	3 pairs of sheets	1141	2 fire pans
352	3 cushions	547	2 pairs of sheets	1177	1 table
359	1 cushion	549	1 pair of sheets	1180	3 trestles
399	1 cushion	550	4 sheets	1192	2 stools
403	1 cushion	551	3 sheets	1198	4 chests
417	25 cases for cushions	554	2 sheets	2305	1 sheet
418	6 cases for cushions	555	4 sheets	2363	2 pillows
419	13 cases for chairs	559	9 pairs of pillow-beres	3312	1 footstool
434	3 carpets	560	5 pairs of pillow-beres and	3325	1 cushion
435	4 carpets		1 single pillow-bere	3327	2 cushions
436	1 counterpoint	561	5 pairs of pillow-beres	3332	6 cushions
442	1 bedstead with apparel	562	2 pairs of pillow-beres	3483	2 stools
443	1 bedstead with apparel	563	9 pairs of pillow-beres	3493	1 quilt
447	1 bedstead with apparel	564	2 pillow-beres	3494	2 pillows
449	1 bedstead with apparel	567	1 pillow-bere	3546	6 pieces of tapestry
451	1 bedstead with apparel	568	3 pillow-beres	3678	2 footstools
453	1 bedstead with apparel	569	7 pillow-beres	3687	1 damask
460	1 scarlet	1019	1 sacrament cloth	3704	1 chair
510	1 fustian	1020	1 mass book	3761	1 corporal case
511	1 quilt	1021	1 corporal case		

To William Griffiths, Keeper of the Wardrobe of the Beds at Richmond, 22 August 1 Ed VI

238	2 chairs	329	1 cushion	376	3 cushions
239	3 chairs	341	1 cushion	383	3 cushions
240	2 chairs	343	2 cushions	391	1 cushion
244	1 chair	350	1 cushion	417	10 cases for cushions
251	1 chair	354	2 cushions	418	11 cases for cushions
258	1 chair	358	1 cushion	419	4 cases for chairs
263	1 chair	359	2 cushions	3323	1 cushion
265	1 chair	360	2 cushions	3331	3 cushions
313	2 cushions	362	2 cushions		

To Hans Hunter, Keeper of the Armoury at Whitehall, 22 August 1 Ed VI

951	1 pair of quishes	983	2 swords	989	2 skenes
976	1 quiver	984	1 sword	990	1 skene
977	2 long bows	985	6 swords	992	1 short hanger
979	1 sword	986	2 swords	993	2 wood knives
980	1 sword	987	1 sword		
982	3 swords	988	1 skene		

To Edmund Pigeon, Clerk of the Wardrobe, 25 August 1 Ed VI

236	1 cloth of estate	476	1 celure and tester	1039	1 vestment
249	2 chairs	477	1 celure and tester	1040	3 vestments
252	1 chair	478	1 celure and tester	1041	1 vestment
254	1 chair	479	1 celure and tester	1042	1 vestment
262	1 chair	480	1 celure and tester	1043	2 vestments
266	1 chair	481	1 celure and tester	1044	1 vestment
267	1 chair	482	1 celure and tester	1045	1 vestment
268	6 stools	483	1 celure and tester	1048	1 vestment
269	7 stools	484	1 celure and tester	1049	1 vestment
270	7 stools	485	1 celure and tester	1163	3 cupboards
271	10 stools	486	1 celure and tester	1177	3 tables
273	1 stool	487	1 celure and tester	1180	3 pairs of trestles
275	2 stools	488	1 celure and tester	1198	2 chests
288	5 footstools	489	1 celure and tester	1204	1 cabinet
291	2 footstools	490	1 celure and tester	1205	1 cabinet
300	5 cushions	491	1 celure and tester	1206	1 cabinet
313	1 cushion	492	1 celure and tester	1207	1 cabinet
321	3 cushions	493	1 counterpoint	1218	1 folding lectern
324	3 cushions	508	4 curtains	1227	1 church cloth
350	2 cushions	509	4 curtains	1228	1 church cloth
365	3 cushions	522	1 bedstead	1229	1 altar frontal
367	3 cushions	523	1 bedstead	1230	1 altar frontal
370	3 cushions	524	4 pillars	2293	1 counterpoint
375	3 cushions	525	4 pillars	2294	1 counterpoint
377	1 cushion	526	canvas to cover bedsteads	2307	1 sheet
382	2 cushions	533	2 cases for bedsteads	2348	1 celure and tester
388	1 cushion	534	3 cases for bedsteads	2349	1 celure and tester
392	1 cushion	535	4 cases for bedsteads	2388	1 cabinet
395	2 cushions	536	2 cases for bedsteads	3315	9 footstools
397	1 cushion	537	3 cases for bedsteads	3317	4 footstools
398	2 cushions	538	2 cases for bedsteads	3318	4 footstools
401	1 cushion	539	1 case for a bedstead	3320	1 cushion
402	1 cushion	540	5 cases for bedsteads	3321	1 cushion
404	1 cushion	542	1 case for a bedstead	3323	1 cushion
405	1 cushion	812	2 pictures	3325	1 cushion
406	1 cushion	1017	2 altar frontals	3330	1 cushion
407	1 cushion	1018	2 vestments	3337	1 counterpoint
408	1 cushion	1024	2 altar frontals	3338	1 counterpoint
411	1 cushion	1025	2 vestments	3346	2 cushions
412	1 cushion	1028	1 altar cloth	3347	2 cushions
413	1 cushion	1029	2 altar frontals	3349	4 footstools
417	5 cases	1031	1 altar frontal	3705	1 cushion
418	11 cases	1033	2 altar frontals	3708	2 footstools
419	7 cases	1034	2 altar frontals	3709	2 footstools
457	1 bedstead	1035	2 altar frontals	3710	2 footstools
458	1 bedstead	1036	3 vestments	3765	6 footstools
473	1 sparver	1037	6 vestments	3766	4 footstools
475	1 celure and tester	1038	1 vestment		

To Philip Van Wilder, of the King's Privy Chamber, Keeper of the King's Instruments, 2 September 1 Ed VI

881	1 mirror	907	1 pair of double virginals	929	1 recorder with case
888	1 pair of double regals	908	1 pair of single virginals	930	4 recorders with case
889	1 pair of double regals	909	1 pair of single virginals	931	9 recorders with case
890	1 pair of double regals	910	2 pairs of single virginals	932	1 case with 6 recorders
891	1 pair of single regals	911	1 pair of single virginals	934	1 case with 8 recorders
892	1 pair of single regals	912	1 pair of double virginals	935	2 recorders
893	1 pair of single regals	913	1 pair of clavichords	936	4 recorders
894	1 pair of double regals	914	1 pair of clavichords	937	1 pipe for a tabor
895	5 pairs of single regals	915	11 vials, great and small	939	8 shawms with 3 cases
896	1 pair of double regals	916	4 gitterons and 4 cases	940	1 case with 7 shawms
897	1 pair of single regals	917	2 gitterons	942	1 case with a shawm
898	1 pair of single virginals and 1 single regal	918	14 gitteron pipes in a bag	943	1 bagpipe
		919	20 lutes and cases	1177	1 table
899	1 pair of single regals	920	1 gitteron and 1 lute	1180	1 pair of trestles
900	1 pair of single regals	921	4 cases with 4 lutes in, 1 case with 3 flutes in	1198	1 chest
901	1 pair of single regals			1203	2 chests for instruments
902	1 pair of double regals and 1 double virginal	922	1 case with 15 lutes	2353	1 vial
		923	1 case with 10 lutes	2354	1 shawm
903	1 instrument that 'goith with a whele'	924	1 case with 7 lutes	2355	1 pair of virginals
		925	5 flutes with case	3354	3 lutes with 3 cases
904	2 pairs of double virginals	926	4 flutes with case	3495	7 vials
905	1 pair of single virginals	927	1 case with 7 crumhorns		
906	1 pair of single virginals	928	6 recorders with case		

To Sir Thomas Cawarden, for Nonsuch, 29 September 1 Ed VI

210	1 carpet	425	1 carpet	467	1 trussing bedstead with apparel
216	2 pieces of verdure	427	1 carpet	471	1 trussing bedstead with apparel
218	20 pieces of verdure	428	1 carpet		
220	3 window pieces of verdure	429	1 carpet	472	1 folding bedstead with apparel
221	13 carpets	430	1 carpet	2296	4 beds
225	7 pieces of arras	431	2 carpets	2297	4 bolsters
261	1 chair	432	1 carpet	3549	1 piece of tapestry
422	1 carpet	433	1 carpet	3550	1 piece of tapestry
423	1 carpet	435	22 carpets		

To Philip Hoby, Master of Ordnance, by the Clerk of the Ordnance, 1 Ed VI

945	2 targets	953	1 pollaxe	961	5 morris-pikes
946	33 targets	954	37 partisans	972	7 crossbows
947	23 targets	955	3 partisans	973	1 quiver
948	5 targets	956	2 partisans	974	1 crossbow
949	2 targets	957	38 partisans		
952	21 pollaxes	959	6 forest bills		

To James Rufforth, Deputy Keeper of the Palace of Whitehall ('as good'), 27 February 2 Ed VI

1	1 gown	588	1 tablecloth	885	2 pairs of playing tables with pieces
2	1 gown	589	1 tablecloth	886	1 pair of playing tables with a bag
3	1 gown	590	1 tablecloth		
4	1 gown	591	1 tablecloth	887	1 pair of playing tables with chessmen
5	1 gown	592	1 tablecloth		
6	1 gown	593	1 tablecloth	1061	3 glass bottles or flagons
7	3 gowns	595	1 tablecloth	1062	2 glass bottles or flagons
8	1 mantle	596	1 tablecloth	1063	12 glass bottles or flagons
9	1 kirtle	598	1 tablecloth	1064	2 earth flagons
10	3 mantles	599	1 tablecloth	1065	1 glass basin and layer
11	2 kirtles	600	1 tablecloth	1066	1 glass basin and 2 layers
12	1 coat	601	1 tablecloth	1067	12 glass basins and 13 ewers and layers
13	2 coats	603	1 tablecloth		
14	1 coat	605	1 tablecloth	1068	1 marble basin and ewer
15	1 coat	606	1 tablecloth	1069	1 earth basin and ewer
16	1 coat	607	1 tablecloth	1070	3 glass bowls
17	1 doublet	608	5 napkins	1071	12 glass bowls
18	1 doublet	609	20 napkins	1072	34 glass bowls
19	1 doublet	610	8 napkins	1073	2 glass bowls
20	1 doublet	611	3 cupboard cloths	1074	4 glass cups
21	1 doublet	613	1 towel	1075	30 glass cups
22	4 shirt bands	614	1 towel	1076	14 glass cups
23	4 shirt bands	615	1 towel	1077	1 glass cup
24	1 pair of sable skins	617	1 towel	1078	2 glass cups
29	1 case for a gown	620	1 towel	1079	2 glass cups
30	4 cases for doublets	622	1 towel	1080	16 glass goblets
548	14 pairs of sheets	623	1 towel	1081	7 glass pots
549	2 pairs and 1 sheet	627	1 towel	1082	1 glass pot
551	5 sheets	628	1 towel	1083	3 glass pots
552	9 pairs and 1 sheet	629	1 towel	1084	3 glass pots
553	2 pairs and 1 sheet	636	1 towel	1085	1 glass pot
556	3 sheets	638	1 towel	1086	1 glass pot
557	4 sheets	639	1 towel	1087	1 glass pot
558	18 trussing sheets	640	1 towel	1088	1 glass cup
565	8 pillow-beres	641	1 towel	1089	1 glass cup
566	1 pillow-bere	642	1 sewer's towel	1090	1 glass cup
570	5 coifs	643	1 sewer's towel	1091	1 glass cup
571	13 kerchiefs	644	1 sewer's towel	1092	24 glass cups
572	6 double rails	645	1 coverpane	1093	1 glass cup
573	6 double stomachers	646	1 coverpane	1094	1 glass cup
574	3 pairs of slops	647	1 coverpane	1095	12 glass cruses
575	6 aprons	648	1 coverpane	1096	15 glass cruses
576	4 handkerchiefs	649	1 coverpane	1097	1 glass cruse
577	11 handkerchiefs	650	3 coverpanes	1098	2 glass cruses
578	25 rubbers of linen	651	1 coverpane	1099	1 glass layer
579	4 tablecloths	652	2 coverpanes	1100	1 glass layer
580	1 tablecloth	653	1 coverpane	1101	8 glass layers
581	1 tablecloth	654	1 coverpane	1102	12 earth cups
582	1 tablecloth	655	1 coverpane	1103	1 glass
583	1 tablecloth	656	1 coverpane	1104	1 crystal glass
584	1 tablecloth	662	10 chamber-water pots	1105	4 glasses
585	1 tablecloth	860	1 globe	1106	1 glass
586	1 tablecloth	883	6 standishes	1107	9 glass spice plates
587	1 tablecloth	884	2 standishes		

1108	7 glass spice plates	2118	1 gown	2171	1 pair of sleeves
1109	1 glass candlestick	2119	1 gown	2172	1 pair of sleeves
1110	3 glass candlesticks	2120	1 gown	2173	1 pair of sleeves
1111	4 glass candlesticks	2121	1 kirtle	2174	1 pair of sleeves
1112	3 glass altar candlesticks	2122	1 kirtle	2175	1 pair of sleeves
1114	6 glass trenchers	2123	1 kirtle	2176	1 pair of sleeves
1115	6 glass trenchers	2124	1 kirtle	2177	1 pair of sleeves
1116	4 spoons	2125	1 kirtle	2178	1 pair of sleeves
1117	2 forks	2126	1 kirtle	2179	1 pair of sleeves
1118	66 glass plates, dishes and saucers	2127	1 kirtle	2180	1 pair of sleeves
		2128	1 kirtle	2181	1 pair of sleeves
1119	2 earth platters	2129	1 kirtle	2182	1 pair of sleeves
1120	6 earth saucers	2130	1 kirtle	2183	1 pair of sleeves
1121	1 glass casting bottle	2131	1 kirtle	2184	1 pair of sleeves
1122	1 glass basket	2132	1 base of a kirtle	2185	1 pair of sleeves
1123	2 glass conserve pots	2133	1 kirtle	2186	1 pair of sleeves
1124	1 glass holy-water stock	2134	1 kirtle	2187	1 pair of sleeves
1125	divers conceits of earth[9]	2135	1 kirtle	2188	1 pair of sleeves
1140	1 fire pan	2136	1 cloak	2189	1 pair of sleeves
1177	1 table	2137	1 pair of sleeves	2190	1 pair of sleeves
1179	1 pair of trestles	2138	1 pair of sleeves	2191	1 pair of sleeves
1192	1 stool	2139	2 pairs of sleeves	2192	1 pair of sleeves
1196	1 chest	2140	1 pair of sleeves	2193	1 pair of sleeves
1198	7 chests	2141	1 pair of sleeves	2194	1 pair of sleeves
1201	1 trunk	2142	1 pair of sleeves	2195	1 pair of sleeves
1214	1 walking staff	2143	1 pair of sleeves	2196	1 pair of sleeves
1215	3 staves	2144	1 pair of sleeves	2197	1 pair of sleeves
1219	1 pair of scales	2145	1 pair of sleeves	2198	1 pair of sleeves
1220	1 pair of scales	2146	1 pair of sleeves	2199	1 pair of sleeves
1232	1 trunk 'to shoot in'	2147	1 pair of sleeves	2200	3 placards
2095	1 gown	2148	1 pair of sleeves	2201	5 placards
2096	1 gown	2149	1 pair of sleeves	2202	8 placards
2097	1 gown	2150	1 pair of sleeves	2203	14 placards
2098	1 gown	2151	1 pair of sleeves	2204	1 stomacher
2099	1 gown	2152	1 pair of sleeves	2205	2 stomachers
2100	1 gown	2153	1 pair of sleeves	2206	1 stomacher
2101	1 gown	2154	1 pair of sleeves	2207	1 stomacher
2102	1 gown	2155	1 pair of sleeves	2208	1 stomacher
2103	1 gown	2156	1 pair of sleeves	2209	1 stomacher
2104	1 gown	2157	1 pair of sleeves	2210	1 stomacher
2105	1 gown	2158	1 pair of sleeves	2211	1 stomacher
2106	1 gown	2159	1 pair of sleeves	2212	1 stomacher
2107	1 gown	2160	1 pair of sleeves	2213	1 stomacher
2108	1 gown	2161	1 pair of sleeves	2214	1 stomacher
2109	1 gown	2162	1 pair of sleeves	2215	1 stomacher
2110	1 gown	2163	1 pair of sleeves	2216	10 frontlets
2111	1 gown	2164	1 pair of sleeves	2217	3 frontlets
2112	1 gown	2165	1 pair of sleeves	2218	2 frontlets
2113	1 gown	2166	1 pair of sleeves	2219	1 French hood
2114	1 gown	2167	1 pair of sleeves	2220	1 biliment
2115	1 gown	2168	1 pair of sleeves	2221	1 biliment
2116	1 gown	2169	1 pair of sleeves	2222	3 coifs
2117	1 gown	2170	1 pair of sleeves	2223	1 partlet

9   Possibly decorative ceramic centrepieces for a dining table.

2224	6 partlets	2311	1 tablecloth	2379	1 terracotta
2225	2 partlets	2312	1 tablecloth	2380	2 terracottas
2226	1 muffler	2316	1 tablecloth	2381	1 terracotta
2227	1 muffler	2317	1 towel	2382	1 terracotta
2228	1 hat	2318	1 towel	2383	1 terracotta
2229	1 hat	2319	1 towel	2384	1 terracotta
2230	1 waistcoat	2320	1 towel	2385	1 terracotta
2231	1 waistcoat	2321	1 towel	2386	1 terracotta
2232	1 waistcoat	2322	1 towel	2389	1 comb case
2233	1 pair of short hose	2324	1 towel	2390	1 set of chessmen
2234	1 sampler	2325	1 towel	2391	10 vizers
2235	1 chest	2327	1 towel	*27 February 2 Ed VI*	
2236	1 chest	2328	1 towel	2398–2435	books
2237	1 chest	2329	1 towel	2436–2474	books
2238	2 coffers	2330	1 towel	2475–2514	books
2239	1 coffer	2332	1 towel	2515–2553	books
2240	1 mirror	2334	1 towel	2554–2591	books
2241	3 comb cases	2336	1 towel	2592–2625	books
2242	1 standish	2337	1 towel	2626–2661	books
2243	1 walking staff	2339	1 towel	2662–2698	books
2244	1 pair of playing tables	2341	1 cupboard cloth	2699–2735	books
2245	1 pair of playing tables	2344	3 napkins	2736–2772	books
2246	1 case of carving knives	2345	12 dozen napkins	2773–2811	books
2247	1 baby	2346	3 coverpanes	2812–2849	books
2248	2 babies	2347	1 coverpane	2850–2888	books
2249	1 glass	2356	14 standishes	2889–2926	books
2250	1 tower of wood	2357	3 standishes	2927–2961	books
2251	1 piece of arras	2358	1 globe	2962–2970	books
2252	1 side of a cushion	2359	2 globes	2971–2987	books
2253	1 piece of cloth of gold	2365	1 table	2988–3020	books
2254	1 box	2366	1 table	3021–3053	books
2255	1 lily pot	2367	1 table	3054–3087	books
2256	1 coverpane	2372	4 coffers	3088–3121	books
2257	1 coverpane	2373	2 coffers	3122–3154	books
2258	1 waist smock	2374	1 coffer	3155–3190	books
2259	1 calico cloth	2375	1 coffer	3191–3223	books
2305	2 pairs of sheets	2376	2 coffers	3224–3257	books
2306	5 pairs of sheets	2377	1 picture	3258–3287	books
2309	1 tablecloth	2378	1 terracotta	3288–3305	books

To James Rufforth, Deputy Keeper of the Palace of Whitehall ('as refuce'),[10] *27 February 2 Ed VI*

414	1 cushion	494	1 counterpoint	502	1 counterpoint
415	2 cushions	495	4 counterpoints	504	1 counterpoint
434	1 carpet	496	2 counterpoints	505	1 counterpoint
435	1 carpet	497	1 counterpoint	514	8 pillows
462	1 trussing bedstead	498	1 counterpoint	519	1 traverse
463	1 trussing bedstead	499	2 counterpoints	548	2 pairs of sheets
469	1 trussing bedstead	500	1 counterpoint	550	1 sheet
470	1 trussing bedstead	501	1 counterpoint	551	1 pair of sheets

10   No date is given for the delivery of the refuse items, but it is likely that Rufforth received them on 27 February along with the good items.

558	12 trussing sheets	634	1 towel	2333	1 towel
570	1 coif	635	1 towel	2335	1 towel
594	1 tablecloth	637	1 towel	2338	1 towel
595	1 tablecloth	1003	10 curtains[11]	2340	1 cupboard cloth
597	1 tablecloth	1198	4 chests	2343	1 cupboard cloth
602	1 tablecloth	1238	1 trivet	2344	2 napkins
608	4 napkins	2299	1 counterpoint	2345	41 napkins
609	12 napkins	2301	1 counterpoint	2369	2 mirrors
610	12 napkins	2302	1 counterpoint	2370	1 mirror
616	1 towel	2303	1 counterpoint	2371	1 mirror
618	1 towel	2308	3 trussing sheets	3308	3 wooden bowls
621	1 towel	2310	1 tablecloth	3316	2 footstools
624	1 towel	2313	1 tablecloth	3676	2 chairs called trams
625	1 towel	2314	1 tablecloth	3677	1 chair called a tram
626	1 towel	2315	1 tablecloth	3680	1 chair
630	1 towel	2323	1 towel	3767	2 curtains
632	1 towel	2326	1 towel		
633	1 towel	2331	1 towel		

To Sir Anthony Denny, Keeper of the Palace of Whitehall ('on his new charge')

211	6 pieces of verdure	676	1 picture	707	1 picture
214	7 pieces of verdure	677	1 picture	708	1 picture
220	4 window pieces of verdure	678	1 picture	709	1 picture
457	1 bed, 1 bolster, 1 pillow, 3 quilts, 2 fustians	679	1 picture	710	1 picture
		680	1 picture	711	1 picture
458	1 bed, 1 bolster, 2 pillows, 3 quilts, 2 fustians	681	1 picture	712	1 picture
		682	1 picture	713	1 picture
466	1 trussing bedstead with apparel	683	1 picture	714	1 picture
		684	1 picture	715	1 picture
468	1 trussing bedstead with apparel	685	1 picture	716	1 picture
		686	1 picture	717	1 picture
503	1 counterpoint	687	1 picture	718	1 picture
506	1 counterpoint	688	1 picture	719	1 picture
507	1 counterpoint	689	1 picture	720	1 picture
549	2 pairs of sheets	690	1 picture	721	1 picture
550	1 sheet	691	1 picture	722	1 picture
551	3 pairs of sheets	692	1 picture	723	1 picture
553	3 pairs and 1 sheet	693	1 picture	724	1 picture
663	3 cisterns for a close stool	694	1 picture	725	1 picture
664	1 picture	695	1 picture	726	1 picture
665	1 picture	696	1 picture	727	1 picture
666	1 picture	697	1 picture	728	1 picture
667	1 picture	698	1 picture	729	1 picture
668	1 picture	699	1 picture	730	1 picture
669	1 picture	700	1 picture	731	1 picture
670	1 picture	701	1 picture	732	1 picture
671	1 picture	702	1 picture	733	1 picture
672	1 picture	703	1 picture	734	1 picture
673	1 picture	704	1 picture	735	1 picture
674	1 picture	705	1 picture	736	1 picture
675	1 picture	706	1 picture	737	1 picture

11   The entry records the yardage, not the number of curtains, delivered to Rufforth; it amounts to ten-twelfths of the total.

738	1 picture	791	1 picture	848	1 map
739	1 picture	792	1 picture	849	1 map
740	1 picture	793	1 picture	850	1 map
741	1 picture	794	1 picture	851	1 map
742	4 pictures	795	1 picture	852	1 map
743	1 picture	796	1 picture	853	1 map
744	2 slates	797	1 picture	854	1 map
745	1 picture	798	1 picture	855	1 map
746	1 picture	799	1 picture	856	1 map
747	1 picture	800	1 picture	857	1 map
748	1 picture	801	1 picture	858	1 map
749	1 picture	802	1 picture	859	1 map
750	1 picture	803	1 picture	862	1 mirror
751	1 picture	804	1 picture	863	1 mirror
752	3 pictures	805	1 picture	864	1 mirror
753	1 picture	806	1 picture	865	1 mirror
754	1 picture	807	1 picture	866	3 mirrors
755	1 picture	808	1 picture	868	1 mirror
756	1 picture	809	1 picture	869	1 mirror
757	1 picture	810	1 picture	870	1 mirror
758	1 picture	811	1 picture	872	1 mirror
759	1 picture	813	1 picture	873	1 mirror
760	1 picture	816	1 stained cloth	876	1 mirror
761	1 picture	817	1 stained cloth	877	1 mirror
762	1 picture	818	1 stained cloth	879	1 mirror
763	1 picture	819	1 stained cloth	880	1 mirror
764	1 picture	821	1 stained cloth	1003	2 curtains[12]
765	1 picture	822	1 stained cloth	1004	6 curtains
766	1 picture	823	1 stained cloth	1005	2 curtains
767	1 picture	824	1 terracotta	1006	7 curtains
768	1 picture	825	1 terracotta	1007	2 curtains
769	1 picture	826	1 terracotta	1008	3 curtains
770	1 picture	827	1 terracotta	1009	2 curtains
771	1 picture	828	1 terracotta	1010	1 curtain
772	1 picture	829	1 terracotta	1011	4 curtains
773	1 picture	830	1 terracotta	1012	10 curtains
774	1 picture	831	1 terracotta	1013	1 curtain
775	1 picture	832	1 terracotta	1014	1 curtain
776	1 picture	833	1 terracotta	1015	9 curtains
777	1 picture	834	1 terracotta	1016	2 curtains
778	1 picture	835	1 terracotta	1051	1 clock
779	1 picture	836	1 terracotta	1052	1 larum
780	1 picture	837	1 map	1058	1 clock
781	1 picture	838	1 map	1126	1 pair of andirons
782	1 picture	839	1 map	1127	1 pair of andirons
783	2 pictures	840	1 map	1128	1 pair of andirons
784	2 pictures	841	1 map	1129	8 pairs of andirons
785	1 picture	842	1 map	1130	1 pair of andirons
786	1 picture	843	1 map	1131	1 pair of andirons
787	1 picture	844	1 map	1132	2 pairs of andirons
788	1 picture	845	1 map	1133	1 pair of andirons
789	1 picture	846	1 map	1134	19 pairs of andirons
790	1 picture	847	1 map	1135	15 fire forks

12 The entry records the yardage, not the number of curtains, delivered to Denny; it amounts to two-twelfths of the total.

1136	11 fire pans	1178	1 table	2368	1 form
1137	15 pairs of tongs	1179	3 pairs of trestles	2393	1 lantern
1138	9 pairs of bellows	1180	20 pairs of trestles	3336	1 table
1145	1 candlestick	1181	1 form	3353	3 curtains
1146	1 candlestick	1182	64 forms	3356	2 curtains
1147	17 candlesticks	1183	1 stool	3357	1 table
1148	2 candlesticks	1184	1 stool	3471	1 map
1149	1 cupboard	1185	1 stool	3472	1 table
1150	1 cupboard	1186	1 stool	3490	1 form
1151	1 cupboard	1187	2 stools	3491	2 stools
1152	1 cupboard	1188	2 stools	3492	4 footstools
1153	3 cupboards	1189	1 stool	3597	1 pair of andirons
1154	2 cupboards	1190	1 stool	3598	1 hearth
1155	3 cupboards	1191	59 stools	3599	1 fire pan
1156	2 cupboards	1192	3 stools	3600	1 fire fork
1157	3 cupboards	1193	4 footstools	3601	1 pair of tongs
1158	2 cupboards	1194	23 footstools	3602	1 rake
1159	3 cupboards	1195	2 chests	3603	1 toasting fork
1160	1 cupboard	1197	1 chest	3688	2 curtains
1161	1 cupboard	1198	17 chests	3689	2 curtains
1162	1 cupboard	1199	2 chests	3690	2 curtains
1163	27 cupboards	1200	1 chest	3691	2 curtains
1165	1 table	1201	1 trunk	3692	4 curtains
1166	1 table	1202	3 chests	3693	1 curtain
1167	1 table	1210	1 screen	3694	1 curtain
1168	1 table	1211	6 screens	3695	1 curtain
1169	2 tables	1216	3 staves	3696	1 stained cloth
1170	1 table	1221	5 snuffers	3697	1 stained cloth
1171	1 table	1231	1 lantern	3698	1 stained cloth
1172	1 table	2296	2 beds	3699	1 map
1173	1 table	2297	2 bolsters	3700	1 map
1174	2 tables	2298	1 counterpoint	3768	2 curtains
1175	1 table	2307	1 sheet	3769	2 curtains
1176	2 tables	2351	3 curtains	3770	1 curtain
1177	32 tables	2352	1 curtain	3771	1 curtain

BRIEF LIVES:
THE PEOPLE OF THE 1542 INVENTORY

THE 1542 INVENTORY is chiefly concerned with three individuals – Henry VIII, who had commissioned the inventory, Sir Anthony Denny, as palace keeper who used the document and Nicholas Bristow, the clerk who compiled it. However, a far larger circle of people were recorded within the text including Henry VIII's children, keepers of other properties owned by the king, merchants, craftsmen and members of the royal household. These short biographies are intended to provide background details on the people mentioned in the 1542 Inventory, focusing on the period covered by the working life of the document (1542–7). Many of them are also mentioned in the three smaller documents included in this volume; for reasons of space those individuals who are mentioned only in the latter are not included. For some individuals very little information is available but what there is, is given here.

Cross-references to other entries in this section are given, except for Henry VIII, his wives and children and Sir Anthony Denny.

Addington, Catherine
Initially worked as a silk woman. 1524: received a royal appointment. 1542: m. Thomas Jenyn (appointed King's Skinner on 6 November 1511). After Jenyn's death m. Thomas Addington, a former apprentice of the skinner John Ring and Master of the Skinners' Company (appointed king's skinner 23 April 1533). December 1543: after Addington's death in that month, held the office of king's skinner. February 1546: undertook to hold the post of king's skinner with Richard Brykett.

Albert, Francis
Milliner who did business with the royal household.

Aucher, Sir Anthony
Master of the Jewel House; Joint Master of the Tents; Controller and Paymaster of Works at Dover; Chief Victualler at Boulogne.

Bandeson, Alan
The king's gunsmith; listed as Keeper of one of the armouries at Whitehall in the 1547 Inventory.

Basset, Anne
Daughter of Honor, Lady Lisle, by her first marriage; stepdaughter of Edward IV's illegitimate son Arthur Plantagenet (Lord Lisle and Lord Deputy of Calais); one of Jane Seymour's ladies-in-waiting and continued in this post under Anne of Cleves, Catherine Howard and Catherine Parr.

Beverley, Robert (*c.* 1522–1558/63)
Listed in the 1542 Inventory as a member of the Lady Elizabeth's household. By 1543: Chief Clerk of the Kitchen in the household of Prince Edward. 1547: received warrants of approximately £500 for the use of the Lady Elizabeth; Second Clerk of the Kitchen in the household of Edward VI. 1548:

granted the reversion of the lease of the manor of Cainhoe, Bedfordshire. March 1553: Member of Parliament for Mitchell; October 1553: Member of Parliament for Bossiney. 1558: Chief Clerk of the Spicery; attended funeral of Queen Mary.

Boleyn, Anne (?1501–1536) (ex.)
Queen consort
Second daughter of Sir Thomas Boleyn, later Earl of Wiltshire and Ormond. Spent some time in France. By 1522: at court. 1533: m. Henry VIII as his second wife (their marriage was one cause of the English Reformation); mother of the Lady Elizabeth, born 7 September. 29 January 1536: gave birth to a stillborn son; 2 May: arrested; 19 May: executed for treason.

Boleyn, George (ex. 1536)
Viscount Rochford
Son of Sir Thomas Boleyn and brother of Anne; page to Henry VIII. 1526: Wolsey had him removed from the post of page. 1528: Master of the Buckhounds: Chief Steward of the Honour of Beaulieu. 1529: made a Gentleman of the Privy Chamber; sent as an ambassador to France with JOHN STOKESLEY. 1530: created Viscount Rochford. 1533: present at the christening of the Lady Elizabeth. 1534: Warden of the Cinque Ports; received the French admiral on his visit to England. 1535: went to France to discuss the Lady Elizabeth's betrothal to the Duke of Angoulême. 1536: implicated in Anne's fall from favour; 2 May: arrested for incest and treason; 17 May: executed.

Boleyn, Jane (ex. 1542)
Lady Rochford
Widow of GEORGE BOLEYN; member of Catherine Howard's household. 1541: implicated in the latter's fall. 1542: executed with her mistress; some of her possessions were then incorporated into Denny's charge.

Bray, Dorothy
Lady-in-waiting to Catherine Parr. m. Edmund Brydges (son of Sir John Brydges); granted manor of Mintey in Wiltshire.

Bristow, Nicholas (d. 1584)
1538: described as Denny's clerk. 1540: Steward of the manors of Aston and Sawbridgeworth in Hertfordshire and Houghton in Bedfordshire. 1541: appointed Clerk to the Wardrobes of the Robes and Beds: compiled inventory of Catherine Howard's jewellery. 1542: appointed Keeper of the Little Wardrobe of the Beds at the Tower (with HUMPHREY ORME). 1544: Clerk of the Jewels. 1546: member of the Commission for Chantries in Essex, Hertfordshire and Colchester.

Brown, Baptist
Milliner who did business with the royal household.

Browne, Sir Anthony (c. 1500–48)
Son of Sir Anthony Browne. 1518: made Surveyor and Master of the Hunt, Castles and Lordship of Hatfield, Thorne and Conisbrough in Yorkshire. 1518-19: to France. 1522: a Knight of the Body. 1525: Lieutenant of the Isle of Man. 1526: Gentleman of the Privy Chamber. 1527: invested Francis I of France with the Order of the Garter. 1528–46: Standard-bearer of England (with Sir Edward Guildford until 1534). 1533: sent to Francis I for discussions on the divorce of Henry VIII and Catherine of Aragon. 1539: made Master of the Horse. 1539/40: appointed Captain of the Gentlemen Pensioners. 1540: made Knight of the Order of the Garter. 1542 and 1543: Member of Parliament for Surrey. 1543: Master of the King's Harriers. 1547: made guardian of Prince Edward and the Lady Elizabeth; one of the executors of Henry VIII's will; left a legacy of £300 by Henry VIII; went to Hereford to inform Prince Edward that he was now king: as Master of the Horse, rode with him into London.

Carcano, Christopher *see* Milliner, Christopher

Carew, Sir Wymond (c. 1498–1549)
c. 1519: m. Martha, daughter of Sir Edmund Denny (thus brother-in-law to Sir Anthony Denny). c. 1529: Deputy Receiver General of the Duchy of Cornwall. 1536: Justice of the Peace for Cornwall and Devon. 1537: Receiver General of Jane Seymour's lands. 1540: Treasurer of Anne of Cleves's household. 1544: Treasurer of Catherine Parr's household. 1545: Treasurer of the Courts of Augmentations and First Fruits and Tenths. 1546: member of the Commission for Chantries of Middlesex, London and Westminster. 1547: Member of Parliament for Peterborough.

Carsidony, Anthony
Florentine merchant trading in silk cloth, rope, armour and weapons with the royal household.

Cawarden, Sir Thomas (c. 1514–59)
Son of William Cawarden, a citizen and fuller of London; apprenticed to Owen Hawkins, a London mercer; follower of reformed religious ideas. 1536: appointee of SIR THOMAS CROMWELL to the Privy Chamber. 1540: made a Gentleman of the Privy Chamber and Keeper of the manor of Bletchingly. 1543: received, with his wife, a pardon for heresy. 1544: joined the king's army in France; knighted at Boulogne; made Steward and Bailiff of Nonsuch. 1545: made first permanent Master of the Revels. 1547: picked as

Sheriff for Surrey; Justice of the Peace for Surrey; member of the Commission for Chantries in Surrey, Sussex and Southwark. 1547–53: remained in favour during Edward VI's reign. 1554: suspected of involvement in Wyatt's rebellion. 1557: committed to the Fleet as a consequence of suspected involvement in that rebellion and released a few months later. 1558: Lieutenant of the Tower of London with Sir Edward Warner.

Cecil, Richard (c. 1495–1553)

Son of David Cecil, a member of Henry VII's household; acquired extensive quantities of monastic land, mainly in Rutland and Northampton; father of William Cecil (later Lord Burghley). By 1517: a Page of the Chamber. 1520: attended the Field of The Cloth of Gold. By 1528: Groom of the Robes; Porter of Warwick Castle. 1539: Yeoman of the Robes; High Sheriff of Rutland; Member of Parliament for Stamford; Justice of the Peace for Northamptonshire. 1547: left a legacy in Henry VIII's will; listed as Yeoman of the Robes in the 1547 Inventory. 1548: member of the Commission for Chantries in Northamptonshire, Oxfordshire, Oxford and Rutland. 1553: Commissioner for the Survey of Church Goods in Lincolnshire and Northamptonshire.

Chapel, Thomas

London upholsterer.

Cranmer, Thomas (1489–1556)

Archbishop of Canterbury

1529: wrote a treatise defending Henry VIII's divorce. 1530: part of the embassy to Charles V, King of Spain and Holy Roman Emperor. 1533: made Archbishop of Canterbury. 1536: declared Henry's marriage to Anne Boleyn invalid. 1539: supported Henry's marriage to Anne of Cleves. 1541: told Henry about Catherine Howard's adultery. 1542: defended the Great Bible against religious conservatives. 1547: appointed a member of Edward VI's Privy Council. 1553: witnessed Edward VI's will, which excluded the Lady Mary from the succession.

Cromwell, Sir Thomas (?1485–1540) (ex.)

Earl of Essex

Son of a smith and fuller from Putney; travelled in Europe, trading in Florence and Antwerp. By c. 1513: practising as a lawyer. 1523: Member of Parliament (constituency unknown). From 1520: retained by Wolsey, making an inquiry into the smaller monasteries in late 1520s. c. 1529: went into Henry VIII's service on Wolsey's fall. 1529: Member of Parliament for Taunton. 1531: member of the Privy Council. 1532: Master of the King's Jewels;

Master of the Court of Wards; Clerk of the Hanaper. 1533: Chancellor of the Exchequer. 1534: King's Secretary and Master of the Rolls. 1535: Vicar-General and Vice-Regent in Spirituals. 1536: Lord Privy Seal and Baron Cromwell of Ockham; Member of Parliament for Kent (?). 1537: Knight of the Order of the Garter; Dean of Wells. 1539: Great Chamberlain of England; negotiated Henry VIII's fourth marriage, to Anne of Cleves. 1540: created Earl of Essex; 10 June: arrested; 23 July: executed.

Denny, Sir Anthony (1501–49)

Educated at St Paul's School and St John's College, Cambridge; subsequently joined household of Sir Francis Bryan; a supporter of reformed religious ideas; m. Joan, daughter of Sir Philip Champernon and a member of Anne Boleyn's household. c. 1533: Groom of the Privy Chamber. 1536: Keeper of the Palace of Whitehall. 1537: Yeoman of the Wardrobe of the Robes. 1539: a Chief Gentlemen of the Privy Chamber, replacing Sir Francis Bryan. 1544: given wardship of Margaret, heiress of Thomas, Lord Audley; knighted at Boulogne. 1546: Groom of the Stool and First Gentleman of the Privy Chamber; empowered to use the dry stamp to affix the king's sign manual to all warrants issued in his name; an executor of Henry VIII's will; left a legacy of £300 by Henry; appointed a Privy Counsellor to Edward VI.

Douglas, Lady Margaret (1515–78)

Countess of Lennox

Daughter of Henry VIII's sister Margaret Tudor and Lord Archibald Douglas; a Catholic claimant to the English throne; mother of Charles Stewart, Earl of Lennox and Henry Stewart, Lord Darnley; grandmother of Arabella Stewart and James VI of Scotland. 1521: accompanied her father into exile in France. 1528: returned to England. 1531: joined the household of the Lady Mary at Beaulieu; lady-in-waiting to Anne Boleyn. 1536: clandestine romance with Thomas Howard (youngest son of the 2nd Duke of Norfolk). 1540: lady-in-waiting to Anne of Cleves. 1544: m. MATTHEW STEWART, EARL OF LENNOX; 1565: imprisoned in the Tower for arranging the marriage of Henry, Lord Darnley to Mary, Queen of Scots. 1567: denounced Mary (Stuart) for murder of Darnley. 1572: reconciled with Mary (Stuart).

Dudley, Sir Andrew (c. 1507–59)

Dudley's career prior to 1540 is obscure. 1540: described as a client of 3rd Duke of Norfolk and a member of the royal household. 1544: an officer of the King's Stable; attended Henry VIII during the French campaign. 1546: sent with a gift of horses and dogs to the Regent in the Low Countries.

1547: one of the four principal Gentlemen of Edward VI's Privy Chamber (the others being Sir Edward Rogers, Sir Thomas Darcy and Sir Thomas Wroth); Keeper of the Palace of Whitehall; managed the privy coffer finances for the king. 1547–9: served in the Scottish wars. 1551: appointed as Captain of Guisnes. 1553: served as Member of Parliament for Oxfordshire; supported the Duke of Northumberland against Mary; arrested as a traitor (later released).

Dudley, John (1502–53) (ex.)
Duke of Northumberland
Son of Edmund Dudley, Henry VII's leading minister, who was executed shortly after Henry VIII's accession. 1513: attainder revoked. 1523: knighted in Calais by Charles Brandon, Duke of Suffolk. 1538: Deputy Governor of Calais. 1542: created Viscount Lisle, Warden of the Scottish Marches and Lord High Admiral. 1543: Privy Counsellor; made Knight of the Order of the Garter. 1544: led the attack on Boulogne. 1547: an executor of Henry VIII's will; created Earl of Warwick and High Chamberlain of England; defeated the Scots at Pinkie. 1549: put down Kett's rebellion. 1551: Earl Marshal and created Duke of Northumberland. 1553: supported claim of Lady Jane Grey to the throne; executed for resisting the accession of Mary.

Edward (b. 12 October 1537, succ. 1547, d. 6 July 1553)
Prince of Wales
Son of Henry VIII and his third wife Jane Seymour; born at Hampton Court; given a classical education by Richard Cox, Roger Ascham and Sir John Cheke. 28 January 1547: succeeded to the throne, aged nine. 1553: willed the succession to Lady Jane Grey.

Elizabeth (b. 7 September 1533, succ. 1558, d. 1603)
Second daughter of Henry VIII, by his second wife, Anne Boleyn. 1536: declared illegitimate. 1549: educated by Roger Ascham. 1553: accompanied her half-sister the Lady Mary as the latter entered London. 1554: imprisoned in the Tower; later released to Woodstock Palace. 1558: succeeded to the throne.

Erizo, Dominico
Venetian merchant. March 1535: received his denization. Listed in the 1547 Inventory as supplying cloth of gold, tissue, velvet and other textiles.

FitzAlan, Henry (1511–80)
12th Earl of Arundel
Eldest son of 11th Earl of Arundel; Deputy of Calais. 1530: one of the group that petitioned Henry VIII to save

Cardinal's College, Oxford. 1542: appointed to Commission of the Peace in Hampshire and Surrey. Summer 1545: made leader of the Army in the West, one of three armies raised by Henry VIII to defend England against a threat of invasion. July 1546: joined coalition of the Duke of Somerset and JOHN DUDLEY, Viscount Lisle (later Duke of Northumberland); December: added to Henry VIII's will as an assistant to the executors. 1547–50: Lord Chamberlain.

Frenior, Richard
1547: received selection of pewter from the palace, at the command of the Lord Protector.

Gates, John (*c.* 1504–53) (ex.)
Son of Sir Geoffrey Gates (a member of the Essex gentry); m. Mary, sister of Sir Anthony Denny. 2 August 1523: called to the Bar of Lincoln's Inn. By 1537: a Page of the Robes. 1540: Groom of the Wardrobe of the Robes; Commissioner of the Peace for Essex. ?1542 Member of Parliament for Chipping Wycombe. 1542: Groom of the Privy Chamber. 1545: Member of Parliament for New Shoreham. 1546: appointed to administer the dry stamp (with Denny). 1547: Member of Parliament for Southwark; Member of Parliament for Essex. 1550: replaced Sir Edward Rogers as one of the four Chief Gentlemen of the Privy Chamber.

Gostwick, Sir John (1493–1545)
Educated at Potton. By 1514: entered Wolsey's household. 1516: admitted to the Merchant Adventurers. 1523: granted an auditorship and began working with SIR THOMAS CROMWELL; appointed as Treasurer of the Court of First Fruits and Tenths; acted as personal treasurer to Cromwell. 1529: left Wolsey's household. 1539: Member of Parliament for Bedfordshire; 1540: knighted; survived Cromwell's fall.

Gresham, Sir John (d. 1556)
Born at Holt, in Norfolk; younger brother of SIR RICHARD GRESHAM. His main trade was with the Levant; Merchant of the Staple and a member of the Merchant Adventurers. 1517: entered the Mercers' Company; acted as agent for Wolsey and SIR THOMAS CROMWELL. 1526: made a Gentleman Pensioner. 1537: Sheriff of London. 1547: Lord Mayor of London. 1555: founder member of the Russia Company.

Gresham, Sir Richard (1486–1549)
Born at Holt, in Norfolk; elder brother of SIR JOHN GRESHAM. Apprenticed to John Middleton, a mercer. Became a leading London merchant and a Merchant of the Staple at Calais. Had close links with Wolsey. Died a very wealthy man, with property in St Lawrence Jewry,

Bethnal Green, Norfolk, Suffolk and Yorkshire. 1507: admitted to the Mercers Company. 1525: supported the Amicable Grant; acted as financial agent for the Crown. 1536: promoted the Act of Paul Wilhypoll, regulating the manufacture of wool. 1537: Lord Mayor of London, with plans to build a bourse in London. 1539 and 1545: Member of Parliament for London.

Griffiths, William

1539: granted two tenements called Le Tenys Play in Little All Hallows; Keeper of the Wardrobe of the manor of Horsleigh. 1542: licence to keep a tennis play. 1545: received wages as a Yeoman of the Chamber. 1547: listed in the 1547 Inventory as Keeper of the Wardrobe of the Beds at Richmond.

Hales, John (c. 1516–72)

A supporter of reformed religious ideas. 1535: servant of SIR THOMAS CROMWELL. 1537: Keeper of Writs for the King's Bench; Principal Auditor to the Office of General Surveyors; Clerk of the Court of First Fruits and Tenths. By 1541: deputy to SIR RALPH SADLER at the Hanaper. 1543: working for Sadler, Master of the Great Wardrobe. 1545: Clerk of the Hanaper; licensed to establish a school in the former St John's Hospital in Coventry (sponsored by Denny). 1547: Member of Parliament for Preston; member of the Privy Council; Justice of the Peace for Middlesex and Warwickshire.

Harper, William

1543–4: took delivery of chapel stuff granted to Catherine Parr.

Heneage, Sir Thomas (d. 21 August 1553)

Gentleman Usher to Wolsey, who moved him into the Henry VIII's Privy Chamber to try to counter Anne Boleyn's influence on Wolsey's fall; Heneage supported SIR THOMAS CROMWELL and his religious policy. 1536: attacked while suppressing the Cistercian abbey near Louth. 1537: knighted. 1537–46: held the posts of Groom of the Stool and Chief Gentleman of the Privy Chamber.

Henry VIII (1491–1547)

Second son of Henry VII and Elizabeth of York; 28 June 1491: born; 23 June 1503: betrothal to Catherine of Aragon; 22 April 1509: death of Henry VII; accession of Henry VIII; 11 June 1509: marriage to Catherine of Aragon; 10 Sept 1515: Thomas Wolsey made a cardinal; 18 Feb 1516: birth of princess Mary; 7–24 June 1520: The Field of The Cloth of Gold; 1529: fall of Wolsey; 1531: appointment of Thomas Cromwell as a councilor; Jan 1535: marriage to Anne Boleyn; 7 Sept 1533 birth of Princess Elizabeth; 7 Jan 1536: death of Catherine of Aragon; 19 May 1536: execution of Anne Boleyn; 30 May 1536: marriage to Jane Seymour; 22 July 1536: death of Henry Fitzroy, duke of Richmond; 12 Oct 1537: birth of Prince Edward; 24 Oct 1537: death of Jane Seymour; 1540: fall and exectuion of Cromwell; 28 July 1540: marriage to Catherine Howard; 13 Feb 1542: execution of Catherine Howard; 12 July 1543: marriage to Catherine Parr; 28 Jan 1547: died; accession of Edward VI.

Hobbs, Robert

1530: receiving wages as Keeper of the Wardrobe of the Beds at The More. 1547: still in post; mentioned in the 1547 Inventory.

Hoby, Sir Philip (1505–58)

Appointed to the Privy Chamber by SIR THOMAS CROMWELL. 1535–6: employed on diplomatic service in Spain and Portugal. By 1538: a Groom of the Privy Chamber. By 1540: Gentleman Usher. 1543: accused of heresy. 1543–8: member of the council serving Catherine Parr. 1543–54: Gentleman Usher of the Black Rod; Knight of the Order of the Garter. 1544: recovered the king's favour; took part in the siege of Boulogne and knighted. 1545: appointed Master of the Ordnance in the North. 1547: Member of Parliament for Cardiff Boroughs; Justice of the Peace for Middlesex. May 1548–August 1550: ambassador to Charles V, King of Spain and Holy Roman Emperor.

Holt, William

Merchant Taylor of London; the king's tailor.

Howard, Agnes (d. 1545)

Dowager Duchess of Norfolk

Born Agnes Tilney; second wife of 2nd Duke of Norfolk; stepmother to 3rd Duke; step-grandmother and guardian of the young Catherine Howard; buried with her husband in the Norfolk chapel at Lambeth. 1533: carried the Lady Elizabeth at her christening and was one of her godmothers (with Margaret, Marchioness of Dorset). 1540: groomed Catherine Howard as successor to Anne of Cleves.

Howard, Catherine (1520/1–1542) (ex.)

Queen consort

Daughter of Lord Edmund Howard, younger son of 2nd Duke of Norfolk. 1539–40: promoted by Bishop Gardiner as an alternative to Anne of Cleves, fourth wife of Henry VIII. 28 July 1540: m. Henry VIII as his fifth wife. 1541: accused by Cranmer of adultery with Thomas Culpepper and Francis Dereham while on the royal progress. 13 February 1542: executed.

Hunter, Hans
Armourer. Listed in the 1547 Inventory as Keeper of two of the armouries at Whitehall.

Lentall, Philip
Possibly an armourer; received a velvet kirtle 'to couer halbertes'.

Lock, William (1480–1550)
A London mercer; Henry VIII's factor in Antwerp; bought books for Anne Boleyn in the Low Countries; a promoter of reformed religious ideas, as recorded by his daughter, Rose Hickman; knighted and served as an alderman of London.

Mary (b. 1516, succ. 1553, m. 1554, d. 1558)
Third child of Henry VIII by his wife Catherine of Aragon, but the only one to survive early childhood. 1518: betrothed to the Dauphin. 1522: betrothed to Charles V, King of Spain and Holy Roman Emperor. 1525: made Princess of Wales and sent to Ludlow. 1531: separated from her mother. 1533: declared illegitimate and lost the title of Princess of Wales. 1536: reconciled to Henry VIII. 1537: chief mourner at Jane Seymour's funeral. 1544: restored to the succession. 1553: Edward VI willed the succession to Lady Jane Gray. Succeeded to the throne on the death of Edward VI after challenging the right of Lady Jane Grey to the throne.

Maynman, Thomas
1539: appointed Keeper of the Wardrobe of the Beds at Greenwich with 8d a day, on surrender of the patents by David Vincent. 1540: made a survey of the Greenwich Wardrobe (with Rowland Ridgeley, David Vincent and James Joskyn). 1547: listed in the 1547 Inventory as still in post.

Mildmay, Sir Walter (?1520–89)
1540s: educated at Christ's College, Cambridge and Gray's Inn. 1545: Surveyor General of the Court of Augmentations. 1547: knighted and made Revenue Commissioner. 1550: auditor of the Mint accounts.

Milliner, Christopher
Also known as Christopher Carcano. From 1528 onwards: made hats for Henry VIII (and others); also sold jewellery and furs to the king and others. 1544: imported a variety of luxury items under licence. Described as the 'king's milliner'. Mentioned in the 1547 Inventory as having supplied two sets of doublets and hose made from knitted silk.

North, Sir Edward (c. 1496–1564)
1st Baron North
Educated at Peterhouse, Cambridge and then entered the Inns of Court. 1531: Clerk of the Parliaments. March 1540–April 1544: Treasurer of the Court of Augmentations. 1541: knighted. 1542: Member of Parliament for Cambridgeshire. 1544: deputed to receive the Great Seal from Lord Audley (with Sir Thomas Pope). April–July 1544: Chancellor of the Court of Augmentations (with Sir Richard Rich); July 1544–August 1548: sole Chancellor. 1546: member of the Privy Council. 1547: Member of Parliament for Cambridgeshire; named as one of the executors of Henry VIII's will and left a legacy of £300; on Edward VI's accession forced to resign as Chancellor of the Court of Augmentations. 1553: Member of Parliament for Cambridgeshire.

Orme, Humphrey
1538: granted the lease of the site of the manor of West Deeping, Lincolnshire; made a Page of the Wardrobe of the Beds. 1540: granted the lease of the farm of the manor of Kylford and Rekwall, in Denbigh. 1542: Keeper of the Little Wardrobe in the Tower, with 12d a day (with NICHOLAS BRISTOW). 1544: the king's army in France. 1547: listed in the 1547 Inventory as Keeper of the Wardrobe of the Beds in the Tower and the Removing Wardrobe Attendant on the king.

Parr, Catherine (1512–48)
Queen consort
Daughter of Sir Thomas Parr of Kendall. 1543: m. Henry VIII as her third husband (and his sixth wife). 1544: assumed regency when Henry VIII was on campaign in France, a position threatened by her reformed religious views. 1547: secretly m. Sir Thomas Seymour. 1548: died after giving birth to a daughter.

Paston, Sir Thomas (c. 1517–50)
1533: Gentleman of the Privy Chamber; Keeper of the Gallery Armoury at Greenwich. 1542: appointed to the Commission for the Peace for Norfolk and the Commission of Oyer and Terminer on the Eastern Circuit; received grants of monastic land in Norfolk. 1544: went on the French campaign; knighted at Boulogne. 1545: Member of Parliament for Norfolk. 1547: left a legacy of £200 by Henry VIII; 15 March: Steward for Duchy of Lancaster in Cambridgeshire, Norfolk and Suffolk.

Paulet, Sir William (c. 1485–1572)
Lord St John, Earl of Wiltshire
1512, 1519, 1523, 1527: Sheriff of Hampshire. 1525: knighted. 1526: appointed Master of the King's Wards (with Thomas

Englefield); member of the Privy Council. 1529–36: sat as knight of the shire for Hampshire in the Reformation Parliament. 1532: made Comptroller of the Household. 1533: accompanied the Duke of Norfolk to France. 1535: judge at the trial of Fisher and More. 1536: judge at the trial of the men arrested with Anne Boleyn; took charge of the royal forces sent against the Pilgrimage of Grace. 1537–9: Treasurer of the Household. 1543: Knight of the Order of the Garter. 1545–50: Great Master of the King's Household. 1547: one of the executors of Henry VIII's will.

Peckham, Sir Edmund (c. 1495–1564)
Catholic; friend and relative of SIR THOMAS WRIOTHESLEY; entered the king's household as a counting-house clerk. 1520: attended Henry on his visit to Gravelines. 1524: Cofferer. 1526: Clerk of the Greencloth. 1533: Member of Parliament for Buckinghamshire. 1542: knighted. 1546–64: Treasurer of the Mint, with a house at the Blackfriars: began the 'great debasement' and oversaw the reforms under Mary and Elizabeth. 1547: one of the executors of Henry VIII's will; left a legacy of £200. 1549: served briefly as a member of the Privy Council. 1554: Member of Parliament for Buckinghamshire.

Pigeon, Edmund
Described as servant to NICHOLAS BRISTOW; Clerk of the Jewel House. 1544: Clerk of the Wardrobes of the Robes and Beds.

Potter, Richard
1545: fined by WILLIAM STANFORD, attorney to the Court of General Surveyors.

Reconger, John
London merchant. 1545: fined for failing to deliver wine to the royal household.

Reed, John
1530: listed in the Chamber accounts as Keeper of the Wardrobe of the Beds at York Place. 1533: appointed Keeper of the King's Wardrobe of the Beds (6d a day) and Vestry (2d a day) at the Palace of Whitehall. 1535: granted a 50-year lease on the lands of the Prebend of St Paul's. 1542: appointed to the Commission for the Peace in Lincolnshire. 1547: still in office, and listed in the 1547 Inventory.

Rock, John
Deputy to SIR JOHN GOSTWICK.

Rogers, John
Clerk of the Ordnance; Surveyor of Works at Boulogne.

Roper, William (1495/6–1578)
Catholic who served under Mary; educated at Oxford and then Lincoln's Inn. c. 1518: entered Sir Thomas More's household; m. More's daughter Margaret; brought before Wolsey on a heresy charge (subsequently dropped). 1529: Member of Parliament for Bramber. 1543: Member of Parliament for Rochester; imprisoned in the Tower of London for giving alms to John Bekinsau, who was involved in the Prebends' Plot against Cranmer. 1547: Member of Parliament for Rochester. 1553: Member of Parliament for Winchelsea. 1554: Member of Parliament for Rochester. 1555, 1558: Member of Parliament for Canterbury.

Rous, Sir Anthony
1544: Master of the Jewel House; Controller of Calais. 1545: Treasurer of the Chamber.

Rufforth, James (d. 1550)
Denny's servant and deputy at the Palace of Whitehall. 1547: responsible for sections of the palace in his own right.

Russell, John (1486–1555)
1st Earl of Bedford
Gentleman of the Privy Chamber under Henry VII; continued under Henry VIII. 1513: went to France as a captain; distinguished himself at the sieges of Therouanne and Tournay; knighted. 1519: commissioner for the surrender of Tournay. 1520: at the Field of The Cloth of Gold. 1523: made Knight Marshal of the Household. 1527: ambassador to Pope Clement VII. 1536: helped to put down the Pilgrimage of Grace. 1550: created Earl of Bedford. 1553: supported Lady Jane Grey but switched allegiance to Mary. 1554: ambassador to Spain to arrange Mary's marriage to Philip.

Sadler, Sir Ralph (1507–87)
Member of household of SIR THOMAS CROMWELL as a young man. 1536: became a Gentleman of the Privy Chamber; Member of Parliament for Hindon (?). 1537: sent to Scotland to improve Anglo-Scottish relations. 1539: Member of Parliament for Middlesex. 1540: sent to Scotland again. 1541: appointed as one of Henry's two secretaries (with SIR THOMAS WRIOTHESLEY). 1542: knighted, sent to Scotland to arrange a marriage between Prince Edward and Mary, Queen of Scots; made a Privy Counsellor; Member of Parliament for Hertfordshire. 1543: replaced as Secretary of State by William Paget but given the office of Master of the Great Wardrobe. 1545: Member of Parliament for Preston. 1547: left a legacy in Henry VIII's will. 1553: Member of Parliament for Hertfordshire.

Seymour, Sir Edward (1506–52) (ex.)
Duke of Somerset
Brother of Jane Seymour, Henry VIII's third wife. 1514: retained as 'enfant d'honneur' to Henry's sister Mary Tudor on her marriage to Louis XII of France. 1523: joined Duke of Suffolk's expedition to France; knighted during the campaign. 1525: appointed Master of the Horse to the Duke of Richmond. 1527: accompanied Wolsey to France. 1535–6: Gentleman of the Privy Chamber. 1537: Earl of Hertford; member of the Privy Council. 1541: Knight of the Order of the Garter. 1542: Lord High Admiral. 1544: led the English army into Scotland. 1547: victory over the Scots at Pinkie: made Protector. 1549: imprisoned in the Tower. 1550: deposed as Protector. January 1552: executed.

Seymour, Jane (?1509–37)
Queen consort
Eldest child of Sir John Seymour and his wife Margaret; lady-in-waiting to Catherine of Aragon and Anne Boleyn. 20 May 1536: m. Henry VIII as his third wife (the day after Anne's execution). 1537: gave birth to Prince Edward (later Edward VI) but died shortly after.

Southwell, Sir Richard (1504–64)
Son of Sir Francis Southwell, a wealthy Norfolk squire; brought up with Henry Howard, Earl of Surrey. 1532: pardoned for murder. 1534: appointed Sheriff of Norfolk and Suffolk. 1535: present during Sir Thomas More's inter-rogation. 1536: helped to put down the Pilgrimage of Grace. 1537: painted by Holbein. August 1538: Receiver of the Court of Augmentations. 1539: attended the Duke of Norfolk at the reception for Anne of Cleves; chosen as Member of Parliament for Norfolk. 1540: knighted. 1542: sent as a commissioner to the borders of Scotland; member of the Privy Council; knighted. 1546: amongst the accusers of Henry Howard Earl of Surrey. March 1547–July 1548: member of the Privy Council under Edward VI. 1549–50: imprisoned for declaring his Catholic faith. 1553–8: member of the Privy Council under Mary.

Stanford, William (1509–58)
Son of a London mercer; after Oxford, entered Gray's Inn; a close friend of SIR THOMAS WRIOTHESLEY. 1536: called to the bar. 1542: appointed to the Court of the General Surveyors as attorney, with £40 a year (with SIR BRIAN TUKE) responsible to the Surveyors (Sir John Daunce, Sir Richard Pollard and Sir Thomas Moyle); Member of Parliament for Stafford; granted custody of Nicholas Witherys, a haberdasher and lunatic of London. 1545: Member of Parliament for Stafford. 1547: Member of Parliament for Newcastle-under-Lyme. Remained in Edward VI's service in spite of being a Catholic. Promoted by Mary to the post of Queen's Serjeant and judge.

Stokesley, John (*c.*1475–1539)
Bishop of London
Encouraged the Carthusians to submit to the king but was opposed to doctrinal change. Through the influence of Richard Fox, Bishop of Winchester, became a chaplain and almoner to Henry VIII; later a member of the Privy Council. 1520: attended the Field of the Cloth of Gold and Gravelines as Henry's chaplain. 1523: tried petitions from Gascony at Parliament; Dean of the Chapel Royal. 1529: accompanied GEORGE BOLEYN as ambassador to France in place of Sir Francis Bryan. 1530: Bishop of London; present at Dunstable with Cranmer when Henry VIII's divorce from Catherine of Aragon was pronounced. 1533: christened the Lady Elizabeth at the Greyfriars church, Greenwich.

Stewart, Matthew (d. 1571)
Earl of Lennox
1543: arrived in Scotland with French money amongst rumours of rebellion against the Governor. 1544: Henry VIII sought to gain control of Scotland through Lennox and the pro-English party; June: married MARGARET DOUGLAS. 1545: received at the English court, with the Lord of the Isles; involved in the formation of a plan to invade Scotland: the invasion was unsuccessful, and the Scottish Privy Council, supported by French troops, prepared to attack the English border.

Thorpe, William
1542: appointed to the Commission of the Peace for Hampshire; appointed to the Western Circuit; appointed a Commissioner of Gaol Delivery in Winchester Castle; Collector of the Customs in the port of Southampton.

Tildesley, William
Page of the Chamber. 1532: granted 'the messuage called the henchmen's chamber' at the Palace of Whitehall (above the king's bakehouse). 1534: grant in reversion of Keepership of the king's library at Richmond 'or elsewhere it shall happen to be' with £10 a year, as held by Giles Duwes. 1536: death of Giles Duwes – £10 annuity to be paid out of the customs of the port of Bristol. 1538: supported Sir Thomas Elyot's project to produce a dictionary: and along with Denny and SIR THOMAS CROMWELL helped him gain access to the king's books. 1539: Groom of the Beds; Keeper of the Wardrobe of the Beds and the King's Armoury in Windsor Castle at 6*d* a day (assisted by a Yeoman Deputy at 3*d* a day). 1547: listed in the 1547 Inventory as Keeper of the Windsor Wardrobe.

Tuke, Sir Brian (d. 1545)
1509: made Clerk of the Signet. 1510: a clerk of the Council of Calais. 1512: appointed to the Commission for the Peace in Kent. 1516: made a Knight of the Body. 1517: Governor of the King's Posts; acted as a secretary to Wolsey. 1522: made Henry VIII's French Secretary. 1523: Clerk of the Parliaments. 1528: Treasurer of the Chamber. 1530, 1531: associated with Sir Edward North as Clerk of the Parliaments. 1533: Sheriff for Essex and Hertfordshire. 1538: Treasurer of the Court of General Surveyors.

Tunstal, Cuthbert (1474–1559)
Bishop of Durham
Educated at Oxford, Cambridge and Padua. 1516: Master of the Rolls. 1522–30: Bishop of London. 1523: Keeper of the Privy Seal. 1530: Bishop of Durham. 1537: President of the Council of the North. 1552: deprived as Bishop of Durham. 1553: restored as Bishop of Durham. 1559: refused to swear the Oath of Supremacy to Elizabeth; deprived as Bishop of Durham.

Vaughan, Stephen (d. 1549)
Follower of reformed religious ideas; m. Margery, the queen's silk woman. c. 1520: Vaughan met SIR THOMAS CROMWELL. 1524: Cromwell's servant (mainly commercial activities). c. 1530: became Henry VIII's financial agent in Antwerp, his chief task being to raise loans from the Fuggers. Vaughan succeeded John Hutton as Governor of the Merchant Adventurers' Company and President of the Factory of English merchants at Antwerp. c. 1530–46: King's Factor to the Netherlands. 1531: appointed as Writer of the King's Books; charged by Henry to persuade Tyndale to return to England (failed). 1532: heresy charges brought against him by one George Constantine. August 1536: appointed to the post of writing the king's accounts; later in 1536: Under-Treasurer at the Mint. 1547: Member of Parliament for Lancaster.

van der Wilder, Philip (c. 1500–53)
Born in the Netherlands; lived in Hart Street in the city of London (in the parish of St Olave's-near-the-Tower); four sons (Henry, Edward, William and John) and one daughter (Catherine); his only surviving English anthem is *Blessed art thou that fearest God*; a number of secular pieces have also survived. 1526: mentioned in the royal accounts; November: received a licence to import 800 tuns of Toulouse wood and Gascon wine. 1529: described as one of the king's lute players (with Gyles, Arthur Dews and Peter

van Wilder). October 1532: accompanied the king when he went to meet Francis I of France. February 1537: m. Frances. April 1537: received a reward for teaching the Lady Mary to play the lute. 1538: son Henry born. 1539: became a naturalized citizen or denizen. c. 1540: made a Gentleman of the Privy Chamber. July 1546: teaching Prince Edward to play the lute. 1547: Keeper of the king's musical instruments. 1551: led a group of 'singing men and children' in the privy chamber. 24 January 1553: died.

Williams, Sir John (c. 1503–59)
Of Welsh descent. c. 1526: an official of Chancery. 1530: made Joint Master of the Jewel House with SIR THOMAS CROMWELL. 1536: involved in the dissolution of the monasteries. 1540: survived the fall of Cromwell and made sole Master of the Jewel House. 1542: Master of the Cygnets on the Thames; Treasurer of the Court of Augmentations; Member of Parliament for Oxfordshire. 1544: appointed High Steward of Oxfordshire. 1547: Member of Parliament for Oxfordshire. ?1553: Chamberlain to Philip II of Spain: Member of Parliament for Oxfordshire. 1555, 1559: President of the Council of the Marches.

Wolf, Morgan
Alias Morgan Philip; the king's goldsmith.

Woodhall, John
Under-Treasurer of the war in the north.

Wotton, Sir Edward
Treasurer of Calais.

Wriothesley, Sir Thomas (1505–50)
1st Earl of Southampton
A religious conservative; made Knight of the Order of the Garter. c. 1530: Clerk of the Signet. 1535: engraver to the Mint. 1538–46: joint ambassador to the Queen of Hungary; secretary to SIR THOMAS CROMWELL. 1540: Wriothesley changed allegiance just before Cromwell's fall, inheriting much of his influence (e.g. surrendered his post of Chief Secretary to Wriothesley and SIR RALPH SADLER). 1543: Treasurer of the Wars. 1544: made Lord Chancellor on Audley's death. 1546: Chamberlain of the Receipt of the Exchequer. January 1547: announced Henry VIII's death to the House Lords; February: made Earl of Southampton; 5 March: forced to resign as Chancellor by the Duke of Somerset.

CONCORDANCES
AND APPENDICES

CONCORDANCE I

THE DUPLICATE ENTRIES IN THE 1542 INVENTORY

Some objects are recorded twice in the 1542 Inventory, and consequently have been allocated two numbers. Objects of this type fall into one of four categories:

A. perquisites given either on Henry VIII's death to those officiating at his funeral, to Sir Anthony Denny as Groom of the Stool, or on Edward VI's coronation to those officiating there;

B. items found to be missing when Denny was discharged as Keeper of the Palace of Whitehall;

C. totals relating to the lengths and remnants of cloth kept at the palace;

D. furnishings given to the lady Elizabeth to provide her with a Removing Wardrobe like that already provided for her sister the Lady Mary and for Prince Edward.

The first of each pair of entries is given in bold in numerical order, and is followed by the brief description of the item; the second 1542 Inventory number is given in square brackets.

An asterisk indicates where there are some discrepancies in the length and number of pieces.

A. Perquisites

Sir Anthony Denny

280	2 close stools	[4021]
281	1 close stool	[4022]
282	2 close stools	[4023]
284	2 close stools	[4024]
285	1 close stool	[4025]
657	10 pewter bowls for close stools	[4026]
658	5 pewter bowls for close stools	[4027]
659	1 pewter bowl for a close stool	[4028]
660	5 pewter cisterns for close stools	[4029]
661	4 small pewter cisterns for close stools	[4030]
3348	1 close stool	[4023]
3350	1 leather case for a close stool	[4031]

The Earl of Warwick

223	5 hangings of scarlet	[3763/4033*]
224	6 window pieces of scarlet	[3764/4034*]
239	1 chair	[4041]
345	1 cushion	[4042]
434	1 carpet	[4036]
435	1 carpet	[4035]
436	1 bedstead with apparel	[4032]
447	1 counterpoint	[4037]
543	1 pair of sheets	[4038]
550	1 sheet	[4039]
559	1 pair of pillow-beres	[4040]
568	1 pillow-bere	[4040]

The Earl of Arundel

1053	1 clock	[4043]

B. Missing items[1]

4	2 buttons from a gown [**3977**]	867	the royal arms off a mirror [**3961**]
168	1 knife [**3978**]	875	1 square mirror [**3959**]
238	6 chair roundels [**3979**]	882	30 silver counters [**3958**]
239	2 chair roundels [**3979**]	894	1 trymmer for a pair of regals [**3998**]
240	3 chair roundels [**3979**]	941	1 great shawm with a case [**3999**]
244	3 chair roundels [**3979**]	969	1 iron gun on wheels [**4000**]
247	1 chair roundel [**3979**]	970	2 touch boxes and a case for a gun [**4001**]
248	1 chair roundel [**3979**]	1012	8 curtains [**4002**]
259	2 chair roundels [**3979**]	1027	1 corporal case [**3973**]
279	1 footstool [**3966**]	1036	1 fanon [**3974**]
306	1 button and tassel for a cushion [**3965**]	1048	2 cuffs for a vestment [**3975**]
398	3 buttons and tassels for cushions [**3965**]	1050	3 linen altar cloths [**3976**]
440	pearls from a bedstead [**3981**]	1080	6 of 11 drinking glasses [**4003**]
444	2 cups for a bedstead [**3987**]	1087	1 of 11 drinking glasses [**4003**]
444	fringe on bed hangings [**3982**]	1089	1 glass [**4006**]
447	4 bed vanes from a bedstead [**3988**]	1090	1 glass [**4005**]
447	fringe on a counterpoint [**3985**]	1094	1 of 11 drinking glasses [**4003**]
449	fringe on bed hangings [**3983, 3984**]	1095	3 of 11 drinking glasses [**4003**]
452	fringe on bed hangings [**3985**]	1096	3 glass covers [**4004**]
455	fringe on bed hangings [**3980**]	1109	1 socket for a glass candlestick [**4007**]
460	fringe on bed hangings [**3986**]	1111	1 glass bell candlestick [**4008**]
534	5 girths for leather cases [**3989**]	1113	1 salt of earth galley making [**4010**]
568	2 pillow-beres [**3956**]	1114	1 glass trencher [**4009**]
569	2 pillow-beres [**3956**]	1135	1 fire fork [**4011**]
577	1 handkerchief [**3955**]	1136	4 pans of iron [**4013**]
604	1 tablecloth [**3954**]	1137	3 pairs of tongues [**4012**]
612	1 cupboard cloth [**3952**]	1138	6 pairs of bellows [**4015**]
619	1 towel [**3951**]	1140	1 round pan of iron on wheels [**4014**]
628	part of a towel [**3951**]	1175	1 table [**3967**]
631	1 towel [**3951**]	1191	14 joined stools [**3968**]
716	precious stones from an embroidery of the Passion [**3990**]	1194	3 foot stools [**3969**]
		1198	1 chest [**4016**]
736	1 sarsenet curtain for a picture [**3991**]	1211	5 wicker screens [**3971**]
740	1 sarsenet curtain for a picture [**3991**]	1212	1 walking staff [**4017**]
800	1 sarsenet curtain for a picture [**3991**]	1213	1 walking staff [**4017**]
806	1 sarsenet curtain for a picture [**3991**]	1214	1 walking staff [**4017**]
814	1 stained cloth [**3992**]	1220	1 copper weight [**4018**]
815	1 stained cloth [**3993**]	1226	1 needlework castle [**3997**]
820	1 stained cloth [**3994**]	2300	1 counterpoint [**4019**]
825	1 box or case for a terracotta [**3996**]	2301	1 counterpoint [**4020**]
827	1 box or case for a terracotta [**3996**]	2308	1 trussing sheet [**3950**]
828	1 box or case for a terracotta [**3996**]	2342	2 cupboard clothes [**3952**]
829	1 box or case for a terracotta [**3996**]	2345	4 dozen and 7 napkins [**3953**]
830	1 box or case for a terracotta [**3996**]	2357	1 standish [**3957**]
832	1 box or case for a terracotta [**3996**]	2392	2 gunpowder horns and 2 purses [**4001**]
833	1 box or case for a terracotta [**3995**]	2411	1 book [**3962**]
866	1 mirror decoration [**3960**]	2416	1 book [**3962**]

1   The marginal comment after entry **1238** records that the foot from a small iron trivet was missing but it was not acknowledged in the list of missing items at the end of the 1542 Inventory (fos 148v–150r) and so does not appear in this concordance.

2425	5 books [3962]		2935	1 book [3962]
2445	1 book [3962]		2941	1 book [3962]
2454	1 book [3962]		2961	1 book [3962]
2457	1 book [3962]		2962	1 book [3962]
2484	1 book [3962]		2999	1 book [3962]
2490	1 book [3962]		3026	1 book [3962]
2515	1 book [3962]		3028	1 book [3962]
2553	1 book [3962]		3031	1 book [3962]
2595	1 book [3962]		3043	1 book [3962]
2596	1 book [3962]		3068	1 book [3962]
2625	1 book [3962]		3089	1 book [3962]
2627	1 book [3962]		3101	1 book [3962]
2638	1 book [3962]		3117	1 book [3962]
2698	1 book [3962]		3131	2 books [3962]
2700	1 book [3962]		3139	1 book [3962]
2719	3 books [3962]		3142	1 book [3962]
2720	3 books [3962]		3166	1 book [3962]
2724	1 book [3962]		3169	1 book [3962]
2764	1 book [3962]		3176	1 book [3962]
2791	1 book [3962]		3184	1 book [3962]
2797	1 book [3962]		3187	1 book [3962]
2817	1 book [3962]		3194	1 book [3962]
2825	1 book [3962]		3239	1 book [3962]
2834	1 book [3962]		3264	1 book [3962]
2836	1 book [3962]		3279	1 book [3962]
2838	1 book [3962]		3288	1 book [3962]
2845	1 book [3962]		3347	1 cushion [3963]
2854	1 book [3962]		3352	6 joined stools [3968]
2870	1 book [3962]		3762	1 box for the host [3972]
2874	1 book [3962]		3765	2 footstools [3970]
2885	1 book [3962]		3779	length of cloth of gold [3944]
2886	1 book [3962]		3781	length of cloth of gold [3945]
2893	1 book [3962]		3782	length of cloth of gold [3946]
2901	1 book [3962]		3805	length of satin [3947]
2916	1 book [3962]		3848	length of Milan fustian [3948]
2918	1 book [3962]		3851	length of kersey [3949]
2920	2 books [3962]			

C. Totals relating to the lengths and remnants of cloth kept at the palace

1900	damask [3911][2]		3783	cloth of gold [3871]
3774	tissue [3863]		3784	cloth of silver [3872]
3775	cloth of gold [3864]		3785	baudekin [3873]
3776	cloth of gold [3865]		3786	tinsel [3874]
3777	cloth of gold [3866]		3787	velvet [3875]
3778	cloth of gold [3867]		3788	velvet [3876]
3779	cloth of gold [3868]		3789	velvet [3885]
3781	cloth of gold [3869]		3790	velvet [3886]
3782	cloth of gold [3870]		3791	velvet [3877]

2   This entry, relating to the total of ash colour damask, is out of sequence because only one length of this fabric is recorded in the inventory. Conseqently, there is no summary describing how the cloth was distributed, so the final total has to relate to the initial entry.

3792 velvet [**3878**]
3793 velvet [**3879**]
3794 velvet [**3880**]
3795 velvet [**3881**]
3796 velvet [**3882**]
3797 velvet [**3883**]
3799 velvet [**3884**]
3800 velvet [**3887**]
3801 satin [**3889**]
3802 satin [**3888**]
3803 satin [**3890**]
3804 satin [**3891**]
3805 satin [**3892**]
3806 satin [**3893**]
3807 satin [**3894**]
3808 satin [**3895**]
3809 satin [**3899**]
3810 satin [**3896**]
3811 satin [**3897**]
3812 satin [**3898**]
3813 damask [**3900**]
3814 damask [**3901**]
3815 damask [**3902**]
3816 damask [**3903**]
3817 damask [**3904**]
3818 damask [**3905**]
3819 damask [**3906**]
3820 damask [**3907**]
3821 damask [**3908**]
3822 damask [**3910**]
3823 damask [**3909**]
3824 damask [**3912**]
3825 taffeta [**3913**]

3826 taffeta [**3914**]
3827 taffeta [**3915**]
3828 taffeta [**3916**]
3829 taffeta [**3917**]
3830 taffeta [**3918**]
3831 taffeta [**3919**]
3832 taffeta [**3920**]
3833 taffeta [**3921**]
3834 taffeta [**3922**]
3836 sarsenet [**3923**]
3838 sarsenet [**3924**]
3839 sarsenet [**3925**]
3840 sarsenet [**3926**]
3841 sarsenet [**3928**]
3842 sarsenet [**3927**]
3843 sarsenet [**3929**]
3845 silk of new making [**3930**]
3847 Bridges satin [**3931**]
3848 Milan fustian [**3932**]
3849 baudekin [**3933**]
3850 camlet [**3934**]
3851 kersey [**3949**]
3852 Brussels ticks [**3935**]
3853 holland [**3936**]
3854 Normandy cloth [**3937**]
3855 Brussels cloth [**3943**]
3856 nettle-cloth [**3938**]
3857 cambric [**3939**]
3859 passementerie [**3940**]
3860 passementerie [**3941**]
3861 fringe [**3942**]

D. Furnishings given to the Lady Elizabeth

208 12 pieces of tapestry [**4062**]
209 1 window piece of tapestry [**4063**]
212 9 pieces of verdure [**4065**]
213 2 pieces of verdure [**4064**]
216 23 pieces of verdure [**4066**]
217 24 pieces of verdure [**4067**]
218 44 pieces of verdure [**4068**]
220 19 window pieces of verdure [**4069**]
239 2 chairs [**4074**]
349 3 cushions [**4075**]
351 1 cushion [**4076**]
354 2 cushions [**4077**]
371 3 cushions [**4078**]
393 2 cushions [**3964**]
400 1 cushion [**4082**]
402 2 cushions [**4083**]

409 1 cushion [**4084**]
434 2 carpets [**4070**]
435 9 carpets [**4071**]
517 1 traverse [**4072**]
520 1 traverse [**4073**]
1018 2 altar frontals [**4054**]
1030 2 altar frontals [**4055**]
1032 2 altar frontals [**4056**]
1036 1 set of vestments [**4058**]
1037 2 sets of vestments [**4061**]
1038 1 set of vestments [**4057**]
1047 1 set of vestments [**4059**]
1048 1 set of vestments [**4060**]
3326 2 cushions [**4079**]
3327 1 cushion [**4081**]
3330 1 cushion [**4080**]

CONCORDANCE II

ITEMS THAT APPEAR IN BOTH THE 1542 AND THE 1547 INVENTORIES

Many of the furnishings and other objects recorded in the 1542 Inventory are also listed in the 1547 Inventory. The chief exceptions are the books and lengths of silk. However, after the reorganization of the Palace of Whitehall many objects were at different locations. Concordance II seeks to reconcile the numbers given to the objects in the 1542 Inventory with those in the 1547 Inventory.

A few objects listed in the 1542 Inventory were altered after the initial description was written (for example, **625**: 'one towel' became 'two towels'). In these cases, the final number of pieces is given. There are also entries in the 1547 Inventory which only record some of the items listed in 1542 because objects had been lost or removed: for example, entry **64** in the 1542 Inventory records twenty-four gilt spoons, and a marginal note states that 12 were delivered to Sir Anthony Aucher (**1226**) and twelve sent to Sir Edmund Peckham at the Mint and melted down. Finally, some large groups of objects were split up and sent to several different locations, and so one 1542 entry may have a number of equivalent entries in the 1547 Inventory.

Some objects recorded at the Palace of Whitehall in the 1547 Inventory were listed twice or three times. This happened because new inventories were taken of sections of the palace in 1549, after the arrest of the Protector, the Duke of Somerset, and in 1550, after the death of James Rufforth. However, in this concordance only the first number allocated to an object in the 1547 Inventory is given.

The 1542 entries are given in bold, in numerical order, followed by a brief description of the item; the 1547 Inventory number is given in parentheses.

1	1 gown (**11211**)	85	1 gilt cup (**593**)	160	1 taste (**603**)
2	1 gown (**11212**)	86	1 gilt cup (**594**)	161	2 white perfume pans (**1997**)
3	1 gown (**11213**)	87	1 gilt cup (**595**)	162	1 snuffer (**1176**)
4	1 gown (**11214**)	88	2 gilt cups (**596**)	164	2 white perfume pans (**1996**)
5	1 gown (**11215**)	90	1 gilt cup (**597**)	165	1 superaltar (**2000**)
6	1 gown (**11216**)	103	2 gilt candlesticks (**1172**)	166	1 case of knives (**1751**)
7	3 gowns (**11217**)	104	1 lantern (**1990**)	167	1 case of knives (**1750**)
8	1 mantle (**11243**)	108	1 hour glass (**1991**)	168	1 case of knives (**1752**)
9	1 kirtle (**11244**)	109	1 clock (**1384**)	169	1 case of knives (**1753**)
10	3 mantles (**11245**)	111	1 gilt perfume pan (**1992**)	170	2 mazers (**822**)
11	3 kirtles (**11246**)	112	1 gilt casting bottle (**1066**)	171	1 hanging (**9191**)
12	1 coat (**11247**)	113	1 gilt candlestick (**1173**)	172	2 window pieces (**9192**)
13	2 coats (**11248**)	114	1 snuffer (**1174**)	173	1 hanging (**9193**)
14	1 coat (**11249**)	115	1 image (**247**)	174	3 window pieces (**9194**)
15	1 coat (**11250**)	116	1 image (**248**)	175	1 hanging (**9195**)
16	1 coat (**11251**)	117	1 image (**249**)	176	2 window pieces (**9196**)
17	1 doublet (**11252**)	118	1 image (**250**)	177	1 hanging (**9197**)
18	1 doublet (**11253**)	119	1 image (**251**)	178	2 window pieces (**9198**)
19	1 doublet (**11254**)	120	1 gilt pyx (**378**)	179	1 hanging (**9199**)
20	1 doublet (**11255**)	121	1 gilt water pot (**990**)	180	4 window pieces (**9200**)
21	1 doublet (**11256**)	122	1 table (**216**)	181	1 hanging (**9201**)
22	4 shirt bands (**11257**)	123	3 gilt casting bottles (**1067**)	182	2 window pieces (**9202**)
23	4 shirt bands (**11258**)	124	2 gilt casting bottles (**1068**)	183	1 hanging (**9203**)
24	sables (**11392**)	125	1 gilt pyx (**377**)	184	2 window pieces (**9204**)
29	1 case (**11259**)	126	1 image (**252**)	185	1 hanging (**9205**)
30	4 cases (**11260**)	127	1 image (**253**)	186	2 window pieces (**9206**)
31	2 gold casting bottles (**180**)	128	1 image (**254**)	187	1 tent hanging (**8790**)
32	2 gold spoons (**127**)	129	1 image (**255**)	188	1 tent hanging (**8791**)
34	1 pair of gilt flagons (**1063**)	130	2 gilt altar basins (**1520**)	189	2 window pieces (**8792**)
37	1 pair of gilt pots (**981**)	131	2 altar candlesticks (**284**)	190	1 tent hanging (**8793**)
41	1 pair of gilt pots (**983**)	132	2 gilt cruets (**325**)	191	1 tent hanging (**8794**)
46	1 pair of gilt pots (**984**)	133	1 holy-water stock (**301**)	192	2 window pieces (**8795**)
47	1 pair of gilt pots (**985**)	134	1 gilt chalice (**353**)	193	12 pieces of arras (**9209**)
48	1 pair of gilt pots (**986**)	135	1 image (**256**)	194	2 pieces of arras (**9210**)
49	1 pair of gilt pots (**987** (?))	136	2 images (**257**)	195	1 piece of arras (**9211**)
50	3 gilt bowls (**814**)	137	2 images (**258**)	196	2 pieces of arras (**9214**)
51	4 gilt bowls (**815**)	138	2 gilt altar basins (**1521**)	197	2 pieces of arras (**9215**)
52	3 gilt bowls (**816**)	139	2 gilt candlesticks (**285**)	198	6 pieces of tapestry (**9731**)
58	1 gilt bowl (**817**)	140	1 gilt pyx (**379**)	199	9 pieces of tapestry (**9732**)
60	1 gilt basin and ewer (**1514**)	141	2 gilt cruets (**324**)	200	5 pieces of tapestry (**9733**)
61	1 gilt basin and ewer (**1515**)	142	1 gilt chalice (**354**)	201	7 pieces of tapestry (**9734**)
64	24 gilt spoons (**1226**)	143	1 gilt sakering bell (**413**)	202	7 pieces of tapestry (**9735**)
65	1 gilt strainer (**1989**)	147	1 parcel-gilt barber's basin (**1518**)	203	8 pieces of tapestry (**9293**)
66	1 gilt spice box (**429**)	148	1 parcel-gilt standish (**1994**)	204	8 pieces of tapestry (**9736**)
68	24 gilt trenchers (**1717**)	149	2 parcel-gilt perfume pans (**1998**)	205	6 pieces of tapestry (**12624**)
69	4 gilt standing trenchers (**1718**)	150	2 parcel-gilt lavatory basins (**1523, 1524**)	206	6 pieces of tapestry (**9737**)
70	2 gilt salts (**1381**)			207	6 pieces of tapestry (**9738**)
75	3 gilt salts (**1382**)	151	1 parcel-gilt sakering bell (**416**)	208	12 pieces of tapestry (**12625, 15267**)
76	1 gilt layer (**1588**)	152	1 parcel-gilt holy-water pot (**304**)		
78	6 gilt chandeliers (**1170**)			209	20 window pieces (**9740, 15268**)
79	5 gilt chandeliers (**1171**)	154	3 white barber's basins (**1519**)	210	1 carpet (**13026**)
81	8 gilt cups (**591**)	155	3 white water pots (**992**)	211	20 pieces of verdure (**10545, 12626**)
83	1 gilt cup (**592**)	156	1 white ladle (**1917**)		

212 23 pieces of verdure (**12627, 15274**)

213 16 pieces of verdure (**12628, 15275**)

214 7 pieces of verdure (**10546**)

215 5 pieces of verdure (**12629**)

216 23 pieces of verdure (**13021, 15276**)

217 24 pieces of verdure (**15277**)

218 44 pieces of verdure (**12630, 13022, 15278**)

219 10 pieces of verdure (**13361**)

220 19 pieces of verdure (**10547, 13025, 15279**)

221 23 carpets (**12724, 13027**)

222 1 hanging (**9207**)

225 7 hangings (**13020**)

226 1 hanging (**9212**)

227 1 piece of arras (**9213**)

228 1 cloth of estate (**9216**)

229 1 cloth of estate (**12982**)

230 1 cloth of estate (**9217**)

231 1 cloth of estate (**12983**)

232 1 cloth of estate (**12711**)

233 2 cloths of estate (**9762, 12712**)

234 1 cloth of estate (**13070**)

236 1 cloth of estate (**13259**)

237 1 celure (**9218**)

238 16 chairs (**9244, 9784, 12737, 12962, 13082, 13539**)

239 16 chairs (**9785, 12963, 13540, 15287**)

240 3 chairs (**13083, 13541**)

241 3 chairs (**12738, 12964, 13084**)

242 1 chair (**12965**)

243 2 chairs (**12739**)

244 4 chairs (**12961, 13085, 13542**)

245 3 chairs (**9786, 12740, 12966**)

246 2 chairs (**12741, 12967**)

247 1 chair (**9787**)

248 1 chair (**9788**)

249 2 chairs (**9428**)

250 2 chairs (**9789, 12960**)

251 2 chairs (**13422, 13543**)

252 1 chair (**9431**)

253 3 chairs (**13423**)

254 1 chair (**9429**)

255 1 chair (**13424**)

256 2 chairs (**13425**)

257 2 chairs (**12968**)

258 2 chairs (**13426,[1] 13544**)

259 2 chairs (**13427**)

260 2 chairs (**9790, 9794**)

261 1 chair (**13039**)

262 1 chair (**9430**)

263 2 chairs (**13428, 13545**)

264 2 chairs (**9791, 13086**)

265 2 chairs (**13429, 13546**)

266 1 chair (**13280**)

267 4 chairs (**9792, 13087, 13288**)

268 6 folding stools (**12915**)

269 7 folding stools (**12916**)

270 7 folding stools (**12917**)

271 10 folding stools (**12918**)

272 2 stools (**12743, 12907**)

273 2 stools (**9432, 9895**)

274 2 stools (**9896, 12744**)

275 5 stools (**9433, 9897, 12098**)

276 1 stool (**9899**)

277 1 stool (**9898**)

278 2 stools (**9900**)

280 5 close stools (**12746, 12912**)

282 1 close stool (**12745, 12911**)

283 1 close stool (**12750**)

286 2 foot stools (**13171**)

287 2 foot stools (**13172**)

288 9 foot stools (**13173, 13290**)

289 1 foot stool (**9901**)

290 2 foot stools (**9902**)

291 6 foot stools (**9434, 9903**)

293 2 cushions (**9232**)

294 1 cushion (**9225**)

295 1 cushion (**9226**)

296 1 cushion (**9227**)

297 1 cushion (**9228**)

298 1 cushion (**9229**)

299 1 cushion (**9230**)

300 5 cushions (**9420**)

301 3 cushions (**9231**)

302 2 cushions (**9805**)

303 1 cushion (**9234**)

304 1 cushion (**9233**)

305 3 cushions (**9806**)

306 1 cushion (**9235**)

307 1 cushion (**9236**)

308 1 cushion (**9807**)

309 1 cushion (**9808**)

310 1 cushion (**12930**)

311 1 cushion (**9809**)

312 3 cushions (**12958**)

313 3 cushions (**9406, 13577**)

314 2 cushions (**12935**)

315 1 cushion (**9237**)

316 3 cushions (**9238, 13106**)

317 3 cushions (**9810**)

318 3 cushions (**9238, 13107**)

319 3 cushions (**9240, 13108**)

320 6 cushions (**12936**)

321 5 cushions (**9241, 9419**)

322 2 cushions (**13109**)

323 3 cushions (**9811**)

324 3 cushions (**9407**)

325 1 cushion (**13110**)

326 1 cushion (**13111**)

327 1 cushion (**13112**)

328 1 cushion (**13113**)

329 1 cushion (**13578**)

330 1 cushion (**13114**)

331 1 cushion (**13115**)

332 1 cushion (**13116**)

333 1 cushion (**13117**)

334 1 cushion (**13118**)

335 1 cushion (**13119**)

336 1 cushion (**13120**)

337 1 cushion (**13121**)

338 1 cushion (**13122**)

339 1 cushion (**13123**)

340 1 cushion (**13124**)

341 1 cushion (**13574**)

342 3 cushions (**12771**)

343 5 cushions (**9812, 13575**)

344 3 cushions (**9813, 13125**)

345 3 cushions (**9814**)

346 3 cushions (**12931**)

347 1 cushion (**9815**)

348 3 cushions (**12932**)

349 4 cushions (**13126, 15288**)

350 3 cushions (**9408, 13576**)

351 3 cushions (**12772, 15289**)

352 5 cushions (**9816, 12773, 12933**)

353 2 cushions (**12934**)

354 4 cushions (**13579, 15290**)

355 1 cushion (**12774**)

356 1 cushion (**12775**)

357 3 cushions (**12776**)

358 4 cushions (**12777, 13127, 13580**)

359 3 cushions (**9817, 13581**)

360 2 cushions (**13582**)

361 1 cushion (**12937**)

362 3 cushions (**12778, 13583**)

363 3 cushions (**13128, 13406**)

364 3 cushions (**12940**)

---

1   Here they are described as two chairs rather than one, possibly a scribal error.

365 3 cushions (**9409**)
366 1 cushion (**12938**)
367 3 cushions (**13305**)
368 3 cushions (**12943**)
369 1 cushion (**12944**)
370 3 cushions (**13307**)
371 3 cushions (**15292**)
372 3 cushions (**12941**)
373 2 cushions (**12955**)
374 2 cushions (**12956**)
375 3 cushions (**13308**)
376 3 cushions (**13584**)
377 1 cushion (**13309**)
378 3 cushions (**12939**)
379 2 cushions (**13407**)
380 3 cushions (**12779, 12947**)
381 2 cushions (**12946**)
382 2 cushions (**13306**)
383 3 cushions (**13585**)
384 1 cushion (**12949**)
385 1 cushion (**12952**)
386 2 cushions (**12942**)
387 2 cushions (**12954**)
388 1 cushion (**13304**)
389 1 cushion (**12948**)
390 3 cushions (**12780, 12951**)
391 2 cushions (**12950, 13586**)
392 2 cushions (**13310**)
393 7 cushions (**12782, 13408**)
394 3 cushions (**13409**)
395 2 cushions (**13311**)
396 3 cushions (**12953**)
397 1 cushion (**13297**)
398 2 cushions (**13298**)
399 1 cushion (**9818**)
400 1 cushion (**15295**)
401 1 cushion (**9421**)
402 2 cushions (**9425, 15296**)
403 1 cushion (**9819**)
404 1 cushion (**9422**)
405 1 cushion (**9418**)
406 1 cushion (**9410**)
407 1 cushion (**13300**)
408 1 cushion (**9411**)
409 1 cushion (**15297**)
410 1 cushion (**12781**)
411 1 cushion (**9426**)
412 1 cushion (**9423**)[2]
413 1 cushion (**9412**)
415 2 cushions (**11801**)

416 1 case for a cushion (**9249**)
417 163 cases for cushions (**9250, 9427, 9824, 12784, 12957, 12959, 13170, 13672**)
418 28 cases for cushions (**9823, 13313,**[3] **13673**)
419 69 cases for chairs (**9248, 9825, 12742, 12969, 13169, 13292, 13430, 13671**)
420 1 carpet (**9219**)
421 1 carpet (**9220**)
422 1 carpet (**13034**)
423 1 carpet (**13037**)
424 1 carpet (**9222**)
425 1 carpet (**13029**)
426 1 carpet (**9221**)
427 1 carpet (**13028**)
428 1 carpet (**13030**)
429 1 carpet (**13031**)
430 1 carpet (**13032**)
431 2 carpets (**13033**)
432 1 carpet (**13035**)
433 1 carpet (**13036**)
434 7 carpets (**9756, 11802, 15280**)
435 55 carpets (**9742, 11803, 13038, 13160, 15281**)
437 1 bedstead with apparel (**13143**)
438 1 bedstead with apparel (**9251**)
439 1 bedstead with apparel (**13144**) with 1 damask (**12973**)
440 1 bedstead with apparel (**9255**)
441 1 bedstead with apparel (**12896**)
442 1 bedstead with apparel (**9767**)
443 1 bedstead with apparel (**9768**)
444 1 bedstead with apparel (**13148**)
445 1 bedstead with apparel (**12893**)
446 1 bedstead with apparel (**12894**)
447 1 bedstead with apparel (**9769**)
448 1 bedstead with apparel (**12895**)
449 1 bedstead with apparel (**9770**)
450 1 bedstead with apparel (**9252**)
451 1 bedstead with apparel (**9771**)
452 1 bedstead with apparel (**13145**)
453 1 bedstead with apparel (**9772**) with 1 damask (**12974**)
455 1 bedstead with apparel (**13149**)
456 1 bedstead with apparel (**13146**)
457 1 bedstead with apparel (**9440**) with bed, bolster, pillow, quilts and fustians (**10549**)

458 1 bedstead with apparel (**9441**) with bed, bolster, pillow, quilts and fustians (**10552**)
459 1 bedstead with apparel (**9253**)
460 1 bedstead with apparel (**9258**)
461 1 folding bedstead with apparel (**9254**)
462 1 trussing bedstead with apparel (**11805**)
463 1 trussing bedstead with apparel (**11806**)
466 1 trussing bedstead with apparel (**10548**)
467 1 trussing bedstead with apparel (**13040**)
468 1 trussing bedstead with apparel (**10551**)
469 1 trussing bedstead with apparel (**11807**)
470 1 trussing bedstead with apparel (**11808**)
471 1 trussing bedstead with apparel (**13041**)
472 1 folding bedstead with apparel (**13042**)
473 1 sparver (**13266**)
475 1 celure and tester (**11541**)
476 1 celure and tester (**11542**)
477 1 celure and tester (**11543**)
478 1 celure and tester (**11544**)
479 1 celure and tester (**11545**)
480 1 celure and tester (**11546**)
481 1 celure and tester (**11547**)
482 1 celure and tester (**11548**)
483 1 celure and tester (**11549**)
484 1 celure and tester (**11550**)
485 1 celure and tester (**11551**)
486 1 celure and tester (**11552**)
487 1 celure and tester (**11553**)
488 1 celure and tester (**11554**)
489 1 celure and tester (**11555**)
490 1 celure and tester (**11555a**)
491 1 celure and tester (**11555b**)
492 1 celure and tester (**11555c**)
493 1 counterpoint (**13628**)
494 3 counterpoints (**11809**)
495 5 counterpoints (**11810**)
496 2 counterpoints (**11811**)
497 2 counterpoints (**11812**)

2   There is a slight discrepancy between the descriptions.
3   The description matches but there is a discrepancy in the numbers.

498 1 counterpoint (**11813**)
499 2 counterpoints (**11814**)
500 1 counterpoint (**11815**)
501 1 counterpoint (**11816**)
502 1 counterpoint (**11817**)
503 1 counterpoint (**10553**)
504 1 counterpoint (**11818**)
505 1 counterpoint (**11819**)
506 1 counterpoint (**10550**)
507 1 counterpoint (**10555**)
508 4 curtains (**13661**)
509 4 curtains (**13662**)
511 1 quilt (**9775**)
512 2 quilts (**9777**)
513 2 pillows (**9773**)[4]
514 8 pillows (**11420**)
515 1 scarlet (**12970**)
516 1 scarlet (**12971**)
517 2 traverses (**9758, 15285**)
518 1 traverse (**13185**)
519 1 traverse (**11824**)
520 1 traverse (**15286**)
521 1 traverse (**9759**)
522 1 bedstead (**11568**)
523 1 bedstead (**11567**)
524 4 pillars (**11569**)
525 4 pillars (**11570**)
526 pieces of canvas (**9256, 9909, 13174, 13450**)
527 1 cloth sack (**13186**)
528 1 cloth sack (**13187**)
529 1 cloth sack (**13188**)
530 1 cloth sack (**13189**)
531 1 cloth sack (**13190**)
532 1 cloth sack (**13191**)
533 2 cases (**13320**)
534 3 cases (**13321**)
535 4 cases (**13322**)
536 2 cases (**13323**)
537 3 cases (**13324**)
538 2 cases (**13325**)
539 1 case (**13326**)
540 5 cases (**12919**)
541 1 case (**9259**)
542 1 case (**13327**)
543 8 pairs of sheets (**9851**)
544 8 pairs of sheets (**9852, 12975**)
545 3 pairs of sheets (**9853, 12976**)
546 3 pairs of sheets (**9854**)
547 2 pairs and 1 sheet (**9855**)
548 16 pairs of sheets (**11421, 11834**)

549 5 pairs and 1 sheet (**9857, 10558, 11422**)
550 8 sheets (**9859, 10560, 11424, 11836**)
551 6 pairs of sheets (**9858, 10559, 11423, 11835**)
552 9 pairs and 1 sheet (**11426**)
553 6 pairs of sheets (**10561, 11428**)
554 4 pairs of sheets (**9861, 12977**)
555 4 sheets (**9862**)
556 3 sheets (**11429**)
557 4 sheets (**11430**)
558 30 sheets (**11431, 11837**)
559 10 pairs of pillow-beres (**9865**)
560 5 pairs of pillow-beres (**9866**)
561 8 pairs of pillow-beres (**9867, 12979**)
562 3 pairs of pillow-beres (**9868, 12978**)
563 9 pairs of pillow-beres (**9869**)
564 2 pillow-beres (**9871**)
565 8 pillow-beres (**11432**)
566 1 pillow-bere (**11433**)
567 1 pillow-bere (**9870**)
568 7 pillow-beres (**9872, 12980**)
569 10 pillow-beres (**9873, 12981**)
570 6 coifs (**11521, 11871**)
571 13 kerchers (**11522**)
572 6 double rails (**11523**)
573 6 double stomachers (**11524**)
574 3 pairs of slops (**11525**)
575 6 aprons (**11526**)
576 4 handkerchiefs (**11527**)
577 12 handkerchiefs (**11528**)
578 25 rubbers (**11529**)
579 4 tablecloths (**11434**)
580 1 tablecloth (**11435**)
581 1 tablecloth (**11436**)
582 1 tablecloth (**11437**)
583 1 tablecloth (**11438**)
584 1 tablecloth (**11439**)
585 1 tablecloth (**11440**)
586 1 tablecloth (**11441**)
587 1 tablecloth (**11442**)
588 1 tablecloth (**11443**)
589 1 tablecloth (**11444**)
590 1 tablecloth (**11445**)
591 1 tablecloth (**11446**)
592 1 tablecloth (**11447**)
593 1 tablecloth (**11448**)
594 1 tablecloth (**11838**)

595 1 tablecloth (**11449, 11839**)
596 1 tablecloth (**11450**)
597 1 tablecloth (**11840**)
598 1 tablecloth (**11451**)
599 1 tablecloth (**11452**)
600 1 tablecloth (**11453**)
601 1 tablecloth (**11454**)
602 1 tablecloth (**11841**)
603 1 tablecloth (**11455**)
605 1 tablecloth (**11456**)
606 1 tablecloth (**11457**)
607 1 tablecloth (**11458**)
608 10 napkins (**11463, 11846**)
609 32 napkins (**11464, 11847**)
610 20 napkins (**11465, 11848**)
611 3 cupboard cloths (**11468**)
612 1 cupboard cloth (**11469**)
613 1 towel (**11470**)
614 1 towel (**11471**)
615 1 towel (**11472**)
616 1 towel (**11853**)
617 1 towel (**11473**)
618 3 towels (**11854**)
620 1 towel (**11474**)
621 1 towel (**11855**)
622 1 towel (**11476**)
623 1 towel (**11477**)
624 1 towel (**11856**)
625 2 towels (**11857**)
626 1 towel (**11858**)
627 1 towel (**11478**)
628 1 towel (**11501**)
629 1 towel (**11475**)
630 1 towel (**11859**)
632 1 towel (**11860**)
633 1 towel (**11861**)
634 1 towel (**11862**)
635 1 towel (**11863**)
636 1 towel (**11479**)
637 1 towel (**11864**)
638 1 towel (**11480**)
639 1 towel (**11481**)
640 1 towel (**11482**)
641 1 towel (**11483**)
642 1 towel (**11502**)
643 1 towel (**11503**)
644 1 towel (**11504**)
645 1 coverpane (**11505**)
646 1 coverpane (**11506**)
647 1 coverpane (**11507**)
648 1 coverpane (**11508**)

4   Possibly two of the four listed.

649	1 coverpane (**11509**)	703	1 picture (**10608**)	756	1 picture (**10659**)
650	3 coverpanes (**11510**)	704	1 picture (**10609**)	757	1 picture (**10660**)
651	1 coverpane (**11511**)	705	1 picture (**10610**)	758	1 picture (**10661**)
652	2 coverpanes (**11513**)	706	1 picture (**10611**)	759	1 picture (**10662**)
653	1 coverpane (**11512**)	707	1 picture (**10612**)	760	1 picture (**10663**)
654	1 coverpane (**11514**)	708	1 picture (**10613**)	761	1 picture (**10664**)
655	1 coverpane (**11519**)	709	1 picture (**10614**)	762	1 picture (**10665**)
656	1 coverpane (**11520**)	710	1 picture (**10615**)	763	1 picture (**10666**)
657	22 bowls of pewter (**12747,**	711	1 picture (**10616**)	764	1 picture (**10667**)
	12751, 12913)	712	1 picture (**10617**)	765	1 picture (**10669**)
660	11 cisterns of pewter (**12747,**	713	1 picture (**10618**)	766	1 picture (**10670**)
	12751, 12914)	714	1 picture (**10619**)	767	1 picture (**10668**)
662	10 chamber-water pots (**11406**)	715	1 picture (**10620**)	768	1 picture (**10671**)
663	3 cisterns (**10857**)	716	1 picture (**10622**)	769	1 picture (**10672**)
664	1 picture (**10569**)	717	1 picture (**10623**)	770	1 picture (**10673**)
665	1 picture (**10570**)	718	1 picture (**10624**)	771	1 picture (**10675**)
666	1 picture (**10571**)	719	1 picture (**10625**)	772	1 picture (**10676**)
667	1 picture (**10572**)	720	1 picture (**10621**)	773	1 picture (**10674**)
668	1 picture (**10573**)	721	1 picture (**10626**)	774	1 picture (**10677**)
669	1 picture (**10574**)	722	1 picture (**10627**)	775	1 picture (**10678**)
670	1 picture (**10575**)	723	1 picture (**10628**)	776	1 picture (**10679**)
671	1 picture (**10576**)	724	1 picture (**10629**)	777	1 picture (**10680**)
672	1 picture (**10577**)	725	1 picture (**10630**)	778	1 picture (**10681**)
673	1 picture (**10578**)	726	1 picture (**10632**)	779	1 picture (**10682**)
674	1 picture (**10579**)	727	1 picture (**10631**)	780	1 picture (**10683**)
675	1 picture (**10580**)	728	1 picture (**10633**)	781	1 picture (**10684**)
676	1 picture (**10581**)	729	1 picture (**10634**)	782	1 picture (**10685**)
677	1 picture (**10582**)	730	1 picture (**10635**)	783	1 picture (**10686**)
678	1 picture (**10583**)	731	1 picture (**10636**)	784	1 picture (**10687**)
679	1 picture (**10584**)	732	1 picture (**10638**)	785	1 picture (**10688**)
680	1 picture (**10585**)	733	1 picture (**10637**)	786	1 picture (**10689**)
681	1 picture (**10586**)	734	1 picture (**10639**)	787	1 picture (**10690**)
682	1 picture (**10587**)	735	1 picture (**10640**)	788	1 picture (**10691**)
683	1 picture (**10588**)	736	1 picture (**10641**)	789	1 picture (**10692**)
684	1 picture (**10589**)	737	1 picture (**10642**)	790	1 picture (**10693**)
685	1 picture (**10590**)	738	1 picture (**10644**)	791	1 picture (**10694**)
686	1 picture (**10591**)	739	1 picture (**10643**)	792	1 picture (**10695**)
687	1 picture (**10592**)	740	1 picture (**10645**)	793	1 picture (**10696**)
688	1 picture (**10593**)	741	1 picture (**10646**)	794	1 picture (**10697**)
689	1 picture (**10594**)	742	1 picture (**10647**)	795	1 picture (**10698**)
690	1 picture (**10595**)	743	1 picture (**10706**)	796	1 picture (**10699**)
691	1 picture (**10596**)	744	1 picture (**10649**)	797	1 picture (**10700**)
692	1 picture (**10597**)	745	1 picture (**10717**)	798	1 picture (**10701**)
693	1 picture (**10598**)	746	1 picture (**10650**)	799	1 picture (**10702**)
694	1 picture (**10599**)	747	1 picture (**10648**)	800	1 picture (**10703**)
695	1 picture (**10600**)	748	1 picture (**10651**)	801	1 picture (**10704**)
696	1 picture (**10601**)	749	1 picture (**10652**)	802	1 picture (**10705**)
697	1 picture (**10602**)	750	1 picture (**10653**)	803	1 picture (**10708**)
698	1 picture (**10603**)	751	1 picture (**10654**)	804	1 picture (**10709**)
699	1 picture (**10604**)	752	1 picture (**10655**)	805	1 picture (**10710**)
700	1 picture (**10605**)	753	1 picture (**10656**)	806	1 picture (**10711**)
701	1 picture (**10606**)	754	1 picture (**10657**)	807	1 picture (**10712**)
702	1 picture (**10607**)	755	1 picture (**10658**)	808	1 picture (**10713**)

809	1 picture (**10714**)	866	4 mirrors (**10797, 13180**)	916	4 gitterons (**11901**)
810	1 picture (**10715**)	867	1 mirror (**13181**)	917	2 gitterons (**11902**)
811	1 picture (**10716**)	868	1 mirror (**10799**)	918	14 gitterons (**11903**)
812	1 picture (**11582**)	869	1 mirror (**10792**)	919	24 lutes (**11905**)
813	1 picture (**10707**)	870	2 mirrors (**10793, 13179**)	920	1 gitteron and 1 lute (**11904**)
816	1 stained cloth (**10722**)	871	1 mirror (**13184**)	921	24 flutes (**11906**)
817	1 stained cloth (**10723**)	872	1 mirror (**10796**)	922	15 flutes (**11907**)
818	1 stained cloth (**10724**)	873	1 mirror (**10798**)	923	10 flutes (**11908**)
819	1 stained cloth (**10725**)	874	1 mirror (**13182**)	924	7 flutes (**11909**)
821	1 stained cloth (**10726**)	875	1 mirror (**13183**)	925	5 flutes (**11910**)
822	1 stained cloth (**10727**)	876	1 mirror (**10794**)	926	4 flutes (**11911**)
823	1 stained cloth (**10728**)	877	1 mirror (**10800**)	927	15 crumhorns (**11912**)
824	1 terracotta (**10734**)	879	1 mirror (**10801**)	928	6 recorders (**11917**)
825	1 terracotta (**10733**)	880	1 mirror (**10802**)	929	1 recorder (**11918**)
826	1 terracotta (**10735**)	881	1 mirror (**11930**)	930	4 recorders (**11919**)
827	1 terracotta (**10736**)	885	2 pairs of playing tables (**11396**)	931	9 recorders (**11920**)
828	1 terracotta (**10737**)	886	1 pair of playing tables (**11397**)	932	6 recorders (**11913**)
829	1 terracotta (**10738**)	887	1 pair of playing tables (**11398**)	933	7 recorders (**11914**)
830	1 terracotta (**10739**)	888	1 pair of double regals (**11872**)	934	16 recorders (**11914**)
831	1 terracotta (**10740**)	889	1 pair of double regals (**11874**)	935	2 recorders (**11915**)
832	1 terracotta (**10741**)	890	1 pair of double regals (**11873**)	936	4 recorders (**11916**)
834	1 terracotta (**10742**)	891	1 pair of single regals (**11877**)	937	1 pipe for a tabor (**11921**)
835	1 terracotta (**10743**)	892	1 pair of single regals (**11878**)	939	8 shawms (**11922**)
836	1 terracotta (**10744**)	893	2 pairs of single regals (**11879**)	940	7 shawms (**11923**)
837	1 map (**10747**)	894	1 pair of double regals (**11875**)	942	1 shawm (**11924**)
838	1 map (**10748**)	895	6 pairs of single regals (**11880**)	943	1 bagpipe (**11926**)
839	1 map (**10749**)	896	1 pair of double regals (**11876**)	945	2 targets (**3862**)
840	1 map (**10750**)	897	1 pair of single regals (**11881**)	946	56 targets (**3865**)
841	1 map (**10751**)	898	1 single virginal (**11885**)	947	37 targets (**3866**)
842	1 map (**10752**)	899	1 pair of single regals (**11882**)	948	6 targets (**3864**)
843	1 map (**10753**)	900	1 pair of single regals (**11883**)	949	2 targets (**3863**)
844	1 map (**10754**)	901	1 pair of single regals (**11884**)	951	1 pair of quishes (**8260**)
845	1 map (**10755**)	902	1 double regal (**11886**)	952	22 poleaxes (**3859**)
846	1 map (**10756**)	903	1 'instrument that goeth on a wheel' (**11887**)	953	1 poleaxe (**3860**)
847	1 map (**10757**)			954	37 partisans (**3857**)
848	1 map (**10758**)	904	2 pairs of double regals (**11888**)	955	3 partisans (**3856**)
849	1 map (**10759**)	905	2 pairs of single virginals (**11892**)	956	2 partisans (**3855**)
850	1 map (**10760**)			957	98 partisans (**3858**)
851	1 map (**10761**)	906	1 pair of single virginals (**11891**)	959	6 forest bills (**3854**)
852	1 map (**10762**)	907	1 pair of double virginals (**11889**)	961	6 morris-pikes (**3861**)
853	1 map (**10764**)			972	10 crossbows (**3867**)
854	1 map (**10763**)	908	1 pair of single virginals (**11893**)	973	1 quiver (**3870**)
855	1 map (**10765**)	909	2 pairs of single virginals (**11894**)	974	1 crossbow (**3869**)
856	1 map (**10766**)			976	2 quivers (**8261**)
857	1 map (**10767**)	910	2 pairs of single virginals (**11895**)	977	2 long bows (**8259**)
858	1 map (**10768**)	911	1 pair of single virginals (**11896**)	979	1 sword (**8246**)
859	1 map (**10769**)	912	1 pair of double virginals (**11890**)	980	1 sword (**8247**)
862	1 mirror (**10789**)			982	3 swords (**8248**)
863	1 mirror (**10790**)	913	1 pair of clavichords (**11898**)	983	2 swords (**8249**)
864	1 mirror (**10791**)	914	1 pair of clavichords (**11899**)	984	1 sword (**8250**)
865	1 mirror (**10795**)	915	11 viols (**11900**)[5]	985	6 swords (**8251**)

5   There is a discrepancy between the numbers recorded in 1542 and 1547.

986	2 swords (**8252**)
987	1 sword (**8253**)
988	1 skene (**8255**)
989	2 skenes (**8256**)
990	1 skene (**8254**)
992	1 short hanger (**8257**)
993	3 wood knives (**8258**)
1003	12 curtains (**11825**)
1017	2 altar frontals (**9881**)
1018	2 altar frontals and 2 vestments (**9882, 15259**)
1019	1 sacrament cloth (**9889**)
1020	1 mass book (**9891**)
1021	1 corporal case (**9890**)
1022	2 altar frontals (**9884**)
1023	2 vestments (**9887**)
1024	2 altar frontals (**12985**)
1025	2 vestments (**13474**)
1026	1 mass book (**9892**)
1028	1 altar cloth (**8985**)
1029	2 altar frontals (**13316**)
1030	2 altar frontals (**15260**)
1031	1 altar frontal (**12986**)
1032	4 altar frontals (**9885**)
1033	2 altar frontals (**9882**)
1034	2 altar frontals (**12987**)
1035	2 altar frontals (**12988**)
1036	4 vestments (**9883, 15263**)
1037	8 vestments (**13317, 13475, 15266**)
1038	4 vestments (**8982, 9886, 15262**)
1039	1 vestment (**12989**)
1040	3 vestments (**8983**)
1041	1 vestment (**13318**)
1042	1 vestment (**13319**)
1043	2 vestments (**12990**)
1044	1 vestment (**12991**)
1045	1 vestment (**12992**)
1047	1 vestment (**15264**)
1048	2 vestments (**8984, 15265**)
1049	1 vestment (**12993**)
1050	5 altar cloths (**9888**)
1051	1 clock (**10782**)
1052	1 larum (**10784**)
1054	1 clock (**13175**)
1055	1 clock (**13176**)
1057	1 clock (**13178**)
1058	1 clock (**10783**)
1059	1 clock (**13177**)
1061	3 glass bottles (**10894**)

1062	2 glass bottles (**10895**)
1063	12 glass bottles (**10896**)
1064	2 earth flagons (**10897**)
1065	1 glass basin and layer (**10898**)
1066	1 glass basin and 2 layers (**10899**)
1067	12 glass basins and 13 ewers and layers (**10900**)
1068	1 marble basin and ewer (**10901**)
1069	1 earth basin and ewer (**10902**)
1070	3 glass bowls (**10903**)
1071	12 glass bowls (**10904**)
1072	34 glass bowls (**10905**)
1073	2 glass bowls (**10906**)
1074	4 glass cups (**10907**)
1075	30 glass cups (**10908**)
1076	14 glass cups (**10909**)
1077	1 glass cup (**10910**)
1078	2 glass cups (**10911**)
1079	2 glass cups (**10912**)
1080	16 glass goblets (**10913**)
1081	7 glass pots (**10914**)
1082	1 glass pot (**10915**)
1083	3 glass pots (**10916**)
1084	3 glass pots (**10917**)
1085	1 glass pot (**10918**)
1086	1 glass pot (**10919**)
1088	1 glass cup (**10920**)
1089	1 glass cup (**10921**)
1092	24 glass cups (**10922**)
1093	1 glass cup (**10923**)
1095	12 glass cruses (**10924**)
1096	15 glass cruses (**10925**)
1097	1 glass cruse (**10926**)
1098	2 glass cruses (**10927**)
1099	1 glass layer (**10928**)
1100	1 glass layer (**10929**)
1101	8 glass layers (**10930**)
1102	12 earth cups (**10931**)
1103	1 glass (**10932**)
1104	1 crystal glass (**10933**)
1105	4 glasses (**10934**)
1106	1 glass (**10935**)
1107	9 glass spice plates (**10936**)
1108	7 glass spice plates (**10937**)
1109	1 glass candlestick (**10938**)
1110	3 glass candlesticks (**10939**)
1111	4 glass candlesticks (**10940**)
1112	3 glass altar candlesticks (**10941**)
1114	6 glass trenchers[6] (**10942**)
1115	6 glass trenchers (**10943**)

1116	4 spoons (**10944**)
1117	2 forks (**10945**)
1118	66 glass plates, dishes and saucers (**10946**)
1119	2 earth platters (**10947**)
1120	6 earth saucers (**10948**)
1121	1 glass casting bottle (**10949**)
1122	1 glass basket (**10950**)
1123	2 glass conserve pots (**10951**)
1124	1 glass holy water stock (**10952**)
1125	'divers conceits of earth' (**10953**)
1126	1 pair of andirons (**10866**)
1127	1 pair of andirons (**10860**)
1128	1 pair of andirons (**10861**)
1129	8 pairs of andirons (**10862**)
1130	1 pair of andirons (**10863**)
1131	1 pair of andirons (**10864**)
1132	2 pairs of andirons (**10867**)
1133	1 pair of andirons (**10865**)
1134	19 pairs of andirons (**10868**)
1135	16 fire forks (**10871**)
1136	15 fire pans (**10876**)
1137	18 pairs of tongues (**10873**)
1138	15 pairs of bellows (**10875**)
1139	1 round pan (**11660**)
1140	6 round pans (**9224, 9913, 11405**)
1141	7 square pans (**9914**)
1143	1 banner (**15136**)
1144	2 banners (**15137**)
1145	1 candlestick (**10803**)
1146	1 candlestick (**10804**)
1147	17 candlesticks (**10805**)
1148	2 candlesticks (**10806**)
1149	2 cupboards (**10842**)
1150	1 cupboard (**10843**)
1151	1 cupboard (**10844**)
1152	1 cupboard (**10845**)
1153	3 cupboards (**10846**)
1154	2 cupboards (**10847**)
1155	3 cupboards (**10849**)
1156	2 cupboards (**10848**)
1157	3 cupboards (**10850**)
1158	2 cupboards (**10851**)
1159	3 cupboards (**10852**)
1160	1 cupboard (**10853**)
1161	1 cupboard (**10854**)
1162	1 cupboard (**10855**)
1163	40 cupboards (**10856**)
1165	1 table (**10807**)
1166	1 table (**10808**)

6   There is a discrepancy between this entry and the number given in the marginal note.

1167 1 table (**10809**)	1216 3 staves (**10888**)	2072 diaper (**15121**)
1168 1 table (**10810**)	1217 2 perfume pans (**1993**)	2073 diaper (**15122**)
1169 2 tables (**10811**)	1218 1 folding lectern (**8978**)	2074 diaper (**15123**)
1170 1 table (**10812**)	1219 1 pair of bellows (**11403**)	2077 diaper (**15124**)
1171 1 table (**10813**)	1220 1 pair of scales (**11404**)	2078 diaper (**15125**)
1172 1 table (**10814**)	1221 5 snuffers (**10878**)	2079 diaper (**15126**)
1173 1 table (**10815**)	1227 1 cloth for a church (**8979**)	2080 diaper (**15127**)
1174 2 tables (**10816**)	1228 1 cloth for a church (**8980**)	2081 diaper (**15128**)
1176 2 tables (**10817**)	1229 1 altar frontal (**8981**)	2082 diaper (**15129**)
1177 38 tables (**9908, 10822, 11530,**	1230 1 altar frontal (**12984**)	2083 diaper (**15130**)
11583, 11929)	1231 1 lantern (**10787**)	2084 diaper (**15131**)
1178 1 frame for a table (**10818**)	1232 1 trunk to shoot in (**11399**)	2091 Brussels tick (**15077**)
1179 4 pairs of trestles (**10823, 11531**)	1238 2 trivets (**11830**)	2092 Brussels tick (**15078**)
1180 25 pairs of trestles (**9908, 10824,**	2029 passement (**15134**)	2093 Brussels tick (**15078**)
11583, 11929)	2036 nettle-cloth (**15084**)	2094 Brussels tick (**15079**)
1181 1 form (**10827**)[7]	2038 diaper (**15085**)	2095 1 gown (**11218**)
1182 64 forms (**10828**)	2039 diaper (**15086**)	2096 1 gown (**11219**)
1183 1 stool (**10829**)	2040 diaper (**15087**)	2097 1 gown (**11221**)
1184 1 stool (**10830**)	2041 diaper (**15088**)	2098 1 gown (**11220**)
1185 1 stool (**10831**)	2042 diaper (**15089**)	2099 1 gown (**11222**)
1186 1 stool (**10832**)	2043 diaper (**15090**)	2100 1 gown (**11223**)
1187 2 stools (**10834**)	2044 diaper (**15091**)	2101 1 gown (**11224**)
1188 5 stools (**10835**)	2045 diaper (**15092**)	2102 1 gown (**11225**)
1189 1 stool (**10837**)	2046 diaper (**15093**)	2103 1 gown (**11226**)
1190 1 stool (**10836**)	2047 diaper (**15094**)	2104 1 gown (**11227**)
1191 73 stools (**10839**)	2048 diaper (**15095**)	2105 1 gown (**11228**)
1192 6 stools (**9906, 10838**)	2049 diaper (**15096**)	2106 1 gown (**11229**)
1193 4 footstools (**10840**)[8]	2050 diaper (**15097**)	2107 1 gown (**11230**)
1194 27 footstools (**10841**)	2051 diaper (**15098**)	2108 1 gown (**11231**)
1195 2 chests (**10879**)	2052 diaper (**15099**)	2109 1 gown (**11232**)
1196 1 chest (**11418**)	2053 diaper (**15100**)	2110 1 gown (**11233**)
1197 5 chests (**10880**)	2054 diaper (**15101**)	2111 1 gown (**11234**)
1198 40 chests (**9223, 9257, 9912,**	2055 diaper (**15102**)	2112 1 gown (**11235**)
10883, 11419, 11832, 11928,	2056 diaper (**15104**)	2113 1 gown (**11236**)
13674)	2057 diaper (**15105**)	2114 1 gown (**11237**)
1199 2 chests (**10882**)	2058 diaper (**15106**)	2115 1 gown (**11238**)
1200 1 chest (**10881**)	2059 diaper (**15107**)	2116 1 gown (**11239**)
1201 1 trunk (**11833**)	2060 diaper (**15108**)	2117 1 gown (**11240**)
1202 3 cases (**10884**)	2061 diaper (**15109**)	2118 1 gown (**11241**)
1203 2 chests (**11927**)	2062 diaper (**15103**)	2119 sleeve linings (**11340**)
1204 1 cabinet (**11574**)	2063 diaper (**15110**)	2120 2 gowns (**11242**)
1205 1 cabinet (**11571**)	2064 diaper (**15111**)	2121 1 kirtle (**11261**)
1206 1 cabinet (**11572**)	2065 diaper (**15112**)	2122 1 kirtle (**11262**)
1207 1 cabinet (**11573**)	2066 diaper (**15115**)	2123 1 kirtle (**11263**)
1208 1 screen (**10463**)[9]	2067 diaper (**15116**)	2124 1 kirtle (**11264**)
1210 1 screen (**10858**)	2068 diaper (**15117**)	2125 1 kirtle (**11265**)
1211 11 screens (**10859**)	2069 diaper (**15118**)	2126 1 kirtle (**11266**)
1214 2 walking staves (**11400**)	2070 diaper (**15119**)	2127 1 kirtle (**11267**)
1215 3 staves (**11401**)	2071 diaper (**15120**)	2128 1 kirtle (**11268**)

7   See also entries **2368** and **3490**.
8   See also entry **3492**.
9   There is a slight discrepancy between the two descriptions.

2129 1 kirtle (**11269**)
2130 1 kirtle (**11270**)
2131 1 kirtle (**11271**)
2132 1 kirtle (**11272**)
2133 1 kirtle (**11273**)
2134 1 kirtle (**11274**)
2135 1 kirtle (**11275**)
2136 1 cloak (**11276**)
2137 1 pair of sleeves (**11277**)
2138 1 pair of sleeves (**11278**)
2139 2 pairs of sleeves (**11279**)
2140 1 pair of sleeves (**11280**)
2141 1 pair of sleeves (**11281**)
2142 1 pair of sleeves (**11282**)
2143 1 pair of sleeves (**11283**)
2144 1 pair of sleeves (**11284**)
2145 1 pair of sleeves (**11285**)
2146 1 pair of sleeves (**11286**)
2147 1 pair of sleeves (**11287**)
2148 1 pair of sleeves (**11288**)
2149 1 pair of sleeves (**11289**)
2150 1 pair of sleeves (**11290**)
2151 1 pair of sleeves (**11291**)
2152 1 pair of sleeves (**11292**)
2153 1 pair of sleeves (**11293**)
2154 1 pair of sleeves (**11294**)
2155 1 pair of sleeves (**11295**)
2156 1 pair of sleeves (**11296**)
2157 1 pair of sleeves (**11297**)
2158 1 pair of sleeves (**11298**)
2159 1 pair of sleeves (**11299**)
2160 1 pair of sleeves (**11300**)
2161 1 pair of sleeves (**11301**)
2162 1 pair of sleeves (**11302**)
2163 1 pair of sleeves (**11303**)
2164 1 pair of sleeves (**11304**)
2165 1 pair of sleeves (**11305**)
2166 1 pair of sleeves (**11306**)
2167 1 pair of sleeves (**11307**)
2168 1 pair of sleeves (**11308**)
2169 1 pair of sleeves (**11309**)
2170 1 pair of sleeves (**11310**)
2171 1 pair of sleeves (**11311**)
2172 1 pair of sleeves (**11312**)
2173 1 pair of sleeves (**11313**)
2174 1 pair of sleeves (**11314**)
2175 1 pair of sleeves (**11315**)
2176 1 pair of sleeves (**11316**)
2177 1 pair of sleeves (**11317**)
2178 1 pair of sleeves (**11318**)
2179 1 pair of sleeves (**11319**)
2180 1 pair of sleeves (**11320**)
2181 1 pair of sleeves (**11321**)

2182 1 pair of sleeves (**11322**)
2183 1 pair of sleeves (**11323**)
2184 1 pair of sleeves (**11324**)
2185 1 pair of sleeves (**11325**)
2186 1 pair of sleeves (**11326**)
2187 1 pair of sleeves (**11327**)
2188 1 pair of sleeves (**11328**)
2189 1 pair of sleeves (**11329**)
2190 1 pair of sleeves (**11330**)
2191 1 pair of sleeves (**11331**)
2192 1 pair of sleeves (**11332**)
2193 1 pair of sleeves (**11333**)
2194 1 pair of sleeves (**11334**)
2195 1 pair of sleeves (**11335**)
2196 1 pair of sleeves (**11336**)
2197 1 pair of sleeves (**11337**)
2198 1 pair of sleeves (**11338**)
2199 1 pair of sleeves (**11339**)
2200 3 placards (**11341**)
2201 5 placards (**11342**)
2202 8 placards (**11343**)
2203 14 placards (**11344**)
2204 1 stomacher (**11345**)
2205 2 stomachers (**11346**)
2206 1 stomacher (**11347**)
2207 1 stomacher (**11348**)
2208 1 stomacher (**11349**)
2209 1 stomacher (**11350**)
2210 1 stomacher (**11351**)
2211 1 stomacher (**11352**)
2212 1 stomacher (**11353**)
2213 1 stomacher (**11354**)
2214 1 stomacher (**11355**)
2215 1 stomacher (**11356**)
2216 10 frontlets (**11357**)
2217 3 frontlets (**11358**)
2218 2 frontlets (**11359**)
2219 1 French hood (**11360**)
2220 1 biliment (**11361**)
2221 1 biliment (**11362**)
2222 3 coifs (**11363**)
2223 1 partlet (**11364**)
2224 6 partlets (**11365**)
2225 2 partlets (**11366**)
2226 1 muffler (**11367**)
2227 1 muffler (**11368**)
2228 1 hat (**11369**)
2229 1 hat (**11370**)
2230 1 waistcoat (**11371**)
2231 1 waistcoat (**11372**)
2232 1 waistcoat (**11376**)
2233 1 pair of short hose (**11373**)
2234 1 sampler (**11374**)

2235 1 chest (**11415**)
2236 1 chest (**11416**)
2237 1 chest (**11417**)
2238 2 coffers (**11408**)
2239 1 coffer (**11409**)
2240 1 mirror (**11375**)
2241 3 comb cases (**11377**)
2242 1 standish (**11379**)
2243 1 walking staff (**11402**)
2244 1 pair of playing tables (**11394**)
2245 1 pair of playing tables (**11395**)
2246 1 case with knives (**1755**)
2247 1 baby (**11381**)
2248 2 babies (**11382**)
2250 1 tower of wood (**11383**)
2251 1 piece of arras for a cushion
         (**11384**)
2252 1 cushion (**11385**)
2253 cloth of gold (**11386**)
2254 1 box (**11387**)
2255 1 lily pot (**11388**)
2256 1 coverpane (**11515**)
2257 1 coverpane (**11518**)
2258 1 waist smock (**11389**)
2259 1 calico cloth (**11390**)
2295 2 knives (**1754**)
2296 4 pallet beds (**13043**)
2297 4 bolsters (**13044**)
2299 1 counterpoint (**11820**)
2301 1 counterpoint (**11821**)
2302 1 counterpoint (**11822**)
2303 1 counterpoint (**11823**)
2304 2 pairs of sheets (**9856**)
2305 2 pairs and 1 sheet (**9860**, **11428**)
2306 5 pairs and 1 sheet (**11427**)
2307 1 pair of sheets (**10562**, **11576**)
2308 4 trussing sheets (**11837**)
2309 1 tablecloth (**11459**)
2310 1 tablecloth (**11842**)
2311 1 tablecloth (**11460**)
2312 1 tablecloth (**11461**)
2313 2 tablecloths (**11843**)
2314 2 tablecloths (**11844**)
2315 2 tablecloths (**11845**)
2316 1 tablecloth (**11462**)
2317 1 towel (**11484**)
2318 1 towel (**11485**)
2319 2 towels (**11486**)
2320 2 towels (**11487**)
2321 1 towel (**11488**)
2322 1 towel (**11489**)
2323 1 towel (**11865**)
2324 1 towel (**11490**)

2325 1 towel (**11491**)
2326 1 towel (**11866**)
2327 1 towel (**11492**)
2328 1 towel (**11493**)
2329 1 towel (**11494**)
2330 1 towel (**11495**)
2331 1 towel (**11867**)
2332 1 towel (**11496**)
2333 1 towel (**11868**)
2334 1 towel (**11497**)
2335 1 towel (**11869**)
2336 1 towel (**11498**)
2337 1 towel (**11499**)
2338 1 towel (**11870**)
2339 1 towel (**11500**)
2340 1 cupboard cloth (**11851**)
2341 1 cupboard cloth (**11469**)
2343 1 cupboard cloth (**11852**)
2344 5 napkins (**11466, 11849**)
2345 20 dozen napkins (**11467, 11850**)
2346 3 coverpanes (**11516**)
2347 1 coverpane (**11517**)
2348 1 celure and tester (**11556**)
2349 1 celure and tester (**13264**)
2350 1 bedstead with apparel (**13147**)
2354 1 shawm (**11925**)
2355 1 pair of single virginals (**11933**)[10]
2363 2 pillows (**9774**)
2368 1 form (**10827**)[11]
2369 2 mirrors (**11827**)
2370 1 mirror (**11828**)
2371 1 mirror (**11829**)
2372 4 coffers (**11410**)
2373 2 coffers (**11411**)
2374 1 coffer (**11412**)
2375 1 coffer (**11413**)
2376 2 coffers (**11414**)
2388 1 cabinet (**11575**)
2389 1 comb case (**11378**)
2390 1 set of chessmen (**11391**)
2391 10 vizers (**11407**)
2393 1 lantern (**10788**)
3308 3 bowls (**11831**)
3311 2 footstools (**12909**)
3312 3 footstools (**9904, 12748**)
3313 2 footstools (**12749**)
3314 2 footstools (**12910**)
3315 11 footstools (**12749, 13289**)

3316 2 footstools (**11804**)
3317 4 footstools (**12920**)
3318 4 footstools (**12921**)
3319 1 cushion (**9242**)
3320 1 cushion (**9413**)
3321 1 cushion (**9414**)
3322 1 cushion (**12783**)
3323 2 cushions (**9415, 13587**)
3324 1 cushion (**12945**)
3325 2 cushions (**9416, 9820**)
3326 2 cushions (**15291**)
3327 3 cushions (**9821, 15294**)
3328 2 cushions (**13410**)
3329 2 cushions (**13411**)
3330 4 cushions (**13412, 15293**)
3331 3 cushions (**13588**)
3332 6 cushions (**9822**)
3333 1 hanging (**9208**)
3334 7 pieces of arras (**9214**)
3335 5 pieces of arras (**9215**)
3336 1 table (**10819**)
3337 1 counterpoint (**13629**)
3338 1 counterpoint (**13272**)
3344 1 cloth of estate (**12710**)
3345 1 chair (**9245**)
3346 2 cushions (**13312**)
3347 3 cushions (**9424**)
3349 4 foot stools (**9435**)
3357 1 table (**10820**)
3471 1 stained cloth (**10770**)
3472 1 table (**10821**)
3479 2 barehides (**13192**)
3483 2 stools (**9907**)
3490 1 form (**10827**)[12]
3491 2 stools (**10833**)
3492 4 footstools (**10840**)[13]
3493 1 quilt (**9776**)
3494 2 pillows (**9773**)
3496 1 bed and 2 pillows (**9251**)
3497 1 bed, 1 bolster and 2 pillows
        (**9255**)
3546 6 pieces of tapestry (**9739**)
3547 8 pieces of tapestry (**9288**)
3548 7 pieces of verdure (**9295**)
3549 11 pieces of verdure (**12876,
        13023**)
3550 4 pieces of verdure (**12877,
        13024**)

3597 1 pair of andirons (**10869**)
3598 1 hearth (**10886**)
3599 1 fire pan (**10877**)
3600 1 fire fork (**10872**)
3601 1 pair of tongues (**10874**)
3602 1 fire rake (**10885**)
3603 1 toasting fork (**10887**)
3676 2 chairs (**11798**)
3677 1 chair (**11799**)
3678 1 footstool (**9905**)
3680 1 chair (**11800**)
3681 sables (**11393**)
3696 1 stained cloth (**10729**)
3697 1 stained cloth (**10730**)
3698 1 stained cloth (**10731**)
3699 1 map (**10771**)
3700 1 map (**10772**)
3701 1 double regal (**13193**)
3702 1 chair (**9247**)
3703 1 chair (**9246**)
3704 1 chair (**9793**)
3705 1 cushion (**9417**)
3706 1 cushion (**9243**)
3707 1 cushion (**13413**)
3708 2 footstools (**9436 or 9437**)[14]
3709 2 footstools (**9438**)
3710 2 footstools (**9439**)
3711 1 gold spoon (**128**)
3712 1 pair of gilt flagons (**1064**)
3713 1 pair of gilt flagons (**1065**)
3714 1 pair of gilt pots (**988**)
3715 1 pair of gilt pots (**989**)
3716 1 gilt bowl (**818**)
3717 3 gilt bowls (**819**)
3718 3 gilt bowls (**821**)
3719 1 gilt cup (**598**)
3720 1 gilt cup (**599**)
3721 1 gilt cup (**600**)
3722 1 gilt basin and ewer (**1516**)
3723 1 gilt layer (**1589**)
3724 1 gilt layer (**1590**)
3725 1 gilt salt (**1383**)
3726 1 jug (**1314**)
3727 1 jug (**1315**)
3728 1 gilt chaffing dish (**1667**)
3729 1 parcel-gilt basin and ewer (**1517**)
3731 1 pair of parcel-gilt flagons
        (**1069**)

10 There is a slight discrepancy between the two descriptions.
11 See also entries **1181** and **3490**.
12 See also entries **1181** and **2368**.
13 See also entry **1193**.
14 The wording of the entries is identical.

3734 1 pair of parcel-gilt pots (**991**)

3736 3 parcel-gilt bowls (**820**)

3738 3 parcel-gilt goblets (**1273**)

3739 2 parcel-gilt goblets (**1274**)

3740 1 parcel-gilt cup (**601**)

3741 1 parcel-gilt cup (**602**)

3743 1 parcel-gilt cruse (**1275**)

3744 1 parcel-gilt cruse (**1276**)

3745 1 parcel-gilt chafing dish (**1668**)

3746 1 parcel-gilt chafing dish (**1669**)

3747 1 white cup (**604**)

3748 1 white cruse (**1277**)

3750 2 white candlesticks (**1175**)

3751 1 lantern (**1995**)

3752 1 gilt cross (**202**)

3753 1 pair gilt altar candlesticks (**286**)

3754 2 gilt altar basins (**1522**)

3755 1 gilt chalice (**355**)

3756 2 gilt cruets (**326**)

3757 1 gilt sakering bell (**414**)

3758 1 gilt holy-water pot (**302**)

3759 1 gilt holy-water sprinkle (**303**)

3760 1 superaltar (**1999**)

3761 1 corporal case (**9893**)

3763 see entry **223**

3764 see entry **224**

3765 8 footstools (**12922**)

3766 4 footstools (**13291**)

3767 2 curtains (**11826**)

3774 tissue (**14981, 14982, 14983, 14984**)

3775 cloth of gold (**14985, 14986**)

3776 cloth of gold (**14987**)

3777 cloth of gold (**14988**)

3778 cloth of gold (**14989**)

3779 cloth of gold (**14990**)

3781 cloth of gold (**14993**)

3782 cloth of gold (**14994, 14995**)

3783 cloth of gold (**14991, 14992**)

3784 cloth of silver (**14997, 14998**)

3785 baudekin (**14996**)

3786 tinsel (**14999**)

3787 velvet (**15001, 15019**)

3788 velvet (**15008**)

3789 velvet (**15002**)

3790 velvet (**15011**)

3791 velvet (**15003**)

3792 velvet (**15004, 15017**)

3793 velvet (**15005, 15012**)

3794 velvet (**15006, 15013**)

3795 velvet (**15014**)

3796 velvet (**15007, 15018**)

3797 velvet (**15015**)

3799 velvet (**15010**)

3800 velvet (**15016**)

3801 satin (**15022**)

3802 satin (**15020, 15021**)

3803 satin (**15023**)

3804 satin (**15024, 15025, 15026**)

3805 satin (**15027**)

3806 satin (**15028**)

3807 satin (**15029**)

3808 satin (**15030**)

3809 satin (**15031, 15032**)

3810 satin (**15033**)

3811 satin (**15034**)

3812 satin (**15035**)

3813 damask (**15036**)

3814 damask (**15038**)

3815 damask (**15038**)[15]

3816 damask (**15039**)

3817 damask (**15040**)

3818 damask (**15041**)

3819 damask (**15043**)

3820 damask (**15044**)

3821 damask (**15042**)

3822 damask (**15045**)

3823 damask (**15046**)

3824 damask (**15037**)

3825 taffeta (**15050**)

3826 taffeta (**15051**)[16]

3827 taffeta (**15052**)

3828 taffeta (**15053**)

3829 taffeta (**15055**)

3830 taffeta (**15056**)

3831 taffeta (**15057**)

3832 taffeta (**15059**)

3833 taffeta (**15058**)

3834 taffeta (**15054**)

3836 sarsenet (**15060, 15061**)

3838 sarsenet (**15062, 15063**)

3839 sarsenet (**15064**)

3840 sarsenet (**15065**)

3841 sarsenet (**15068, 15069**)

3842 sarsenet (**15066, 15067**)

3843 sarsenet (**15070**)

3845 silk of newmaking (**15048**)

3846 flannel (**11797**)

3847 Bridges satin (**15074, 15075**)

3848 Milan fustian (**15076**)

3849 baudekin (**15049**)

3850 camlet (**15071, 15072, 15073**)

3851 kersey (**11796**)

3852 Brussels ticks (**15077, 15078, 15079**)

3853 holland (**15080**)

3854 Normandy cloth (**15801**)

3855 Brussels cloth (**15802**)

3856 nettle-cloth (**15084**)

3857 cambric (**15083**)

3859 passement (**15132, 15133**)

3860 passement (**15134**)

3861 fringe (**15135**)

3863 see entry 3774

3864 see entry 3775

3865 see entry 3776

3866 see entry 3777

3867 see entry 3778

3868 see entry 3779

3869 see entry 3781

3870 see entry 3782

3871 see entry 3783

3872 see entry 3784

3873 see entry 3785

3874 see entry 3786

3875 see entry 3787

3876 see entry 3788

3877 see entry 3791

3878 see entry 3792

3879 see entry 3793

3880 see entry 3794

3881 see entry 3795

3882 see entry 3796

3883 see entry 3797

3884 see entry 3799

3885 see entry 3789

3886 see entry 3790

3887 see entry 3800

3888 see entry 3802

3889 see entry 3801

3890 see entry 3803

3891 see entry 3804

3892 see entry 3805

3893 see entry 3806

3894 see entry 3807

3895 see entry 3808

3896 see entry 3810

3897 see entry 3811

3898 see entry 3812

15 The damask was listed under separate headings of purple and blue in the 1542 Inventory and under purple in the 1547 Inventory.

16 The taffeta was described as incarnate in the 1542 Inventory and as carnation in the 1547 Inventory.

3899 see entry 3809

3900 see entry 3813

3901 see entry 3814

3902 see entry 3815

3903 see entry 3816

3904 see entry 3817

3905 see entry 3818

3906 see entry 3819

3907 see entry 3820

3908 see entry 3821

3909 see entry 3823

3910 see entry 3822

3911 see entry 1900

3912 see entry 3824

3913 see entry 3825

3914 see entry 3826

3915 see entry 3827

3916 see entry 3828

3917 see entry 3829

3918 see entry 3830

3919 see entry 3831

3920 see entry 3832

3921 see entry 3833

3922 see entry 3834

3923 see entry 3836

3924 see entry 3838

3925 see entry 3839

3926 see entry 3840

3927 see entry 3842

3928 see entry 3841

3929 see entry 3843

3930 see entry 3845

3931 see entry 3847

3932 see entry 3848

3933 see entry 3849

3934 see entry 3850

3935 see entry 3852

3936 see entry 3853

3937 see entry 3854

3938 see entry 3856

3939 see entry 3857

3940 see entry 3859

3941 see entry 3860

3942 see entry 3861

3943 see entry 3855

3944 see entry 3779

3945 see entry 3781

3946 see entry 3782

3947 see entry 3805

3948 see entry 3848

3949 see entry 3851

3950 see entry 2308

3951 see entries 619, 628, 631, 2320

3952 see entries 612, 2342

3953 see entries 608, 2345

3954 see entry 604

3955 see entry 577

3956 see entries 568, 569[17]

3957 see entry 2357

3958 see entry 882

3959 see entry 875[18]

3960 see entry 866

3961 see entry 867

3962 see entries 2411, 2416, 2425,
        2445, 2454, 2457, 2484,
        2490, 2515, 2553, 2595–
        2596, 2625, 2627, 2638,
        2698, 2700, 2719–2720,
        2724, 2764, 2791, 2797,
        2817, 2825, 2834, 2836,
        2838, 2845, 2854, 2870,
        2874, 2885–2886, 2893,
        2901, 2916, 2918, 2920,
        2935 2941, 2961–2962,
        2999, 3026, 3028, 3031,
        3043, 3068, 3089, 3101,
        3117, 3131, 3139, 3142,
        3166, 3169, 3176, 3184,
        3187, 3194, 3239, 3264,
        3279, 3288

3963 see entry 3347

3964 see entry 393

3965 see entries 306, 398

3966 see entry 279

3967 see entry 1175

3968 see entry 1191

3969 see entry 1194

3970 see entry 3765

3971 see entry 1211

3972 see entry 3762

3973 see entry 1027

3974 see entry 1036

3975 see entry 1048

3976 see entry 1050

3977 see entry 4

3978 see entry 168

3979 see entries 238, 239, 240, 244,
        247, 248, 259

3980 see entries 437, 443, 444, 450

3981 see entry 440

3982 see entry 455

3983 see entry 449

3984 see entry 449

3985 see entry 452

3986 see entry 460

3987 see entry 444

3988 see entry 477

3989 see entry 534, 541

3990 see entry 716

3991 see entries 736, 740, 800, 806

3992 see entry 814

3993 see entry 815

3994 see entry 820

3995 see entry 833

3996 see entries 825, 827, 828, 829,
        830, 832

3997 see entry 1226

3998 see entry 894

3999 see entry 941

4000 see entry 969

4001 see entries 970, 2392

4002 see entry 1012

4003 see entries 1080, 1087, 1094,
        1095

4004 see entry 1096

4005 see entry 1090

4006 see entry 1089

4007 see entry 1109

4008 see entry 1111

4009 see entry 1114

4010 see entry 1113

4011 see entry 1135

4012 see entry 1137

4013 see entry 1136

4014 see entry 1140

4015 see entry 1138

4016 see entry 1198

4017 see entries 1212, 1213, 1214

4018 see entry 1220

4019 see entry 2300

4020 see entry 2301

4021 see entry 280

4022 see entry 281

4023 see entries 282, 3348

4024 see entry 284

4025 see entry 285

4026 see entries 657, 3483

4027 see entry 658

4028 see entry 659

4029 see entries 660, 3484

17   While entry **3956** records three missing pillow-beres, the marginal notes to entries **568** and **569** state that a total of four are missing.

18   The marginal note to entry **875** entry records part of the mirror's decoration as missing, not the whole mirror.

4030	see entry **661**	**4055**	see entry **1030**	**4070**	see entry **434**
4031	see entry **3350**	**4056**	see entry **1032**	**4071**	see entry **435**
4032	see entry **436**	**4057**	see entry **1038**	**4072**	see entry **517**
4033	see entries **223, 3763**	**4058**	see entry **1036**	**4073**	see entry **520**
4034	see entries **224, 3764**	**4059**	see entry **1047**	**4074**	see entry **239**
4035	see entry **435**	**4060**	see entry **1048**	**4075**	see entry **349**
4036	see entry **434**	**4061**	see entry **1037**	**4076**	see entry **351**
4037	see entry **447**	**4062**	see entry **208**	**4077**	see entry **354**
4038	see entry **543**	**4063**	see entry **209**	**4078**	see entry **371**
4039	see entry **550**	**4064**	see entry **213**	**4079**	see entry **3326**
4040	see entries **559, 568**	**4065**	see entry **212**	**4080**	see entry **3330**
4041	see entry **239**	**4066**	see entry **216**	**4081**	see entry **3327**
4042	see entry **345**	**4067**	see entry **217**	**4082**	see entry **400**
4043	see entry **1053**	**4068**	see entry **218**	**4083**	see entry **402**
4054	see entry **1018**	**4069**	see entry **220**	**4084**	see entry **409**

CONCORDANCE III

THE RELATIONSHIP BETWEEN THE 1542 INVENTORY AND THREE SMALLER DOCUMENTS RELATING TO SIR ANTHONY DENNY'S DISCHARGE FROM OFFICE AS PALACE KEEPER

The three documents described below are much smaller than the 1542 Inventory, and each one deals with a specific aspect of Sir Anthony Denny's role as Keeper.

DOCUMENT A (PRO E101/427/2) lists all the missing items for which Denny was called to account when he was discharged as Keeper. It also records perquisites given to him, along with items distributed at Henry VIII's funeral and Edward VI's coronation. A variant of this list was written into the back of the 1542 volume (fos 148v–151r) [**3944–4043**].

DOCUMENT B (BL LANSDOWNE ROLL 14) is a review of the money which passed through Denny's hands as Keeper of the Palace of Whitehall (1542–7) and as Groom of the Stool (1546–7). Sections of this document are closely related to the section of the 1542 volume which records the money received by Denny (PRO E315/160, fos 264r–271v) [**4085–4156**].

DOCUMENT C (BL LANSDOWNE ROLL 15) is much briefer than PRO E101/427/2 but it is also concerned with Denny's discharge from office. It deals with those items still missing from the Palace of Whitehall shortly after Denny's death and for which his widow Joan was then answerable. The descriptions given in this document are much briefer than those in the 1542 Inventory and consequently it is not always possible to link objects in the two lists with any degree of certainty. Some of the numbers given in square brackets are therefore qualified with a question mark.

The entries are given in bold, in numerical order, followed by a brief description of the item; the 1542 Inventory number is given in square brackets. Only entries with an equivalent in the 1542 Inventory are shown.

Document A: PRO E101/427/2

A1	cloth of gold [3779, 3944]	A29	5 screens [1211, 3971]	A61	11 drinking glasses [1080, 1087, 1094, 1095, 4003]
A2	cloth of gold [3781, 3945]	A30	1 box for the host [3762, 3972]		
A3	cloth of gold [3782, 3946]	A31	1 corporal case [1027, 3973]	A62	3 covers for glasses [1096, 4004]
A4	satin [3805, 3947]	A32	1 fanon [1036, 3974]		
A5	Milan fustian [3848, 3948]	A33	2 cuffs [1048, 3975]	A63	1 glass [1090, 4005]
A6	kersey [3851, 3949]	A34	3 altar linen cloths [1050, 3976]	A64	1 glass [1089, 4006]
A7	1 trussing sheet [2308, 3950]	A35	2 buttons from a gown [4, 3977]	A65	1 socket for a glass candlestick [1109, 4007]
A8	3 towels [619, 628, 631, 2302, 3951]	A36	1 knife [168, 3978]		
		A37	18 chair roundels [238, 239, 240, 244, 247, 248, 259, 3979]	A66	1 glass bell candlestick [1111, 4008]
A9	part of a towel [2302, 3951]				
A10	4 dozen and 8 napkins [608, 2345, 3953]	A38	fringe & pearls from bed hangings [437, 440, 443, 444, 450, 3980, 3981]	A67	1 glass trencher [1114, 4009]
				A68	1 salt of earth galley making [1113, 4010]
A11	1 tablecloths [604, 3954]				
A12	1 handkerchief [577, 3955]	A39	fringe from bed hangings [455, 3982]	A69	1 fire fork [1135, 4011]
A13	4 pillow-beres [568, 569, 3956]			A70	1 pair of fire tongues [1137, 4012]
A14	3 cupboard cloths [612, 2342, 3952]	A40	fringe from bed hangings [449, 3984]	A71	1 fire pan [1136, 4013]
				A72	1 fire pan [1140, 4014]
A15	1 standish [2357, 3957]	A41	fringe from bed hangings [449, 3983]	A73	1 pair of bellows [1138, 4015]
A16	30 silver counters [882, 3958]			A74	1 chest [1198, 4016]
A17	1 mirror [875, 3959]	A42	fringe from bed hangings [452, 3985]	A75	4 walking staves [1212, 1213, 1214, 4017]
A18	1 mirror decoration [866, 3960]				
A19	1 royal coat of arms from a mirror [867, 3961]	A43	fringe from bed hangings [460, 3986]	A76	1 weight [1220, 4018]
				A77	1 counterpoint [2300, 4019]
A20	77 books [2411, 2416, 2425(5), 2445, 2454, 2457, 2484, 2490, 2515, 2553, 2595, 2596, 2625, 2627, 2638, 2698, 2700, 2719(3), 2720(3), 2724, 2764, 2791, 2797, 2817, 2825, 2834, 2836, 2838, 2845, 2854, 2870, 2874, 2885, 2886, 2893, 2901, 2916, 2918, 2920(2), 2935, 2941, 2961, 2962, 2999, 3026, 3028, 3031, 3043, 3068, 3089, 3101, 3117, 3131(2), 3139, 3142, 3166, 3169, 3176, 3184, 3187, 3194, 3239, 3264, 3279, 3288, 3962] [only 76 books identified]	A44	2 bed vanes [444, 3987]	A78	part of a counterpoint [2301, 4020]
		A45	4 bed vanes [447, 3988]		
		A46	8 girths for cases [534, 541, 3989]	A79	2 close stools [280, 4021]
				A80	1 close stool [281, 4022]
		A47	11 counterfeit stones for a picture [716, 3990]	A81	3 close stools [282, 4023]
				A82	2 close stools [284, 4024]
		A48	4 sarsenet curtains for pictures [736, 740, 800, 806, 3991]	A83	1 close stool [285, 4025]
				A84	12 bowls [657, 3483, 4026]
		A49	1 stained cloth [814, 3992]	A85	5 bowls [658, 4027]
		A50	1 stained cloth [815, 3993]	A86	1 bowl [659, 4028]
		A51	1 stained cloth [820, 3994]	A87	6 cisterns [660, 3484, 4029]
		A52	1 terracotta picture [833, 3995]	A88	4 cisterns [661, 4030]
		A53	6 boxes or cases for pictures [825, 827, 828, 829, 830, 832, 3996]	A89	1 case [3350, 4031]
				A90	1 bedstead [447, 4032]
A21	1 cushion [3347, 3963]	A54	1 castle of needlework [1226, 3997]	A91	4 hangings of scarlet [223, 3763, 4033]
A22	2 cushions [393, 3964]				
A23	4 buttons with tassels for cushions [306, 398, 3965]	A55	1 tinner for a pair of regals [894, 3998]	A92	10 hangings of scarlet [224, 3764, 4034]
A24	1 table [1175, 3967]	A56	1 great shawm [941, 3999]	A93	2 carpets [435, 4035]
A25	20 stools [1191, 3352, 3968]	A57	6 boxes or cases for pictures [see A53]	A94	1 carpet [434, 4036]
A26	3 foot stools [1194, 3969]			A95	1 counterpoint [447, 4037]
A27	2 foot stools [3765, 3970]	A58	1 model gun [969, 4000]	A96	1 pair of sheet [543, 4038]
A28	1 stool [279, 3966]	A59	2 gun powder horns, 2 purses and 2 touch boxes [970, 2392, 4001]	A97	1 sheet [550, 4039]
				A98	3 pillow-beres [559, 568, 4040]
		A60	curtains [1012, 4002]	A99	1 chair [239, 4041]
				A100	1 cushion [345, 4042]
				A101	1 clock [1053, 4043]

Document B: BL Lansdowne Roll 14

B1　money: to Henry VIII [**4085, 4089, 4086, 4087**]

B2　money: to Stephen Vaughan [**4088**]

B3　money: to Henry VIII [**4091, 4092, 4093, 4094, 4095, 4096, 4097, 4098, 4099, 4100, 4101, 4102, 4104, 4105**]

B4　money: to Sir Brian Tuke [**4090, 4103**]

B5　money: to Henry VIII [**4106, 4111, 4112, 4113, 4114, 4115, 4116, 4117, 4118, 4121, 4122, 4123, 4124**]

B6　money: to Sir Anthony Denny [**4107**]

B7　money: to William Thorp [**4108**]

B8　money: to Sir Edmund Peckham [**4109, 4110, 4119**]

B9　money: to William Stamford [**4120**]

B10　money: to Henry VIII [**4128, 4129, 4130, 4131**]

B11　money: to Sir John Gostwick [**4125**]

B12　money: to Sir Edmund Peckham [**4126, 4127**]

B13　money: to Henry VIII [**4132, 4133, 4134, 4135, 4136, 4137, 4138, 4440**]

B14　money: to Sir Wymond Carew [**4141, 4142**]

B15　money: to Sir John Williams [**4139**]

B18　money: to Sir Wymond Carew [**4143, 4146, 4147, 4148**]

B19　money: to the Lord St John [**4145**]

B20　money: to Sir Edmund Peckham [**4144**]

B21　money: to Sir Wymond Carew [**4149**]

B53　jewels, plate, cloth of gold etc. [**3333–3334**]

Document C: BL Lansdowne Roll 15

C1　1 full length portrait of the Duchess of Milan [**675**]

C3　1 clock or watch [**1052**]

C4　1 antique head from a mirror [**866**]

C5　11 forms [**1182** (?)]

C6　2 joined stools [**1184, 1185**]

C7　1 foot of timber from a screen [**1211** (?)]

C9　3 copper rings from andirons [**1132**]

C10　1 fire fork [**1133** or **3600**]

C11　3 pairs of tongs [**1137**]

C12　1 pair of bellows [**1138**]

C14　3 staves to draw curtains [**1216**]

C15　3 toasting forks [**3600**]

CONCORDANCE IV

THE RELATIONSHIP BETWEEN THE IDENTIFYING NUMBERS USED
IN THIS EDITION AND THOSE USED BY W A SHAW

In 1937 W A Shaw published the section of the 1542 Inventory that records the King's 'tables with pictures'.[1] He compared the 1542 entries with those found in the 1547 Inventory. The latter form two distinct lists: the items at Whitehall and other properties (excluding St James's Palace) in 1547 and the pictures at St James's Palace in 1549. Shaw numbered the entries in the 1547 Inventory, rather than those in the 1542 Inventory. As a few items had been either lost or acquired between 1542 and 1547, or were recorded in a slightly different order, there are a few small discrepancies between the numerical order of the 1542 Inventory and the sequences of numbers from the 1547 Inventory and Shaw.

Concordance IV reconciles the entry numbers used by Shaw, those used in this edition and those used for the printed edition of the 1547 Inventory.[2] The number given in bold is that of the entry in the 1542 Inventory, and it is followed by the five-figure 1547 Inventory reference number in parentheses. There is then a brief description of the subject of the picture: these descriptions are based on the 1542 Inventory. Finally, Shaw's number is given in curly brackets.

1 Shaw, *Inventories of Pictures*.
2 Starkey, ed, *Inventory*.

'Tables with pictures' (paintings, with some embroideries, relief sculpture and inlaid work)

664 (**10569**) The Five Wounds {1}

665 (**10570**) St Jerome with a dead man's head {2}

666 (**10571**) A naked woman, with a scripture {3}

667 (**10572**) St John the Baptist {4}

668 (**10573**) A woman playing a lute (with an old man) {5}

669 (**10574**) A woman playing a lute (with a book) {6}

670 (**10575**) St Michael and St George {7}

671 (**10576**) The French King, in a crimson doublet {8}

672 (**10577**) The French Queen [Eleanor] {9}

673 (**10578**) The three children of the King of Denmark {10}

674 (**10579**) A man holding St John's head {11}

675 (**10580**) The Duchess of Milan {12}

676 (**10581**) St George {13}

677 (**10582**) A naked woman on a rock, with a scripture {14}

678 (**10583**) The naked truth {15}

679 (**10584**) The old emperor, the current emperor and Ferdinand {16}

680 (**10585**) Our Lady holding Our Lord taken down from the cross {17}

681 (**10586**) Lady Margaret, Duchess of Savoy {18}

682 (**10587**) *Filius Prodigus* {19}

683 (**10588**) A woman holding a vernicle {20}

684 (**10589**) Mary Magdalene, with a cup {21}

685 (**10590**) Mary Magdalene, looking at a book {22}

686 (**10591**) An old man dallying with a woman {23}

687 (**10592**) The feast of Assuerus and Vaschtie {24}

688 (**10593**) The nativity of Our Lord {25}

689 (**10594**) A woman with a monkey {26}

690 (**10595**) Frederick, Duke of Saxony {27}

691 (**10596**) Philip, Archduke of Austria {28}

692 (**10597**) Elizabeth, Queen of Austria {29}

693 (**10598**) The Queen of Hungary {30}

694 (**10599**) Our Lady and Christ sucking {31}

695 (**10600**) Prince Arthur {32}

696 (**10601**) Our Lord appearing to Mary Magdalene {33}

697 (**10602**) A woman holding a unicorn {34}

698 (**10603**) St John the Evangelist {35}

699 (**10604**) *Christiana paciencia* {36}

700 (**10605**) The Passion {37}

701 (**10606**) The salutation of Our Lady {38}

702 (**10607**) Our Lady and St Anne {39}

703 (**10608**) The three kings of Cologne {40}

704 (**10609**) Our Lord {41}

705 (**10610**) Henry VII {42}

706 (**10611**) Queen Elizabeth {43}

707 (**10612**) His Majesty being young {44}

708 (**10613**) His Majesty and Queen Jane {45}

709 (**10614**) My Lord Prince {46}

710 (**10615**) My Lord Prince {47}

711 (**10616**) The countess of Richmond {48}

712 (**10617**) Henry V {49}

713 (**10618**) Henry VI {50}

714 (**10619**) Queen Elizabeth, Edward's wife {51}

715 (**10620**) Edward IV {52}

716 (**10622**) The Passion {54}

717 (**10623**) Mary Magdalene, sitting by a bed {55}

718 (**10624**) *Lucrecia Romana* {56}

719 (**10625**) *Lucrecia Romana* {57}

720 (**10621**) The King of Castile's children {53}

721 (**10626**) Our Lady with Our Lord sleeping on her breast {58}

722 (**10627**) The parable of Matthew, chapter 18 {59}

723 (**10628**) St George {60}

724 (**10629**) The burial of Our Lord {61}

725 (**10630**) King Midas and misery {62}

726 (**10632**) The King standing upon a mitre {64}

727 (**10631**) Our Lady with Our Lord in her arms {63}

728 (**10633**) St George {65}

729 (**10634**) The Nativity {66}

730 (**10635**) *Lucrecia Romana* {67}

731 (**10636**) The Salutation of Our Lady {68}

732 (**10638**) Our Lady holding Our Lord in her arms {70}

733 (**10637**) Our Lady with Our Lord sleeping on her breast {69}

734 (**10639**) The French King, his wife and the fool {71}

735 (**10640**) Our Lady holding Our Lord in her arms {72}

736 (**10641**) A woman with a bracelet {73}

737 (**10642**) *Lucrecia Romana* {74}

738 (**10644**) Lewis the French King {76}

739 (**10643**) The Queen of Castile {75}

740 (**10645**) The French King when he was young {77}

741 (**10646**) One with long hair, being crowned and wearing a robe of cloth of gold {78}

742 (**10647**) Hampton Court, Amboise, Cognac and Gandit [Ghent] {79}

743 (**10706**) The Duchess of Milan {138}

744 (**10649**) Eight tables of slate {81}

745 (**10717**) Christ taken down from the cross {149}

746 (**10650**) Richard IIII[3] {82}

747 (**10648**) A young man with three brooches {80}

748 (**10651**) Barsele, Countess of 'Corn' {83}

749 (**10652**) Charles VIII {84}

750 (**10653**) Our Lady, Our Lord and Joseph {85}

751 (**10654**) The Duke of Bourbon {86}

752 (**10655**) Our Lord {87}

753 (**10656**) Our Lady {88}

754 (**10657**) Our Lord bearing the cross {89}

755 (**10658**) Pilot bringing forth Christ {90}

3   A scribal error for Richard III.

756 (10659) The Holy Ghost and the Five Wounds {91}

757 (10660) Our Lady, Our Lord and St Anne {92}

758 (10661) Our Lady holding Our Lord in her arms {93}

759 (10662) Our Lady holding Our Lord at her breast {94}

760 (10663) St Jerome with a dead man's head {95}

761 (10664) The decollation of St John the Baptist {96}

762 (10665) His Majesty when young {97}

763 (10666) Prince Arthur, wearing a red cap and a collar of red and white roses {98}

764 (10667) The Emperor {99}

765 (10669) One being in black with this scripture: *Glorificamus te sancte dei genetrix et cetera* {100}

766 (10670) Charles, Duke of Burgundy {101}

767 (10668) The birth of Christ / The three Kings of Cologne / Our Lady giving suck {102}

768 (10671) Isabel, Queen of Castile {103}

769 (10672) A woman with a French hood {104}

770 (10673) Our Lady holding Our Lord in her lap {105}

771 (10675) A woman, her head and neck bare {107}

772 (10676) Joan, Archduchess of Austria {108}

773 (10674) The seven sorrows of Our Lady {106}

774 (10677) One having a black cap and a collar of scallop shells {109}

775 (10678) Philip, Duke of Burgundy {110}

776 (10679) A woman having a 'tyer' on her head {111}

777 (10680) Julius Caesar {112}

778 (10681) Philip, Duke of Hardy {113}

779 (10682) Charles, the great emperor {114}

780 (10683) The Salutation of Our Lady {115}

781 (10684) Our Lady with Our Lord in her arms {116}

782 (10685) Frederick III, Holy Roman Emperor {117}

783 (10686) *Lucrecia Romana* {118}

784 (10687) Mary Magdalene in red robes {119}

785 (10688) Our Lady with Our Lord in her arms sleeping {120}

786 (10689) Our Lord crowned with thorns {121}

787 (10690) Our Lady with Christ sucking on her breast {122}

788 (10691) Our Lord crowned with thorns {123}

789 (10692) *Lucrecia Romana* {124}

790 (10693) Adam and Eve {125}

791 (10694) St George {126}

792 (10695) Our Lord blessing with one hand and with the other hand on the world {127}

793 (10696) Our Lady holding Our Lord in her arms {128}

794 (10697) Our Lady with Our Lord in her arms sucking {129}

795 (10698) The Duke of Sabandy {130}

796 (10699) Duke John {131}

797 (10700) Our Lord and Our Lady holding the arms of the Passion {132}

798 (10701) A woman in a French hood {133}

799 (10702) Jacob [James], King of Scots {134}

800 (10703) Ferdinand, King of Aragon {135}

801 (10704) The birth and passion of Christ {136}

802 (10705) The birth and passion of Christ {137}

803 (10708) The wife of Lord Fiennes {140}

804 (10709) The siege of Pavia {141}

805 (10710) Our Lady with Our Lord sitting on her lap {142}

806 (10711) St George {143}

807 (10712) Our Lady with Our Lord dead in her lap {144}

808 (10713) A woman called Michaell with a red Rose and a dog {145}

809 (10714) Jesus and the four evangelists {146}

810 (10715) John Frederick, Duke of Saxony {147}

811 (10716) Orpheus with beasts and monsters {148}

812 (11582) 2 tables of sundry coloured woods {~}

813 (10707) The Salutation of Our Lady / The three Kings of Cologne / Our Lady giving Our Lord suck {~}

Stained cloths

814 (~) A preacher preaching in a pulpit {~}

815 (~) The history of Hester {~}

816 (10722) Charles the emperor {1}

817 (10723) The Prince of Orange {2}

818 (10724) Men and women at a banquet {3}

819 (10725) Men and women at a banquet {4}

820 (~) *Filius prodigus* {~}

821 (10726) Phoebus {5}

822 (10727) The history of Judith {6}

823 (10728) Suleiman the Turk {7}

3471 (10770) The description of Florence {~}

3696 (10729) King Aza breaking the altars {~}

3697 (10730) Judith striking Holofernes {~}

'Pictures of earth' (terracottas)

824 (**10734**) Moses {2}

825 (**10733**) A woman with a carnation robe {1}

826 (**10735**) A woman with an orange coif {3}

827 (**10736**) A women in a purple garment {4}

828 (**10737**) A woman in a robe of ash colour {5}

829 (**10738**) A Morian boy {6}

830 (**10739**) A woman in a crimson garment {7}

831 (**10740**) A woman in a carnation garment {8}

832 (**10741**) A woman in a green garment {9}

833 (~)   A man in a gown {~}

834 (**10742**) St John's head {10}

835 (**10743**) Balthasar, one of the three kings of Cologne {12}

836 (**10744**) A woman with a child in her arms {11}

2377 (~)   A head of white marble {~}

2378 (~)   The Queen of Hungary {~}

2379 (~)   A man with a coif {~}

2380 (~)   Men in harness {~}

2381 (~)   A man with a garland about his head {~}

2382 (~)   A woman with a blue lace about her neck {~}

2383 (~)   A man being naked {~}

2384 (~)   A Morian boy {~}

2385 (~)   A Morian boy {~}

2386 (~)   A woman with a 'cipers' about her neck {~}

APPENDIX I

INVENTORIES OF HENRY VIII'S POSSESSIONS

This appendix lists all surviving inventories of Henry VIII's possessions in readily accessible collections. The entries are listed under the document title (which usually gives the type of object or objects under consideration) in date order; the manuscript number and its reference in Letters and Papers are also given.[1] A number of the inventories are in BL Cotton MS Appendix 28. This document has been reclassified as BL Cotton Appendix 89 and it is listed here under that reference. A list of the surviving accounts produced annually by the Great Wardrobe (which included a summary of the lengths of cloth in hand at the year's end) is also included.

Arms and armour in Calais and Flanders
8 April 1514
PRO SP1/7, fos 181r–186v (*LP* I.ii, 2812)

The king's ships in the Thames
27 July 1514
PRO E36/13

Receipt by Henry VIII of jewels from Sir Henry Wyat
25 December 1514
Bod Lib Rawlinson MS A 290, f. 4r (*LP* I.i, 3571)

The manor of Beaulieu
20 September 1516
PRO E101/622/31

The Wardrobe of the Robes
20 December 1516
BL Harley MS 2284

Revels stuff
July 1517
PRO E36/228, fos 9v–16v (*LP* II.ii, 1517)

Tents, halls and pavilions
July 1517
PRO E36/228, fos 17r–20v (*LP* II.ii, 1510–11)

Bards, bases, saddles and horse harness
July 1517
PRO E36/228, fos 1r–5r (*LP* II.ii, 1515–17)

Armoury items at Greenwich in the keeping of George Lovekyn
1 May 1519
PRO SP1/29, fos 191r–205v (*LP* III.ii, 1548)

Jewels in the keeping of Sir William Compton
6 October 1519
PRO SP1/19, fos 43r–46v, 47r–59v, 60r–68v
(*LP* III.i, 463)

A brief inventory of jewels and plate in use by the king and various officers of the household
1520
PRO SP1/232, fos 237r–238v (*LP* Add. I.i, 300)
[mutilated]

Equipment on the *Henry Grace à Dieu*
10 January 1521
PRO SP1/21, fos 166r–167v (*LP* III.i, 1128)

The Wardrobe of the Robes
March 1521
BL Harley MS 4217

---

1   This appendix draws on Hayward, 'Possessions', appendix 1, 238–47.

The jewel house
1521
Original MS lost.
See Trollope, 'Henry VIII's jewel book'.

Ordnance in the Tower
21 September 1523
PRO SP1/28, fos 221r–228v (*LP* III.ii, 3351)

Ships at Portsmouth and on the Thames
22 October 1525
BL Royal MS 14B.XXIIA (*LP* IV.i, 1714)

Ships for the king's use
22 October 1525
BL Royal MS 14B.XXIIB (*LP* IV.i, 1714)

Account of ships
22 October 1525
BL Otho MS E.IX 64b (*LP* IV.i, 1714)

Shirts and other stuff delivered to Henry Norris by Sir William Compton
18 January 1526
PRO SP1/37, fos 32r–41v (*LP* IV.i, 1906)

Jewels delivered to Henry Norris at Eltham
18 January 1526
BL Royal MS 14B.XLIII (*LP* IV.i, 1907)

Jewels delivered to Robert Amadas at Greenwich
18 January 1526
BL Royal MS 7C.XVI, f. 38r (*LP* IV.i, 1907)

A view taken at Portsmouth by Cornelius Johnson
25 April 1526
PRO SP1/38, fos 55r–v (*LP* IV.i, 2123)

Stuff and plate in the custody of Richard Rawson, Chaplain and Clerk of the Closet, Geoffrey Wren, late Clerk of the Closet and Sir Henry Wyat
April 1527
PRO SP1/41, fos 201r–203v (*LP* IV.ii, 3085)

Jewels delivered to the king
December 1527
PRO SP1/46, f. 46r (*LP* IV.ii, 3746)

Jewels in certain boxes and coffers
December 1528
PRO SP1/52, fos 25r–39v (*LP* IV.ii, 5114)

Memorandum of the delivery by Cornelius Hayes to Henry VIII at Windsor
21 April 1530
BL Royal MS 7C.XVI, f. 53r (*LP* IV.iii, 6349)

The king's scullery
22 December 1530
PRO SP1/58, fos 218r–219v (*LP* IV.iii, 6771)

The king's jewellery
1530
PRO SP1/58, fos 237r–273v (*LP* IV.iii, 6789)

Jewels delivered to the king since 1 August 1530 by Cornelius Hayes
May 1531
PRO SP1/66, fos 39r–45v (*LP* V, 276)

The jewel house
2 June 1532
PRO E36/85 (*LP* V, 1799)

Jewels sent from Greenwich by Henry Norris to the king at Hampton Court
21 September 1532
BL Royal MS 7C.XVI, f. 71r (*LP* V, 1335)

Jewels delivered by the king to Thomas Cromwell
1 October 1532
BL Royal MS 7C.XVI, fos 40r–46r (*LP* V, 1376)

Jewels returned by Cromwell to the king
4 October 1532
BL Cotton MS Appendix 89, f. 37r (*LP* V, 1385)

The *Great Bark*
6 October 1532
BL Cotton MS Appendix 89 (*LP* V, 469)

Receipt of jewels by Henry Norris from the king
7 October 1532
BL Royal MS 7C.XVI, f. 50r (*LP* V, 1399)

Delivery of jewels to the king by Cromwell.
7 October 1532
BL Cotton MS Appendix 89, f. 36r (*LP* V, 1399)

Plate to be broken
13 April 1533
PRO SP1/75, fos 96r–101v (*LP* VI, 338)

Henry VIII's banqueting plate
13 April 1533
PRO SP1/75, fos 102r–149v (*LP* VI, 339)

Plate
April 1533
PRO SP1/74, fos 9r–10v (*LP* VI, 13)

Gold, silver gilt, parcel gilt and white plate delivered to the Tower
28 October 1533
PRO SP1/80, fos 41r–47v (*LP* VI, 1364)

Survey of Berwick
1533
PRO E36/173

Clothes and jewels delivered to Thomas Alvard
16 November 1534
BL Royal MS 7F.XIV, f. 124r (*LP* VII, 1432)

Plate delivered by Henry Norris to Whitehall
13 January 1535
PRO SP1/89, fos 24r–27v (*LP* VIII, 44)

Precious stones, pearls and gold delivered by the king to Cornelius Hayes
13 February 1535
BL Royal MS 7C.XVI, f. 48r (*LP* VIII, 206)

Inventory of Hackney
5 March 1535
PRO E101/421/19

Gold plate delivered by Thomas Cromwell to the jewel house
November 1535
PRO SP1/99, fos 121r–122v (*LP* IX, 909)

A book of ... house at ... stuff delivered to Edmund Harman [Inventory of Parlands: the bulk of the material was later delivered to Oatlands]
June 1536
BL Cotton MS Appendix 89, fos 54r–66r (*LP* X, 1240)

Inventory of the Little Park of Windsor
BL Cotton MS Appendix 89, f. 66v (*LP* X, 1240)

Ordnance, artillery and munitions at Calais in the charge of Sir Christopher Morris
23 September 1536
PRO SP1/106, fos 194r–211v (*LP* XI, 488)

Swords for the king
December 1536
PRO SP1/113, f. 121r (*LP* XI, 1431)

Silks and velvets
13 April 1537
BL Cotton Appendix 89, fos 47r–53v (*LP* XII.i, 925)

Daggers and swords remaining with Maryon
10 October 1537
PRO SP1/125, fos 175r–178v (*LP* XII.ii, 877)

The queen's jewels
October 1537
BL Royal MS 7C.XVI, fos 18r–31v (*LP* XII.ii, 973)

Certain jewels trussed and enclosed within a desk
December 1537
BL Cotton MS Appendix 89, f. 27 (*LP* XII.ii, 1315)

Jewels
December 1537
BL Cotton MS Appendix 89, f. 31 (*LP* XII.ii, 1315)

Pontefract Castle and Sandall Castle
12 January 1538
PRO E36/159 (*LP* XIII.i, 72)

The king's robes
29 June 1538
PRO SP1/133, fos 234r–235v (*LP* XIII.i, 1278) [draft of title page only]

Receipt of jewels from the king by Cornelius Hayes
September 1538
BL Royal MS 7C.XVI, f. 55r

Memorandum by Cornelius Hayes of receipt of diamonds and other jewels received from the king
September 1538
BL Royal MS 7C.XVI, f. 57r (*LP* XIII.ii, 478)

Ships in the Thames
26 January 1539
Hatfield MS (*LP* XIV.i, 143)

The Wardrobe of the Beds in Windsor Castle
26 March 1539
BL Additional MS 10602, fos 1r–6r (*LP* XIV.i, 607)

Apparel taken out of the Tower
4 November 1539
PRO SP1/154, fos 122r–123v (*LP* XIV.ii, 457)

Ordnance in the Tower and elsewhere and in the king's ships
13 February 1540
PRO E101/60/3 (*LP* XV, 196)

Unappointed Wardrobe stuff at Whitehall
18 May 1540
BL Royal MS 7C.XVI, fos 60r–64r (*LP* XV, 686)

Gold, silver, jewels and money delivered to the king by John Williams
26 June 1540
(*LP* XV, 809)

Dress given away
Stuff issued for the officer's fee
26 June 1540
PRO SP1/164, fos 126r–129v, 130r (*LP* XVI, 402)

The king's robes
1. Items delivered to Robert Horden, yeoman
2. Items delivered to Richard Egleston, servant to John Malt
6 April 1541
PRO SP1/168, fos 199r–208v (*LP* XVI, Appendix 3)

Jewels given by the king to Catherine Howard at their marriage
November 1541
BL Stowe MS 559, fos 55r–68r (*LP* XVI, 1389)

Inventory of the Palace of Whitehall
24 April 1542
PRO E315/160 (*LP* XVII, 267)
[Transcribed as BL Additional MSS 4729 and 25469]

Tents and pavilions
4 December 1542
GMR LM 4, 45, 49

1. Wardrobe of the Beds at Windsor in the charge of William Tildesley
2. Stuff received from the Wardrobe at Whitehall from John Reed
3. Stuff received from Nicholas Bristow on 21 November 1542 from persons attainted
4. Stuff received from Nicholas Bristow on 10 April 1544 from persons attainted
5. Stuff sent from Hampton Court to Windsor, August 1546
February 1543
BL Additional MS 30367, fos 2r–31v (*LP* XVIII.i, 224)

Tents and pavilions
1544
GMR LM 6

Plate and jewels
22 February 1545
BL Egerton MS 2679, fos 3r–6v (*LP* XX.i, 247)

The king's ships and merchant ships appointed for war service
19 April 1545
PRO SP1/200, fos 25r–28v (*LP* XX.i, 543)

Ordnance, shot, gunpowder and munitions at Carlisle
26 April 1545
PRO SP1/200, fos 67r–69v (*LP* XX.i, 580.2)

Ordnance, artillery, munitions and habiliments of war at Berwick
April 1545
PRO SP1/200, fos 70r–72v, 73r–v (*LP* XX.i, 581)

The fleet
10 August 1545
PRO SP1/205, fos 160r–165v (*LP* XX.ii, 88)

Ordnance, gunpowder and munitions shipped to Calais
24 December 1545
BL Additional MS 5753, f. 29 (*LP* XX.ii, 1032)

The king's ships (The Anthony Roll)
1546
Magdalene College, Cambridge, Pepys MS 2991 and BL Additional MS 22047
See Knighton and Loades, *Anthony Roll*

Ships appointed for the Narrow Seas
March 1546
PRO SP1/216, fos 45r–52v (*LP* XXI.i, 498)

Tents and pavilions
31 January 1547
GMR LM 28

Revels and masking garments
1 April 1547
Folger Shakespeare Library MS Lb.319
See Feuillerat, *Documents*, 9–17

Revels stuff in the custody of Sir Thomas Cawarden
May 1547
Folger Shakespeare Library MS Lb.112
See Feuillerat, *Revels at Court*, 18–21

Stuff delivered to Humphrey Orme, Keeper of the Tower Wardrobe, by Sir Anthony Denny
9 July 1547
BL Additional MS 30367, fos 32r–end

Plate moved from Windsor to the Tower
26 July 1547
PRO E101/419/16, fos 125–7

The 1547 Inventory of Henry VIII
14 September 1547
SA MS 129; also BL Additional MS 46348, BL Harley MS 1419 (*LP* XXI.ii, 754)
See Starkey, ed, *Inventory*

The rough book of James Rufforth relating to the palace at Whitehall
c. 1547
PRO E101/419/16

The declaration of the account of Sir Anthony Denny
30 June 1549
PRO E101/427/2

1510–44: the accounts of the Great Wardrobe

The section for the Great Wardrobe in the 1547 Inventory follows the format of the annual accounts produced by the Master; a list of the surviving annual accounts, account books and particulars is therefore included here.

1510–11
PRO E101/417/4

1511–12
PRO E101/417/5

1516–17
PRO E101/418/9

1518–19
PRO E101/418/14

1519–20
PRO E101/418/20

1519–20
PRO E101/419/3

1524–5
PRO E101/419/12

1524–5
PRO E36/224

1526–7
PRO E101/419/18

1526–7
PRO E101/419/20

1527–8
PRO E101/420/5

1530–1
PRO E101/420/13

1530–1
PRO E101/420/14

1531–2
PRO E101/421/2

1531–2
PRO E101/421/3

1533–4
PRO E101/421/16

1534–5
PRO E101/422/2

1535–6
PRO E315/455

1538–9
PRO E101/422/11

1538–9
PRO E315/456

1540–1
[heading only]
PRO E101/422/20

1542–3
PRO E101/423/6

1543–4
PRO E101/423/9

1543–4
PRO E101/423/10

APPENDIX II

OFFICES, GRANTS AND ANNUITIES GIVEN
TO SIR ANTHONY DENNY

This appendix contains three separate lists of the offices, land grants and annuities given by Henry VIII to Denny between 1536 and 1545. Where the exact month is unclear a dash has been used.

Offices

January 1536
Keeper of the new park near Westminster and the lodges therein; Keeper of the play houses called 'les Tenys playes, bowlynge aleyes, Cocke place and Fesauntecourts'; Bailiff and Receiver of the Rents of the king's messuages near Charing Cross and of all the messuages lately acquired by the king from the abbot and convent of Westminster with fees of 8*d* a day and the usual profits. (*LP* X, 226.33)

Keeper of the place or messuage called York Place, Westminster, and of the gardens and orchards of the same with fees of 12*d* a day. (*LP* X, 226.34)

September 1537
Keeper of the royal household in the palace of Westminster with fees of 6*d* a day. (*LP* XI, 796.13; repeated in September 1538: *LP* XIII, 491.11)

October 1538
Grant in survivorship with Sir Thomas Heneage: Bailiff of the manor or lordship of Cheshunt, Hertfordshire; Keeper of Brantingeshey Park, Hertfordshire with fees of 4*d* a day. (*LP* XIII.ii, 734.10)

December 1539
Steward and Bailiff of the manors of Bedwell and Berkhamsted, Hertfordshire; Keeper of Bedwell Park and hunt of deer; Keeper of the king's mansion of Bedwell and the little garden with 40*s* a year as steward and £10 a year for the other offices, herbage and pannage in the

park, free warren and two pastures next to the park, the 'Great Copie' and the 'Little Copie'. (*LP* XIV.ii, 780.27)

March 1541
One of the Customers and Collectors of Tonnage and Poundage in the Port of London with a licence to act by deputy.[1] (*LP* XVI, 678.27)

January 1542
Sheriff of the lordship or manor of Cheshunt, Hertfordshire with fees of 40*s* a year. (*LP* XVII, 71.14)

— 1542
Keeper of the mansion and garden of Hatfield manor, Hertfordshire, and the park called Innings in Hertfordshire; Bailiff and Chief Steward of the Manor of Hatfield, Hertfordshire; Keeper of the site and chief messuage at Waltham monastery, Essex, and of the waters of Waltham Holy Cross, Essex; Keeper of the great garden called Covent Garden in the parish of St Margaret's, Westminster, and of the chief mansion of Marylebone, Middlesex, and of all the woods there; Keeper of the Great Wood and Middle Park at Hatfield with Peter Browne. (*LP* XVII, Appendix 17, p. 692)

— 1542
Keeper of Tyburn manor in Marylebone parish, Middlesex, except the mansions, gardens and lands enclosed in Marylebone park. (*LP* XVII, Appendix 17, p. 703)

---

1   Sir William Compton also held this office: *LP* I.i, 94.27.

Grants

January 1536

Grant in reversion of the tenements etc. in the Palace of Westminster, the houses and mansions called Paradise and Hell in Westminster Hall; the lands and tenements Will Fryes lately held; the house or mansion called Purgatory which Nich [indecipherable] held; the house under the Exchequer called Potans House; the tower which John Cateby held; the house called Green Lathys in which Thomas Cony now dwells with the custody of the of the place, which premises were granted to James ap Jenkins (dec.) and William Butteler, serjeant-at-arms Westminster. (*LP* X, 226.35)

September 1536

The site and priory of the nuns of St Mary Cheshunt, Hertfordshire, now dissolved; all messuages, houses, dovecotes, gardens etc. therein; all lands lately belonging to the priory in Cheshunt, 'Brokesborne', Berkhamsted, 'Morles', Amwell, Mimms, Wormley, Tunford and Hertford, Hertfordshire; Waltham and 'Heyrothing', Essex; Enville, Middlesex and in London; a fair to be held at the Chapel of St Giles near Enville Chase, Hertfordshire, on the feast of St Giles the Abbot and the two days preceding; free warren in all the grantee's demesne land with an annual value of £20, to be held at a rent of 40*s*. (*LP* XI, 519.12)

February 1538

Grant in fee of the site etc. of the dissolved priory of St Mary, near Hertford; the manors of Hertford Priory alias the Prior of Hertford's manor, Pirton and Bibbesworth, Hertfordshire, and Ickington, Warwickshire; the advowsons and rectories of the churches of St John Evangelist in Hertford, Pirton and Amwell (all in Hertfordshire) and Ickington (Warwickshire), with tithes and advowsons of the vicarages of the same, all annuities and liberties; with an annual value of £72, for a rent of £7 4*s*. (*LP* XIII.ii, 384.47)

August 1540

Grant in tail male of the manor of Amwell, Hertfordshire, of the dissolved monastery of St Peter, Westminster; the messuage called Le Trynyte in Hertford belonging to the late prior of the Crossed Friars, Mussenden, Kent; other land. (*LP* XV, 1027.25)

February 1541

Grant in tail male of the manor of Leving alias Parlaunt, Buckinghamshire; the park; the advowson of the chantry of Colbroke Chapel in Colbroke, Buckinghamshire. (*LP* XVI, 580.42)

— 1541

Grant of Waltham Grange in Waltham, Essex, except the forge and the stable for the king's chariot horses; the demesne lands of Waltham Holy Cross monastery; the rectory of Waltham Holy Cross, provision out of Wormley rectory and Epping vicarage; the manor and rectory of Nazeing, Essex. (*LP* XVI, 1500)

April 1542

Grant of the site, church etc. of the dissolved chantry or college of St Mary, Mettingham; the manors or lordship of Mettingham, Broomfield and Mellis, Suffolk, and 'Peryhall', Howe, Holme Hale and Lyng, Norfolk; all other possessions of the college which came to the king by grant of Thomas, Bishop of Ipswich, late Master and Chaplain of the Brethren. (*LP* XVII, 283.43)

February 1543

Licence to alienate the manor of Bibesworth, Hertfordshire. (*LP* XVIII.i, 226.82)

March 1544

Licence to alienate Cheshunt rectory, Hertfordshire, to Anthony Denny.[2] (*LP* XIX.i, 278.25; see also ibid, 76)

Annuities

August 1540

[Grant to Sir John Gresham of monastic land in Westerham and Edenbridge, Kent, of the dissolved monastery of St Peter, Westminster, whence] annuity of £4 due from the manor of Westerham. (*LP* XV, 1027.34)

May 1544

Annuity of £20 out of lands in Essex which belonged to Robert Dacre, deceased; the wardship with marriage of

George, son and heir of Robert. (*LP* XIX.i, 610.5)

March 1545

Annuity of £50 out of the manors of 'Broughery', 'Comebury', Westmill and Little Hormead, Hertfordshire, which belonged to Lord Chancellor Audley, deceased; the wardship of Margaret Audley, daughter and co-heiress with Mary Audley of Lord Chancellor Audley. (*LP* XX.i, 465.88)

---

2   The Dean and Chapter of Westminster Abbey were granted a mortmain licence to acquire land to the value of £40, and Denny's licence was part of that grant.

APPENDIX III

KEEPERS APPOINTED TO CARE FOR HENRY VIII'S POSSESSIONS

This appendix[1] gives as full a list as possible of the Keepers appointed to look after specific groups of Henry VIII's movable goods. It focuses chiefly upon the groups of possessions found within the 1542 Inventory, and this wide-ranging selection has many parallels with the contents of the 1547 Inventory. To complete the network of Keepers, the officers responsible for the King's ships, horses, tents and revels have also been included; however, the men appointed to keep the series of forts and castles are not listed.

The Armouries

Master of the Armouries
Sir Edward Guilford – g. November 1509 (*LP* I.i, 257.73)
Sir Thomas Darcy – in office in 1547 (SA MS 129, f. 429r)

Keeper of the Greenwich Armoury
John Diconson – named in successor's grant (*LP* V, p. 320)
Hans Clerk – g. July 1530 (ibid, p. 320)
Erasmus Kirkener, armourer – in office in 1547 (SA MS 129, f. 433v)

Keeper of the Long Gallery in the Tilt-yard, Greenwich
George Lovekyn – in office in 1519 (*LP* III.ii, p. 1548)
John Dudley – named in successor's grant (*LP* XIII.i, 1309.36)
Thomas Culpepper – g. 27 June 1538 (ibid)
Sir Thomas Paston – g. December 1541 (*LP* XVI, 1488.26); in office in 1547 (SA MS 129, f. 438v)

Keeper of the Hampton Court Armoury
Thomas Wolner, armourer – in office in 1547 (SA MS 129, f. 440v)

Keeper of the Whitehall Armouries
Hans Hunter, armourer – in office in 1547 (SA MS 129, f. 429r)
Alan Bawdesonne – in office in 1547 (ibid, f. 431r)
John Lyndsey, armourer – in office in 1547 (ibid, f. 440v)

Books

The King's Librarian
Quentin Poulet – gdp. 7 April 1492 (*CPR 1485–94*, 378); gl. 20 January 1494 (ibid, 455)

Gilles Duwes – g. 2 February 1516 (*LP* VII, 419.11); d. 12 April 1536
William Tyndesley – gr. 11 March 1534 (ibid); g. April 1536 (*LP* X, 776.5)

---

1   This appendix draws on Hayward, 'Possessions', 295–304.

Chapel Stuff

Serjeant and Yeoman of the Vestry
William Tebbe – g. 28 January 1510 (*LP* I.i, 417.3)
Geoffrey Wright – serjeant by 1520[2]
Richard Green – serjeant by February 1530[3]
Ralph Tapping – yeoman in 1535/8; serjeant by August 1544; in office in 1547 (SA MS 129, f. 463r)

Clerk of the Closet
Geoffrey Wren – in office on 5 December 1509 (*LP* I.i, 263)
Richard Rawson – in office by Easter 1518[4]
Thomas Westby – in office by 25 March 1525[5]
George Wolfet – in office by 6 October 1533[6]
Edward Leighton – in office by Michaelmas 1538[7]
John Rudd – in office by 25 March 1545[8]

The Great Wardrobe

Keepers
Sir Andrew Windsor – in office on 30 September 1509 (*LP* I.i, 186)
Sir Ralph Sadler – g. 9 May 1543 (*LP* XVIII.i, 623.61); in office in 1547 (BL Harley MS 1419, f. 416r)

Clerks
Laurence Gower – in office on 27 February 1511 (*LP* I.i, 707)
John Porth – g. 1 June 1511 (ibid, 804.1)
John Plofield – in office by April 1529 (*LP* V, p. 311)
John Briggs – in office by April 1530 (ibid, p. 318)
James Joskyn – g. 5 September 1537 (*LP* XII.ii, 796.6)
Nicholas Bristow – g, 10 January 1541 (*LP* XVI, 503)
Edmund Pigeon – gr. June 1544 (*LP* XIX.i, 812.97)

Porters
Richard Gibson – gdp. 13 June 1509 (*LP* I.i, 94.48)
Ralph Worsley – g. November 1534 (*LP* VII.ii, 1498.14)

Yeoman Tailors
Richard Gibson – gdp. 13 June 1509 (*LP* I.ii, 94.48)
John Malt – g. 14 November 1534 (*LP* VII.ii, 1498.18)

Arras makers
'buying and repairing of the king's arras'
Cornelius van der Strete – gdp. October 1509 (*LP* I.i, 218.16)
Peter Gengham – in office by January 1510 (ibid, 357.11)
Thomas Garton – named in successor's grant (*LP* XII.i, 795.22)
John Lysen – named in successor's grant (ibid)
John Musting – g. 6 March 1537 (ibid)
Cornelius Mustring – g. July 1546 (*LP* XXI.i, 1383.52)

Horses

Master of the Horse
Sir Thomas Brandon – April 1509 (*LP* I.i, 20)
Sir Thomas Knyvet – g. 8 February 1510 (*LP* I.i, 381.76)
Charles Brandon, Duke of Suffolk – 1512[9]
Sir Henry Guildford – 6 November 1515 (*LP* II.i, 1114)
Sir Nicholas Carew – g. 18 July 1522 (LP III.ii, 2395)
Sir Anthony Browne – in office in 1539; in office in 1547 (SA MS 129, f. 444r)

Stud at Warwick
Christopher Erington – in office in 1547 (SA MS 129, f. 445r)

Stud at Malmesbury
Lancelot Sacker – in office in 1547 (SA MS 129, f. 446r)

Stud at Eskermayne, Wales
Thomas Guillliam – in office in 1547 (SA MS 129, f. 447r)

Stud in Wales
Rice ap Moris – in office in 1547 (SA MS 129, f. 447v)

---

2   Kisby, 'Royal Household Chapel', appendix 1.
4   Bickersteth and Dunning, *Clerks of the Closet*, 12–14.
6   Ibid.
9   Reese, *Royal Office of Master of the Horse*, 342–3.

3   Ibid.
5   Ibid.
7   Ibid.
8   Ibid.

The Jewel House

Masters
Sir Henry Wyatt – gdgc. May 1513 (*LP* I.ii, 1948.92)[10]
Robert Amadas – g. 20 April 1526 (*LP* IV.i, 2114)
Thomas Cromwell – g. 14 April 1532 (*LP* V, 978.13)
Thomas Cromwell and Sir John Williams – gs. 1535/6 (*LP* XIX.i, 610.3)
Sir John Williams – g. 28 July 1540 (*LP* XIX.i, 610.3)

Anthony Rous – g. 1 May 1544 (ibid)
Sir Anthony Aucher – in office on 25 November 1545 (*LP* XX.ii, 910.58); in office in 1547 (SA MS 129, f. 4r)

Clerks
John Williams – gr. May 1531 (*LP* V, 278.10)

Musical Instruments

Keeper of the King's Instruments
William Lewes – in office on 11 June 1514 (*LP* II.ii, p.1464)
Philip van Wilder – in office in 1547 (BL Harley MS 1419, f. 200r)

Ordnance

Masters
Sir Samson Norton – in office on 26 August 1511 (*LP* I.i, 849)
Sir William Skerington – g. 30 May 1515 (*LP* II.i, 530)
Sir Christopher Morris – g. February 1536 (*LP* X, 392.17)
Sir Thomas Seymour – g. 18 April 1544 (*LP* XIX.i, 442.23)
Sir Philip Hoby – in office in 1547 (SA MS 129, f. 251r)

Revels Stuff

Yeomen
Richard Gibson – in office by February 1510 (*LP* II.ii, p.1499)
John Farlyon – g. 20 November 1534 (*LP* VII, 1498.41)
John Bridges – g. 21 October 1539 (*LP* XIV.ii, 435.48)

Masters
Sir Henry Guildford – in office in 1511 (PRO E36/217, f. 38r)
Sir Thomas Cawarden – g. 5 March 1545 (backdated to 16 March 1544) (*LP* XX.i, 465.28); in office in 1547 (SA MS 129, f. 449r)

Clerk Controllers *see* tents

Ships

Keepers or Clerks
Robert Briggandine – in office on 19 May 1495 (*CPR 1494–1509*, 17)
Thomas Jermyn – in office in 1523 (*LP* III, 2992); until February 1538
Edmund More – g. 5 February 1538 (*LP* XIV.i, 384)
Edward Water – in office in December 1540 (*LP* XVI, 1056)
William Holstok – g. 20 April 1546 (paid from 25 December 1545) (*LP* XXI.i, 718.9)

Clerk Controllers
John Hopton – in office in 1512 (*LP* I.i, 3318.30)
Sir Thomas Spert – in office in 1524 (*LP* IV.i, 309)
John Osborne – gr. July 1540 (*LP* XV, 942.104)
William Broke – g. 20 April 1546 (paid from 25 December 1545) (*LP* XXI.i, 718.10)

Keeper of the Store Houses at Erith and Deptford
John Hopton – gl. January 1514 (*LP* II.i, 2617)
William Gonson – g. 25 September 1524 (*LP* IV.i, 693)
Richard Howlett – g. 14 January 1545 (*LP* XX.i, 58); g. 20 April 1546 (paid from 25 December 1545) (ibid, 718.2)

---

10 Wyatt had been in office since 13 September 1492: see Collins, *Jewels and Plate of Elizabeth 1*, 257.

Council for Marine Causes[11]

Lieutenant or Vice-Admiral
Sir Thomas Clere – g. 20 April 1546 (paid from 25 December 1545) (*LP* XXI.i, 718.5)

Treasurer
Robert Legge – g. 20 April 1546 (paid from 25 December 1545) (*LP* XXI.i, 718.8)

Surveyor and Rigger
Benjamin Gonson – g. 20 April 1546 (paid from 25 December 1545) (*LP* XXI.i, 718.6)

Master of Naval Ordnance
Sir William Woodhouse – g. 20 April 1546 (paid from 25 December 1545) (*LP* XXI.i, 718.1)

Tents

Serjeants
John Morton – g. 28 November 1496 (*CPR 1494–1509*, 72–3)
Sir Christopher Garnesche – in office in 1513 (*LP* II.ii, 2349, 2480.8)
Richard Gibson – in office by August 1518 (*LP* II.ii, p. 1479)
John Parker – g. 8 December 1534 (*LP* VII, 1601.19)
John Farlyon – g. August 1538 (*LP* XIII.ii, 249.15)
John Travers – g. 28 September 1539 (*LP* XVI.ii, 264.30)

Grooms
Thomas Hale – g. 15 November 1541 (*LP* XV, 1391)

Master[12]
Sir Thomas Cawarden and Anthony Aucher – gs. 5 March 1545 (backdated to 16 March 1544) (*LP* XX.i, 465.27); Cawarden in office in 1547 (SA MS 129, f. 457v)

Yeoman
Richard Gibson – in office in 1513 (*LP* I.ii, 2349, 2480.8)
Richard Longman – g. 19 August 1538 (*LP* XIII.ii, 249.12)
John Bridges and Richard Longman – gs. 15 November 1541 (*LP* XVI, 1391.34)

Clerk (of Tents and Revels)
Thomas Philips – g. 4 May 1546 (*LP* XXI.i, 970.15)

Clerk Controller (of Tents and Revels)
John Bernard – g. 5 March 1545 (*LP* XX.ii, 465.29)

Wardrobe of the Beds

Yeomen
John Ashkirk – g. 14 May 1509 (LP I.i, 54.27)
William Cheyney – g. 18 May 1509 (ibid, 54.53)
Ralph Jenet – g. 2 November 1509 (ibid, 257.72)
Rowland Ridgely – in office by March 1540 (*LP* XVI, 380)
Humphrey Orme – in office in 1547 (BL Harley MS 1419, f. 394r)

Grooms
John Pate – g. 20 May 1509 (*LP* I.i, 54.7)
Robert Little – g. 22 May 1509 (ibid, 54.85)
Rowland Ridgeley – g. January 1536 (*LP* X, 226.15)
Lancelot Alforde – g. June 1537 (*LP* XII.ii, 291)
Humphrey Orme – 1538 (*LP* XIII.ii, 1280)

David Vincent – g. April 1543 (*LP* XVIII.i, 474.26)
William Tildesley – g. May 1544 (*LP* XIX.i, 610.6)

Pages
Richard Cachemayde – g. 8 February 1510 (*LP* I.i, 381.29)
William Ridgeley – g. 30 September 1511 (ibid, 924.4)
John Sedgewick – g. 8 June 1513 (ibid, 2055.56)
Thomas Garton – g. 22 July 1517 (*LP* II.ii, 3500.36)
Rowland Ridgely – g. October 1530 (*LP* IV.iii, 6709.17)
William Tildesley – g. January 1536 (*LP* X, 226.15)
David Vincent – March 1538 (*LP* XIII.i, 1280)
Richard Bethell – 30 September 1542 (*LP* XVII, 880)
Henry Plesington – 1545 (*LP* XX.ii, Appendix 2)

11 Established 1545.
12 Established 1545.

Standing Wardrobes of the Beds[13]

The Tower of London
Robert Hasilridge – gdp. 18 May 1509 (*LP* I.i, 54.86)
Robert Draper – g. 27 April 1532 (*LP* V, 980.6)
Humphrey Orme and Nicholas Bristow – gs. April 1542 (*LP* XVII, 283.51)
Humphrey Orme – in office in 1547 (BL Harley MS 1419, f. 5r); v. 10 November 1564

Beaulieu (acquired 1516)
Thomas Carvanel – g. 5 December 1519 (*LP* III.i, 581)
William Carey – g. 5 February 1522 (*LP* III.ii, 2074.5)
George Boleyn – g. 15 November 1528 (*LP* IV.ii, 4993.15)
Robert, Earl of Sussex – g. June 1536 (*LP* X, 1256.31)
William, Marquis of Northampton – g. May 1543 (*LP* XVIII.i, 623.88); in office in 1547 (BL Harley MS 1419, f. 360r)

Beddington (acquired 1539)
Edmund Harvey – g. 20 July 1540 (*LP* XV, 942.94)
Sir Michael Stanhope – in office in 1547 (BL Harley MS 1419, f. 373r)

Greenwich (Crown property in 1509)
David Vincent – g. 27 February 1532 (*LP* V, 838)
Thomas Maynman – g. October 29 1539 (*LP* XIV.ii, 435.53); in office in 1547 (BL Harley MS 1419, f. 37r)

Hampton Court (acquired 1525–9)
John Pate – named in successor's grant (*LP* XII.i, 539.12)
Robert Smith – g. February 1537 (ibid)
David Vincent – g. 29 October 1539 (*LP* XIV.ii, 435.54); in office in 1547 (BL Harley MS 1419, f. 206r)

Horsley[14]
William Griffiths – g. 2 December 1539 (*LP* XIV.ii, 780)

The More (acquired 1529)
Richard Hobbes – g. October 1529 (PRO E101/420/11, f. 89r); in office in 1547 (BL Harley MS 1419, f. 328r)

Nonsuch (built 1538 onwards)
Sir Ralph Sadler – g. January 1541 (*LP* XVI, 1500)
Sir Thomas Cawarden – g. 1544 (*LP* XIX.i, 1036); in office in 1547 (BL Harley MS 1419, f. 280r)

Nottingham Castle (Crown property)
William Davies – named in successor's grant (*LP* II.i, 1916)
John Copinger – g. 20 May 1516 (ibid)
Laurence Holland – g. 11 May 1519 (*LP* III.i, 278)
Thomas Cliff – g. October 1537 (*LP* XII.ii, 1008.28); in office in 1547 (BL Harley MS 1419, f. 364r)

Oatlands (acquired 1536)
Edmund Harman – in office by June 1536 (*LP* X, 1240)
Sir Anthony Browne – in office in 1547 (BL Harley MS 1419, f. 254r)

Richmond Palace (Crown property)
John Staunton – g. 11 March 1511 (*LP* I.i, 731.33)
[John Pate – g. 7 October 1515 (*LP* VI, 1195.3) – *see* Whitehall]
[Robert Smith – g. February 1537 (*LP* XII.i, 539) – *see* Whitehall]
Roger Bryne – g. February 1529 (PRO E101/420/11 f. 95r)
David Vincent – g. December 1530 (*LP* IV.iii, 6803.29)
William Griffiths – in office in 1547 (BL Harley MS 1419, f. 343r)

St James's Palace (built 1531–6)
Sir Anthony Denny[15]
Richard Cook – in office in 1548–9 (BL Harley MS 1419, f. 444r)

St Johns (acquired on the dissolution of the priory of St John of Jerusalem)
Sir Anthony Denny – in office in 1547 (BL Harley MS 1419, f. 368r)

Westminster, old Palace (Crown property)
Robert Hasilridge – gdp. 14 November 1509 (*LP* I.i, 257.81)
John Pate – Keeper of the wardrobe 'removed from Westminster to Richmond' – g. 7 October 1515 (*LP* II.ii, 1002)

Whitehall, built on the site of York Place
John Reed – g. February 1529 (PRO E101/420/11, f. 95r)
John Reed – Keeper of Wardrobe and Vestry – g. 4 September 1536 (*LP* VI, 1195.3); in office in 1547 (BL Harley MS 1419, f. 63r)

---

13 The Keeper of the house was also responsible for the Standing Wardrobe for all the properties listed here apart from the Tower of London, Greenwich, Hampton Court, Richmond and Whitehall.
14 The Wardrobe at Horsley was not listed in the 1547 Inventory.
15 Denny was responsible for the fabric of the building, although not named as keeper: BL Lansdowne Roll 14.

Windsor Castle (Crown property)
Ralph Jenet and Robert Little – gs. October 1509 (*LP* I.i, 414.69)
Robert Little – g. 1516 (*LP* II.i, 2736)
William Tildesley – g. 4 February 1539 (*LP* XIV.i, 403); in office in 1547 (BL Harley MS 1419, f. 298r)

Woodstock (Crown property)
John Segewick – g. 4 August 1516 (*LP* II.i, 2245)
Robert Bradshaw – g. 29 September 1533 (*LP* VI, 1195.24)
no name listed in 1547 (BL Harley MS 1419, f. 318r)

Wardrobe of the Robes

Yeomen
Richard Smith – g. 19 May 1509 (*LP* I.i, 54.75)
Robert Rissheton – g. 18 May 1509 (ibid, 54.32)
James Worsley – in office by December 1516 (*LP* II.ii, p. 1473)
John Parker – in office by October 1528 (*LP* V, p. 303)
Anthony Denny – g. September 1537 (*LP* XII.ii, 796.13)
Richard Cecil – in office by March 1539 (paid from December 1538) (*LP* XIV.ii, 781); in office in 1547 (BL Harley MS 1419, f. 398r)

Grooms
William Smith – 1509 (*LP* I.i, 447.8)
James Worsley – g. 30 January 1510 (ibid, 357.40)
John Sharp – g. 15 February 1512 (ibid, 1083.35)
Richard Cecil – g. August 1528 (*LP* IV.ii, 4687.27)
John Gates – 27 July 1540 (*LP* XV, 917)
Thomas Sternold – March 1544 (*LP* XIX.i, 275)

Pages
John Copinger – g. 19 March 1510 (*LP* I.i, 447.8)
Ralph Wursley – g. February 1526 (*LP* IV.i, 2002.27)
Richard Aunsham – in office in 1527 (*LP* IV.ii, 3540)
Richard Agmondsham – in office by February 1536 (*LP* X, 392)
John Gates – in office by October 1537 (*LP* XII.ii, 877)
William Sherington – in office by January 1538 (*LP* XIII.ii, 1280)
John Rowland – in office by September 1542 (*LP* XVII, 880)

Other wardrobe officers
Robert Hordon – in office on 16 September 1530 (*LP* IV.iii, 6621)

APPENDIX IV

THE SIGNIFICANCE OF DONATIONS FROM DENNY'S CHARGE AT WHITEHALL ON THE DEVELOPMENT OF THE WARDROBES OF THE BEDS AT OATLANDS AND NONSUCH, 1542–7

This appendix[1] highlights how many of the furnishings recorded at Oatlands[2] and Nonsuch[3] in the 1547 Inventory had come from Denny's charge at Whitehall, either during Henry VIII's lifetime or shortly after his death. The items in the two Wardrobes which came from Whitehall are analysed in turn, in two formats. First, the list is presented with the numbering of the 1542 Inventory in bold, followed by a brief description of the item; the 1547 Inventory number is given in parentheses. Secondly, the order is reversed with the numbering of the 1547 Inventory in bold and the 1542 Inventory number in square brackets.

The second list for Oatlands also shows the items which had come from Parham (BL Cotton MS Appendix 89, fos 55r–66r); they are marked by an asterisk in the second list, in order to put the donations from Whitehall in context. Items marked with a double asterisk come from Parham but may appear in an earlier inventory: the doubt arises from either a slight discrepancy in the measurements given or from the objects being grouped in different ways.

The dashed line dividing the entries in the second list for Nonsuch indicates the two distinct sections of the entry for this property in the 1547 Inventory.

---

1   This appendix draws on Hayward, 'Possessions', appendix 9, 280–6.
2   BL Cotton MS Appendix 89, fos 55r–66r; PRO E315/160; BL Harley MS 1419, fos 245r–279r.
3   PRO E315/160; BL Harley MS 1419, fos 280r–297r.

Oatlands

1542 Inventory

205	6 pieces of tapestry (**12624**)	246	1 chair (**12741**)	380	2 cushions (**12779**)
208	7 pieces of tapestry (**12625**)	272	1 stool (**12743**)	390	1 cushion (**12780**)
211	14 verdures (**12626**)	274	1 stool (**12744**)	393	2 cushions (**12782**)
212	14 verdures (**12627**)	280	1 close stool (**12746**)	410	1 cushion (**12781**)
213	14 verdures (**12628**)	282	1 close stool (**12745**)	417	18 cases (**12784**)
215	5 verdures (**12629**)	283	1 close stool (**12750**)	419	6 cases (**12742**)
218	21 verdures (**12630**)	342	3 cushions (**12771**)	657	4 bowls, 2 cisterns of pewter (**12747**)
221	10 carpets (**12724**)	351	2 cushions (**12772**)		
232	1 cloth of estate (**12711**)	352	1 cushion (**12773**)	660	2 bowls, 1 cistern of pewter (**12751**)
233	1 cloth of estate (**12712**)	355	1 cushion (**12774**)		
238	1 chair (**12737**)	356	1 cushion (**12775**)	3312	2 footstools (**12748**)
241	1 chair (**12738**)	357	3 cushions (**12776**)	3315	2 footstools (**12749**)
243	1 chair (**12739**)	358	2 cushions (**12777**)	3322	1 cushion (**12783**)
245	1 chair (**12740**)	362	1 cushion (**12778**)	3344	1 cloth of estate (**12710**)

1547 Inventory

12599	3 pieces of tapestry*	**12675**	5 sheets*	**12739**	1 chair [**243**]
12600	6 pieces of tapestry*	**12676**	3 sheets*	**12740**	1 chair [**245**]
12601	1 piece of tapestry*	**12678**	1 pair of sheets*	**12741**	1 chair [**246**]
12602	1 piece of tapestry**	**12679**	4 pairs of sheets *	**12742**	6 cases [**419**]
12606	4 verdures*	**12680**	1 pair of sheets*	**12743**	1 stool [**272**]
12607	1 verdure**	**12681**	2 pairs of sheets*	**12744**	1 stool [**274**]
12624	6 pieces of tapestry [**205**]	**12682**	5 sheets*	**12745**	1 close stool [**282**]
12625	7 pieces of tapestry [**208**]	**12683**	2 pairs of sheets*	**12746**	1 close stool [**280**]
12626	14 verdures [**211**]	**12684**	7 pairs of sheets (*3 pairs)	**12747**	4 bowls, 2 cisterns of pewter [**657**]
12627	14 verdures [**212**]	**12689**	12 pillow-beres*		
12628	14 verdures [**213**]	**12690**	12 pillow-beres*	**12748**	2 footstools [**3312**]
12629	5 verdures [**215**]	**12698**	1 mass book*	**12749**	2 footstools [**3315**]
12630	21 verdures [**218**]	**12700**	1 standard*	**12750**	1 close stool [**283**]
12636	1 canopy*	**12701**	1 chest*	**12751**	2 bowls, 1 cistern of pewter [**660**]
12637	the apparel of a bed*	**12705**	4 altar frontals, 3 vestments with all the apparel (*1 only)		
12638	1 trussing bedstead*			**12762**	12 cushions (*9 only)
12639	the apparel of a bed*	**12710**	1 cloth of estate [**3344**]	**12765**	1 cushion*
12640	1 trussing bedstead*	**12711**	1 cloth of estate [**232**]	**12766**	1 cushion*
12642	1 trussing bedstead*	**12712**	1 cloth of estate [**233**]	**12767**	2 cushions*
12643	the apparel of a bed*	**12713**	1 carpet*	**12768**	3 cushions*
12644	1 trussing bedstead*	**12718**	1 carpet*	**12771**	3 cushions [**342**]
12645	the apparel of a bed*	**12719**	1 carpet*	**12772**	2 cushions [**351**]
12646	1 trussing bedstead*	**12720**	1 carpet*	**12773**	1 cushion [**352**]
12657	2 beds with bolsters*	**12724**	10 carpets [**221**]	**12774**	1 cushion [**355**]
12658	1 bed with bolster*	**12725**	10 carpets	**12775**	1 cushion [**356**]
12659	1 bed with bolster*	**12734**	1 close stool*	**12776**	3 cushions [**357**]
12661	1 bed [**]	**12735**	1 close stool*	**12777**	2 cushions [**358**]
12667	4 pairs of fustians*	**12736**	1 chair*	**12778**	1 cushion [**362**]
12673	1 pair of sheets *	**12737**	1 chair [**238**]	**12779**	2 cushions [**380**]
12674	1 pair of sheets*	**12738**	1 chair [**241**]	**12780**	1 cushion [**390**]

12781	1 cushion [410]	12818	2 embroideries*	12862	1 kettle*
12782	2 cushions [393]	12819	1 picture*	12863	2 kettles*
12783	1 cushion [3322]	12820	1 picture*	12864	2 frying pans and 1 dripping pan*
12784	18 cases [417]	12821	1 picture*		
12785	18 counterpoints*	12822	1 picture*	12865	2 pots*
12788	1 counterpoint*	12823	2 comb cases*	12866	3 pans*
12789	1 counterpoint*	12824	1 comb case*	12867	2 little pan chafers and 1 pot chafer*
12790	1 counterpoint*	12825	1 mirror*		
12792	2 counterpoints*	12826	8 chamber pots*	12868	2 gridirons*
12793	2 counterpoints*	12827	4 perfume pans*	12869	2 pewter basins for a close stole*
12796	1 counterpoint*	12828	4 pairs of andirons*		
12797	1 counterpoint*	12829	2 fire forks, 1 pair of tongs*	12870	1 basin and ewer of pewter*
12805	4 quilts*	12830	2 candle plates*	12871	24 platters, 24 dishes, 10 saucers of pewter*
12811	6 pillows*	12831	1 coverpane*		
12812	4 pillows*	12843	10 tables (*3 only)	12872	12 candlesticks*
12813	4 pillows*	12851	11 forms (*6 only)	12873	5 spits*
12814	1 pillow*	12853	18 joined stools (*14 only)	12874	2 leather pots*
12815	1 pillow **	12861	1 pair of iron racks*		

Nonsuch

1542 Inventory

210	1 carpet (13026)	348	3 cushions (12932)	428	1 carpet (13030)
216	2 verdures (13021)	352	1 cushion (12933)	429	1 carpet (13028)
218	20 verdures (13022)	353	2 cushions (12934)	430	1 carpet (13032)
220	3 verdures (13025)	361	1 cushion (12937)	431	2 carpets (13033)
221	13 carpets (13027)	364	3 cushions (12940)	435	22 carpets (13038)
225	7 hangings (13020)	366	1 cushion (12938)	439	1 damask (12973)
238	3 chairs (12962)	368	3 cushions (12943)	441	1 bed with apparel (12896)
239	7 chairs (12963)	369	1 cushion (12944)	445	1 bed with apparel (12893)
241	1 chair (12964)	372	3 cushions (12941)	446	1 bed with apparel (12894)
242	1 chair (12965)	373	2 cushions (12955)	448	1 bed with apparel (12895)
244	2 chairs (12961)	374	2 cushions (12956)	453	1 damask (12974)
245	1 chair (12966)	378	3 cushions (12939)	467	1 bed with apparel (13040)
246	1 chair (12967)	380	1 cushion (12947)	471	1 bed with apparel (13041)
250	1 chair (12960)	382	2 cushions (12946)	472	1 bed with apparel (13042)
257	1 chair (12968)	384	1 cushion (12949)	515	1 scarlet (12970)
262	1 chair (13039)	385	1 cushion (12952)	516	1 scarlet (12971)
268	6 folding stools (12915)	386	2 cushions (12942)	540	5 cases (12919)
269	6 folding stools (12916)	387	2 cushions (12954)	544	3 pairs of sheets (12975)
270	7 folding stools (12917)	389	1 cushion (12948)	545	1 pair of sheets (12976)
271	10 folding stools (12918)	390	2 cushions (12951)	554	1 pair of sheets (12977)
272	1 stool (12907)	391	1 cushion (12950)	561	3 pairs of pillow-beres (12979)
280	2 close stools (12912)	396	3 cushions (12953) (2 stolen July 1545)	562	1 pair of pillow-beres (12978)
282	1 close stool (12911)			568	1 pillow-bere (12980)
310	1 cushion (12930)	417	57 cases (12957, 12959)	569	1 pillow-bere (12981)
312	3 cushions (12958)	419	18 cases (12969)	1031	1 altar frontal (12986)
314	2 cushions (12935)	422	1 carpet (13034)	1034	2 altar frontals (12987)
320	6 cushions (12936)	423	1 carpet (13037)	1035	2 altar frontals (12988)
346	3 cushions (12931)	425	1 carpet (13029)	1043	2 vestments (12990)

1044	1 vestment (**12991**)	**2297**	4 bolsters (**13044**)	**3324**	1 cushion (**12945**)
1045	1 vestment (**12992**)	**3311**	2 footstools (**12909**)	**3549**	11 verdures (**12876, 13023**)
1049	1 vestment (**12993**)	**3314**	2 footstools (**12910**)	**3550**	4 verdures (**12877, 13024**)
1230	1 altar frontal (**12984**)	**3317**	4 footstools (**12920**)	**3765**	6 footstools (**12922**)
2296	4 pallet beds (**13043**)	**3318**	4 footstools (**12921**)		

1547 Inventory

12876	10 verdures [**3549**]	**12945**	1 cushion [**3324**]	**12979**	3 pairs of pillow-beres [**561**]
12877	3 verdures [**3550**]	**12946**	2 cushions [**382**]	**12980**	1 pillow-bere [**568**]
12893	1 bed with apparel [**445**]	**12947**	1 cushion [**380**]	**12981**	1 pillow-bere [**569**]
12894	1 bed with apparel [**446**]	**12948**	1 cushion [**389**]	**12984**	1 altar frontal [**1230**]
12895	1 bed with apparel [**448**]	**12949**	1 cushion [**384**]	**12986**	1 altar frontal [**1031**]
12896	1 bed with apparel [**441**]	**12950**	1 cushion [**391**]	**12987**	2 altar frontals [**1034**]
12907	1 stool [**272**]	**12951**	2 cushions [**390**]	**12988**	2 altar frontals [**1035**]
12909	2 footstools [**3311**]	**12952**	1 cushion [**385**]	**12990**	2 vestments [**1043**]
12910	2 footstools [**3314**]	**12953**	3 cushions [**396**] (2 stolen July	**12991**	1 vestment [**1044**]
12911	1 close stool [**282**]		1545)	**12992**	1 vestment [**1045**]
12912	2 close stools [**280**]	**12954**	2 cushions [**387**]	**12993**	1 vestment [**1049**]
12915	6 folding stools [**268**]	**12955**	2 cushions [**373**]		– – – – – – – –
12916	6 folding stools [**269**]	**12956**	2 cushions [**374**]	**13020**	7 hangings [**225**]
12917	7 folding stools [**270**]	**12957**	54 cases [**417**]	**13021**	2 verdures [**216**]
12918	10 folding stools [**271**]	**12958**	3 cushions [**312**]	**13022**	20 verdures [**218**]
12919	5 cases [**540**]	**12959**	3 cases [**417**]	**13023**	1 verdure [**3549**]
12920	4 footstools [**3317**]	**12960**	1 chair [**250**]	**13024**	1 verdure [**3550**]
12921	4 footstools [**3318**]	**12961**	2 chairs [**244**]	**13025**	3 verdures [**220**]
12922	6 footstools [**3765**]	**12962**	3 chairs [**238**]	**13026**	1 carpet [**210**]
12930	1 cushion [**310**]	**12963**	7 chairs [**239**]	**13027**	13 carpets [**221**]
12931	3 cushions [**346**]	**12964**	1 chair [**241**]	**13028**	1 carpet [**429**]
12932	3 cushions [**348**]	**12965**	1 chair [**242**]	**13029**	1 carpet [**425**]
12933	1 cushion [**352**]	**12966**	1 chair [**245**]	**13030**	1 carpet [**428**]
12934	2 cushions [**353**]	**12967**	1 chair [**246**]	**13032**	1 carpet [**430**]
12935	2 cushions [**314**]	**12968**	1 chair [**257**]	**13033**	2 carpets [**431**]
12936	6 cushions [**320**]	**12969**	18 cases [**419**]	**13034**	1 carpet [**422**]
12937	1 cushion [**361**]	**12970**	1 scarlet [**515**]	**13037**	1 carpet [**423**]
12938	1 cushion [**366**]	**12971**	1 scarlet [**516**]	**13038**	22 carpets [**435**]
12939	3 cushions [**378**]	**12973**	1 damask [**439**]	**13039**	1 chair [**262**]
12940	3 cushions [**364**]	**12974**	1 damask [**453**]	**13040**	1 bed with apparel [**467**]
12941	3 cushions [**372**]	**12975**	3 pairs of sheets [**544**]	**13041**	1 bed with apparel [**471**]
12942	2 cushions [**386**]	**12976**	1 pair of sheets [**545**]	**13042**	1 bed with apparel [**472**]
12943	3 cushions [**368**]	**12977**	1 pair of sheets [**554**]	**13043**	4 pallet beds [**2296**]
12944	1 cushion [**369**]	**12978**	1 pair of pillow-beres [**562**]	**13044**	4 bolsters [**2297**]

APPENDIX V

THE DEVELOPMENT OF THE WARDROBE OF THE BEDS
HELD BY JOHN REED AT WHITEHALL IN 1547

This appendix analyses the composition of John Reed's charge for the Wardrobe of the Beds at Whithall as it was recorded in the 1547 Inventory. At this point, Reed's charge contained 233 entries (**9682–9914**). As this list was drawn up after the redistribution of Denny's charge, it is possible to identify how many pieces Reed had received from Denny.

The material follows the order used for Reed's charge in the 1547 Inventory and is organized under the headings used in the document. After each heading, the total number of these items is given in parentheses. Then follows a breakdown of how many of the items had been part of Reed's charge prior to 1547 and how many had come from Denny. The latter is also expressed in terms of the number of entries and as a percentage. The actual items that passed from Denny to Reed are then recorded. The layout of the 1547 Inventory shows that most of the pieces Reed received from Denny were just added to the end of the existing groups of objects in his charge; on the whole, they were added in the same order as in the 1542 Inventory.

The entry number in the 1547 Inventory is given in bold, followed by a brief description; the number from the 1542 Inventory is given in square brackets.

Hangings (total: 277)
Reed 193; Denny 79
From Denny: 10/59 entries (17%)
9731	6 pieces of tapestry [**198**]
9732	9 pieces of tapestry [**199**]
9733	5 pieces of tapestry [**200**]
9734	7 pieces of tapestry [**201**]
9735	7 pieces of tapestry [**202**]
9736	8 pieces of tapestry [**204**]
9737	6 pieces of tapestry [**206**]
9738	6 pieces of tapestry [**207**]
9739	6 pieces of tapestry [**3546**]
9740	19 window pieces [**209**]

Carpets (total: 71)
Reed 64; Denny 7
From Denny: 2/17 entries (12%)
9742	4 carpets [**435**]
9756	3 carpets [**434**]

Traverses (total: 2)
Reed 0; Denny 2
From Denny: 2/2 entries (100%)
9758	2 traverses [**517**]
9759	1 traverse [**521**]

Cloths of estate (total: 3)
Reed 2; Denny 1
From Denny: 1/3 entries (33%)
9762	1 cloth of estate [**233**]

Beds and bedsteads (total: 46)
Reed 30; Denny 16
From Denny: 11/14 entries (79%)
9767	1 bedstead with apparel [**442**]
9768	1 bedstead with apparel [**443**]
9769	1 bedstead with apparel [**447**]
9770	1 bedstead with apparel [**449**]
9771	1 bedstead with apparel [**451**]
9772	1 bedstead with apparel but not the damask [**453**]
9773	4 pillows [**513, 3494**]
9774	2 pillows [**2363**]
9775	1 quilt [**511**]
9776	1 quilt [**3493**]
9777	2 quilts [**512**]

Chairs (total: 21)
Reed 7; Denny 14
From Denny: 11/17 entries (65%)
9784   1 chair [**238**]
9785   3 chairs [**239**]
9786   1 chair [**245**]
9787   1 chair [**247**]
9788   1 chair [**248**]
9789   1 chair [**250**]
9790   2 chairs [**260**]
9791   1 chair [**264**]
9792   4 chairs [**267**]
9793   1 chair [**3704**]
9794   2 chairs [**260**]

Cushions (total: 144)
Reed 65 plus a length of cloth; Denny 79
From Denny: 20/35 entries (57%)
9805   2 cushions [**302**]
9806   3 cushions [**305**]
9807   1 cushion [**308**]
9808   1 cushion [**309**]
9809   1 cushion [**311**]
9810   3 cushions [**317**]
9811   3 cushions [**323**]
9812   3 cushions [**343**]
9813   2 cushions [**344**]
9814   2 cushions [**345**]
9815   1 cushion [**347**]
9816   3 cushions [**352**]
9817   1 cushion [**359**]
9818   1 cushion [**399**]
9819   1 cushion [**403**]
9821   2 cushions [**3327**]
9822   6 cushions [**3332**]
9823   6 cases for cushions [**418**]
9824   25 cases for cushions [**417**]
9825   13 cases for chairs [**419**]

Counterpoints (total: 30)
Reed 30; Denny 0
From Denny: 0/4 entries (0%)

Celures and testers (6)
Reed 6; Denny 0
From Denny: 0/5 entries (0%)

Sparvers (8)
Reed 8; Denny 0
From Denny: 0/8 entries (0%)

Fustians (14 pairs)
Reed 14 pairs; Denny 0
From Denny: 0/1 entries (0%)

Sheets (16 single, 48 pairs)
Reed 27 pairs; Denny 16 single, 21 pairs
From Denny: 12/14 entries (86%)
9851   7 pairs of sheets [**543**]
9852   5 pairs of sheets [**544**]
9853   2 pairs of sheets [**545**]
9854   3 pairs of sheets [**546**]
9855   2 pairs and 1 sheet [**547**]
9856   2 pairs of sheets [**2304**]
9857   2 sheets [**549**]
9858   3 sheets [**551**]
9859   4 sheets [**550**]
9860   1 sheet [**2350**]
9861   2 sheets [**554**]
9862   4 sheets [**555**]

Pillows (total: 6)
Reed 6; Denny 0.
From Denny: 0/1 entries (0%)

Pillow-beres (totals: 20 single, 30 pairs)
Reed 6 single; Denny 14 single, 30 pairs
From Denny: 9/10 entries (90%)
9865   9 pairs of pillow-beres [**559**]
9866   5 pairs of pillow-beres [**560**]
9867   5 pairs and 1 single pillow-beres [**561**]
9868   2 pairs of pillow-beres [**562**]
9869   9 pairs of pillow-beres [**563**]
9870   1 pillow-bere [**567**]
9871   2 pillow-beres [**564**]
9872   3 pillow-beres [**568**]
9873   7 pillow-beres [**569**]

Cupboard cloths (3)
Reed 3; Denny 0
From Denny: 0/3 entries (0%)

Window curtains (7)
Reed 7; Denny 0
From Denny: 0/4 entries (0%)

Ornaments for chapels and closets (22)
Reed 0; Denny 22
From Denny: 13/13 entries (100%)
9881   2 altar frontals [**1017**]
9882   2 altar frontals [**1033**]
9883   3 vestments [**1036**]
9884   2 altar frontals [**1022**]
9885   2 altar frontals [**1032**]
9886   2 vestments [**1038**]
9887   2 vestments [**1023**]
9888   2 altar cloths [**1050**]
9889   1 sacrament cloth [**1019**]
9890   1 corporal case [**1021**]
9891   1 mass book [**1020**]
9892   1 mass book [**1026**]
9893   1 corporal case [**3761**]

Stools and footstools (25?)
Reed 1; Denny 24?
From Denny: 14/15 entries (93%)
9895   1 stool [**273**]
9896   1 stool [**274**]
9897   2 stools [**275**]
9898   1 stool [**277**]
9899   1 stool [**276**]
9900   2 stools [**278**]
9901   1 footstool [**289**]
9902   2 footstools [**290**]
9903   2 footstools [**291**]
9904   1 footstool [**3312**]
9905   2 footstools [**3678**]
9906   stools (no number given) [**1192**]
9907   2 stools [**3483**]
9908   1 table, 3 trestles [**1177, 1180**]

Canvas (unspecified number of pieces)
Reed 0; Denny all.
From Denny: 1/1 entries (100%)
9909   pieces of canvas [**526**]

Chests (8)
Reed 4; Denny 4
From Denny: 1/3 entries (33%)
9912   4 chests [**1198**]

Pans to make fire in (3)
Reed 0; Denny 3
From Denny: 2/2 entries (100%)
9913   1 round pan [**1140**]
9914   2 square pans [**1141**]

BIBLIOGRAPHIES,
GLOSSARY AND INDEXES

MANUSCRIPTS CONSULTED

Cambridge, St John's College
D.91.12

Guildford Muniment Room, Surrey
Loseley Manuscripts GMR LM 11; GMR LM 22/1; 22/2; GMR LM 30/3; GMR LM 59/46; 59/101; 59/112; 59/142; 59/150

Huntingdon, Hertfordshire County Record Office
HCRO MS 10585

Kew, Public Records Office
PRO C66 Patent Rolls C66/666
PRO E36 Exchequer, Treasury of Receipt E36/171; E36/215; E36/216; E36/225; E36/236; E36/236E36/239; E36/251; E36/252
PRO E101 Exchequer, King's Remembrancer: Various Accounts E101/60/23; E101/417/3; E101/419/16; E101/420/11; E101/421/19; E101/423/10; E101/425/14; E101/426/8; E101/427/2; E101/497/1; E101/546/19; E101/622/31
PRO E179 Exchequer, King's Remembrancer: Particulars of Account and other records relating to Lay and Clerical Taxation E179/388/13
PRO E314 Exchequer, Augmentation Office: Miscellaneous E314/79
PRO E315 Exchequer, Pipe Office: Declared accounts, Miscellaneous Books E315/160; E315/249
PRO E321 Exchequer, Court of Augmentation and Court of General Surveyors: Legal Proceedings E321/44/45
PRO E351 Pipe Office: Declared accounts E351/3322
PRO E403 Exchequer of Receipt: Enrolments and Registers of Issues E403/478
PRO LC5 Lord Chamberlain's Department: Record of Special Events LC5/49
PRO LR2 Exchequer (Land Revenue): Surveyors General and Commissioners of Woods etc Accounts to 1893 LR2/115; LR2/119; LR2/121
PRO OBS1 Obsolete Lists, Indices and Miscellaneous Summaries and Reports associated with the National Archives Holdings OBS 1/1419
PRO PROB11 Prerogative Court of Canterbury: Wills PROB 11/32 (37 Populwell)
PRO SP1 State Papers, Domestic: Henry VIII SP1/70; SP1/228; SP1/232
PRO SP10 State Papers, Domestic: Edward VI SP10/6; SP10/9

London, The British Library
BL Additional MSS 10109; 10602; 21116; 30367; 34561; 46348
BL Additional Rolls 63255; 63256; 63259; 63260; 63263; 63264; 63264A; 63266; 63267; 63268; 63271; 63272; 63273; 63275
BL Arundel MS 97
BL Cotton MS Appendices 29; 89 (formerly 28)
BL Egerton MSS 2679B; 2806
BL Harley MSS 599; 1419; 2284; 4217
BL Lansdowne Rolls 14; 15
BL Otho MS C.X
BL Royal MS 7F.XIV
BL Royal MSS 14B.XLVII; 14B.XXIIA; 14B.XXIIB
BL Royal MS 7C.XVI
BL Stowe MSS 557; 559

London, The British Museum
BM 1850-7-13-14

London, Society of Antiquaries
SA MS 129

London, Westminster Abbey Muniment Room
WAM 4708; 37118; 37119; 37157; 37158; 43046; 14298*; 14299

Nottingham University Library
Newcastle Manuscript NUL Ne.01

Oxford, Bodleian Library
Bod Lib MS English History b 192/1
Bod Lib Rawlinson MS D 776

Washington, DC, Folger Shakespeare Library
MS Z d.11

BIBLIOGRAPHY

This bibliography lists all the books, articles, and printed sources cited in this work. The section *Extended Bibliography* (pp. 229–48 below) provides an overview of relevant literature by category. Printed primary sources are given in alphabetical order of editor where possible.

Printed Primary Sources

A. PRINTED TRANSCRIPTS OF THE 1542 INVENTORY

Burtt, J, 'Inventories of certain valuable effects of king Henry the Eighth, in the Palace of Westminster, AD 1542', *Archaeological Journal* 18 (1861) 134–45 [looking-glasses, musical instruments, clocks, glassware: entries **861–881, 888–943, 1051–1060, 1061–1125**]

Carley, J P, ed, *The Libraries of King Henry VIII* (London 2000) [books: entries **2398–3305**]

Monnas, L, 'Tissues in England during the fifteenth and sixteenth centuries', *CIETA Bulletin* 75 (1998) 62–80 [lengths of tissue: entries **1240–1270**]

Shaw, W A, *Three Inventories of Pictures in the Collections of Henry VIII and Edward VI* (London, 1937) [Full but sometimes inaccurate transcripts, by the author's own admission, of entries **664–823**]

B. OTHER PRINTED PRIMARY SOURCES

Arnold, J, ed, *'Lost from Her Majesties Back'*, Costume Society (Extra Series) 7 (1980)

Baker, A C, ed, 'Extracts from the royal accounts of Henry VIII', *London Topographical Record* 19 (1947) 100–16

Bailey, J E and Fishwick, J, eds, 'Inventories of church goods in the churches and chapels of Lancashire taken in the year AD 1552', *Remains Historical and Literary Connected with the Palatine Counties of Lancaster and Chester*, Cheatham Society (old series) 113 (Manchester, 1888) 57–113

Brewer, J S, Gairdner, J and Brodie, R H, eds, *Letters and Papers, Foreign and Domestic, of the Reign of Henry VIII, 1509–1547*, 21 vols and addenda (London, 1862–1932)

Calendar of Patent Rolls, 1377–1509, 22 vols (London, 1895–1963)

Calendar of Patent Rolls, 1547–8 (London, 1924)

Calendar of Patent Rolls, 1550–3 (London, 1926)

Calendar of Patent Rolls, 1558–60 (London, 1939)

Calendar of Patent Rolls, 1560–3 (London, 1948)

Calendar of State Papers, Spanish, ed G A Bergenroth and P de Gayanos (London, 1862–86)

Calendar of State Papers, Venetian, ed R Brown, C Bentinck and H Brown, 9 vols (London, 1864–98)

Dasent, J R *et al*, *Acts of the Privy Council of England*, 46 vols (London, 1890–1964)

Ellis, H, ed, *Original Letters of Eminent Literary Men of the Sixteenth, Seventeenth and Eighteenth Centuries* (London, 1843)

Knighton, C S, ed, *Calendar of State Papers Domestic Series of the Reign of Edward VI 1547–1553* (London, 1992)

Lang, R G, ed, *Two Tudor Subsidy Assessment Rolls for the City of London: 1541 and 1582*, London Record Society 29 (1993)

The Lisle Letters, ed M St Clair Byrne, 6 vols (Chicago and London, 1981)

Luders, A D *et al*, ed, *Statutes of the Realm*, 11 vols (London, 1819–28)

Madden, F, ed, *The Privy Purse Expenses of Princess Mary 1536–1544* (London, 1831)

Millar, O, ed, *Abraham van der Doort's Catalogue of the Collection of Charles I* (1960)

Myers, A R, ed, *The Household of Edward VI. The Black Book and the Ordinance of 1748* (Manchester, 1959)

Nichols, J G, ed, *Literary Remains of King Edward the Sixth*, Roxburgh Club, 2 vols (London 1857)

——, ed, 'View of the wardrobe stuff of Katherine of Aragon, 1535', *Camden Miscellany* 3 (London, 1855) 23–41

Nicolas, N H, ed, *A Collection of Ordinances and Regulations for the Government of the Royal Household* (London, 1790)

——, ed, *The Privy Purse Expenses of Henry VIII* (London, 1827)

——, ed, *Proceedings and Ordinances of the Privy Council of England, 1386–1542*, 7 vols (1834–7)

Pocock, N, ed, *Troubles Connected with the Prayer Book of 1549*, Camden Society (new series) 37 (London, 1884)

Scattergood, J, ed, *John Skelton. The Complete English Poems* (Harmondsworth, 1983)

Starkey, D R, ed, *The Inventory of King Henry VIII* (London, 1998)

State Papers of the Reign of King Henry the Eighth (London, 1830–52)

Steer, F W, ed, *Scriveners' Company Common Paper 1357–1628*, London Record Society 4 (London, 1968)

Stow, J, *A Survey of London Written in the Year 1598* (Stroud, 1997)

Sylvester, R S, ed, *Life and Death of Wolsey*, Early English Text Society (original series) 243 (1963)

Townsend, G, ed, *The Acts and Monuments of John Foxe*, 5 vols (1843–9)

Trollope, E, ed, 'King Henry VIII's jewel book', *Associated Architectectural Societies Reports and Papers*, 17 (London, 1884) 155–229

Turnbull, W B D D, ed, *Account of the Monastic Treasures Confiscated at the Dissolution of the Various Houses in England*, Abbotsford Club (Edinburgh, 1836)

Secondary Sources

UNPUBLISHED THESES AND PAPERS

Hayward, M A, 'The possessions of Henry VIII: a study of inventories', unpublished PhD thesis, London (1997)

Kisby, F L, 'The royal household chapel in early Tudor London, 1485–1547', unpublished PhD thesis, London (1996)

Melograni, A, 'A place to read: libraries and domestic spaces in Renaissance Italy', paper given at 'Representing Design: 1400 to the Present Day', Design Historical Society Annual Conference, 20–22 September 2001

Merritt, J, 'Religion, government and society in early modern Westminster, 1525–1625', unpublished PhD thesis, London (1992)

Starkey, D R, 'The king's privy chamber, 1485–1547', unpublished PhD thesis, Cambridge (1973)

BOOKS AND ARTICLES

Alexander, J and Binski, P, eds, *Age of Chivalry. Art in Plantagenet England 1200–1400* (London, 1988)

Arnold, J, *Queen Elizabeth's Wardrobe Unlock'd* (Leeds, 1988)

Auerbach, E, 'Vincent Volpe, the king's painter', *Burlington Magazine* 92 (1950) 222–7

Ballie, H M, 'Etiquette and the planning of the state apartments in Baroque palaces', *Archaeologia* 101 (1967) 169–99

Barrett, J and Iredale, D, *Discovering Old Handwriting* (Aylesbury, 1995)

Barron, C M, 'Centres of conspicuous consumption: the aristocratic town house in London 1200–1500', *London Journal* 20 (1995) 1–16

Bernard, G W, 'The rise of Sir William Compton, early Tudor courtier', *English Historical Review* 96 (1981) 754–77

Bickersteth, J and Dunning, R W, *Clerks of the Closet in the Royal Household* (Gloucester, 1991)

Bindoff, S T, *The House of Commons 1509–1558: I Appendices, Constituencies, Members A–C* (London, 1982)

——, *The House of Commons 1509–1558: II Members D–M* (London, 1982)

Blair, C, 'The most superb of all royal locks', *Apollo* 84 (1966) 493–4

Blezzard, J and Palmer, F, 'King Henry VIII: performer, composer and connoisseur of music', *Antiquaries Journal* 80 (2000) 249–72

Brigden, S, *London and the Reformation* (Oxford, 1989)

Briquet, C M, *Les Filranes* (Paris, 1907)

Brown, C M and Lorenzoni, A M, 'The *grotta* of Isabella d'Este, part 1', *Gazette des Beaux-Arts* 89 (1977) 155–71

Campbell, T, 'Tapestry quality in Tudor England: problems of terminology', *Studies in Decorative Arts* 3 (1995–6) 29–50

——, 'Cardinal Wolsey's tapestry collection', *Antiquaries Journal* 76 (1996) 76–137

Carley, J P, 'John Leland and the contents of English pre-dissolution libraries: Lincolnshire', *Transactions of the Cambridge Bibliographical Society* 9 (1989) 330–57

——, 'John Leland and the foundation of the royal library: the Westminster inventory of 1542', *Bulletin of the Society of Renaissance Studies* 7 (1989) 13–20

——, 'Greenwich and Henry VIII's royal library' in *European Court*, ed D R Starkey, 155–9

Challis, C E, 'Lord Hastings to the great silver recoinage, 1464–1699', in *A New History of the Royal Mint*, ed C E Challis (Cambridge, 1992) 179–397

Cheyney, C R, *Handbook of Dates*, Royal Historical Society Guides and Handbooks 4 (London, 1945; reprinted 1991)

Chrimes, S B, *Henry VIII* (London, 1972 {1981?})

Clay, C T, 'The keepership of the old palace of Westminster', *English Historical Review* 59 (1944) 1–21

Collins, A J, ed, *Jewels and Plate of Queen Elizabeth I: the Inventory of 1574* (London, 1955)

Colvin, H M *et al, The History of the King's Works*, 6 vols (London, 1963–82)

Cope, R, 'The "long gallery": its origins, development, use and decoration', *Architectural History* 29 (1986) 43–72

Cunnington, C W and Cunnington, P, *Handbook of English Costume in the Sixteenth Century* (London, 1970)

Davies, C S L, 'The administration of the royal navy under Henry VIII: the origins of the navy board', *English Historical Review* 78 (1965) 268–86

Dawson, G E and Kennedy-Skipton, L, *Elizabethan Handwriting 1500–1650* (London, 1966)

Denny, H L L, 'Biography of the right honourable Sir Anthony Denny', *Transactions of the East Hertfordshire Archaeological Society* 3 (1905) 197–216

Doggett, N, 'The demolition and conversion of former monastic buildings in Hertfordshire at the dissolution', in *Hertfordshire in History: Papers Presented to Lionel Munby*, ed D Jones-Baker (Hertfordshire, 1991) 47–64

Dowling, M, 'The gospel and the court: Reformation under Henry VIII', in *Protestantism and the National Church in Sixteenth Century England*, ed P Lake and M Dowling (Beckenham, 1987) 36–77

Elton, G R, *Reform and Reformation* (London, 1977)

Fairbrass, S and Holmes, K, 'The restoration of Hans Holbein's cartoon of Henry VIII and Henry VII', *Conservator* 10 (1986) 12–16

Foister, S and Campbell, L, 'Gerard, Lucas and Susan Horenbout', *Burlington Magazine* 128 (1986) 719–27

Gaimster, D R M, with contributions by J C Thorn and M R Cowell, 'Appendix II: Armorial stove-tiles excavated in 1939' in Thurley, *Royal Palaces*, 149–61

Gillingham, J, *The Wars of the Roses. Peace and Conflict in Fifteenth-century England* (London, 1981)

Goldthwaite, R, *Wealth and the Demand for Art in Italy, 1300–1600* (Baltimore, 1993)

Green, H J M and Thurley, S J, 'Excavations on the west side of Whitehall, 1960–2 part 1: from the building of the Tudor palace to the construction of the modern offices of state', *Transactions of the London and Middlesex Archaeological Society* 38 (1987) 59–130

Grummitt, D, 'Henry VII, chamber finance and the "New Monarchy": some new evidence', *Historical Research* 72 (1999) 229–43

Gunn, S, 'Running into the sand: the last of the Suffolk line', in *Rivals in Power*, ed D R Starkey, 174–183

Guy, J, *Tudor England* (London, 1990)

Harvey, J H, 'Richard II and York', in *The Reign of Richard II*, ed F R H du Boulay and C M Barron (London, 1971) 202–17

Hawkyard, A, 'From painted chamber to St Stephen's chapel: the meeting places of the Houses of Commons at Westminster until 1603', *Parliamentary History* 21 (2002) 62–84

Hayward, M A, 'Luxury or magnificence? Dress at the court of Henry VIII', *Costume* 30 (1996) 37–46

——, 'Repositories of splendour: Henry VIII's wardrobes of the Robes and Beds', *Textile History* 29 (1998) 134–56

——, 'Seat furniture at the court of Henry VIII', in *Upholstery Conservation Principles and Practice*, ed K Gill and D Eastop (Oxford, 2000) 115–32

Hearn, K, ed, *Dynasties: Painting in Tudor and Jacobean England, 1530–1630* (London, 1995)

Hector, L C, *The Handwriting of English Documents* (Dorking, 1988 (reprint))

Hoak, D, 'The secret history of the Tudor court: the king's coffers and the king's purse, 1542–1553', *Journal of British Studies* 26 (1987) 208–31

Houlbrooke, R A, 'Henry VIII's wills: a comment', *Historical Journal* 37 (1994) 891–899

Howard, M, *The Early Tudor Country House: Architecture and Politics 1490–1550* (London, 1987)

Hoyle, R, 'War and public finance', in *The Reign of Henry VIII: Politics, Policy and Piety*, ed D MacCulloch (London, 1995) 75–99

Hudson, W S, *The Cambridge Connection and the Elizabethan Settlement of 1559* (Durham NC, 1980)

Hurstfield, J and Smith, A R G, eds, *Elizabethan People: State and Society* (London, 1972)

Ives, E W, 'Henry VIII's will: a forensic conundrum', *Historical Journal* 35 (1992) 779–804

Jackson-Stops, G, 'Purchases and perquisites: the 6th earl of Dorset's furniture at Knole', *Country Life* (1977) 1620–2

Jardine, L, *Worldly Goods: a New History of the Renaissance* (London, 1996)

Jenkinson, H, *The Later Court Hands in England from the Fifteenth to the Seventeenth Century*, 2 vols (Cambridge, 1927)

Knighton, C S, *Acts of the Dean and Chapter of Westminster. Part I: The First Collegiate Church (1543–1556)* (Woodbridge, 1997)

Knighton, C S and Loades, D M, eds, *The Anthony Roll of Henry VIII's Navy*, Occasional Publications of the Navy Record Society 2 (2000)

Lightbown, R W, *Secular Goldsmiths' Work in Medieval France: a History* (London, 1978)

Loach, J, *Edward VI* (New Haven and London, 1999)

MacCulloch, D, *Tudor Church Militant: Edward VI and the Protestant Reformation* (London, 1999)

Miller, H, 'Henry VIII's unwritten will: grants of land and honours in 1547', in *Wealth and Power in Tudor England: Essays Presented to S T Bindoff*, ed E W Ives, R J Knecht and J J Scarisbrick (London, 1978) 87–105

Mills, J S and White, R, *The Organic Chemistry of Museum Objects* (London, 1987)

Mitchell, D M, 'Coverpanes: their nature and use in Tudor England', *CIETA Bulletin* 75 (1998) 81–96

Monnas, L, 'Loom widths and selvedges prescribed by Italian silk weaving statutes 1265–1512: a preliminary investigation', *CIETA Bulletin* 66 (1988) 35–44

Murphy, J, 'The illusion of decline: the Privy Chamber, 1547–1588', in *English Court from Wars of Roses to Civil War*, ed D R Starkey (1987) 119–46

Oppenheim, M, *A History of the Administration of the Royal Navy and of Merchant Shipping in Relation to the Navy* (London, 1896)

Plumb, J H, *Royal Heritage* (London, 1977)

Prockter, A and Taylor, R, *The A to Z of Elizabethan London* London Topographical Society Publications 122 (London, 1979)

Reese, M M, *The Royal Office of the Master of the Horse* (London 1976)

Richardson, G, '"Most highly to be regarded": The privy chamber of Henry VIII and Anglo-French relations, 1515–1520', *Court Historian* 4 (1999) 119–40

Richardson, W C, *Tudor Chamber Administration 1485–1547* (Baton Rouge, 1952)

——, *History of the Court of Augmentations 1536–1554* (Baton Rouge, 1961)

Roberts, J, *Holbein and the Court of Henry VIII* (London 1993)

Rosser, G A, *Medieval Westminster, 1200–1540* (Oxford, 1989)

Rosser, G and Thurley, S, 'Whitehall Palace and King Street: the urban cost of princely magnificence', *London Topographical Record*, 26 (1990) 57–77

Routh, C R N, *Who's Who in Tudor England* (London, 1964, revised 1990)

Rye, W B, *England as Seen by Foreigners in the Days of Elizabeth and James I* (London, 1865)

Saunders, A, *Regent's Park: a Study of the Development of the Area from 1086 to the Present Day* (London, 1969)

Scammell, G V, 'War at sea under the early Tudors: part 2', *Archaeol Aeliana* (4th series) 39 (1961) 179–205

Scarisbrick, D, *Jewellery in Britain 1066–1837: A Documentary, Social, Literary and Artistic Survey* (Norwich, 1994)

——, *Tudor and Jacobean Jewellery* (London, 1995)

Scarisbrick, J J, *Henry VIII* (London, 1991)

Scott-Fleming, S, *Pen Flourishing in Thirteenth-Century Manuscripts* (Leiden, 1989)

Shirley, T F, *Thomas Thirlby, Tudor Bishop* (London, 1964)

Sil, N P, 'The rise and fall of Sir John Gates', *Historical Journal* 24 (1981) 929–43

——, '"Jentell Mr Heneage": A forgotten Tudor servant', *Notes and Queries* 229 (1984) 169–72

——, 'Sir Anthony Denny: a Tudor servant in office', *Renaissance and Reformation* 8 (1984) 190–201

Slavin, A J, *Politics and Profit: A Study of Sir Ralph Sadler, 1507–1547* (Cambridge, 1966)

Smith, J T, *English Houses 1200–1800: the Hertfordshire Evidence* (London, 1992)

——, *Hertfordshire Houses: Selective Inventory* (London, 1993)

Starkey, D R, 'Representations through intimacy: a study in the symbolism of monarchy and court office in early modern England', in *Symbols and Sentiments: Cross-Cultural Studies in Symbolism*, ed I Lewis (London, 1977) 187–224

——, *The Reign of Henry VIII: Personalities and Politics* (1985, reprinted 1991)

——, 'Introduction: court history in perspective', in *English Court from Wars of Roses to Civil War*, ed D R Starkey (1987) 1–24

——, 'Intimacy and innovation: the rise of the Privy Chamber', in *English Court from Wars of Roses to Civil War*, ed D R Starkey (1987) 71–118

——, 'The legacy of Henry VIII', in *European Court*, ed D R Starkey (1987) 8–13

——, 'Tudor government: the facts?' *Historical Journal* 31 (1988) 923–4

——, *Elizabeth* (London, 2001)

Starkey, D R, ed, *The English Court from the Wars of the Roses to the Civil War* (London and New York, 1987)

——, *Rivals in Power: Lives and Letters of the Great Tudor Dynasties* (London, 1990)

——, *Henry VIII: A European Court in England* (London, 1991)

Stephen, S and Lee, S, eds, *The Dictionary of National Biography from the Earliest Times to 1900*, 22 vols plus supplement (London, 1921–90)

Storey, R L, 'Gentlemen bureaucrats', in *Profession, Vocation and Culture in Later Medieval England*, ed C H Clough (Liverpool, 1982) 90–129

String, T C, 'A neglected Henrician decorative ceiling', *Antiquaries Journal*, 76 (1996) 139–51

Strong, R, *The Renaissance Garden in England* (London, 1979, 1998)

Strype, J, *Ecclesiastical Memorials*, II.ii (Oxford, 1822)

Swaine, M, *Tapestries and Textiles at the Palace of Holyrood House in the Royal Collection* (London, 1988)

Swensen, P C, 'Patronage from the Privy Chamber: Sir Anthony Denny and religious reform', *Journal of British Studies*, 27 (1988) 25–44

Sylvester, R S, ed, *The Life and Death of Cardinal Wolsey*, Early English Text Society 143 (1959)

Thornton, P, *Seventeenth-Century Interior Decoration in England, France and Holland* (New Haven and London, 1978)

Thurley, S J, 'Henry VIII and the building of Hampton Court: a reconstruction of the Tudor palace', *Architectural History* 31 (1988) 1–51

——, 'The domestic building works of Cardinal Wolsey', in *Cardinal Wolsey: Church, State and Art*, ed S J Gunn and P Lindley (Cambridge, 1991) 76–102

——, 'Greenwich Palace' in *European Court*, ed D R Starkey (1991) 20–5

——, *The Royal Palaces of Tudor England: Architecture and Court Life 1460–1547* (New Haven and London, 1993)

——, *The Whitehall Palace Plan of 1670*, London Topographical Society Publications 153 (1998)

——, *Whitehall Palace: an Architectural History of the Royal Apartments, 1240–1690* (New Haven and London, 1999)

Turner, G, 'Lord Pembroke's inventory of 1561', *Journal of the Silver Society*, 11 (1999) 189–195

Wordsworth, C, 'Inventories of plate, vestments etc. belonging to the cathedral church of the blessed Mary of Lincoln', *Archaeologia* 53 (1892) 2–82

EXTENDED BIBLIOGRAPHY

THIS BIBLIOGRAPHY provides a comprehensive, but not exhaustive, overview of the literature relating to the various groups of objects recorded in the 1542 and the 1547 inventories. It includes introductory works and more specialist articles and the inclusion or exclusion of references tends to reflect the bias of the documents themselves. For example, the section on textiles mainly includes articles on silk because silk was the predominant material used for the clothing and furnishings recorded in these inventories. In chronological terms, the bibliography concentrates on the period from *c.*1500 to *c.*1550 but pertinent articles from *c.*1450 to *c.*1600 have been included. Where relevant, some of the entries have been expanded to include references to particular artists or craftsmen who produced the objects or to the individuals within the household who worked with them. The references are arranged by object type:

ARMS, ARMOUR AND ORDNANCE[1]

ART AND ARTISTS

BOOKS

CARPETS

CERAMICS

CLOCKS AND SCIENTIFIC INSTRUMENTS

DAMASK, NAPERY AND DINING

DRESS AND ACCESSORIES

ECCLESIASTICAL TEXTILES

EMBROIDERY

FURNISHINGS AND FURNITURE

FURS

GLASS

HAWKS, HORSES AND HOUNDS

ILLUSTRATED AND ILLUMINATED
    MANUSCRIPTS

JEWELLERY

MAPS AND GLOBES

MISCELLANEOUS

MUSIC AND MUSICAL INSTRUMENTS

PLATE AND MEDALS

SHIPS AND NAVAL ORDNANCE

TAPESTRIES

TEXTILES

---

1 I would like to thank Claude Blair for sending me a detailed bibliography for Henry VIII's arms and armour, which I have made use of here.

ARMS, ARMOUR AND ORDNANCE[1]

Beard, C R, 'The clothing and arming of the Yeomen of the Guard', *Archaeological Journal* 32 (1928) 93

Biasini, V and Cristoferi, E, 'A study of the corrosion products on sixteenth and seventeenth century armour from the Ravenna National Museum', *Studies in Conservation* 40 (1995) 250–6

Blackmore, H L, *Arms and Armour* (New York, 1965)

——, *Royal Sporting Guns at Windsor* (London, 1968)

——, *Hunting Weapons* (London, 1971)

——, *The Armouries of the Tower of London. 1 The Ordnance* (1976)

——, *A Dictionary of London Gunmakers 1350–1850* (London, 1986)

——, 'An archery bill for Henry VIII, 1547', *Journal of the Society of Archer-Antiquaries* 32 (1989) 5–8

Blair, C, *European Armour c. 1066 to c. 1700* (London, 1958)

——, 'New light on four Almain armours, part 1', *Connoisseur* 144 (1959) 17–20

——, 'New light on four Almain armours, part 2', *Connoisseur* 144 (1959) 240–4

——, *European and American Arms, c. 1100–1850* (London, 1962)

——, 'The Emperor Maximilian's gift of armour to King Henry VIII', *Archaeologia* 99 (1965) 1–52

——, 'A royal swordsmith and damascener: Diego de Caias', *Metropolitan Museum Journal* 3 (1970) 149–98

——, 'Comments on Dr Borg's "Horned Helmet"', *Journal of the Arms and Armour Society* 8 (1974–6) 138–85

——, 'King Henry VIII's silvered and engraved armour', *Apollo* 129 (1989) 266–7

——, 'King Henry VIII's tonlet armour', *Journal of the Arms and Armour Society* 15 (1995–7) 85–108

Blair, C and Delamer, I, 'The Dublin civic swords', *Proceedings of the Royal Irish Academy* 88 (1988) 87–142

Borg, A, 'The Rams horn helmet', *Journal of the Arms and Armour Society* 8 (1974–6) 127–37

——, 'A royal axe?' *Connoisseur* 188 (1975) 296–301

——, 'Two studies in the history of the Tower armouries', *Archaeologia* 105 (1976) 317–52

——, 'The Spanish armoury in the Tower', *Archaeologia* 105 (1976) 332–52

Cowgill, J, de Neergaard, M and Griffiths, N, *Knives and Scabbards*, Medieval Finds from Excavations in London 1 (London, 1987)

Credland, A G, 'The pellet bow in Europe and the East', *Journal of the Society of Archer-Antiquaries* 18 (1975) 13–21

——, 'The hunting crossbow in England', *Journal of the Society of Archer-Antiquaries* 30 (1987) 40–60

——, 'The longbow in the sixteenth and seventeenth centuries', *Journal of the Society of Archer-Antiquaries* 32 (1989) 9–23

Dalton, O M, 'A late medieval bracer in the British Museum', *Antiquaries Journal* 11 (1922) 208–10

Dillon, H A, 'Feathers and plumes', *Archaeological Journal* 53 (1896) 126–39

Eaves, I, 'The tournament armours of King Henry VIII of England', *Livrust Kammaren* (1993) 3–45

Edwards, I and Blair, C, 'Welsh bucklers', *Antiquaries Journal* 62 (1982) 74–115

Ffoulkes, C, 'Some aspects of the craft of the armourer', *Archaeologia* 79 (1929) 13–28

Hayward, J F, 'English firearms in the sixteenth century', *Journal of the Arms and Armour Society* 3 (1959) 117–41

——, *The Art of the Gunmaker*, 2 vols (London, 1962–3)

Jackson, H, *English Hand Firearms in the Sixteenth, Seventeenth and Eighteenth Centuries* (London, 1959)

Lumpkin, H, 'The pictures of Henry VIII's army in Cotton Manuscript Augustus III', *Journal of the Arms and Armour Society* 3 (1959–60) 145–70

Mann, J, 'The exhibition of Greenwich armour at the Tower of London', *Burlington Magazine* 43 (1951) 378–83

——, *Wallace Collection Catalogue of European Arms and Armour: volume I, Armour* (London, 1962)

——, *Wallace Collection Catalogue of European Arms and Armour: volume II, Arms* (London, 1962)

Nickel, H, '"Harnes all gilte": a study of the armour of Galiot de Genouilhac and the iconography of its decoration', *Metropolitan Museum Journal* 5 (1972) 75–124

Oman, C C, *The Art of War in the Sixteenth Century* (London, 1937)

Pfaffenbichler, M, *Medieval Craftsmen: Armourers* (London, 1992)

Reid, W, 'A royal crossbow in the Scott collection, part 1', *Scottish Art Review* 7 (1959) 10–13

——, 'A royal crossbow in the Scott collection, part 2', *Scottish Art Review* 7 (1959) 29–30

Schubert, H, 'The first cast iron canon made in England', *Journal of the Iron and Steel Institute* 146 (1942) 13

Stone, G C, *A Glossary of the Construction, Decoration and use of the Arms and Armour in all Countries at All Times* (Portland, Maine, 1934)

Tout, T F, 'Firearms in England in the fourteenth century', *English Historical Review* 26 (1911) 666–702

Watts, K N, 'Henry VIII and the pageantry of the Tudor tournament', *Livrust Kammaren* (1993) 131–41

Williams, A and de Reuck, A, *The Royal Armoury at Greenwich 1515–1649*, Royal Armouries Monograph 4 (Leeds, 1995)

ART AND ARTISTS

Anglo, S, 'The Hampton Court painting of the Field of the Cloth of Gold considered as an historical document', *Antiquaries Journal* 46 (1966) 304–7

Arnold, J, 'The coronation portrait of Elizabeth I', *Burlington Magazine* 120 (1978) 727–41

Auerbach, E, 'Vincent Volpe, the king's painter', *Burlington Magazine* 92 (1950) 222–7

——, 'Holbein's followers in England', *Burlington Magazine*, 93 (1951) 44–51

——, 'Illuminated royal portraits', *Burlington Magazine*, 93 (1951) 300–3

——, *Tudor Artists* (London, 1954)

——, 'Notes on Flemish miniatures in England', *Burlington Magazine*, 96 (1954) 51–3

Binski, P, *Medieval Craftsmen: Painters* (London, 1991)

Black, W H, 'On the date and other circumstances of the death of Hans Holbein', *Archaeologia* 39 (1863) 272–6

Black, W H and Franks, A W, 'Discovery of the will of Hans Holbein', *Archaeologia* 39 (1863) 1–18

Borenius, T, 'Two little known pictures by Holbein in England', *Burlington Magazine* 83 (1943) 285–6

Brown, C M and Lorenzoni, A M, 'The *grotta* of Isabella d'Este, part 1', *Gazette des Beaux-Arts* 89 (1977) 155–71

——, 'The *grotta* of Isabella d'Este, part 2', *Gazette des Beaux-Arts* 91 (1978) 72–82

Campbell, L, 'The art market in the southern Netherlands in the fifteenth century', *Burlington Magazine* 118 (1976) 188–98

——, *The Early Flemish Pictures in the Collection of Her Majesty the Queen* (Cambridge, 1985)

Campbell, L *et al*, 'Quentin Matsys, Desiderus Erasmus, Pieter Gillis and Thomas More', *Burlington Magazine* 120 (1978) 716–24

Carr, D W and Leonard, M, *Looking at Paintings* (Malibu and London, 1992)

Chamberlain, A B, 'Holbein's visit to High Burgony', *Burlington Magazine* 21 (1912) 25–30

Clough, C H, 'Federigo da Montefeltro's private study in his ducal palace of Gubbio', *Apollo* 68 (1967) 278–87

Colding, T H, *Aspects of Miniature Painting* (Copenhagen, 1953)

Cole, A, *Art of the Italian Renaissance Courts* (London, 1995)

Colvin, S, 'On a portrait of Erasmus by Holbein', *Burlington Magazine* 16 (1909–10) 67–71

Cust, L, 'A portrait of Queen Catherine Howard by Hans Holbein the Younger', *Burlington Magazine* 17 (1910) 193–9

Fletcher, J, 'A group of royal portraits painted soon after 1513: a dendrochronological study', *Studies in Conservation* 21 (1976) 171–8

——, 'Tree-ring dating of Tudor portraits', *Proceedings of the Royal Institute of Great Britain* 52 (1980) 81–104

——, 'A portrait of William Carey and Lord Hunsdon's long gallery', *Burlington Magazine* 123 (1981) 304

Fletcher, J and Trapp, M C, 'Hans Holbein the Younger at Antwerp and in England 1526–8', *Apollo* 117 (1983) 87–93

Foister, S, 'Paintings and other works of art in sixteenth-century English inventories', *Burlington Magazine* 123 (1981) 273–82

——, *Drawings by Holbein from the Royal Library, Windsor Castle* (London, 1983)

——, 'Tudor collections and collectors', *History Today* 35 (1985) 20–6

——, 'Holbein as court painter', in *European Court*, ed D R Starkey (1991) 58–63

Foister, S and Campbell, L, 'Gerard, Lucas and Susan Horenbout', *Burlington Magazine* 128 (1986) 719–27

Ganz, P, 'A new portrait of Sir John Godsalve by Hans Holbein the Younger', *Burlington Magazine* 26 (1914) 46–7

——, 'The last work of Hans Holbein the Younger', *Apollo* 2 (1925) 326–7

——, 'A rediscovered portrait of Charles Brandon, Duke of Suffolk by Holbein', *Burlington Magazine* 57 (1930) 59–63

——, 'Henry VIII and his court painter, Hans Holbein', *Burlington Magazine* 63 (1933) 146–55

——, 'Holbein and Henry VIII', *Burlington Magazine* 83 (1943) 269–73

——, *The Paintings of Hans Holbein* (London, 1950)

Grossmann, F, 'Holbein, Torrigiano and some portraits of Dean Collet', *Journal of the Warburg and Courtauld Institutes* 13 (1950) 202–36

——, 'Holbein, Flemish painting and Everhard Jabach', *Burlington Magazine* 93 (1951) 16–25

——, 'Holbein studies, part 1', *Burlington Magazine* 93 (1951) 39–44

——, 'Holbein studies, part 2', *Burlington Magazine* 93 (1951) 111–14

——, 'A religious allegory by Hans Holbein', *Burlington Magazine* 103 (1961) 491–4

Harley, R D, *Artists' Pigments 1600–1835* (London, 1982)

Harvey, J H, 'Some London painters of the fourteenth and fifteenth centuries', *Burlington Magazine* 89 (1947) 303–5

Hearn, K, ed, *Dynasties: Painting in Tudor and Jacobean England 1530–1630* (London, 1995)

Hepburn, F, *Portraits of the Later Plantagenets* (Woodbridge, 1986)

Higgins, A, 'On the work of Florentine sculptors in England in the early part of the sixteenth century', *Archaeological Journal* 51 (1894) 131–99

Hill, G and Pollard, G, *Medals in the Renaissance* (London, 1978)

Ives, E, 'The queen and the painters: Anne Boleyn, Holbein and Tudor royal portraits', *Apollo* 134 (1994) 36–45

James, S E, 'Lady Jane Grey or Queen Kateryn Parr?', *Burlington Magazine* 138 (1996) 20–4

Kosinova, A, 'The conservation of the portrait bust of Giovanni de' Medici (later Pope Leo X)', *V&A Conservation Journal* 17 (1995) 14–15

Lebel, G, 'British-French artistic relations in the late sixteenth century', *Gazette des Beaux-Arts* 32 (1948) 278

Lloyd, C, *The Royal Collection* (London, 1992)

Millar, O, *The Tudor, Stuart and Early Georgian Pictures in the Collections of Her Majesty the Queen*, 2 vols (London, 1963)

Mitchell, M, 'Works of art from Rome for Henry VIII', *Journal of the Warburg and Courtauld Institutes* 34 (1971) 178–203

Necipoglu, G, 'Süleyman the Magnificent and the representation of power in the context of Ottoman-Hapsburg-Papal rivalry', *The Art Bulletin* 71 (1989) 401–27

Nevinson, J L, 'Portraits of the Gentleman Pensioners before 1625', *Walpole Society* 34 (1952–4) 1–13

Nichols, F M, 'On some works executed by Hans Holbein during his first visit to England 1526–9', *Proceedings of the Society Antiquaries* (2nd series) 17 (1897–9) 132–45

Nichols, J G, 'Notice of the contemporaries and successors of Holbein', *Archaeologia* 39 (1863) 19–46

Pächt, O, 'Holbein and Kratzer as collaborators', *Burlington Magazine* 81 (1944) 134–9

Paget, H, 'Gerard and Lucas Hornebolt in England', *Burlington Magazine* 150 (1959) 396–402

Parker, K T, *The Drawing of Hans Holbein in the Collection of His Majesty the King at Windsor* (Oxford and London, 2nd edition, 1945)

Popham, A E, 'Hans Holbein's Italian contemporaries in England', *Burlington Magazine* 84 (1944) 12–17

Reader, F W, 'Tudor domestic wall painting, 1', *Archaeological Journal* 42 (1936) 243–86

——Reader, 'Tudor domestic wall painting, 2', *Archaeological Journal* 43 (1937) 220–62

Reynolds, G, *The Sixteenth- and Seventeenth-Century Miniatures in the Collection of Her Majesty the Queen* (London, 1999)

Rowlands, J, *Holbein: The Paintings of Hans Holbein the Younger* (Oxford, 1985)

Rowlands, J and Starkey, D R, 'An old tradition reasserted: Holbein's portrait of Anne Boleyn', *Burlington Magazine* 125 (1983) 83–92

St John Hope, W H, 'On the sculptured alabaster heads called St John's Heads', *Archaeologia* 52 (1890) 669–708

Scharf, G, 'On a votive painting of St George and the dragon with kneeling figures of Henry VII, his Queen and children, formerly at Strawberry Hill and now in the possession of Her Majesty the Queen', *Archaeologia* 49 (1886) 243–300

Shaw, W A, 'An early English pre-Holbein school of portraiture', *Connoisseur* 30 (1911) 72

——, 'The early English school of portraiture', *Burlington Magazine* 65 (1934) 171–84

Strong, R, 'Holbein's cartoon for the Barber-Surgeons group rediscovered', *Burlington Magazine* 55 (1963) 4–14

——, 'More Tudor artists', *Burlington Magazine* 108 (1966) 83–5

——, *Holbein and Henry VIII* (London, 1967)

——, 'Holbein in England, part 1', *Burlington Magazine* 109 (1967) 276–81

——, 'Holbein in England, part 2', *Burlington Magazine* 109 (1967) 700–2

——, *The National Portrait Gallery: Tudor and Jacobean Portraits*, 2 vols (London, 1969)

——, *Tudor and Jacobean Portraits* (London, 1969)

——, *Artists of the Tudor Court* (London, 1983)

Tatlock, R, 'Sir Bryan Tuke by Holbein', *Burlington Magazine* 43 (1923) 246–51

Winter, C, 'Holbein's miniatures', *Burlington Magazine* 83 (1943) 266–9

Wortley, C S, 'The portrait of Thomas Wriothesley, Earl of Southampton, by Holbein', *Burlington Magazine* 57 (1930) 82–6

BOOKS AND ILLUSTRATIONS

Armstrong, E, 'English purchases of printed books from the Continent, 1465–1526', *English Historical Review* 94 (1979) 268–90

Auerbach, E, 'Early English engravings', *Burlington Magazine* 94 (1952) 326–30

Axton, M and Carley J P, eds, *Triumphs of English: Henry Parker, Lord Morley, Translator to the Tudor Court* (London, 2000)

Birrell, T A, *English Monarchs and Their Books* (London, 1987)

Bosanquet, E F, 'The personal prayer-book of John of Lancaster, Duke of Bedford, KG', *Library* 13 (1933) 148–55

Carley, J P, 'John Leland at Somerset libraries', *Proceedings of the Somerset Archaeological and Natural History Society* 129 (1985) 141–54

——, 'John Leland and the contents of the English pre-Dissolution libraries: Glastonbury Abbey', *Scriptorum* 40 (1986) 107–19

——, 'John Leland and the foundation of the royal library: the Westminster inventory of 1542', *Bulletin of the Society of Renaissance Studies* 7 (1989) 13–20

——, 'John Leland and the contents of the English pre-Dissolution libraries: Lincolnshire', *Transactions of the Cambridge Bibliographical Society* 9 (1989) 330–57

——, 'Books seen by Samuel Ward "In Bibliotheca Regia", circa 1614', *British Library Journal* 16 (1990) 89–98

——, 'Greenwich and Henry VIII's royal library', in *European Court*, ed D R Starkey (1991) 155–9

——, 'The royal library as a source for Sir Robert Cotton's collection', *British Library Journal* 18 (1992) 52–73

——, 'Marks in books and the libraries of Henry VIII', *Papers of the Bibliographical Society of America* 91 (1997) 583–606

——, '"Her moost lovyng and fryndely brother sendeth gretyng": Anne Boleyn's manuscripts and their sources', in *Illuminating the Book: Makers and Interpreters*, ed M P Brown and S McKendrick (London and Toronto, 1998) 261–80

Carley, J P, ed, *The Libraries of King Henry VIII*, Corpus of British Medieval Library Catalogues 7 (London, 2000)

Carley, J P and Tite, C, 'Sir Robert Cotton as collector of manuscripts and the question of dismemberment: British Library MSS Royal 13.D.1 and Cotton Otho D VIII', *Library* (6th series) 14 (1992) 94–9

Davis, N Z, 'Beyond the market: books as gifts in sixteenth-century France', *Transactions of the Royal Historical Society* 33 (1983) 69–88

Dodgson, C, 'Woodcuts designed by Holbein for English printers', *Walpole Society* 27 (1938–9) 1–11

——, 'Additional notes to woodcuts designed by Holbein for English printers', *Walpole Society* 28 (1939–40) 95

Floyer, J K, 'The Medieval library of the Benedictine priory of St Mary in Worcester cathedral church', *Archaeologia* 58 (1902) 561–70

Foot, M M, 'English decorative book bindings', in *Book Production and Publishing in Britain 1375–1475*, ed J Griffiths and D Pearsall (Cambridge, 1989) 65–86

Glenn, J, 'A sixteenth-century library: the Francis Trigge chained library of St Wulfram's church, Grantham', in *Early Tudor England*, ed D Williams, Proceedings of the Harlaxton Symposium 1987 (Woodbridge, 1989) 61–72

Kekewich, M, 'Edward IV, William Caxton and literary patronage in Yorkist England', *Modern Language Review* 66 (1971) 481–7

Liddell, J R, 'Leland's lists of manuscripts in Lincolnshire monasteries', *English Historical Review* 54 (1939) 88–95

Meale, C M, 'Patrons, buyers and owners: book production and social status', in *Book Production and Publishing in Britain 1375–1475*, ed J Griffiths and D Pearsall (Cambridge, 1989) 201–38

Nixon, H M, *Five Centuries of English Bookbinding* (London, 1978)

Rebecchini, G, 'The book collection and other possessions of Baldassarre Castiglione', *Journal of the Warburg and Courtauld Institutes* 61 (1998) 17–52

Saxl, F, 'Holbein's illustrations to the "Praise of Folly" by Erasmus', *Burlington Magazine* 83 (1943) 275–9

Somerville, R, 'The Cowcher books of the duchy of Lancaster', *English Historical Review* 51 (1936) 598–615

Stratford, J, 'The royal library in England before the reign of Edward IV', in *England in the Fifteenth Century*, ed N Rogers, Proceedings of the Harlaxton Symposium 1992 (Stamford, 1994) 187–97

Sutton, A F and Visser-Fuchs, L, *Richard III's Books* (London and Gloucester, 1997)

Tudor-Craig, P, 'The hours of Edward V and William, Lord Hastings: British Library Manuscript Additional 54782', in *England in the Fifteenth Century*, ed D Williams, Proceedings of the Harlaxton Symposium 1986 (Woodbridge, 1987) 351–69

——, 'Henry VIII and King David', in *Early Tudor England*, ed D Williams, Proceedings of the Harlaxton Symposium 1987 (Woodbridge, 1989) 185–205

Weiss, R, 'Henry VI and the library of All Souls College', *English Historical Review* 57 (1942) 102–5

Wormald, F and Wright, C E, eds, *The English Library before 1700* (London, 1958)

CARPETS

King, D, 'The inventories of the carpets of Henry VIII', *Hali* 5 (1983) 287–96

——, 'The carpet collection of Cardinal Wolsey', *Oriental Carpet and Textile Studies* 1 (1985) 41–54

——, 'The carpet collection of Charles I', *Oriental Carpet and Textile Studies* 3 (1987) 22–6

King, D and Sylvester, D, eds, *The Eastern Carpet in the Western World From the 15th to the 17th Century* (London, 1983)

Mills, J, *Carpets in Paintings* (London, 1983)

van de Put, A, 'A fifteenth-century Spanish carpet', *Burlington Magazine* 45 (1924) 119–20

CERAMICS

Eames, E, *Medieval Craftsmen: English Tilers* (London, 1992)

von Erdberg, J P, 'Maiolica by known artists in the collection of the Musée de Cluny', *Burlington Magazine* 92 (1950) 283–7

Godden, G A, *An Illustrated Encyclopaedia of British Pottery and Porcelain* (London, 1966)

Goldthwaite, R A, 'The economic and social world of Italian Renaissance maiolica', *Renaissance Quarterly* 42 (1989) 1–32

Rackham, B, 'Early Tudor pottery', *Transactions of the English Ceramic Circle* 2 (1938) 18

——, *Italian Maiolica* (London, 1952)

CLOCKS AND SCIENTIFIC INSTRUMENTS

Armstrong, C A J, 'An Italian astrologer at the court of Henry VIII', in *England, France and Burgundy in the Fifteenth Century*, ed C A J Armstrong (London, 1983) 157–78

Bruce, J, 'Description of a pocket dial made in 1593 for Robert Devereux, Earl of Essex', *Archaeologia* 40 (1866) 343–56

Cipolla, C M, *Clocks and Culture* (London, 1967)

Dodgson, C, 'Holbein's design for Sir Anthony Denny's clock', *Burlington Magazine* 58 (1931) 226–31

Evans, L, 'On a portable sundial of gilt brass made for Cardinal Wolsey', *Archaeologia* 57 (1901) 331–4

Ginerich, O, 'Apianus' Astronomicum Caesareum', *Journal for the History of Astronomy* 2 (1971) 168–77

Gunther, R T, 'The astrolabe: its uses and derivatives', *Scottish Geographical Magazine* 43 (1927) 135–47

——, *The Astrolabes of the World*, 2 vols (Oxford, 1932)

Heller, B and Heller, H, *The Astronomical Clock at Hampton Court* (London, 1973)

Jagger, C, *Royal Clocks* (London, 1983)

Landes, D S, *Revolution in Time* (Cambridge, MA and London, 1983)

Lloyd, H A, *Some Outstanding Clocks Over Seven Hundred Years 1250–1950* (London, 1958)

Maddison, F R, 'Early astronomical and mathematical instruments', *British Journal for the History of Science* 2 (1963) 17–50

North, J D, 'Nicholas Kratzer: the king's astronomer', in *Studies in Honour of Edward Rosen (Studia Copernica)* 16 (1978) 205–34

Robertson, J D, *The Evolution of Clockwork* (London, 1931)

Tait, H, *Clocks and Watches* (London, 1983)

Tait, H and Coole, P G, *Catalogue of Watches in the British Museum*, I (London, 1987)

Taylor, E G R, *The Mathematical Practitioners of Tudor and Stuart England* (Cambridge, 1967)

Thorndike, L, 'Invention of the mechanical clock about AD 1271', *Speculum* 16 (1941) 242–3

Turner, A J, 'Sundials: history and classification', *British Journal for the History of Science* 27 (1989) 303–18

Turner, G L, 'Mathematical instrument-making in London in the sixteenth century', in *English Map Making 1500–1650*, ed S Tyacke (London, 1983) 93–106

White, G S J, 'A stone polyhedral sundial dated 1520', *Antiquaries Journal* 66 (1987) 372–3

DAMASK, NAPERY AND DINING

Cavallo, A S, 'Continental sources of early damask patterns in Scotland', *Burlington Magazine* 107 (1965) 559–63

Marshall, R K, 'The queen's table', in *Tools and Traditions*, ed H Cheape (Edinburgh, 1993) 138–43

Mitchell, D M, '"By your leave my masters": British taste in table linen in the fifteenth and sixteenth centuries', *Textile History* 20 (1989) 49–76

——, 'Coverpanes: their nature and use in Tudor England', *CIETA Bulletin* 75 (1998) 81–96

——, 'Linen damasks of the early 16th century from written sources', in *Leinendamaste. Produktionszentren und Sammlungen*, ed R Schorta (Riggisberg, 1999) 179–200

Prinet, M, *La Damas de Lin Historic du XVIe au XIXe Siecle Ouvrage de Haute-Lice* (Berne, 1982)

Réunion des Musée Nationaux, *Versailles et les Tables Royales en Europe* (Paris, 1993)

Wilson, C A, ed, *'Banquetting Stuffe': the Fare and Social Background of the Tudor and Stuart Banquet* (Edinburgh, 1991)

van Ysselsteyn, G T, *White Figured Linen Damask from the Fifteenth Century to the Beginning of the Nineteenth Century* (Van Goor Zonen den Haag, 1962)

DRESS AND ACCESSORIES

Arnold, J, 'Decorative features: pinking, snipping and slashing', *Costume* 9 (1975) 22–6

——, 'Fashion in miniature', *Costume* 11 (1977) 45–55

——, *Patterns of Fashion: the Cut and Construction of Clothes for Men and Women c. 1560–1620* (London, 1985, revised 1986)

——, *Queen Elizabeth's Wardrobe Unlock'd* (Leeds, 1988)

——, 'Costumes for masques and other entertainments c. 1500–1650', *Historical Dance*, 3 (1993) 3–20

——, 'Serpents and flowers: embroidered designs from Trevelyon's miscellanies of 160 and 1616', *Costume* 34 (2000) 7–12

Ashelford, J, *A Visual History of Costume: the Sixteenth Century* (London, 1983)

Carter, A, 'Mary Tudor's wardrobe', *Costume* 18 (1984) 9–28

Egan, G and Pritchard, F, *Dress Accessories c. 1150–c. 1450*, Medieval Finds from Excavations in London 3 (1991)

Grew, F and de Neergaard, M, *Shoes and Pattens*, Medieval Finds from Excavations in London 2 (1988)

Hayward, M A, 'Luxury or magnificence? Dress at the court of Henry VIII', *Costume* 30 (1996) 37–46

Marshall, R K, '"Hir Rob Ryall": the costume of Mary of Guise', *Costume* 12 (1978) 1–12

——, '"To be the king's grace ane dowblett": the costume of James V, King of Scots', *Costume* 28 (1994) 14–21

Monnas, M, 'The cloth of gold of the pourpoint of the blessed Charles de Blois: a pannus Tartaricus?', *CIETA Bulletin* 70 (1992) 117–29

Nevinson, J L, 'Prince Edward's clothes', *Costume* 2 (1968) 3–8

Norris, H, *Costume and Fashion: volume III, pt I The Tudors 1485–1547* (London, 1938)

Staniland, K, 'Medieval courtly splendour', *Costume* 14 (1980) 7–23

Sutton, A F, 'The coronation robes of Richard III and Anne Neville', *Costume* 13 (1979) 8–16

——, 'George Lovekyn, tailor to three kings of England, 1470–1504', *Costume* 15 (1981) 1–12

ECCLESIASTICAL TEXTILES

Buckland, A F, 'The Skenfrith cope and its companions', *Textile History* 14 (1983) 125–39

Kendrick, A F, 'A tapestry altar-frontal of the fifteenth century', *Burlington Magazine* 49 (1926) 211–17

Monnas, L, 'The vestments of Sixtus IV at Padua', *CIETA Bulletin* 57 and 58 (1983) 104–25

——, 'The vestments of Henry VII at Stonyhurst College', *CIETA Bulletin* 65 (1987) 69–80

——, 'New documents for the vestments of Henry VII at Stonyhurst College', *Burlington Magazine* 131 (1989) 345–9

——, '*Opus Anglicanum* and Renaissance velvet: the Whalley Abbey vestments', *Textile History* 25 (1994) 3–27

Randall, R H, 'A fourteenth-century altar frontal', *Apollo* 100 (1974) 368–71

Tait, H, 'The hearse cloth of Henry VII belonging to the University of Cambridge', *Journal of the Warburg and Courtauld Institutes*, 19, nos. 3–4 (1956) 294–8

Whiting, M and King, D, 'A Renaissance cope', *Hali* 43 (1986) 14–15

EMBROIDERY

Christie, A G I, *English Medieval Embroidery* (Oxford, 1938)

King, D, 'Medieval and Renaissance embroidery from Spain', *Victoria and Albert Museum Yearbook*, 2 (1970) 55–65

Schuette, M and Müller, S, *The Art of Embroidery* (London, 1964)

Staniland, K, *Medieval Craftsmen: Embroiderers* (London, 1991)

FURNISHINGS AND FURNITURE

Acton-Adams, M, 'Wall seats and settles of the sixteenth century', *Connoisseur* 121 (1948) 16–21

Beard, G, *The National Trust Book of English Furniture* (London, 1985)

Cesarisky, H, 'Two English oak cabinets of the early sixteenth century', *Burlington Magazine* 71 (1939) 187–93

Chinery, V, *Oak Furniture* (Woodbridge, 1979)

Clabburn, P, *The National Trust Book of Furnishing Textiles* (London, 1988)

Darrah, J A, 'Furniture timbers', *V&A Conservation Journal* 4 (1992) 4–6

Dubon, D, 'Masterpieces of the Renaissance collection in the Philadelphia Museum of Art', *Apollo* 100 (1974) 18–27

Eames, P, 'Documentary evidence concerning the character and use of domestic furniture in England in the fourteenth and fifteenth centuries', *Furniture History* 7 (1971) 41–60

——, 'Inventories as sources of evidence for domestic furnishings in the fourteenth and fifteenth centuries', *Furniture History* 9 (1973) 33–40

——, 'An iron chest at Guildhall of about 1427', *Furniture History* 10 (1974) 1–4

Fletcher, J, 'Tree-ring dates for some panel painting in England', *Burlington Magazine* 116 (1974) 251–3

Forman, B M, 'Continental furniture craftsmen in London 1511–1625', *Furniture History* 7 (1971) 94–120

Hayward, M A, 'Appendix 2: Report on the velvet covered box containing the bones', in *Saint Chad of Birmingham*, ed M W Greenslade, Archdiocese of Birmingham Historical Commission Publication No 10 (Birmingham, 1996) 26–8

——, 'The packing and transportation of the goods of Henry VIII, with particular reference to the 1547 inventory', *Costume* 31 (1997) 8–15

——, 'Repositories of splendour: Henry VIII's Wardrobes of the Robes and Beds', *Textile History* 29 (1998) 134–56

——, 'Seat furniture at the court of Henry VIII', in *Upholstery Conservation*, ed K Gill and D Eastop (Oxford, 2000) 115–32

——, 'William Green, coffer maker to Henry VIII, Edward VI and Mary I', *Furniture History* 36 (2000) 1–13

Hewett, C A, *The Development of Carpentry 1200–1700* (Newton Abbot, 1969)

Huth, H, 'A Venetian Renaissance casket', *Museum Monographs* (City Art Museum, St Louis) 1 (1968) 42–50

Jackson-Stops, G, 'Purchases and perquisites: the 6th Earl of Dorset's furniture at Knole', *Country Life* (1977) 1620–2

Jennings, C, *Early Chests in Wood and Iron* (London, 1974)

Mander, N, 'Painted cloths: history, craftsmen and techniques', *Textile History* 28 (1997) 137–40

Mitchell, P, 'Italian picture frames 1500–1825', *Furniture History* 14 (1978) 18–27

Rieder, W, 'French sixteenth-century *Boiserie* and furniture', *Apollo* 106 (1977) 350–1

Robertson, J C, 'Furnishings seized in London, 1575', *Furniture History* 25 (1989) 36–41

Ruggles-Brise, S, 'Some royal coffers', *Connoisseur* 129 (1952) 19–24

Symmonds, R W, 'The chest and the coffer', *Connoisseur* 107 (1941) 15–21

——, 'The craft of the coffer and trunk maker in the seventeenth century', *Connoisseur* 109 (1942) 40–6

——, 'New light on Tudor furniture, Part 2: Queen Elizabeth's coffer makers, John and Thomas Grene', *Country Life* 93 (1943) 1054

——, 'The craft of the joiner in Medieval England, part 1', *Connoisseur* 118 (1946) 17–23

——, 'The craft of the joiner in Medieval England, part 2', *Connoisseur* 118 (1946) 98–104

——, 'Of jakes and close stools – their place in English social history', *Connoisseur* 129 (1952) 86–91

Thornton, P, 'Two problems', *Furniture History* 7 (1971) 61–71

——, 'Canopies, couches and chairs of state', *Apollo* 100 (1974) 292–9

——, *Seventeenth-Century Interior Decoration in England, France and Holland* (New Haven, 1978)

Thornton, P and Tomlin, M, 'The furnishing and decoration of Ham House', *Furniture History* 16 (1980) 36–177

Thornton, P and di Castro, D, 'Some late sixteenth-century Medici furniture', *Furniture History* 14 (1978) 1–9

Thorp, W A, 'A great Baroque bedstead', *Burlington Magazine* 92 (1950) 3–8

Wainwright, C, 'Specimens of ancient furniture', *Connoisseur* 184 (1973) 105–13

FURS

Hunt, J, 'Jewelled neck furs and "flohpelze"', *Pantheon* 21 (1963) 150

Veale, E M, *The English Fur Trade in the Later Middle Ages* (Oxford, 1966)

——, 'On so-called 'flea furs', *Costume* 28 (1994) 10–13

GLASS

Brown, S and O' Connor, D, *Medieval Craftsmen: Glass Painters* (London, 1991)

Charleston, R J, *English Glass and Glass Used in England 400–1940* (London, 1984)

Cook, J M, 'A fragment of medieval glass from London', *Medieval Archaeology* 2 (1958) 173–7

Crossley, D W, 'Glass making in Bagot's Park, Staffordshire, in the sixteenth century', *Post-Medieval Archaeology* 1 (1967) 44–83

——, 'The performance of the glass industry in sixteenth-century England', *The Economic History Review* (2nd series) 25 (1972) 421–33

Crossley, D W and Aberg, F A, 'Sixteenth century glass making in Yorkshire', *Post-Medieval Archaeology* 6 (1972) 107–59

Fowler, J, 'On the process of decay in glass, and incidentally, on the composition and texture at different periods and the history of its manufacture', *Archaeologia* 46 (1881) 65–162

Glanville, P, 'The Parr pot', *Archaeological Journal* 127 (1971) 147–55

——, 'Anglo-Saxon and Medieval glass in Britain', *Medieval Archaeology* 22 (1978) 11–14

D B Harden *et al*, *Masterpieces of Glass* (London, 1968)

Klein, D and Lloyd, W, eds, *The History of Glass* (London, 1984)

Middeldorf, U, 'On the origins of email sur ronde-bosse', *Gazette des Beaux-Arts* (6th series) 55 (1960) 233

Reed, C H, 'On a Saracenic goblet of enamelled glass of medieval date', *Archaeologia* 58 (1902) 217–26

Tait, H, *The Golden Age of Venetian Glass* (London, 1979)

Vickers, M, 'A note on glass medallions in Oxford', *Journal of Glass Studies* 16 (1974) 18–21

HAWKS, HORSES AND HOUNDS

Beard, C R, 'Dog collars', *Connoisseur* 92 (1933) 29–34

——, 'A collection of dog collars', *Connoisseur* 105 (1940) 102–6

Clark, J, ed, *The Medieval Horse and its Equipment, c. 1150–c. 1450*, Medieval Finds from Excavations in London 5 (London, 1995)

Cummins, J, *The Hound and the Hawk: the Art of Medieval Hunting* (London, 1988)

Davis, R H C, *The Medieval Warhorse: Origin, Development and Redevelopment* (London, 1989)

Edwards, E H, *The Encyclopaedia of the Horse* (London, 1994)

Gaimster, D R M, 'A late medieval cast copper alloy stirrup from Old Romney, Kent', *Medieval Archaeology* 34 (1990) 157–60

MacGregor, A, 'The royal stables: a seventeenth-century perspective', *Antiquaries Journal* 76 (1996) 181–200

Prior, C M, *The Royal Studs of the Sixteenth and Seventeenth Centuries* (London, 1935)

Reese, M M, *The Royal Office of the Master of the Horse* (London, 1976)

Sutton, A F, 'John Hertyngton, supplier of saddlery to Richard III', *The Ricardian* 6 (1984) 379–84

Tylden, G, *Horses and Saddlery* (London, 1965)

ILLUSTRATED AND ILLUMINATED MANUSCRIPTS

Alexander, J J G, *Italian Renaissance Illuminations* (London, 1977)

——, 'Painting and manuscript illumination for royal patrons in the later Middle Ages', in *English Court Culture in the Later Middle Ages,* ed V J Scattergood and J W Sherborne (London, 1983) 141–62

——, *Medieval Illuminators and Their Methods of Work* (London, 1992)

——, ed, *The Painted Page: Italian Renaissance Book Illumination 1450–1550* (London, 1994)

Auerbach, E, 'Ornament and decoration in Essex records', *Burlington Magazine* 92 (1950) 324–5

——, 'Illuminated royal portraits', *Burlington Magazine* 93 (1951) 300–3

——, 'An Elizabethan illuminated indenture', *Burlington Magazine* 93 (1951) 319–23

Backhouse, J, *Books of Hours* (London, 1985)

——, 'Founders of the royal library: Edward IV and Henry VII as collectors of illuminated manuscripts', in *England in the Fifteenth Century*, ed D Williams, Proceedings of the Harlaxton Symposium 1986 (Woodbridge, 1987) 23–41

——, 'Illuminated manuscripts and the early development of the portrait miniature', in *Early Tudor England*, ed D Williams, Proceedings of the Harlaxton Symposium 1987 (Woodbridge, 1989) 1–17

——, 'Illuminated manuscripts associated with Henry VII and members of his immediate family', in *The Reign of Henry VII*, ed B Thompson) Proceedings of the Harlaxton Symposium 1993 (Stamford, 1995) 175–87

Dickens, A G, 'A Tudor Percy emblem in Royal MS 18 Dii', *Archaeological Journal* 112 (1955) 95–9

de Hamel, C, *Medieval Craftsmen: Scribes and Illuminators* (London, 1992)

Harrison, K, 'Katherine of Aragon's pomegranate', *Transactions of the Cambridge Bibliographical Society* 2 (1954) 88–92

Kren, T, *Renaissance Painting in Manuscripts: Treasures from the British Library* (London, 1983)

Marks, R and Morgan, N, *The Golden Age of English Manuscript Painting 1200–1500* (London, 1981)

Orth, M, 'A French illuminated treaty of 1527', *Burlington Magazine* 122 (1980) 125–6

Pächt, O, 'Notes and observations on the origin of humanistic book decoration', in *Fritz Saxl 1890–1948*, ed D J Gordon (London, 1957) 184–94

Payne, A, 'Sir Thomas Wriothesley and his heraldic artists', in *Illuminating the Book*, ed M Brown and S McKendrick (London and Toronto, 1998) 148–53

——, 'An artistic survey', in *Anthony Roll*, ed C S Knighton and D M Loades (2000) 20–7

Randall, L M C, 'Pea-pods and molluscs from the Master of Catherine of Cleves Workshop', *Apollo* 100 (1974) 372–9

Trapp, J B, 'Pieter Meghen, yet again', in *Manuscripts in the Fifty Years After the Invention of Printing*, ed J B Trapp (London, 1983) 23–8

JEWELLERY

Arnold, J, 'Sweet England's jewels', in *Princely Magnificence: Court Jewels of the Renaissance 1500–1630*, ed A Somers Cocks (London, 1980) 31–40

Beard, C R, 'The Emperor Maximilian's garter', *Connoisseur* 131 (1953) 108–9

Castle, J, 'Amulets and protection: pomanders', *Bulletin of the Society of Renaissance Studies* 17 (2000) 12–18

Cherry, J, 'The Dunstable swan jewel', *Journal of the British Archaeological Association* (3rd series) 32 (1969) 38–53

——, 'The Medieval jewellery from the Fishpool Hoard, Nottinghamshire', *Archaeologia* 104 (1973) 307–21

——, 'Healing through faith: the continuation of medieval attitudes to jewellery into the Renaissance', *Renaissance Studies* 15 (2001) 154–71

Evans, J, *English Jewellery from the Fifth Century AD to 1800* (London, 1921)

——, *Magical Jewels of the Middle Ages and the Renaissance* (Oxford, 1922)

——, 'Un bijou magique dessiné par Hans Holbein', *Gazette des Beaux-Arts* 14 (1926) 357

——, 'The garter of Charles the Bold, Duke of Burgundy', *Antiquaries Journal* 32 (1952) 70–1

Fortnum, C D, 'Notes on some of the antique and Renaissance gems and jewels in Her Majesty's collection at Windsor Castle', *Archaeologia* 45 (1877) 1–28

Gaimster, D R M and Goodall, J A, 'A Tudor parcel-gilt livery badge from Chelsham, Surrey', *Antiquaries Journal* 79 (1999) 392–9

Godfrey, E S, *The Development of English Glass-Making 1560–1640* (Oxford, 1975)

Hackenbroch, Y, *Renaissance Jewellery* (London, New York and Munich, 1979)

Hartshorne, A, 'Notes on collars of SS', *Archaeological Journal* 34 (1882) 376–7

——, 'The gold chains, the pendants, the paternosters and the zones of the Middle Ages, the Renaissance and later times', *Archaeological Journal* 66 (1909) 77

Lang, A, *Portraits and Jewels of Mary Stuart* (Glasgow, 1906)

Lightbown, R W, *Medieval European Jewellery* (London, 1992)

Maclagan, E and Oman, C C, 'An English gold rosary of about 1500', *Archaeologia* 85 (1936) 1–22

Marshall, R K, 'The jewellery of James V, King of Scots', *Jewellery Studies* 7 (1996) 79–86

Marsham, R, 'On a manuscript book of prayers in a binding of gold, enamelled, said to have been given by Queen Anne Boleyn to a lady of the Wyatt family', *Archaeologia* 44 (1873) 259–72

Oman, C C, 'A miniature triptych of about 1400', *Burlington Magazine* 110 (1968) 93–4

d' Otrange, M L, 'Jewels of the fifteenth and sixteenth centuries', *Connoisseur* 132 (1953) 126–33

Scarisbrick, D, *Jewellery in Britain 1066–1837* (Norwich, 1994)

——, *Tudor and Jacobean Jewellery* (London, 1995)

A Somers-Cocks, ed, *Princely Magnificence: Court Jewels of the Renaissance 1500–1630* (London, 1980)

Spenser, B, 'Fifteenth-century collar of SS', *Antiquaries Journal*, 60 (1985) 449–51

Stone, P, 'Baroque pearls, part 1', *Apollo* 63 (1958) 194

——, 'Baroque pearls, part 2', *Apollo* 64 (1959) 33

Strong, R, 'Three royal jewels: the Three Brothers, the Mirror of Great Britain and the Feather', *Burlington Magazine* 108 (1966) 350–2

Tait, H, 'Tudor hat badges', *British Museum Quarterly* 20 (1955–6) 37

——, 'A Tudor jewel: gold enamelled pendant', *Museums Journal* 56 (1957) 233

——, 'Historiated Tudor jewellery', *Antiquaries Journal* 42 (1962) 232–7

——, 'A Tudor gold enamelled buckle', *British Museum Quarterly* 26 (1962–3) 112

——, 'Anonymous loan to the British Museum: Renaissance jewellery', *Connoisseur* 154 (1963) 147–53

——, 'The girdle-prayer book or "tablett"', *Jewellery Studies* 2 (1985) 29–57

——, *Catalogue of the Waddesdon Bequest in the British Museum: I, The Jewels* (London, 1986)

Tonnochy, A B, 'Jewels and engraved gems at Windsor', *Connoisseur* 95 (1935) 275

Ward, A *et al*, eds, *The Ring: From Antiquity to the Twentieth Century* (London, 1981)

MAPS AND GLOBES

Barber, M, 'Visual encyclopaedias: the Hereford and other *mappae mundi*', *Map Collector* 48 (1989) 2–8

——, 'England I: Pageantry, defence and government: maps at court to 1550', in *Monarchs, Ministers and Maps*, ed D Buisseret (Chicago, 1992) 26–56

——, 'Maps and monarchs in Europe, 1550–1800', in *Royal and Republican Sovereignty in Early Modern Europe*, ed R Oresko, G C Gibbs and H M Scott (Cambridge, 1997) 75–124

Baldwin, R, *Globes* (Cambridge, 1992)

Baynes-Cope, A D, 'Investigation of some globes', *Imago Mundi* 33 (1981) 9–20

Destombes, M, 'Nautical charts attributed to Verrazano', *Imago Mundi* 11 (1954) 57–66

Gairdner, J, 'On a contemporary drawing of the burning of Brighton in the time of Henry VIII', *Transactions of the Royal Historical Society* (3rd series) 1 (1907) 19–31

Harvey, D A, *The History of Topographical Maps* (London, 1980)

——, 'The Portsmouth map of 1545 and the introduction of scale maps into England', in *Hampshire Studies Presented to Dorothy Dymond* (Portsmouth, 1981) 33–49

——, *Maps in Tudor England* (London, 1993)

Kenyon, J R, 'An aspect of the 1550 survey of the Isle of Wight', *Post-Medieval Archaeology* 13 (1979) 61–77

Keuning, J, 'The history of geographical map projects until 1600', *Imago Mundi* 12 (1955) 1–24

van der Krogt, P, *Old Globes in the Netherlands* (Utrecht, 1984)

Macdonald, A, 'Plans of Dover harbour in the sixteenth century', *Archaeologia Cantiana* 49 (1937) 110–12

Merriman, M, 'Italian military engineers in Britain in the 1540s', in *English Map Making*, ed S Tyacke (1983) 57–67

Skelton, R A, *Decorative Printed Maps of the Fifteenth to Eighteenth Centuries* (London, 1952)

——, 'The military surveyor's contribution to British cartography in the sixteenth century', *Imago Mundi* 24 (1970) 77–85

Stevenson, E L, *Terrestrial and Celestial Globes* (New Haven, 1921)

Tooley, R V, *Dictionary of Mapmakers* (Tring, 1989)

Tyacke, S, ed, *English Map Making 1500–1650* (London, 1983)

Wallis, H M, 'The first English globe', *The Geographical Journal* 117 (1951) 275–90

——, 'Further light on the Molyneux globes', *The Geographical Journal* 121 (1955) 304–11

——, 'Globes in England up to 1660', *Geographical Magazine* 35 (1962) 267–79

——, 'The use of terrestrial and celestial globes in England', in *Actes du XIème Congrès International d'Histoire des Sciences, Wroclaw* (London, 1968) 204–12

——, 'Early maps as historical and scientific documents', in *Papers of the Nordenskiold Seminar on the History of Cartography and the Maintenance of Cartographic Archives*, ed K Hakulinen and A Peltonen (Helsinki, 1981) 101–16

Wallis, H M, ed, *The Maps and Text of the 'Boke of Idirography' Presented by Jean Rotz to Henry VIII* (Oxford, 1981)

Yonge, E L, *A Catalogue of Early Globes Made Prior to 1850 and Conserved in the United States* (New York, 1968)

MISCELLANEOUS

Andrews, L L, 'Some notes on the history of spectacles', *Transactions of the Lancashire and Cheshire Antiquarian Society* 43 (1927)

Anglo, S, 'Archives of the English tournament: some cheques and lists', *Journal of the Society of Archivists* 2 (1961) 153–62

Beard, C R, 'English warming pans of the seventeenth century', *Connoisseur* 91 (1933) 4–9

Bell, R C, *Board and Table Games from Many Civilisations*, 2 vols (London, 1969)

Blair, C, 'The most superb of all royal locks', *Apollo* 84 (1966) 493–4

Campbell, M, *An Introduction to Ironwork* (London, 1983)

Cherry, J, 'The Talbot casket and related late medieval leather caskets', *Archaeologia* 107 (1982) 131–40

Dillon, H A, 'Tilting in Tudor times', *Archaeological Journal* 55 (1898) 296–321

——, 'Additional notes illustrative of tilting in Tudor times', *Archaeological Journal* 55 (1898) 329–39

Ffoulkes, C, *Decorative Ironwork from the xith to the xviiith Century* (London, 1913)

Hughes, G B, 'Old English fire-dogs', *Country Life* 117 (1953) 628

Murray, H J R, *A History of Chess* (Oxford, 1913)

——, 'The medieval game of tables', *Medium Aevum* 10 (1941) 57–69

Penzer, N M, 'The royal fire-dogs', *Connoisseur* (1954) 9–11

Peers, C, 'The king's beasts', *Archaeologia* 62 (1910) 309–16

Pintor, E H, *Treen and Other Wooden Bygones* (London, 1969)

Seaby, W A, 'A pair of pre-Plantation spurs', *The Ulster Journal of Archaeol* 29 (1966) 112

Stewart, I J and Watkins, M J, 'An eleventh century bone tabula set from Gloucester', *Medieval Archaeology* 28 (1984) 185–90

Watt, J, 'Surgeons of the *Mary Rose*', *Mariners Mirror* 68 (1983) 3–18

MUSIC, MUSICIANS AND MUSICAL INSTRUMENTS

Ashbee, A, 'Groomed for service: musicians in the privy chamber at the English court c. 1495–1558', *Early Music* 25 (1997) 185–97

Baines, A, *European and American Musical Instruments* (London, 1966)

Barry, W, 'The keyboard instruments of Henry viii', *Organ Yearbook* 13 (1982) 31–45

Bergsagel, J, 'The date and provenance of the Forrest-Heyther collection of Tudor masses', *Music and Letters* 44 (1963) 240–58

Bernstein, J A, 'Philip van Wilder and the Netherlandish chanson in England', *Musica Disciplina* 33 (1979) 55–67

Blezzard, J, 'Church music in Tudor times', *Library* (6th series) 20 (1998) 301–24

Blezzard, J and Palmer, F, 'King Henry viii: performer, connoisseur and composer of music', *Antiquaries Journal* 80 (2000) 249–72

Boalch, D H, *Makers of the Harpsichord and Clavichord 1440–1830* (Oxford, 2nd edition 1974)

Bowers, R, 'The vocal scoring, choral balance and performing pitch of Latin church polyphony in England c. 1500–58', *Journal of the Royal Musical Association* 112 (1987) 57–64

——, 'The cultivation and promotion of music in the household and orbit of Thomas Wolsey', in *Cardinal Wolsey: Church, State and Art*, ed S J Gunn and G Lindley (Cambridge, 1991) 178–218

Bowles, E A, 'Haut and bas: the grouping of musical instruments in the Middle Ages', *Musica Disciplina* 8 (1954) 115–40

Chappell, W, 'Some account of an unpublished collection of songs and ballads by king Henry viii and his contemporaries', *Archaeologia* 41 (1867) 371–86

Clutton, C and Niland, A, *The British Organ* (London, 2nd edition, 1982)

Edwards, W, 'The instrumental music in Henry viii's manuscript', *Consort* 34 (1978) 274–82

Greer, D, 'Henry viii', in *New Grove Dictionary of Music and Musicians*, ed S Sadie, viii (London, 1980) 485–6

Hillebrand, H M, 'The early history of the Chapel Royal', *Modern Philology* 18 (1920) 233–68

Holman, P, 'The English royal violin consort', *Proceedings of the Royal Musical Association* 109 (1982–3) 39–59

——, *Four and Twenty Fiddlers* (Oxford, 1993)

Humphreys, D, 'Philip van Wilder', *Soundings* 9 (1979–80) 13–36

Izon, J, 'Italian musicians at the Tudor court', *Musical Quarterly* 44 (1958) 329–37

Kisby, J, 'Music and musicians in early Tudor Westminster', *Early Music* 23 (1995) 223–40

——, 'Courtiers in the community: the musicians of the royal household chapel in early Tudor Westminster', in *The Reign of Henry VII*, ed B Thompson, Proceedings of the Harlaxton Symposium 1993 (Stamford, 1995) 229–60

——, 'Royal minstrels in the city and suburbs of early Tudor London', *Early Music* 25 (1997) 199–219

Lasocki, D, 'Professional recorder playing in England 1500–1740', *Early Music* 10 (1982) 23–9

——, 'The Anglo-Venetian Bassano family as instrument makers and repairers', *Galpin Society Journal* 38 (1985) 112–32

——, 'The Bassanos: Anglo-Venetian and Venetian', *Early Music* 14 (1986) 558–60

Lowinsky, E E, 'MS 1070 of the Royal College of Music in London', *Proceedings of the Royal Musical Association* 96 (1969–70) 1–19

——, 'A music book for Anne Boleyn', in *Florilegium Historiale*, ed J G Rowe and W H Stockdale (Toronto and Buffalo, 1971) 160–235

Munrow, D, *Instruments of the Middle Ages and the Renaissance* (London, 1976)

Ongaro, M, 'Sixteenth-century Venetian wind instrument-makers and their clients', *Early Music* 13 (1985) 391–7

Price, D C, *Patrons and Musicians of the English Renaissance* (Cambridge, 1981)

Prior, R, 'Jewish musicians at the Tudor court', *Musical Quarterly* 69 (1983) 253–65

Rastall, R, 'Some English consort groupings of the late Middle Ages', *Music and Letters* 4 (1974) 179–202

Rinshaw, M, 'An early seventeenth-century organ', *British Institute of Organ Studies Journal* 4 (1980) 34–42

Russell, R, *The Harpsichord and the Clavichord* (London, 1973)

Sachs, C, *The History of Musical Instruments* (New York, 1940)

Skinner, D, 'William Cornish: clerk or courtier?', *Musical Times* 138 (1997) 5–12

Stevens, J, *Music and Poetry in the Early Tudor Court* (Cambridge, 2nd edition 1979)

——, ed, *Music at the Court of Henry VIII* (London, 1969)

Winternitz, E, *Musical Instruments and Their Symbolism in Western Art* (New York, 1967)

Woodfield, I, 'The early history of the viol', *Proceedings of the Royal Musical Association* 103 (1976–7) 141–57

PLATE AND MEDALS

Alsop, J D, 'The mint dispute of 1530–32', *British Numismatic Journal* 51 (1981) 197–200

Blair, C, 'The Rochester plate', *Connoisseur* 200 (1979) 254–9

Blair, C, ed, *The History of Silver* (London, 1987)

——, *The Jewel House* (London, 1988–9)

Blair, C, Blair, J and Brownsord, R, 'An Oxford brazier's dispute of the 1390's: evidence for brass-making in medieval England', *Antiquaries Journal* 66 (1986) 82–90

Brownsword, R and Pitt, E R H, 'An analytical study of pewterware from the *Mary Rose*', *Journal of the Pewter Society* 7 (1990) 109–25

Campbell, M, 'Bishop Fox's chalice and patern', *Pelican* (1981–2) 20–44

——, 'English goldsmiths in the fifteenth century', in *England in the Fifteenth Century*, ed D Williams, Proceedings of the Harlaxton Symposium 1986 (Woodbridge, 1987) 43–52

——, 'Gold, silver and precious stones', in *English Medieval Industries: Craftsmen, Techniques, Products,* ed J Blair and N Ramsey (London, 1991) 107–66

Cherry, J, *Medieval Craftsmen: Goldsmiths* (London, 1992)

Clifford, H, 'Archbishop Matthew Parker's gifts of plate to Cambridge', *Burlington Magazine* 139 (1997) 4–10

Cooper, J K D, 'A reassessment of some late Gothic and early Renaissance plate: part 1', *Burlington Magazine* 119 (1977) 408–12

——, 'A reassessment of some late Gothic and early Renaissance plate: part 2', *Burlington Magazine* 119 (1977) 475–6

——, 'An assessment of Tudor plate design 1530–60', *Burlington Magazine* 121 (1979) 360–4

Cust, L, 'John of Antwerp, goldsmith, and Hans Holbein', *Burlington Magazine* 8 (1905–6) 356–60

Dalton, O M, *The Royal Gold Cup in the British Museum* (London, 1924)

Dodgson, C, 'The engravers on metal after Holbein', *Burlington Magazine* 83 (1943) 282–5

Gask, N, *Old Silver Spoons of England* (London, 1926)

Glanville, P, 'Bishop Fox's ablution basins', *Pelican* (1983–4) 73–86

——, 'Tudor drinking vessels', *Burlington Magazine* 127 (1985) 19–22

——, 'Robert Amadas, court goldsmith to Henry VIII', *Proceedings of the Silver Society* 3 (1986) 106–13

——, *Silver in England* (London, 1987)

——, *Silver in Tudor and Early Stuart England* (London, 1990)

——, 'Cardinal Wolsey and the goldsmiths', in *Cardinal Wolsey: Church, State and Art*, ed S J Gunn and G Lindley (Cambridge, 1991) 131–48

——, 'The Howard Grace cup', *History Today* 44 (1994) 41–5

Grimwade, A, 'English silver tankards', *Apollo* 57 (1953) 177–9

Harris, J, 'Two Byzantine craftsmen in fifteenth-century London', *Journal of Medieval History* 21 (1995) 387–403

Hatcher, J and Barker, T C, *A History of English Pewter* (London, 1974)

Hayward, J F, *English Cutlery, the Sixteenth to the Eighteenth Centuries* (London, 1957)

——, 'A rock crystal bowl from the treasury of Henry VIII', *Burlington Magazine* 110 (1968) 120–4

——, *Virtuoso Goldsmiths and the Triumph of Mannerism 1540–1620* (London, 1976)

Homer, R F, 'The medieval pewterers of London, c 1190–1457', *Transactions of the London and Middlesex Archaeological Society* 36 (1985) 137–63

——, 'The Pewterers' ordinances of 1455', *Journal of the Pewter Society* 5 (1986) 101–6

——, 'A sixteenth-century London pewterer's workbook fragment', *Journal of the Pewter Society* 7 (1989) 18–22

——, 'A London pewterer's workshop in 1551', *Antiquaries Journal* 79 (1999) 245–55

Hornsby, P, *Pewter, Copper and Brass* (London, 1981)

Juynboll, G H A, 'The attitude to gold and silver in early Islam', in *Pots and Pans: a Colloquium on Precious Metals and Ceramics*, ed M Vickers, Oxford Studies in Islamic Art 3 (Oxford, 1986) 107–15

Lenman, B, 'Jacobean goldsmith-jewellers as credit-creators: the case of James Mossman, James Cockie and George Heriot', *Scottish Historical Review* 74 (1995) 159–77

Lewis, J M, 'Some types of metal chafing dish', *Antiquaries Journal* 53 (1973) 59–172

Lightbown, R W, *Tudor Domestic Silver* (London, 1970)

——, *Secular Goldsmiths' Work in Medieval France* (London, 1978)

Oman, C C, 'The Swinburne pyx', *Burlington Magazine* 92 (1950) 337–9

——, *English Church Plate* (London, 1957)

——, *Medieval Silver Nefs* (London, 1963)

——, 'English medieval base metal church plate', *Archaeological Journal* 119 (1964) 195–208

Peacock, E, *English Church Furniture, Ornaments and Decorations at the Period of the Reformation* (London, 1866)

Peal, C A, 'Pewter from the *Mary Rose*', *Journal of the Pewter Society* 2 (1979) 22–3

——, *Pewter of Great Britain* (London, 1983)

Penzer, N M, 'The Howard Grace cup and the early date letter cycles', *Connoisseur* 117 (1946) 87–92

——, 'Tudor font-shaped cups, *Apollo* 65 (1957) 174–9

Pinter, E H, 'Mazers and their wood', *Connoisseur* 123 (1949) 33–6

Rogers, J M, 'Plate and its substitutes in Ottoman inventories', in *Pots and Pans: a Colloquium on Precious Metals and Ceramics*, ed M Vickers, Oxford Studies in Islamic Art 3 (Oxford, 1986) 117–36

St John Hope, W H, 'English medieval chalices and patterns', *Archaeological Journal* 40 (1887) 137–61

——, 'On English medieval drinking bowls called mazers', *Archaeologia* 50 (1887) 129–93

Schroder, T, 'Sixteenth-century English silver: some problems of attribution', *Proceedings of the Silver Society* 3 (1983) 40–7

——, 'A royal Tudor rock-crystal and silver-gilt vase', *Burlington Magazine* 137 (1995) 356–66

Sitwell, H D, 'The jewel house and the royal goldsmiths', *Archaeological Journal* 117 (1960) 131–51

Syson, L, 'Sperandio's medals', *History Today* 45 (1995) 43–9

Tait, H, 'The Stonyhurst salt', *Apollo* 75 (1964) 270–8

Thornton, D and Cowell, M, '"The Armada service": a set of late Tudor dining silver', *Antiquaries Journal* 76 (1996) 153–80

Toesca, I, 'Silver in the time of François I: a new identification', *Apollo* 90 (1969) 292–7

Weiss, R, 'The medals of Julius II', *Journal of the Warburg and Courtauld Institutes* 28 (1965) 163–82

Wilson, T, 'Bishop Fox's crozier', *Pelican* (1980–1) 8–27

SHIPS AND NAVAL ORDNANCE

Anderson, R C, 'Henry VIII's *Great Galley*', *Mariners Mirror* 6 (1920) 274–81

——, 'The *Mary Gonson*', *Mariners Mirror* 46 (1960) 199–204

Bennell, J E G, 'English oared vessels of the sixteenth century', *Mariners Mirror* 60 (1974) 9–26, 169–185

——, 'The oared vessels', in *Anthony Roll*, ed C S Knighton and D M Loades (2000) 34–8

Corbett, J S, 'Guns and gunnery in the Tudor navy', *Navy Records Society* 2 (1898) Appendix A

Davis, C S L, 'The administration of the royal navy under Henry VIII', *English Historical Review* 78 (1965) 268–86

Glete, J, *Navies and Nations: Warships, Navies and State Building in Europe and America, 1500–1860*, I (Stockholm, 1993)

Goldingham, C S, 'The navy under Henry VII', *English Historical Review* 33 (1918) 472–88

——, 'Warships of Henry VIII', *United Services Magazine* 179 (1919) 453–62

Hildred, A, 'The evidence of the *Mary Rose* excavation, part 2: the munitions', in *Anthony Roll*, ed C S Knighton and D M Loades (2000) 16–19

Hildred, A and Rule, M H, 'Armaments from the *Mary Rose*', *Antique Arms and Militaria* 4 (1984) 17–24

Hogg, O F G, 'The 'gunner' and some other masters of ordnance', *Journal of the Royal Artillery* 62 (1936) 463–73

Howard, G F, 'Gunport lids', *Mariners Mirror* 67 (1981) 64

——, 'Early Tudor rigging', *Mariners Mirror* 68 (1982) 277–8

——, 'Early ships' guns, part 1: built-up breech loaders', *Mariners Mirror* 72 (1986) 439–53

——, 'Early ships' guns, part 2: the swivels', *Mariners Mirror* 73 (1987) 49–55

Knighton, C S and Loades, D M, eds, *The Anthony Roll of Henry VIII's Navy*, Occasional Pubications of the Navy Record Society 2 (London, 2000)

Laughton, L G C, 'Early Tudor ship-guns', *Mariners Mirror* 46 (1960) 242–85

Loades, D M, *The Tudor Navy* (London, 1992)

——, 'The ordnance', in *Anthony Roll*, ed C S Knighton and D M Loades (2000) 12–14

Oppenheim, M, *A History of the Administration of the Royal Navy 1509–1660* (London, 1896)

Padfield, P, *Guns at Sea* (London, 1973)

Perrin, W G, 'Early naval ordnance', *Mariners Mirror* 6 (1920) 51–3

Rodger, N A M, 'The development of broadside gunnery, 1540–1650', *Mariners Mirror* 82 (1996) 301–24

Rule, M H, *Mary Rose: the Excavation and Raising of Henry VIII's Flagship* (London, 1983)

Scammell, G V, 'War at sea under the early Tudors: part 1, *Archaeologia Aeliana* (4th series) 38 (1960) 73–97

——, 'War at sea under the early Tudors: part 2, *Archaeologia Aeliana* (4th series) 39 (1961) 179–205

——, 'English merchant shipping at the end of the Middle Ages', *The Economic History Review* (2nd series) 13 (1961) 327–41

Smith, R D, 'Towards a new typology for wrought iron ordnance', *International Journal of Nautical Archaeology and Underwater Exploration* 17 (1988) 5–16

——, 'Port pieces: the use of wrought iron ordnance in the sixteenth century', *Journal of the Ordnance Society* 5 (1993) 1–8

Vine, S, 'The evidence of the *Mary Rose* excavation, part 1: the ship', in *Anthony Roll*, ed C S Knighton and D M Loades (2000) 15–16

TAPESTRY

Asselberghs, J, 'Charles VIII's Trojan war tapestry', *Victoria and Albert Museum Yearbook* (1969) 80–4

Boccara, J *et al*, 'Frenzy and sobriety: Feuilles de choux tapestries', *Hali* 46 (1989) 15–23

Campbell, T, 'Tapestry quality in Tudor England: problems of terminology', *Studies in Decorative Arts* 3 (1995–6) 29–50

——, 'School of Raphael tapestries in the collection of Henry VIII', *Burlington Magazine* 138 (1996) 69–78

——, 'Cardinal Wolsey's tapestry collection', *Antiquaries Journal* 76 (1996) 73–137

——, 'Henry VIII and the Château of Ecouen *History of David and Bathsheba* tapestries', *Gazette des Beaux-Arts* 128 (1996) 122–40

Cavallo, A S, 'The redemption of man: a Christian allegory in tapestry', *Bulletin of the Museum of Fine Arts, Boston* 56 (1958) 147–68

——, *Medieval Tapestries in the Metropolitan Museum of Art* (New York, 1993)

Delmarcel, G, 'Texts and images: some notes on the *tituli* of Flemish 'Triumphs of Petrarch' series', *Textile History* 20 (1989) 321–9

——, *Flemish Tapestry* (New York and London, 1999)

——, *Los Honores: Flemish Tapestries for the Emperor Charles V* (Amsterdam, 2000)

Hefford, W, 'Bread, brushes and brooms: aspects of tapestry restoration in England 1660–1760', in *Acts of the Tapestry Symposium, November 1976* (San Francisco, 1979) 65–75

Kendrick, A F, 'A tapestry altar-frontal of the fifteenth century', *Burlington Magazine* 49 (1926) 211–17

King, D, 'Tapestries from France and Flanders', *Connoisseur* 195 (1976) 232–7

——, 'The Devonshire Hunts: art and sport in the fifteenth century', *Connoisseur* 196 (1977) 246–53

Marillier, H C, *The Tapestries at Hampton Court* (London, 1951, revised 1962)

McKendrick, S, 'Edward IV: an English royal collector of Netherlandish tapestry', *Burlington Magazine* 129 (1987) 521–4

——, 'Tapestries from the Low Countries in England during the fifteenth century', in *England and the Low Countries in the Late Middle Ages*, ed C M Barron and N Saul (New York and Stroud, 1995) 43–60

Muel, F, *Tenture de l'Apocalypse d'Angers: L'Envers et L'Endroit* (Nantes, 1990)

Ortiz, A D, Carreto, C H and Godoy, J A, eds, *Resplendence of the Spanish Monarchy: Renaissance Tapestries and Armour from the Patrimonio Nacional* (New York, 1991)

Popham, A E, 'The fifteenth-century drawings for tapestry in the British Museum', *Burlington Magazine* 45 (1924) 60–6

Saintenoy, P, 'Les tapisseries de la cour de Bruxelles sous Charles V', *Annals de la Société Royales d'Archéologie de Bruxelles* 30 (1921) 5–31

Salmon, L, 'The Passion of Christ in medieval tapestries', in *Acts of the Tapestry Symposium, November 1976* (San Francisco, 1979) 79–101

Standen, E A, 'The twelve ages of man: a further study of a set of early sixteenth-century Flemish tapestries', *Metropolitan Museum Journal* 2 (1969) 127–68

——, 'Some sixteenth-century Flemish tapestries related to Raphael's workshop', *Metropolitan Museum Journal* 4 (1971) 109–21

——, 'Tapestries in use: indoors', *Apollo* 144 (1981) 6–15

——, 'Tapestries in use: outdoors', *Apollo* 144 (1981) 16–19

——, 'Renaissance and mannerism', *Apollo* 144 (1981) 20–8

——, 'Romans and soldiers: a sixteenth-century set of Flemish tapestries', *Metropolitan Museum Journal* 9 (1974) 211–28

Thomson, W G, *A History of Tapestry from the Earliest Times until the Present Day* (London, 1906, reprinted 1973)

Verdier, P, 'The tapestry of the prodigal son', *Journal of the Walters Art Gallery* 18 (1955) 9–58

White, J and Shearman, J, 'Raphael's tapestries and their cartoons', *The Art Bulletin* 40 (1958) 193–221

Wingfield-Digby, G, *The Victoria and Albert Museum: The Tapestry Collections Medieval to Renaissance* (London, 1980)

Wingfield-Digby, G, with Hefford, W, *The Devonshire Hunting Tapestries* (London, 1971)

Wood, D T B, 'Tapestries of the seven deadly sins: part 1', *Burlington Magazine* 20 (1912) 210–23

——, 'Tapestries of the seven deadly sins: part 2', *Burlington Magazine* 20 (1912) 277–89

——, 'The Credo set of tapestries: part 1', *Burlington Magazine* 22 (1914) 247–54

——, 'The Credo set of tapestries: part 2', *Burlington Magazine* 22 (1914) 309–16

TEXTILES

Cavallo, A S, *Textiles: Isabella Stewart Gardner Museum* (Boston, 1986)

Cobb, H, 'Textile imports in the fifteenth century: the evidence of the customs accounts', *Costume* 29 (1995) 1–11

Crowfoot, E, Pritchard, F and Staniland, K, *Textiles and Clothing, c 1150–c 1450*, Medieval Finds from Excavations in London 4 (1992)

de Francesco, G, 'Silk fabrics in Venetian paintings', *Ciba Review* 29 (1940) 1036–48

Hayward, M A, 'The flags, part 2: fabric', in *Anthony Roll*, ed C S Knighton and D M Loades (2000) 31–3

Hobbs, D, 'Royal ships and their flags in the late fifteenth and early sixteenth centuries', *Mariners Mirror* 80 (1994) 388–94

Hofenk de Graaff, J H, 'The chemistry of red dyestuffs in medieval and early modern Europe', in *Cloth and Clothing in Medieval Europe*, ed N B Harte and K G Ponting (London, 1983) 71–9

Kellenbenz, H, 'The fustian industry of the Ulm region in the fifteenth and early sixteenth centuries', in *Cloth and Clothing in Medieval Europe*, ed N B Harte and K G Ponting (London, 1983) 259–76

King, D, *Textiles in the Tudor Period*, The Connoisseur Period Guides (London, 1956)

——, 'Textile furnishings', in *The Late King's Goods: Collections, Possessions and Patronage of Charles I in the Light of the Commonwealth Sale Inventories*, ed A MacGregor (Oxford 1989) 307–21

Lacey, K, 'The production of 'narrow ware' by silkwomen in fourteenth- and fifteenth-century England', *Textile History* 18 (1987) 187–204

Mitchell, D M and Sonday, M, 'Printed fustians', *CIETA Bulletin* 77 (2000) 99–118

Monnas, L, 'Developments in figured velvet weaving in Italy during the fourteenth century', *CIETA Bulletin* 63 and 64 (1986) 63–100

——, 'Loom widths and selvedges prescribed by Italian silk weaving statutes 1265–1512', *CIETA Bulletin* 66 (1988) 35–44

——, 'Silk clothes purchased for the Great Wardrobe of the kings of England, 1325–1462', *Textile History* 20 (1989) 283–307

——, 'Contemplate what has been done: silk fabrics in paintings by Jan van Eyck', *Hali* 60 (1991) 103–13

——, ''Tissues' in England during the fifteenth and sixteenth centuries', *CIETA Bulletin* 75 (1998) 63–80

Munro, J H, 'The medieval scarlet and the economics of sartorial splendour', in *Cloth and Clothing in Medieval Europe*, ed N B Harte and K G Ponting (London, 1983) 13–70

Pritchard, F, 'Two royal seal bags from Westminster Abbey', *Textile History* 20 (1989) 225–34

Reath, N A, 'Velvets of the Renaissance from Europe and Asia Minor', *Burlington Magazine* 50 (1927) 298–304

Staniland, K, 'The Great Wardrobe accounts as a source for historians of fourteenth-century clothing and textiles', *Textile History* 20 (1989) 275–81

——, 'Clothing provision and the Great Wardrobe in the mid-thirteenth century', *Textile History* 22 (1991) 239–52

Sutton, A F, 'Order and fashion in clothes: the king, his household, and the City of London at the end of the fifteenth century', *Textile History* 22 (1991) 253–76

——, 'Mercery through four centuries, 1130s–c. 1500', *Nottingham Medieval Studies* 41 (1997) 100–25

——, 'Some aspects of the linen trade c 1130s to 1500, and the part played by the Mercers of London', *Textile History* 30 (1999) 155–75

Swain, M, *Tapestries and Textiles at the Palace of Holyrood House in the Royal Collection* (London, 1988)

de Unger, E, 'A Renaissance silk velvet with a phoenix design at the V&A', *Textile History* 20 (1989) 309–20

GLOSSARY

Some definitions in this glossary have been taken from Starkey, ed., *Inventory*, with permission.

AGATE   one of several varieties of banded chalcedony.

AGLET   the metal tag of a lace; metallic ornament on dress.

ALABASTER   translucent white form of gypsum.

ALB   a long white linen tunic with sleeves, sometimes decorated with embroidered panels, or apparels, at the cuffs and hem; worn under the **TUNICLE**, **DALMATIC**, **CHASUBLE** or cope and always with the **AMICE** and **GIRDLE**.

ALKOMEN   meaning uncertain; from the text, it appears to be a type of metal [258].

ALTAR CLOTH   a linen cloth laid over an altar.

ALTAR FRONTAL   a rectangular panel used to decorate the altar; the nether (lower) frontal hangs in front of an altar and the upper frontal hangs on the wall behind the altar.

AMICE   a rectangle of linen worn as a neck cloth, to protect the other vestments from perspiration.

ANDIRON   a metal stand for supporting burning wood on a hearth.

ANGEL   a gold coin with the figure of the archangel Michael piercing the dragon.

ANTIQUE, ANTIQUEWORK   in the classical style of ancient Greece and Rome, also referred to as the **GROTESQUE** style.

APPAREL   a decorative embroidered panel stitched to the **AMICE** and the **ALB**.

ARRAS   a tapestry-woven textile, incorporating wool, silk and metal thread.

ASH   a white/grey colour.

BABY   a fashion doll.

BAIN   a bath.

BALAS   a rose-coloured spinel ruby.

BAREHIDE   a leather covering for a cart.

BASES   base valances to accompany hangings on bedsteads.

BAUDEKIN   a figured silk.

BED   a mattress.

BEDSTEAD   a wooden framework with mattresses and coverings.

BERYL   a transparent precious stone; pale green, light blue, yellow or white.

BICE   a pigment made from blue or green basic copper carbonate, giving a dull shade of blue or green; similar in colour to smalt (deep blue glass).

BILIMENTS   a decorative border on a French hood (a woman's head-dress in the French style).

BIRRAL   a transparent precious stone in a range of colours indicating pale blue, light green, yellow and white. Emeralds and aquamarine also belong to this mineral species.

BLANKET   a white woollen cloth used for bed covers; the best quality came from Spain.

BODKIN   a thick, blunt needle with an eye near the point; kept with knives in the side pocket of a scabbard.

BOLSTER   a long, round pillow.

BRASS   a yellow alloy of copper and zinc.

BRIDGES, BRUGES SATIN   a mixed satin-weave cloth with a warp of silk and a weft of wool, probably made in Brussels.

BRUSSELS TICK, CLOTH   a fine white cloth made in the Brussels area.

BUCKRAM a coarse cloth made from hemp, gummed (i.e. stiffened with starch or a substance such as **GUM ARABIC**) and **CALENDERED**.

BUDGE black imported lambskin.

CAMBRIC a fine, white linen of a plain weave.

CAMEO a precious stone having two layers of different colours, in the upper of which a figure is carved, while the lower acts as a ground

CALENDERED cloth which has been placed under pressure by putting it through rollers to make it smooth or create a decorative pattern, such as watering or wavy lines.

CAMLET a lightweight cloth made of wool, silk, mohair or camel hair.

CASTING BOTTLE a small bottle containing rose-water for sprinkling in church.

CAUL a hairnet or close-fitting cap, covering the ears.

CELURE the horizontal canopy of a set of bed hangings or a **CLOTH OF ESTATE**; used in combination with a **TESTER**.

CHAFING DISH a dish with an outer pan of hot water, or a small brazier, to keep food warm or to cook food at the table.

CHAMBERER a personal attendant, providing service in the chamber.

CHANGEABLE where the warp and the weft are a different colour, giving a 'shot' effect.

CHAPE the metal guard at the point of a scabbard.

CHASE setting for a gemstone.

CHASUBLE vestment worn by the priest while celebrating mass; basically conical in shape, often decorated with orphreys on the front and back.

CHECKED the simplest form of counter-change pattern, with regularly spaced squares of alternating colours.

CHEVERID, CHEVRONED with a simple geometric pattern consisting of *V*s, arranged singly or in vertical strings, forming a zigzag.

CIPHER a monogram, or interlaced initials,

CLAVICHORD a keyboard instrument with strings struck with a **TANGENT**.

CLOCK a mechanical device for telling the time, which often struck the hours.

CLOSE STOOL a chamber pot with water cistern, placed within a fabric- or leather- covered box.

CLOTH OF ESTATE a **CELURE** and **TESTER**, often with valances, used in combination with a chair and **FOOTSTOOL**.

COAT a male outer garment.

COIF either a close-fitting undercap of linen worn by men, or a close-fitting cap of linen worn by women.

COLLET a box setting for gemstones.

CORDAUNT a type of cord or braid, sometimes used for embroidery.

CORPORAL, CORPORAL CLOTH a square piece of white linen upon which the chalice and host rest during the Eucharist. It was kept in a decorative case when not in use.

CORPORAL CASE or **BURSE** a case to protect the **CORPORAL CLOTH**.

CORRODY a pension, annuity or provision for board and accommodation given by religious houses in return for a lump sum paid at the outset.

COUNTERPOINT a decorative bed-covering, a quilt.

COUNTERPOISE a counterbalancing weight, present as part of a clock mechanism.

COVERPANE a cloth used to cover bread.

CREEPER/CREEPERS a small iron 'dog' or fire dog, a pair of which was placed on the hearth between the andirons

CROSSBOW a bow fixed across a wooden stock with a groove for the arrow, bolt etc. and a mechanism for drawing and releasing the string.

CRUCE a small drinking vessel with a pair of handles.

CRUET small vessels to hold wine and water during the celebration of the mass, or holy water on other occasions.

CRUMHORN a wind instrument with double reed and curved end.

CRYSTAL a clear transparent quartz, usually in hexagonal prisms; not a type of glass.

CUP (for a bedstead) a cup-shaped finial at the top of the bedposts, which could hold feathers or vanes.

CUP OF ASSAY a cup for tasting or sampling drink or holding water for washing.

CUPBOARD CLOTH linen used at meals.

DALMATIC a calf-length, T-shaped vestment with sleeves, worn by deacons when assisting the priest at mass.

DAMASK a figured, woven silk with pattern visible on both sides.

DAMASK GOLD a type of gold-wrapped thread, originally associated with Damascus.

DAMASK SILVER a type of silver thread, originally associated with Damascus.

DIAMOND a colourless or tinted brilliant precious stone of pure carbon.

DIAPER a linen fabric woven with a small pattern.

DIAPERWORK a design based on a repeating geometric pattern of a framework filled with motifs such as squares, lozenges or scales.

DOMUS MAGNIFICENCIE the household above stairs, overseen by the Lord Chamberlain and the counterpart to the **DOMUS PROVIDENCIE**.

DOMUS PROVIDENCIE the household below stairs, overseen by the Lord Steward and the counterpart to the **DOMUS MAGNIFICENCIE**.

DORNIX a type of fabric with a linen warp and a wool weft, originating in Dornick (Tournai).

DORSE a hanging for covering the back of an altar.

DOUBLE RAIL a linen neckerchief for the bath.

DOUBLET a men's close-fitting garment for the upper body.

DOWN a bird's under-plumage, used as stuffing.

ELL measurement of length. The English ell was 45ins (1.143m), the Flemish ell 27ins (686mm) and the Scottish ell, 37.2ins (946mm).

EMBOSSING a raised relief pattern on metal, leather or cloth.

EMBROIDER to decorate cloth with stitched motifs which rarely cover the whole of the ground fabric.

ENAMEL a glass-like opaque or semi-transparent coating for metallic surfaces.

ENGRAVE to inscribe or ornament with incised lines.

ERMINE the white winter coat of the ermine or stoat.

EWERY (the Ewery and Napery) a department of the royal household and part of the **DOMUS PROVIDENCIE**; it provided clean **NAPERY** for the king's table and other tables where appropriate, and clean water, for the diners to wash their hands.

FAGGOTS bundles of sticks

FANON a **MANIPLE**, worn over the left arm.

FARDEL a bundle; a measure of quantity for cloth or other items assembled in a bale or bundle of no standard dimensions.

FIFES uncertain meaning

FIRE PAN a vessel (which could be on wheels) to carry hot coals or embers.

FODDER see **FOTHER**.

FOOTSTOOL a low stool, made individually or with a matching chair.

FOREST BILL a **STAFF WEAPON** with a scythe blade mounted at the top.

FOTHER a weight for lead, generally 2,100lb (952.54kg).

FRONTLET an ornamental band worn over the forehead.

FUSTIAN a plain woven cloth with a linen warp and a cotton weft, although in some types either the warp or weft were worsted thread; made in Norwich, Naples and Genoa.

FUSTIANS (pair of) a pair of blankets (?) made from **FUSTIAN**.

GARNET a vitreous silicate material, of which the transparent deep red kind is used as a gem.

GIMP silk or wool thread twisted round a cord or wire core.

GITTERON a plucked stringed instrument with a flat back.

GOWN a loosely cut outer garment for a man.

GROTESQUE style influenced by the designs found on the walls of the *domus aurea* in Rome, the Golden House of the Emperor Nero.

GUARD an ornamental border on a garment.

GUM ARABIC gum exuded by certain species of the acacia tree.

HAGBUSH a muzzle-loading hand firearm; some

were fitted with a matchlock, others were fired using a handheld slowmatch. They were handheld or fired using a support, depending on their size.

HALBERD   a long hafted axe, with the top of the blade pointed for thrusting and a long rearward spike.

HALE   a roofed-over structure, usually open at the sides; a pavilion or tent

HAMMER FOR A HORSEMAN   a war hammer for cavalry: a light weapon with a short shaft and a long, sharp rear spike.

HANAPER, THE   a department of Chancery which received fees for the sealing and enrolling of charters and other documents.

HOLINESS   a club armed with spikes.

HOLLAND   a plain white linen woven originally in Holland; in the sixteenth century the name was applied to any good-quality imported plain linen.

HOLY-WATER STOCK   a stoop or basin to hold holy water.

IN PREST   money advanced on account of work to be done, or not yet completed; part payment in advance to hire a person or thing.

INCARNATE   red.

JASPER   an opaque variety of quartz, usually red, yellow or brown.

JAVELIN   a horseman's spear with a broad leaf-shaped head.

JEAN   from Genoa.

JELLY FLOWERS   pinks or carnations.

JENET   the skin of the civet cat; the black were more valuable than the grey, and both were more expensive than other cat skins.

KERCHER   a kerchief; a cloth used to cover the head or neck.

KERSEY   a double-twilled **SAY**, coarse or fine.

KIRTLE   a woman's dress worn alone or with a gown.

KNOP   an ornamental knob, often a decorative feature of a lid or cover for a piece of plate.

LARUM   a mechanical device to strike the hours.

LATTEN   alloy of copper, zinc, lead and tin.

LAVATORY BASIN   a basin used for washing the hands.

LAYER   a small jug, often filled with water to dilute wine.

LINKS   torches made of tow and pitch

LOCKER, LOCKET   the mount at the mouth of a scabbard and for suspension rings (also on a scabbard).

LUKES   from Lucca, or in the Luccesse style.

LUTE   a plucked stringed instrument with a curved back.

LYE   a water made alkaline by lixiviation (the process of separating a soluble from an insoluble substance by percolation of water) of vegetable ashes; used for washing.

MANIPLE   a short, narrow band worn on the left wrist by an officiating priest.

MARQUETRY   inlaid work in wood, ivory etc.

MAZER   a standing cup, the body of which was often made of maple wood.

MINIVER   a kind of fur used as a lining and trimming in ceremonial costume.

MORIAN   Moorish, a Moor.

MORRIS-PIKE   a long pike believed to be of Moorish origin.

MOTHER-OF-PEARL   the smooth, shining, iridescent substance which forms on the inner surface of a shell, e.g. that of an oyster.

MUFFLER   a scarf or kerchief to cover the neck or face.

MURREY   a dull, red-purple colour.

NAPERY   domestic linen, especially for the table.

NEEDLEWORK   canvas work, usually covering the ground fabric.

NETTLE-CLOTH   a calico or cotton cloth.

NIGHT PLATE   drinking vessels, plates, candlesticks etc. for food and drink consumed at night

NORMANDY CANVAS   a heavyweight linen cloth originating from Normandy.

NORMANDY CLOTH   a plain, white linen cloth made in Normandy.

NUT   a cup made from a coconut.

ORPHREY   an ornamental border on ecclesiastical vestments.

OWTNALL   a type of tapestry-woven hanging from Oudenarde (a Flemish weaving centre).

OYER AND TERMINER   a grant issued to judges, allowing them to hear and determine indictments on particular crimes.

PALING   the action of constructing a fence or enclosing a place with pales; fencing

PALLET BED   a mattress.

PAMPILION   Spanish black lamb skins from Pampeluna.

PANED   having widths or strips of fabric seamed to create a striped furnishing textile (e.g. hangings and curtains) with the stripes running vertically.

PARCEL   (in connection with gilt plate) partially gilded.

PARCHMENT   skin, especially of sheep or goat, prepared for writing or painting.

PARTISAN, PARTIZAN   a long broad blade, sharp on both edges, often with curved lugs at its base, on a long staff.

PARTLET   an article of clothing worn round the neck and over the chest by men and women.

PASSAMAYNE   gold or silver lace, used as a decoration.

PASSEMENT, PASSEMENTERIE   trimmings of lace, **GIMP** or braid made from silk or metal-wrapped thread.

PEARL   a concretion, usually white or bluish-grey, formed within a shell.

PERFUME, PERFUME PAN   a dish or pan containing an aromatic; used to scent the air.

PERQUISITE   a reward additional to normal revenue.

PEWTER   a grey alloy of tin with lead or another metal.

PIETRE DURE   'hard stones' e.g. **AGATE**, **SERPENTINE**.

PIKE   a small diamond-shaped head on a long staff; used by infantry.

PILLOW-BERE   a pillowcase.

PIRL   a cord of twisted gold or silver wire used in embroidered decoration.

PLACARD   a **STOMACHER** worn by men and women to fill the open front of a **COAT**, **DOUBLET** or **GOWN**.

PLAT   a map or plan.

PLUMMET   a weight for a clock.

POLLAXE   a long-handled **STAFF WEAPON**.

POMMEL   an oval or spherical form on the uprights of upholstered furniture.

POPINJAY   a green or blue colour, or a mixture of the two.

PORTAGUES   uncertain meaning

PORTATIVE   a small, easily portable organ.

PREST   an advance of money

PRICKETS   candles

PURE   trimmed **MINIVER**.

PYX   a vessel used to store the consecrated host.

QUARREL   a bolt shot from a **CROSSBOW**: these were short and thick in comparison to those shot from the longbow.

QUISH   obsolete form of *cuisse*: armour for protecting the front part of the thighs; in singular, a thigh-piece.

RABASKWORK   patterns in the arabesque style.

RAIL   a linen garment for use in the bath.

REBEC   a three-stringed musical instrument played with a bow.

RECORDER   a vertical flute.

REDORSE   a hanging for covering the wall at the back of an altar.

REGAL   an organ with a regal or reed stop.

REVELS   small plays or interludes; the Revels was the department of the royal household that was responsible for organizing masks and disguisings.

RUBBER   a coarse linen towel for rubbing hair to remove grease.

RYAL   an English gold coin originally worth 10*s*, first issued by Edward IV in 1465.

SABLE   a brown fur of a small arctic or sub-arctic mammal related to the marten (*see also* **TIMBER**).

SACKBUT   a kind of trombone.

SAD   a dull or neutral colour.

SAKERING BELL   a bell used during the liturgy.

SAPPHIRE   a transparent blue precious stone consisting of corundum (a crystallized mineral).

SARSENET   a fine, soft silk fabric of **TAFFETA** weave, used mainly for linings; either plain or striped.

SAY   a fine cloth made of silk, wool or a combination of silk and wool.

SCABBARD   two strips of wood shaped to fit the blade of a sword or dagger and covered in leather, fabric or metal. Until 1500 the scabbard was usually laced to a belt; thereafter it was usually attached to the belt by rings (**LOCKERS** or **LOCKETS**) fixed to metal mounts on the scabbard.

SCARLET   an expensive, very fine worsted cloth.

SCARLETS   (a pair) blankets (?) made from **SCARLET**.

SERPENTINE   a soft rock, consisting mainly of hydrated magnesium silicate; usually dark green; takes a high polish and was used as a decorative material.

SEWER   an attendant present at meals, who supervised the arrangement of the table, the tasting and serving of dishes and hand-washing arrangements.

SEWER'S TOWEL   a towel used by a **SEWER**, usually worn over the shoulder during meals.

SHAWM   a woodwind instrument similar to the oboe, with a conical bore and a double reed.

SHEMEWE   a man's gown cut in the middle (similar to a **COAT**).

SHORT HANGER   a short sword.

SIGNET, CLERK OF THE   clerk of the king's smallest seal, used by his Secretary.

SKENE   a Gaelic dagger used in Ireland and Scotland.

SLOPS   loose breeches with wide legs.

SOULTWICH   a type of canvas.

SPARVER   a canopy.

STAFF WEAPON   a weapon mounted on a shaft or staff, such as a lance or spear.

STANDISH   a stand or desk containing ink and other writing materials.

STOMACHER   a covering for the chest, worn by men and women.

SUMPTERMAN   the man that looks after and leads a sumpter horse (a horse used to carry luggage packed in chests or bundles)

SUPERALTAR   a portable stone slab consecrated for use upon an unconsecrated altar.

TABLE WITH A PICTURE   a painting on panel.

TABLE or **TABLET**   a small devotional image.

TABOR   a small drum.

TAFFETA   a plain tabby-woven silk textile.

TALFHIDES   uncertain meaning

TANGENT   a small piece of metal, which strikes a string in a **CLAVICHORD**.

TAPESTRY   a tapestry-woven textile, incorporating wool and silk thread.

TARTARON   a cheap silk cloth (though more expensive than **TAFFETA**) of eastern origin but copied in Europe; it could be plain or striped with silver and gold, and of either a tabby or tabby and twill weave.

TASTE   a cup for tasting or sampling food or drink.

TAWNY   a brownish-yellow or brownish-orange colour.

TESTER   a head cloth, often used in combination with a celure.

TICK   a twill woven linen fabric used to make mattresses; mattresses could be referred to as ticks

TIMBER   a package of forty sable furs.

TINSEL   silk textile incorporating silver or silver-gilt metal strips.

TISSUE   cloth of gold with uncut loops of metal thread.

TRAVERSE   a curtain used to divide a room.

TRIVET   an iron bracket which hooks on the bars of a grate.

TRYMMER   a canopy

TRUSSING BEDSTEADS   bed frames, with or without hangings, that were collapsible for easy transportation; they could be packed or trussed for carriage by wrapping them in cloth and binding with cord or placing them in trunks or cases.

TUNICLE   a small vestment, similar to the **DALMATIC**, worn by subdeacons.

TURQUOISE   an opaque or translucent sky-blue or greenish-blue precious stone.

VALANCE   a narrow border of fabric hung around the **CELURE** of a bedstead or a **CLOTH OF ESTATE**. Base valances were hung around the base of a **BEDSTEAD**.

VANE   a decorative finial placed at the corners of a bed-frame.

VELVET   a silk textile with a pile, which could be cut or uncut, voided (lacking pile) or of more than one length.

VENICE GOLD   a silver-gilt or gold-wrapped thread imported from Venice.

VENICE SILVER   a silver-wrapped thread imported from Venice.

VERDURE   tapestry depicting landscapes: made from wool only or with very small quantities of silk.

VERNICLE   a cloth or handkerchief said to have belonged to St Veronica and used by her to wipe Christ's face on his way to Calvary; an image of Christ's features appeared miraculously on the cloth.

VESTMENT   a set of vestments included a **CHASUBLE** or **TUNICLE** for a priest, a **DALMATIC** for a deacon and a tunicle for a subdeacon.

VIOL   a bowed stringed instrument with a fretted fingerboard, like a guitar.

VIRGINALS, PAIR OF   a legless, early form of the spinet in a box, used in the sixteenth and seventeenth centuries.

VIZER   a mask worn at the **REVELS**.

WAINSCOT   wooden panelling or boarding, often of oak.

WHITE LIGHTS   candles, possibly made of beeswax rather than tallow

WHITE PLATE   silver plate.

WORKS   a pattern, either embroidered or woven.

WROUGHT   worked, meaning either embroidered or woven.

DOCUMENT INDEX

THIS INDEX IS ARRANGED in a single alphabetical sequence and, for simplicity, it uses modern spelling only. It records the objects and the individuals associated with them. Additional details such as colour, materials, motifs and decorative techniques are also listed. For the objects and their associated details, the items are identified using their number. However, people and places are recorded either by folio, if mentioned in a heading, or by the entry number if mentioned in the marginal notes.

This index focuses upon the objects in the 1542 Inventory – to trace items cited within the other three documents associated with Denny, consult Concordance Three. However, the people and places that appear in these other documents are recorded here by their document reference and entry numbers. Any specialist words and terms are defined in a separate glossary.

For the decorative techniques, such as gilding and painting, the types of object that they were used on have been given. For the decorative motifs and coats of arms, the details relate to the type of technique used. As the inventory makes a distinction between embroidery and needlework, this has been observed here. The word metalwork has been used to denote items made from both precious and base metals. In many cases it is not possible to be more explicit and to state a particular technique. When describing the types of plate, the terms used in the inventory – gold, gilt, parcel gilt and white (i.e. silver) – have been followed. The colours of objects have been itemised and are listed separately, with the exception of the liturgical textiles, where colour is a key form of classification. With the section covering 'coats of arms, badges and ciphers', only includes features specifically described as such in the inventory. All other motifs are listed under the 'decorative motif' heading. Some of these motifs may well be badges, such as crowned falcon and a falcon on a branch which could be Anne Boleyn's badge, but as it is not possible to be certain no assumptions have been made. This is also true of the way the pictures have been recorded. The index entries follow the inventory's descriptions, without elaboration.

The quantity of detail given for a particular item, or group of items, is dependent upon the length of the entries recorded in the inventory. As much of the information has been included as possible, with the exception of the books. As their titles are given in roughly alphabetical order, to index them would just duplicate the text of the inventory. Instead supplementary details, such as language, size, binding and number of volumes, have been given. In order to keep cross references to a minimum, a selection of generic headings have been included to group related entries. These headings are given on the following page.

Generic Headings Used in the Document Index

BEDDING

CERAMICS

CHAPEL GOODS

COFFERS AND OTHER PACKING MATERIALS

COLOURS

CONSTRUCTION TECHNIQUES

CUTLERY

DECORATIVE TECHNIQUES

DRESS

FIRE FURNITURE

FUR

FURNISHINGS

FURNITURE

GEM STONES

GLASSWARE

JEWELLERY

MATERIALS

METALS

MUSICAL INSTRUMENTS

NAPERY

PASSEMENTERIE

PATTERNS

PLATE

STUFFING MATERIALS

TEXTILES

WEAPONS AND ACCESSORIES

WOODS

[Decorative motifs, *cont.*]

mayling
embroidery **1391**
woven **1391**
man, men
metalwork **1053, 1055**
needlework **1226**
man in harness with club and shield
metalwork **109**
men's heads, with caps and feathers
metalwork **3736–3737**
milpikes, half milpikes
embroidery **450, 452, 469**
naked woman holding a child
painted **867**
oak leaves
metalwork **3712–3713**
old man with a shield and a club
metalwork **90**
old man with a shield and a pollaxe
metalwork **93**
old men's heads
metalwork **152**
ostrich feathers
woven **1045**
Our Lady holding Our Lord
embroidery **2273**
Our Lady with angels
woven **226**
Our Lord in the sepulchre
embroidery **1230**
Our Saviour
embroidery **1028**
pansy, pansies
metalwork **45, 124, 144**
Passion, the
embroidery **1030, 1033, 1228, 4055**
peacock feathers
woven **1045**
pelican with a wheat ear in its feet
metalwork **134, 142**
woven **268**
pillars
metalwork **3721, 3725**
pinks
embroidery **298**
planets
painted **455**
pomegranates
embroidery **503**
metalwork **108, 159, 3759**
woven **213–214, 216, 259, 303, 337, 4064, 4066**
portcullises
metalwork **77**
woven **233, 331**
pots
woven **213, 4064**
rams' heads
metalwork **72, 105**
rayed
woven **1815**
rebecks
metalwork **60, 75**

[Decorative motifs, *cont.*]

root of Jesse
embroidery **2269**
roses
embroidery **233, 257–258, 280–281, 283–284, 295, 299–300, 436–437, 451, 503, 1149, 3337, 3348, 3680, 4021–4024**
gilding **953**
metalwork **32–33, 42, 49, 54, 61, 72, 101–102, 108, 139, 149, 255–256, 262, 3723, 3727, 3730, 3734, 3748, 3754**
painted **251, 253, 258, 260, 3701**
woven **213, 246, 259, 278, 303, 308, 310, 337, 358–362, 370–371, 451, 1268–1270, 4064, 4078**
roses, branches of
metalwork **3726**
roses, crowned
embroidery **461, 889, 3337**
roses, crowned, in a garland
embroidery **447, 4037**
roses, double red and white
embroidery **452**
rose garlands
embroidery **222**
roses in sunbeams
embroidery **450**
rose trails
embroidery **229**
woven **235, 393, 3064**
roses and pelicans
woven **368, 389**
roses and pomegranates
woven **259, 303, 337, 392**
roses and portcullises
carved **1162**
embroidery **229**
metalwork **101**
woven **1029**
roses, red
metalwork **31, 3726**
roses, red and white
embroidery **295, 420–421**
metalwork **72**
needlework **2255**
roses, white
embroidery **299, 438**
metalwork **3726**
roses and trails
metalwork **3730**
woven **393**
rose bushes
embroidery **302**
roses with another flower
embroidery **282**
roses with trails
embroidery **235**
roundels
woven **212**
rows [stripes]
woven **242, 289, 372, 425, 432–433, 499, 501–502, 1760, 2019**
St James's shells
metalwork **132**

GENERAL INDEX